DATE DUE

MEXICAN CONSULS AND LABOR ORGANIZING

GILBERT G. GONZÁLEZ

Mexican Consuls and Labor Organizing
Imperial Politics in the American Southwest

University of Texas Press, *Austin*

peared as "The Los Angeles County
ience, Volume 20 No. 4, December
arfax Publishing Limited, P.O. Box
ngdom.

Chapter Five in revised form first appeared as "Company Unions, the
Mexican Consulate, and the Imperial Valley Agricultural Strikes, 1928–
1934" in the *Western Historical Quarterly,* Volume 37 No. 1, Spring 1996.

Copyright © 1999 by the University of Texas Press
All rights reserved
Printed in the United States of America
First edition, 1999

Requests for permission to reproduce material from this work
should be sent to Permissions, University of Texas Press, P.O. Box 7819,
Austin, TX 78713-7819.

∞ The paper used in this book meets the minimum requirements of
ANSI/NISO Z39.48-1992 (R1997) (Permanence of Paper).

Library of Congress Cataloging-in-Publication Data

González, Gilbert G., 1941–
    Mexican consuls and labor organizing : imperial politics in the American
Southwest / by Gilbert G. González.
        p.   cm.
    Includes bibliographical references and index.
    ISBN 0-292-72823-9 (cl. : alk. paper). — ISBN 0-292-72824-7 (pbk. :
alk. paper)
    1. Mexican Americans—Employment—Southwestern States.
    2. Mexican American agricultural laborers—Southwestern States.
    3. Trade—unions—Mexican American membership—Southwestern
States.   4. Consuls—Mexico.   I. Title.
    HD8081.M6G665   1999
    331.6'272076—dc21   99-20648

The Secretariat under my command has named F. Peralta to take charge of an active campaign to organize Mexican workers in the jurisdictions of California, Texas, Arizona, and Nuevo Mexico.... Mr. Peralta was selected so that he may work for the unification of the Mexican laboring classes in foreign territory....

—Ramón P. de Negri, Mexican Secretary of Industry, Commerce, and Labor, 1929

In search of economic benefits, numerous Mexicans in [El Paso, Texas] have formed the Society of Manufacturing Workers which numbers more than three hundred members.... All the labor of unification and organization of Mexican workers . . . has been under the active direction of Señor Benito Rodríguez, Head of the Department of Protection and Repatriation of the Mexican Consulate General in El Paso, Texas.

—Los Angeles *La Opinión*, May 1933

The Mexican consul brought in as always in Southern California agricultural strikes to split the ranks by dividing the workers along racial lines.

—*The Western Worker*, 1934

At the moment those who get jobs in the fields must join the Mexican Association recently organized by the Mexican consul under the grower's sponsorship.

—Helen Marston, ACLU, 1934

The attempt to set up separate unions along racial lines has been disastrous.

—Ernesto Galarza, National Farm Labor Union, 1949

Contents

Preface and Acknowledgments   ix

Introduction   1

CHAPTER 1
The 1910 Mexican Revolution, the United States,
and *México de afuera*   11

CHAPTER 2
Organizing *México de afuera* in Southern California   37

CHAPTER 3
The Los Angeles County Strike of 1933   82

CHAPTER 4
The San Joaquin Valley Strike of 1933   122

CHAPTER 5
The Imperial Valley Strikes of 1933–1934   159

CHAPTER 6
Denouement and Renaissance   197

Notes   229

Bibliography   261

Index   271

Illustrations follow page 121

Preface and Acknowledgments

The United States and Mexico have an economic and political relationship that is, on the one hand, extraordinary, and on the other, not uncommon in the history of international relations. They share a common border, which, unlike any other existing national boundary, serves to divide the most powerful nation in the world from a poor undeveloped nation. The more important linkages between the two nations are cut from the traditional pattern characteristic of relations between an imperial power and its colonies. An economic satellite of the United States throughout the twentieth century, Mexico has been dependent upon the United States for investment capital, technology, and trade and as an outlet for surplus labor, and it remains generally dominated by the political power of the northern military giant. Mexico's subordination to foreign capital for modernization projects, established during the era of Porfirio Díaz, survived the 1910 Mexican Revolution. The consequences for Mexico were as significant as were those of the War of 1848. As one Mexican scholar put it, in 1848 half of Mexico was annexed to the United States; in the twentieth century the other half fell via an open door to finance capital.[1]

Ironically, over the past century Mexico has contributed significantly to its northern neighbor's economic well-being while remaining one of the world's poverty-stricken nations. Mexico's chief exports, able-bodied workers, have abandoned their homeland (or better, have been forced out), according to economic cycles and trends in foreign investment, and moved north. Large-scale agriculture, mining, railroad construction, and manufacturing have historically relished and depended upon the unimpeded flow of legal, illegal, and contract labor.

Beginning in the Porfirian period, and extending into the postrevolutionary era, Mexico's compliant governmental policies have complemented that demand and ensured labor availability. An oversupply of labor caused by the Porfirian and later Revolutionary Mexico's "Open Door" foreign investment policy (a policy demanded by Washington), coupled with the voracious appetite for Mexican labor of large-scale corporations (often the very same investing in Mexico) together acted as an international economic infrastructure that stabilized the Mexican immigrant community as a permanent component and ethnicity within the United States working class. Not only was an incipient sector of the regional working class formed in the early decades of this century, but it continued to grow in subsequent years through various forms of legal and illegal immigration in response to capital's requirements for workers. More often than not "illegal" immigration constituted a form of state-sanctioned labor border crossing to satisfy peak periods of corporate demand. Continually arriving and settling into older barrios and creating new communities separate from the host country's dominant groups, these economically active workers quickly assimilated into the national economic system.

Indeed, by 1920 the Mexican community had emerged as a major participant in the capitalist development of the southwestern region of the United States, integrated into the corporate industries then experiencing unprecedented growth. And yet these same economically productive workers were segregated in work, religion, occupation, recreation, housing, and education. An apparent irony and contradiction was set in motion: integrated into a system of production dominated by monopolistic capital, Mexican immigrants found themselves segregated from nearly all other aspects of society. The irony is only illusionary; social and political segregation and economic integration manifested an identical process, were one and the same. The social and economic conditions that were to characterize the Mexican community throughout the century had made an auspicious presence over the first two decades, a period during which the modern Chicano community made its historical entrance onto the U.S. social stage.

A measure of Mexico's annexation (economic, not geopolitical) can be calibrated by examining the ways in which the Mexican immigrant community has been politically socialized and controlled while in the United States. The analysis must include a wide transnational context, one in which the Mexican state plays a critical role in fashioning a policy intended to politically dominate the immigrant labor force. In this role the Mexican state has complemented the various ways in which U.S. capital has preferred to recruit and organize its labor force, particularly its cheapest labor pool. In effect, this study will argue that the Mexican state has been central to the implementation of key labor policies of the northern power and thus to the political history relative to the Mexican immigrant community.

Trends in recent scholarship relating to the Chicano community and to transnational issues have channeled the discourse onto matters of culture and cultural relations between the dominant and nondominant communities. Consequently, in terms of Chicano history, we have a complex of studies building upon notions of cultural identity and derivative themes. Interest in searching for associations between migrations and the imperial power and policies of the United States is notably absent from these studies. We have no information regarding the linkages between migration and empire, and we are in the dark regarding the international political forces which have attempted, and at times succeeded, to orchestrate the political history of the Mexican immigrant community. The analysis that follows centers upon the methods that the Mexican state has employed, in cooperation with the U.S. State Department and other authorities, to control the community's political discourse, culture, and action. This study intends to establish a place for the Mexican state, an economic dependency of the United States, within the historiography of the Chicano community. In the process, the international political factors that bear upon Chicano history, U.S. labor history, and U.S.–Mexico relations are drawn forth.

Hopefully, this study will initiate an interest in examining the ways in which an international collusion, albeit between a powerful country and a weak subordinate neighbor, has sought to shape the political experience of an immigrant community. This is not to imply a "victimology," that is, a top-down history; on the contrary, the immigrant community has impeded and at times temporarily defeated the internationally based policies. At a deeper level, the purpose here acknowledges the larger, more fundamental transnational issues that have confronted one segment of the U.S. working class, the Chicano community. It is also a statement of the need to focus upon and authenticate that reality and thereby clarify the full range of items on the political agenda of Chicano labor in particular, and the working class in general.

Many individuals assisted me with their expertise, comments, and suggestions, and I am indebted to them. I could never have accomplished this work without a team of researchers. I thank the following for their many valuable contributions: Gaspar Rivera, Stuart Lawrence, José Alamillo, Robert Hayden, Kathryn Azevedo, and José Amaya. I was also fortunate to have the assistance of several undergraduates, and I hope that their university experience was enriched by having worked on this project. I enjoyed having Evelyn Bethencourt, Sandra Sosa, Jaime Ruiz, Chris Ynostroza, and Joseph O'Connell-González aboard. Finally, I want to thank Barbara Bronte Bernal for her adept editing of a draft of the manuscript and Edna Mejía for her many contributions.

The librarians and archivists at a number of institutions were invaluable collaborators in this study; their expertise opened doors to the pleasure of discovery. The librarians and archivists at the Bobst Library and the Tamiment Library/Wagner Library at New York University; the Walter Ruether Library at Wayne State University; the Bancroft Library at the University of California, Berkeley; the Department of Special Collections, University Research Library at UCLA; the National Archives in Washington, D.C., and Suitland, Maryland; the Southern California Library for Social Studies and Research in Los Angeles; the Archivo General de la Nación and the Archivo de la Secretaría de Relaciones Exteriores, both in Mexico City; the Imperial County Historical Society in Imperial, California; and the Main Library at UC Irvine led me and my assistants through the thickets of information. My sincere appreciation extends to them.

Financial assistance from the University of California Office of the President's Senate Concurrent Resolution 43 funds for research into California Latino public policy issues provided the wherewithal to initiate and complete the project. The intellectual interest that generated this study began many years ago when I first arrived at UC Irvine and began my career in the Program in Comparative Culture. Several colleagues created an intellectual atmosphere which I was fortunate to experience, an atmosphere that continues today. I thank them for it.

My colleagues at the Center for the Study of Chicano Latinos in a Global Society and in the Focused Research Program in Labor Studies, both at UC Irvine, also made for a camaraderie that welcomed the opportunity to discuss and debate. At the University of California Humanities Research Institute, where I spent a yearlong fellowship, I presented incipient expositions of what was to become an article and later a chapter in this book.

Beyond the confines of academia, family plays a major role in nurturing, expanding, and keeping creative energies flowing. The fundamental research plan which I utilized, the employment of a team approach, I owe to my wife, Frances. A scholar in a field remote from the humanities, she organizes her work without regard to rank, but with an eye for teamwork. I found that applying those principles worked well in the historian's retreat. Frances, together with our children Antonio and Alicia, accompanied me on several research ventures and turned my frequent stops at the Bancroft Library from work into a pleasure. I look back fondly on those trips. Finally, to Ramón, my happy congratulations, and to Xochitl, keep up the great work.

MEXICAN CONSULS AND
LABOR ORGANIZING

Introduction

In early 1994 twelve prominent southern California Chicano political figures met with Santiago Oñate Laborde, the personal emissary for then Mexican presidential candidate Donaldo Colossio. The Mexican representative initiated the encounter to discuss ways in which the Mexican state might engender closer ties with *México de afuera,* literally Mexico outside of Mexico. The Chicano group opened with a specific agenda. Over Mexican sweet breads, hot chocolate, and coffee, the Chicanos discussed ways in which the Mexican state might open professional and business opportunities for qualified Chicanos. The Mexican government, guided by the Partido Revolucionario Institucional (PRI) for nearly 70 years, had a distinct agenda, one scripted to develop political support from the region's expatriate community for the PRI in the upcoming presidential elections. After a lengthy but friendly engagement at a downtown Los Angeles hotel, both sides departed pleased with the meeting. The Chicano group was particularly impressed by Oñate's responses to its ideas.[1]

Meetings like the Los Angeles conclave had been held from time to time in the 1980s and 1990s, but more importantly for this study, these encounters also carried forward a long history of Mexico to *México de afuera* relations. Dating back to the postrevolutionary period of the late teens and twenties, such contacts have taken a number of forms, but always with the same objective: to extend official Mexican domestic policy into the emigrant community. In regard to such contacts, the Mexican immigrant community is unique in comparison with other immigrant groups. Among the hallmarks that distinguish Mexican immigrant history from the Asian and European experiences, the long-standing interventionist policy sponsored by various Mexican administrations is of vital significance. Not only does the pattern of intervention differentiate Mexican immigrant experience from other immigrant groups; it also contributes in important ways to shaping Chicano political history. Whereas historical accounts of European and Asian immigrants scarcely mention their respective home governments, the Mexican case is substantially dissimilar.

Indeed, students of Chicano history, Southwest labor, and U.S.–Mexico relations cannot avoid bumping into archival documentation that testifies to the significant presence and activism of the Mexican government via its consulate corps within the expatriate communities across the United States. With the exception of Mexican historiography (which traditionally expresses little interest in matters north of the border), numerous published studies verify that consuls actively engaged an interest in the political affairs of the immigrant *colonias* between 1920 and 1940, the period of interest to this study. Several strands of twentieth-century Chicano history—in particular, community organizing, political development, union organizing, and the California agricultural labor strikes of the 1930s—defy explanation without reference to the high-level interventions by various Mexican consuls.

Although nearly every historical account of Mexican immigrants devotes varying degrees of attention to the consuls, a comprehensive examination of this important and fascinating matter is unfortunately absent. Nor is there a shared understanding and explanation for consular conduct. Thirty years of Chicano historiography have delivered neither a basic understanding of the importance and effects of consular interaction nor a sustained interest and discussion. On the contrary, we have neither disagreement nor debate. The issue seems to list this way and that, consequently languishing on the research margins. Yet, if we examine the record we find abundant material demonstrating that the consulates sponsored a wide variety of organizations, from self-help *mutualistas* to political and labor groups. Consuls established community organizations, sought union leadership, polarized political factions, and, among other interventions, generated serious political conflicts within the *colonias* and with other ethnic communities, particularly Filipinos. Moreover, that intervention with variations has continued into the 1990s.

The Debate

Many *emigrados* voiced complaints concerning the consuls, while others expressed deep satisfaction that the consuls took an abiding interest in their welfare. An interpreter for the Detroit International Institute confided, "The Mexicans in the past have not been very fortunate as to their consuls. I do not think that they have tried to do anything for the common people."[2] Not a few immigrants agreed that the consuls were uninterested in the plight of the "common people." By 1930 the volume of complaints had induced the Secretariat of Foreign Relations to issue a public relations bulletin defending the consulates. Notwithstanding the "praise expressed for Mexico's consulates by colleagues from other nations," read the bulletin, "disgracefully, only vituperations come from Mexican elements."[3] The Secretariat correlated the negative response with the level of honesty of the individual consuls who had been instructed to deal equally and without favoritism with their compatriots. Anastacio Torres was one of those who felt the apparent callousness of the consuls toward their compatriots. Torres recollected that he had thought of "going to ask the Mexican consul there [Kansas City] to help me but some countryman told me not to go to that consul because he didn't help anybody."[4] Gonzalo Clark, a small bookshop owner in Tucson, Arizona, proudly published an independent humorous weekly that targeted the consuls. "A few times," stated Clark, "I have had some scraps with the Mexican consuls who don't attend to the interests of the Mexicans here or who think that they are sent to enjoy their salary. I have attacked them in my paper freely and faithfully but as they can't do anything here they don't bother me."[5] Mexican labor leader Vicente Lombardo Toledano expressed similar misgivings in an interview with a Mexico City journalist in 1937. In Lombardo Toledano's opinion, the Mexican government implemented "no program for the protection of Mexican workers in the United States. . . . The majority of consuls dedicate themselves, placidly, to play golf and bridge, without attending the most urgent problems affecting thousands of workers."[6]

Others disagreed that the consuls comprised a shabby lot, and some offered opposing views of consular involvement. Longtime civil rights and union activist Bert Corona recalls that the civil rights organization Asociación Nacional México Americana, founded in 1949, "developed a very good relationship with the Mexican consulate in San Francisco." Further on, Corona contends that from 1934 to 1940, consuls appointed by President Lázaro Cárdenas "were very sympathetic to . . . the labor movement in the United States."[7] Official bulletins periodically briefed the *colonias* with information that supported the positive portrayal sketched by Corona. Annual reports from Mexico's Secretariat of Foreign Relations related impressive data on services rendered by the consuls. According to the 1931 bulletin, nearly 38,000 cases of "direct intervention by consuls exercising their good services in favor of our nationals" were registered.[8]

Consuls reportedly comforted the sick, helped the indigent, assisted the injured to seek compensatory damages, and more. These protective actions, announced the Secretariat, can be explained by "the desire of the Secretariat of Foreign Relations that the consular corps render good services for Mexicans abroad and has given instructions so that in those cases where action is necessary to realize what our nationals justly require, that the consuls do not limit their service to mere sympathy, on the contrary [the Secretariat] has recommended the greatest activism without omitting any effort."[9]

Local consulates also issued annual bulletins of services rendered to the *colonias*. For the month of June 1934, Los Angeles Consul Alejandro Martínez reported impressive data to the Secretariat of Foreign Relations relating to assistance provided by the consulate to 950 Mexican citizens. The consulate intervened in a wide variety of cases, from assisting fellow citizens held in county and state prisons, counseling those detained on immigration violations, to visiting the infirm in county hospitals; at least forty were assisted in repatriating.[10] Consul Martínez also expressed his support, promising his complete cooperation to local garment workers who had charged that their employer mistreated them. He counseled the women to identify their just grievances for "constructing a solid foundation for a formal and energetic representation before the authorities." His office, he assured, would meanwhile carry out its own investigations in a show of solidarity.[11]

Many observers, however, were far from convinced that the consulates contributed to the well-being of the community. On the contrary, they alleged that the consulates harmed *México de afuera*. Anthropologist Ruth Tuck's study of a Los Angeles County urban *colonia, Not with the Fist: Mexican Americans in a Southwest City* (1946), severely criticized the Mexican consulate for fostering *mexicanismo*. Tuck alleged that this "attempt to strengthen ties with Mexico" contributed to a timid and inactive *colonia* leadership. Tuck submitted that *mexicanismo* was "simply nostalgia, a warm relaxing bath into which immigrants can fall back." Unfortunately, she wrote, it was "a devotion which every consulate has ardently encouraged." Furthermore, the nationalist exercise conformed with the dominant community's intent to withhold from the Mexican American community full participation and equality with the larger society. Consequently, in Tuck's view, *mexicanismo* inadvertently strengthened the subordinate status of the Mexican community vis-à-vis the dominant classes.[12]

Mexicanismo spilled over the generational divide, as sons and daughters of *emigrados* were well within earshot of the nationalistic messages. And like their parents, the Mexican American generation had opinions concerning the consuls. Mexican American civil rights activists found substance in these critiques, contending that the matter required their attention. Some militant activists of that era went further than Tuck. Ignacio López, the noted southern California civil rights activist, newspaper publisher, and muckraker, complained that Tuck failed to take the consulate sufficiently to task for harming the *colonia*'s interests through foisting *mexicanismo* upon it.[13] Although Tuck raised serious misgivings relating to the political impact of the consuls, Lopez's charges take on greater significance and offer an insight into the internal conflicts generated by the political presence displayed by the consuls. The two perspectives collide, not only within the voices of the past generations, but within the literature on Chicano history and California agricultural labor history, where they continue to resonate.

Just as in the past, so in the present there exists a division of opinion that in turn lends an air of historiographical dissension to the subject. At least four strands of opinions and conclusions regarding the historical role, significance, and objectives of the consulates permeate the literature. The marketplace condition suggests that readers choose between works which portray the consulates as protectors of the *colonia,* and the opposing studies, like that of Ruth Tuck, which argue that the consuls represented interests far removed from the *colonias* they allegedly served.

The first variant contends that the consuls played a central role in *colonia* affairs and in doing so provided protection of the interests of the expatriate community. This perspective traces its lineage, in part, to Stuart Jameison's 1938 study of agricultural unionism in the United States, sections of which highlighted the Depression-era strikes involving Mexican workers. Jameison reported that "Consular officials were perhaps their main source of protection in California. On numerous occasions in later years these officers mediated labor disputes, served as official representatives in collective bargaining agreements, and even organized labor unions among their compatriots."[14] More recently, that tradition has been embraced by several scholars. The most prominent among them is Francisco Balderrama, who wrote the pioneering study *In Defense of La Raza: The Los Angeles Mexican Consulate and the Mexican Community, 1929–1936.* This study remains the only work that effectively places the consul at the center of the *colonia* experience. Contemporary scholarship reiterates Balderrama's main thesis, that "the Los Angeles Consulate provided effective assistance to the more than 170,000 Mexicans and Mexican Americans during the twentieth century's most severe crisis."[15]

In the second, counter current, the consulates provided minimal protection, and their participation is recognized primarily for maintaining the community in a politically subordinate position, both to the Mexican government (consuls represented the policies of the Mexican government) and to the employers in the United States. The tradition begins with the stinging critiques published in the mid-forties by anthropologists Ruth

Tuck and Beatrice Griffith that acknowledged the significance of the consuls in community affairs but rebuked them for hindering the political development and action of the Mexican American community. Griffith underscored her argument with a statement by a high school teacher who charged: "The consuls retard us . . . they hold us back. There is no doubt about it. The only thing they do is get visas for Mexico and be important at the [national] Holidays."[16] Not to be outdone, Tuck offered a most unflattering view of the consul: "a nice fellow, from the *gente decente* of Mexico, mildly ambitious, somewhat narrow in outlook, and given, like most officialdom, to the pious hope that he will never stick his neck out and get himself into trouble."[17] That tradition continues with Clete Daniel's examination of California agricultural labor, which blisters the consuls for their conduct and paints a convincing portrait of consular deception and collaboration with the very economic and political forces that oppressed the *colonia*.[18] Devra Weber's study of the 1933 cotton strike shows that Consul Enrique Bravo exerted "little effort to support workers in relation to growers."[19] Further, Bravo's interventions were not consistent with the strikers' objectives: he opposed the striking compatriots, cooperated with growers to break the strike, and conspired with growers to form a company union. My own studies of the 1936 citrus picker strike and the 1933–1934 Imperial Valley strikes sustain the conclusions reached by Daniel and Weber.

Other studies extend the critique beyond the union movement, citing community organizing, political activities, and repatriations. Camille Guerin-Gonzales counters the thesis that consuls offered much-needed assistance to expatriates who were being forcibly returned to their native land during the repatriation drives of the 30s.[20] Her analysis provides substantial evidence that the consuls did more than merely feed and transport the departing thousands; she shows that consuls collaborated with U.S. authorities in all aspects of the repatriation campaign. George Sánchez goes one step further and finds that the Mexican government was as central to the repatriation campaigns as were the authorities in Los Angeles who sought the mass return of excess Mexican labor. Both studies strongly suggest that without the collaboration of Mexican authorities the repatriation drives would have remained inoperative or, at the very least, far less extensive.

The third current of thought on the issue claims a middle ground, that the consuls acted positively here, negatively there, depending on the circumstances and on the good intentions of specific consuls. Juan Gómez Quiñones, among others, provides an example of this line of analysis. He writes:

The administrations of Obregón-Calles (1920–1924 and 1924–1928) and Cárdenas (1934–1940) were generally sympathetic to Mexican residents in the United States and to Mexican workers in particular, often taking specific steps to provide aid and assistance to Mexicans abroad through giving orders to consulates or by providing resources. If a consul acted negatively, it was due less to standing government policy and was more the result of personal bias. The contribution of the consul to a community organization role must be viewed through specific situations. . . . Mexican consular officials became involved in strikes, sometimes favoring owners and at other times the workers.[21]

Ricardo Romo suggests a similar interpretation in his study of East Los Angeles during the 1920s.[22]

Finally, the fourth view either marginalizes the consul to the periphery, transforming him into a bit player, or omits the consul altogether. In a few cases the omission is quite obvious, as in several studies that touch upon important agricultural strikes in which Mexican workers and the Mexican consulate figured prominently.[23] An example of this line comes from the work of anthropologist Carlos G. Vélez Ibáñez, *Border Visions: Mexican Cultures of the Southwest United States*.[24] Although Vélez Ibáñez's study is not primarily concerned with union issues, he devotes several pages to union organizing, in particular, the Mexican union, the Confederación de Uniones Obreros Mexicanos, founded in Los Angeles in 1927. Several works, including the 1920s research of Paul S. Taylor, show conclusively the leadership displayed by Consul F. Alfonso Pesqueira in the organizing and development of that union. More recently, Devra Weber, Clete Daniel, Abraham Hoffman, and Charles Wollenberg, among others, have verified the fundamental participation of consuls in the disputes that a number of scholars examine with minimal attention to the consul. Vélez Ibáñez, however, emphasizes border cultural practices but misses the international dimension of the union drive. Whereas a few scholars omit mention of the consular tutelage, other works marginalize, practically to the point of extinguishing, the involvement of the consul. In their impressive study of California agribusiness and the state, Linda C. Majka and Theo J. Majka briefly discuss the consulate-controlled Confederación de Uniones Obreras Mexicanas, but they, too, overlook the critical participation of the consul in unionization drives. Later, their discussion of repatriation and the strikes of 1933 and 1934 involving Mexican workers conforms to the pattern: consuls were simply unimportant understudies to the events.[25]

These, then, comprise the four main interpretations. The question remains: Which of the four accurately reflects the historical record? That question frames the parameters of this study. Meeting that challenge requires a comprehensive examination and analysis of the broad scope of consular policies, actions, and outcomes. Though mention is most often made of individual acts of consular interventions, markedly absent is a comprehensive study that investigates whether a pattern of consulate involvement appears. If a discernible pattern exists, did a central policy guide consulate actions? In pursuing these matters, other important lines of inquiry will surface: What policy or policies guided consular conduct? Did this policy correspond to the needs of the community? What role did the Mexican government have in shaping that policy and in directing the conduct of the consulates? Finally, were the activities of the consulates a contributing factor in the economic subordination of the Mexican community? The purpose of this study is to explore these questions, and, hopefully, explain and illuminate the obscure area that reaches beyond Chicano and labor history to embrace Mexican political history and international politics.

This study resumes an interest that began with an exploration into the history of citrus worker villages in southern California. In that work I found ample evidence of high-level consular involvement, particularly in relation to political acculturation and labor organizing. Indeed, in the Orange County citrus picker strike of 1936, the largest strike ever to affect the industry, the Mexican consulate played a major role in the eventual outcome. I concluded that the consul succeeded in shaping union politics along quite conservative and nationalistic lines and, in doing so, badly divided the union ranks.[26] The present work enlarges upon that theme to explore the role of the Mexican consulate in community organizing and the unionization campaigns and strikes of the 1920s and 1930s in Los Angeles County, the San Joaquin Valley, and the Imperial Valley. Again, the question to be addressed revolves around consular patterns of action as well as their political objectives. In order to adequately investigate these problems, the analysis must examine the politics of the Mexican revolutionary regimes, especially those of the 1920s and 1930s. After all, it was the Mexican state that administered and directed the consulate enterprise.

The analysis then moves to a discussion of the community organizations fostered by the Los Angeles consulate that held jurisdiction over much of southern California. With well over 200,000 Mexican immigrants in the area, the consulate made it a matter of high priority to organize and monitor the political activities in the community. George Sánchez reports that the Mexican consul "emerged as the central organizer of community leadership" within the Los Angeles city *colonia*.[27] Evidence shows that the consul was deeply involved beyond the city and had extended organizing throughout the southern and central California regions. The questions remain: What political objectives guided the consulate's organizing efforts? Did a Mexican middle-class outlook shape the contours of consular community activities? I will argue that the Mexican civil war, popularly known as the 1910 Revolution, and the political forces and their ideology that reformed (but did not revolutionize) the Mexican nation and state constituted the critical factors shaping consular interventions. Ultimately, the objective of the Mexican government in organizing the expatriate community did not originate with "encouraging return migration" or with the "preservation of cultural integrity of Mexican emigrants."[28] The long-term goal had more to do with Mexican domestic politics in the postrevolutionary period.

During the regimes of Obregón through Cárdenas, dating from 1920 to 1940, an authoritarian corporate state institution underwent construction. The first example of that institutionalized state apparatus, the Partido Nacional Revolucionario, made its debut in 1929, succeeded by the Partido Revolucionario Mexicano in 1938. Within these state institutions, government-sponsored labor and peasant organizations were extended the opportunity to participate, but only on the condition of their loyalty, dependence, and subordination to the ruling party and state bureaucracy. This domestic policy objective ultimately guided the conduct of the consuls who followed on the heels of emigrants as they crossed borders. Whereas emigrants searched for survival, work, and a better life, the Mexican government endeavored to define the parameters of that search and incorporate *México de afuera* into a political ideology and social relations consonant with the interests of the ruling upper classes in Mexico. Within that fundamental guiding principle, consulates fostered *mexicanismo,* organized unions, developed community leadership, offered legal protections, spied upon the *colonia,* facilitated emigration, and, when required, participated in the massive removal of its citizens from U.S. territory.

Mexican state political involvement in U.S. territory was not an entirely novel departure from past practices. Dirk Raat's study of the Porfirio Díaz regime's persecution of the Flores Magón brothers and their Mexican Liberal Party adherents by U.S. agents in collaboration with Mexican government undercover men provides an early-twentieth-century example of international political intrigues.[29] After the fall of Díaz, the revolutionary regimes recognized that the border region still served as a harbor for all sorts of disaffected elements. With the mass emigration of a million or more between 1900 and 1930 and the potential for their adverse political socialization and return, it became imperative that the postrevolutionary governments that feared the potential for working-class political rebellion inoculate themselves against antigovernment activities, especially the radical and leftist political versions. In tandem with domestic policy, consulates were directed to enforce that policy bearing upon the relation of the state to the working class. In performing their duties the consulates were quintessential expressions of the politics engendered by the Mexican revolution and seldom acted out of individualistic impulses. As we shall see, positions in the consular corps were awarded to those who could demonstrate their complete personal allegiance to the governing regimes. Defining the interventions of the consulate requires, therefore, an overview of the politics of the 1910 Mexican Revolution. Included in this overview are summary analyses of revolutionary policies toward land reform, foreign capital, labor, criteria for selecting consuls, emigration, and repatriation.

One last but most important point remains to be made. The significance of the imperialist conduct of the United States for explaining Mexican public policy, particularly emigration, has unfortunately been muffled, if not silenced. The reader will note an analytical thread extending throughout this study, specifically regarding the political implications of Mexico's subordination to the economic power of the United States. Only by way of reference to the imperialist relationship can the conduct of the Mexican state, via the consulates, be explicated. Or put another way, the Mexican state, especially in its policies toward the expatriate community, operated within the parameters of an empire administered by its northern neighbor. Mexican emigrant policy, in the final analysis, emanated from Mexico's status as an economic satellite of the United States.

CHAPTER 1

The 1910 Mexican Revolution, the United States, and *México de afuera*

The violence of the Mexican Revolution left an estimated million and a half dead, villages plundered, fields devastated, and an economy in shambles. Conventional histories have claimed that the revolution tore down the Porfirian socioeconomic edifice and paved the way for the new, modern Mexico. Many, however, doubt that a revolution ever occurred, and recent scholarship has marshaled a strong case for defining the revolution as *Porfirismo* in new dress. If the latter is closer to "the truth," and there is good reason to believe that a fundamental reordering of society did not happen, then the questions arises: What does this mean for explaining the policies and programs Mexico directed at the expatriate community in the 1920s and 1930s? Answering this question requires that we examine in detail the evidence that supports the *continuismo* interpretation. By comparing basic Porfirian policies and juxtaposing them to those of the post-Díaz governments, we may gain a clearer impression of the continuity between the two eras. This in turn can lend insight into the policies adopted by Mexican revolutionary administrations regarding its expatriate community.

Porfirian Modernization

Under Díaz, Mexico enjoyed a period of unprecedented economic growth and modernization, due in large measure to an enforced social discipline tied to foreign capital. With the protection of a political stability induced by Díaz's strong-arm tactics, foreign investors built railroads, developed industries, exploited natural resources, and propelled the development of the modern working class. Modernization, however, failed to eradicate the large disparities among sectors of the economy, nor did it disturb social relations permeated with medievalism, which continued as before. In truth, continuity and moderate to conservative reforms dominated the politics of postrevolutionary Mexico, while the great migrations treaded northward, recruited by agencies operating the same corporations that reshaped Mexico's centuries-old demographic pattern.

Mexico exhibited two faces. The first was characterized by the feudal hacienda, an inheritance from the colonial era that remained untouched and dominated the countryside, where 80 percent of the population resided, half in a state of servile labor subordinated to the powerful hacendados. Nearly 97 percent of "rural households held no land whatsoever," while twenty thousand owners laid claim to one half of the national territory.[1] In the state of Morelos, the center of the Zapata peasant rebellion, seventeen individuals held title to twenty-four sugar factories and thirty-six haciendas and "owned twenty-five percent of the state's land area." [2]

In stark contrast, the second face originated from within industrialized capitalist nations. This face reflected modern techniques of oil exploration, extraction, and processing; the newest railroad engines and cars; and up-to-date technology in mining and smelting, all under the aegis of corporations such as Anaconda; Phelps Dodge; U.S. Mining, Smelting, and Refining; Doheny; Hearst; Rockefeller; and Texas Oil, which stood like citadels on a feudal plain. By 1911, foreigners owned as much as 20 percent of Mexico's land, and the majority of its eighty largest commercial establishments. Monopolistic corporations may have revolutionized methods of production in particular branches of the economy, but these had little effect upon the national economic and social backbone, the hacienda. Except for some rural commercial ventures, the countryside stood still. And even when commerce entered the hacienda, servile labor, rather than free wage labor, using backward instruments of production, predominated.

Modernization, by way of foreign financing, generated no fundamental (i.e., capitalist) transformation of society. Mining and petroleum concerns produced for export; railroads were laid out to facilitate that export; textile mills were placed near ports for easy transport overseas. Mexico's extraction-oriented economy fed American industry while Mexico itself remained a predominantly rural society. Simultaneous with the beat of modern economic exploitation, the hacienda, ironically, increased in significance. An extensive landed estate, the hacienda was usually owned by one individual, or family, who often lived in an urban center and left the administration to a *mayordomo*. Generally managed cautiously, the hacienda was relatively self-sufficient, employed a resident labor force, and utilized "backward production methods" to satisfy its needs.[3]

The 1910 Civil Rebellion

A growing number of scholars are convinced that the Mexican Revolution of 1910 was not, in the strict sense of the word, a revolution. James D. Cockroft, for example, notes that "the Revolution of 1910–1920 did not succeed; nor was it aborted or 'interrupted,' it was defeated."[4] John Womack Jr. agrees with Cockroft on that score. "The difference the so-called Revolution made to the country's modern history, was, therefore, not a radical transformation but simply a reform, accomplished by violent methods within already established limits." Later Womack adds, "the Revolution would represent not a historic replacement of the ancient regime by a new republic, but the historic failure of the Mexican bourgeoisie ever to shape [itself] as a ruling class. . . ."[5] Ramón Eduardo Ruiz finds common ground with Cockroft and Womack. "The evidence indicates," writes Ruiz, "that the views of current scholars, who doubt the existence of a revolution, defined in terms of fundamental socio-economic change, are close to the truth."[6]

Interpretations like the above had been voiced long ago, before the ink of the revolution was dry. Intrigued by the revolution and attracted by the rich cultural tableaux of Mexico, many Americans flocked to Mexico in anticipation of a great social reconstruction. Not a few, particularly liberals, were greatly disappointed. In an article for the *New Republic,* Carleton Beals abandoned his former enthusiasm and argued that by 1926 reactionaries were in control of the revolution and that "the old economic doctrines . . . of Díaz" had triumphed.[7]

The revolution which tore Mexico apart for the better part of a decade simply never uprooted the fundamental political and economic forces, nor the social classes, extant under the *Porfiriato*. Certainly, change did occur. Realignments of the distribution of political power and economic resources brought new figures into power. But in the end the process more resembled a "circulation of elites" than that of an entirely new class supplanting the old. The evidence strongly indicates that the old feudalistic landed order remained as before the revolution, with modifications to be sure. A rudimentary commercial and manufacturing capitalist class joined with the old landed classes, and new members came from the revolution's victorious armies, but these did not carve out a new society. Moreover, Mexico's historical subjection to foreign investors and the political and economic influence of its northern imperialist neighbor, the United States, continued basically intact. New ruling groups inherited a history, and rather than discard it, they used it as the foundation for the reformist reconstruction of the nation.

Commentaries of the era described the political leaders of the twenties as the "Revolutionary plutocrats." Lesley Byrd Simpson contended that they virtually joined league "with their ancient enemies, old hacendado-clergy-foreign complex of Don Porfirio's day" and lived in "palaces in Cuernavaca . . . medieval castles . . . tennis courts, swimming pools." The "new millionaires," the "heroes of the Revolution," came into their wealth "in the service to their country."[8] Some, like Plutarco Elías Calles, simply expanded their wealth. At the age of seventeen, Calles's son was bequeathed a fifteen-thousand-acre hacienda. And how did the rural peasantry fare?

Land Reform

Nearly twenty years after the 1917 Constitution laid the legal basis for land reform, Margaret Clark observed that the Mexican peasantry's "gain over its semi-feudal position was neither very extensive nor very great." Later, she added, the "peasant is probably worse off today, materially, than he was in the colonial epoch."[9] Those grim observations were echoed forty years later by James Cockroft, whose investigations explain why land reform made little headway into land tenure patterns: "Commercial hacendados, particularly those producing for export, were protected from agrarian reform legislation and favored by credit policies."[10] In the Yucatan and the Laguna regions, protection from expropriation secured the survival of "many of the largest land holdings." Díaz-era henequen plantations retained their prerevolutionary social relations, and plantation owners and majordomos managed to "retain control of most of the area's peasants." Cockroft adds that in spite of the celebrated Cárdenas land distributions, the government's own accounting showed that "Mexico continued to be fundamentally a country of estates of more than 5,000 hectares in size." The popular *ejido* program, which was supposed to reestablish traditional communal landholdings, actually tells a story of the retention of colonial land laws and distribution patterns. Agrarian reform, argues Cockroft, did allow the confiscation and distribution of "many latifundistas' unproductive or idle lands." However, echoing Simpson, he adds that "many hacendados had survived to rebuild or expand their estates, their ranks swelled by the so-called revolutionary landlords—military officers and politicians who, with state encouragement, had amassed immense amounts of land. . . . Not untypically when distributing land to rural proletarians . . . Cárdenas left the lands of the principal producers . . . untouched."[11]

Clearly, the peasant was not the primary beneficiary, and the fact that the wealthy Cárdenas owned at least three estates may explain his flawed vision of land reform. Not only were the successful estates sidestepped for expropriation, but also agrarian reform conveniently passed over latifundias owned by former military and political cohorts. John W. Hart has argued that Cárdenas spared "the latifundia complex in Sonora owned by his old chief, Alvaro Obregón, in his agrarian reform package." [12] Special entitlements insured that some would remain lords over estates and in political control of the peasantry. Nearly a century has passed since the first land reform laws were enacted. That the peasantry continues to demand land, rebelling in Guerrero and Morelos, old bastions of *Zapatismo*, signifies that land reform remains an unfulfilled demand for millions of Mexicans. Did the revolution affect foreign investments in a similar manner?

Foreign Capital and Investments

The character of the Mexican Revolution is reflected in its policy toward foreign investment. Throughout Mexico's period of civil strife and the era of political consolidation, Washington's policy stressed one central objective: maintain the Díaz open-door policy and legal protections for foreign capital, particularly U.S. capital. Washington ignored government corruption but feared that the economic nationalism would erect walls against the continued flow of American investment not only into Mexico, but into Central and South America as well. U.S. foreign policy considered Mexico the linchpin for the whole of Latin America, feared the spread of economic nationalism, and therefore spared no effort to steer Mexico into acquiescing to U.S. policy. The administrations of Woodrow Wilson to Herbert Hoover struggled to shape a Mexico where foreign "investment could flourish." [13] Washington followed a simple dictum, that the U.S. by virtue of natural law and a higher form of civilization had the right to dictate Mexico's internal policy, and further held that anything other than complete acceptance of that policy implied "Bolshevism."

Ultimately Washington succeeded, but that success should have been anticipated. Mexican leaders never sought the complete elimination of the dominant presence of foreign investment; rather they hoped for a larger share of the receipts, and perhaps a role in decisions concerning the regulation of investments. Limited control and a partnership in the investment decision making comprised Mexico's main nationalistic economic ideology and strategy. Leading political figures of the revolution did not enunciate an ideology that flatly opposed foreign investment but rather challenged uncontrolled foreign investment.[14] Ambivalent revolutionaries, as Ramón Eduardo Ruiz titled the generation of leaders, products of a "rudimentary capitalistic structure," with one foot in the medieval hacienda economy and the other in some form of capitalism, eventually succumbed.

With the 1923 signing of the Bucareli Agreements, Mexico essentially agreed to abide by the terms of U.S. policy and promised to "safeguard the interests of foreign capitalists." Revolutionary rhetoric declared Mexico's economic independence, but the record shows that in the 1920s foreign investments either held a steady course or increased compared to those of the Díaz period. The limited sanctions enforced by the revolutionary governments delighted U.S. investors and Washington officials and prompted one manufacturer of farm machinery to declare that Obregón was "by far the best ruler Mexico has had since Díaz . . . and in some respects is superior to Díaz." The revolution, one might say, was a bonanza for U.S. banks and corporations investing in Mexico.

Evidence records that Mexico's dependence upon U.S. capital, technology, trade, expertise, and tutelage retained its Porfirian-era profile. Contemporary data demonstrates the growing, rather than the lessening, subordination of the Mexican economy to the northern world power. As the 1920s came to a close, foreign interests owned 98 percent of all mining operations, two thirds of all coffee plantations, 86 percent of all cotton production, 100 percent of bananas and other fruits, 95 percent of refined sugar, and 94 percent of petroleum operations. "In most areas," summarizes Robert Freeman Smith, "the United States expanded its presence." Smith adds that "fears that the U.S. predominance in the Mexican economy would be eliminated . . . proved to be wrong."[15] U.S. corporate investors like Thomas Lamont, a partner in the J. P. Morgan firm, and Judge E. J. Gary, of U.S. Steel, among others, found in Revolutionary Mexico "a government endeavoring to do the right thing."[16]

Labor and Labor Politics

As the revolution affirmed the Porfirian open-door investment policy, labor policies followed a similar path and contained many of the strategies of the old regime. These policies are critical for explaining consular interventions in the 1920s and 1930s. David W. Walker argues persuasively that the post-Díaz administrations did not create a new public policy toward labor but applied a variety of tried and tested practices to promote desired forms of labor organization. Walker contends that the "Díaz government promoted modes of organization which retarded labor militancy, sponsored informal as well as official mediation between workers and employers during strikes and other conflicts, and disseminated propaganda and instituted educational programs . . . designed to promote labor's identification of its own well-being with the interests of the state. While the Revolution of 1910 and the later developments of the Cárdenas era institutionalized state-labor relations as never before, the objectives and instrumentalities of contemporary labor relations have their origin in the Porfiriato." [17] Walker concludes that "[c]lose examination, then, shows few fundamental differences in labor policy before or after the Revolution of 1910." Walker's interpretation runs against the grain of conventional wisdom, that is, the contention that the 1917 Constitution guaranteed labor rights and privileges not found in the most advanced industrial democracies of the day. Mexican workers obtained (or better were given) legal protection for an eight-hour day, minimal wage, a maximum work week of six days, overtime pay, the right to organize unions and bargain collectively, as well as other rights. The Constitution was one thing; its enforcement was an entirely different matter. Seldom were constitutional guarantees acted upon. Margaret Clark, among others, observed while studying Mexican labor sixty years ago: "Nowhere does a greater difference exist between written law and practice than in Mexico." [18] Much of the responsibility for the glaring gap between law and practice must be handed to the astute political sense of Mexico's leaders, for it was they who cynically engineered the subordination of labor by way of a government-controlled labor central, the Confederación Regional Obrera Mexicana, or CROM.

With blueprints borrowed from Porfirio Díaz, CROM was founded in 1918 as a mechanism to ensure labor's fealty. In return, those who pledged their support to the regime could expect government patronage. An array of government sinecures, bribes, emoluments, and patronage, combined with severe and systematic repression of leftist and radical challenges, allowed CROM to effectively shape and then channel working-class political interests favorable to state objectives. Led by the notoriously corrupt Luis Morones, CROM effectively dominated labor from 1918 to the late 1920s and held considerable power through the 1950s (it exists even today), promoting a conservative and limited labor politics that revolved within pro-government parameters. Shortly after its founding, CROM not only secured the enforced loyalty of labor, a vital and important segment of Mexican society, but also ensured the subjugation of that sector to the dictates of the dominant political forces.

Patronage and repression, the Porfirian *pan o palo* (the bread or the stick), became an institutionalized method for coercing labor's acquiescence. Ideology counted for little as CROM supported whichever candidate lined their pockets, especially those of CROM's inner circle of labor politicians, the Grupo Acción. All important union decisions were made by the Grupo Acción's twenty appointed, not elected, individuals who acted as an authoritarian board of directors. Special privileges accrued to members of the secretive inner circle comprised of an old network of cronies. Three examples convey the picture. In 1920 President Obregón named Luis Morones director of federal military factories; Celestino Gasca became the governor of the Federal District, and Eduardo Moneda "earned" the directorship of the newly established Department of Social Provisions.[19] One American, the self-styled socialist Robert Haberman, sat on the Grupo Acción and was reported to be an informant, in other words, a spy for J. Edgar Hoover in the U.S. Justice Department.[20]

CROM kept labor "on a leash," but CROM itself was useful only as long as its leaders were tethered to the state. The implicit bargain brought official labor inside the inner walls of the state, but the state and a handful of labor cronies, not labor, were the beneficiaries. Luis Morones continued his starry, if opportunistic, political climb and was appointed secretary of industry, commerce, and labor in the cabinet of President Calles. In keeping with Porfirian tradition, Morones's appointment meant for him an independent source of lucrative handouts, privileges, and political clout, all of which he used for Grupo Acción's aggrandizement. If the bribe failed, CROM was not averse to using systematic labor repression, including assassinations. These practices soon became a trademark of state policy.

CROM not only capitalized on its official privileges but also sought to ensure a monopoly and eliminate all opposition. Expediency determined whether to support or suppress a strike, and often secret agreements signed with employers, without the knowledge or acceptance of the rank and file, brought an end to a strike. Not surprisingly, Morones and his closest allies made "the most from labor and political connections" and amassed a large personal fortune while labor made very little headway, "unable to increase [its] share of national income" during the same time frame.[21]

CROM's free use of violence to pacify labor descended from its status as a government tool. An American Federation of Labor (AFL) committee charged with informing on the organization's international relations reported that "the relations between the Mexican labor movement and the Mexican government are very intimate."[22] "Very intimate" was putting it mildly. Frank Tannenbaumn, one of a group of firsthand observers of the early years of the revolutionary administrations, wrote many decades ago that Mexico's "labor unions and labor movement are essentially creatures and instruments of the government."[23] One only needs to add that the practice was a political device inherited from the Porfiriato, an era that, according to the nationalistic rhetoric of the day, was supposedly buried by the revolution.

Gompers, the AFL, and CROM

The dark side of the revolution failed to deter the AFL under Samuel Gompers from forging an international alliance with CROM, an alliance that, in addition to impacting the emigrant work force, was particularly useful and advantageous for both parties. Throughout the Carranza (1915–1920) and Obregón (1920–1924) periods and until Gompers's untimely death in 1924 while returning home (after attending Calles's inauguration as a special guest who had been formally introduced on the presidential platform), the AFL president enjoyed "most cordial relations" with CROM and Morones.[24] After Gompers's demise, the alliance, based on fraternal cooperation, continued. Each side entered into celebrated agreements and, as fraternal delegates, attended and addressed the other's national conventions. Gompers's ebullience toward CROM, Morones, Obregón, and Calles exemplified the alliance. In an outburst of emotion, Gompers praised presidential candidate Calles as a "friend of labor and champion of those principles for which we all stand."[25]

After Calles's election in 1924, the president-elect journeyed to the United States, where he met with Gompers at the AFL headquarters. Their greeting, described by Gompers's personal secretary, exhibited the cordial relations between CROM and the AFL: "General Calles' greeting to Mr. Gompers was most affectionate—put his arms around Mr. Gompers and gave him a genuine Latin embrace. The two sides accompanying likewise were very cordial in their greetings."[26]

More fundamental reasons account for the AFL-CROM collaboration. Gompers advocated U.S. economic domination in Latin America—in particular, the maintenance of U.S. investments in Mexico. Gompers strayed but little from the State Department's immediate objectives regarding the Mexican Revolution. With a firm conviction that the mastery of the world's economy was the United States's "manifest destiny and our duty," he set out to assist the organization of the Mexican labor movement.[27] It is hard to make the argument that Gompers's first goal was the organization of labor in Mexico. Studies show that his primary objective was a Mexican administration accommodated to U.S. demands regarding foreign capital. However, Gompers's concerns moved beyond the key economic goal that he shared with the State Department and corporate investors.

He had a keen interest in the politics of the Mexican labor movement, and he worried over labor's political perspective on capital, foreign and national. By 1915, reports had begun filtering in of a growing Industrial Workers of the World (IWW) and anarcho-syndicalist influence within the main Mexican labor organization, the Casa del Obrero Mundial. Spurred by this news, Gompers assumed an activist role in the Mexican labor movement. Fearing the potential for a rise of the left within organized labor, he intended to intervene and steer it, if at all possible, onto safe political terrain. With anarchist and leftist politics infiltrating Mexican labor, the possibility loomed that the American labor movement might then be infected. With rising Mexican immigration, such ideological aberrations might well seep by way of the migrants into the ranks of American labor. However, before Mexican labor could be correctly organized, Mexico required a policy adjusted to the requirements that Wilson and his successors defined as fundamental to international relations. Underdeveloped countries shouldered the obligation to honor, protect, and welcome foreign investment, for the good of their nation required it. Once in place, proper domestic policy ensured an abiding respect for the rights of all capital, foreign and national. Upon that foundation a correct labor movement might then freely evolve. Gompers hoped for two things: a government friendly to the United States and a reformist, gradualist, and collaborationist labor movement. Both wishes were fulfilled.

The new Mexican labor leadership, Morones among them, guided labor away from anarchism and Marxist sympathies toward the conservative trade union ideals of the imperial AFL. Shortly after its founding, CROM began an official cooperative exchange with the AFL and indicated that the Mexican federation would "organize along the lines of the AFL."

We should not be surprised that former President Obregón received an honorary membership in an AFL affiliate, the International Association of Machinists (IAM), nor that the AFL assigned an IAM organizer, one Joe Kelly, to CROM's Mexico City headquarters to help develop that organization, an assignment which gave him access to the president. Kelly later served as a special Mexican propagandist in the United States under the pay of the Mexican government, receiving $600 a month for his services.[28] Luis Morones established a tradition when he attended the 1919 AFL convention in a display of "international labor solidarity." Five years later, at the 1924 convention, the alliance still in force, Gompers assured the large gathering, which included fraternal CROM delegates (representing the Grupo Acción), "that the AFL would stand 'shoulder to shoulder' with the CROM in its future labor struggles." [29]

Pax Mexico-Americana

Gross misinterpretations of the 1910 Revolution by U.S. diplomats (and many Mexican archconservatives) led to labeling leaders like Obregón, Calles, and Morones as "Bolshevists" and "socialists," epithets often thrown with great rancor at the Mexican Revolutionary clique. Eventually State Department officials realized the folly and grew confident regarding the intentions of the government. In practice, Mexican leaders convinced the State Department that the revolution harbored no thoughts of a socialist takeover and that it, like the political colleagues CROM and the AFL, stood "shoulder to shoulder" with their northern neighbor on the matter of economic policy.

Symbolic nationalistic rhetoric, often peppered with Marxist-sounding phrases, was useful for generating public support for the revolutionary administrations, particularly among the working class and intellectuals. However, the rhetoric of class struggle (mixed with doses of nationalistic *indigenismo*) contrasted with the reigning ideology, theory, and practice. It was one thing to talk "revolution," another to practice it. In practice, the Mexican Revolution stopped far short of a socialist program, although speeches by Morones and other CROM leaders contained tinges of Marxist terminology and could confuse the listener. Such was the situation at the 1926 AFL convention when Ricardo Treviño, of Grupo Acción, sounded quite radical in his address to the convention. "It is an undisputed fact," he stated, "that we in Mexico, as you in the United States, are both under the same influence and the exploitation of the same capitalist forces. . . . they employ the same methods in their attacks . . . against the organized labor movement." [30] When Luis Morones rose before the 1927 convention of the Pan-American Federation of Labor (an invention of Gompers), he described the AFL as an organization that has "never . . . allied with American capital," the only true defender of the American working class.[31] Rhetoric obfuscated the glaring contradictions. That year, at the forty-seventh annual AFL convention in Los Angeles, the California delegation, led by Paul Scharrenberg, succeeded in passing a resolution calling for a quota on Mexican immigration. After deliberations, CROM and the AFL agreed upon reviving voluntary restrictions by Mexican authorities.

As the Mexican Revolution and the United States came to terms by the early 1920s, the gestating Mexican state apparatus eventually emerged in

1929 as the authoritarian one-party corporate institution that would come to dominate the Mexican state to the end of the century. As the state matured, CROM weakened. President Calles feared that Morones held too much power in addition to pretensions to the presidency, and so he pulled out of the compact around 1928. Without strong-man support, CROM declined, although it retained a large share of unionized labor and still held considerable power. Despite CROM's fall from official grace, Mexican labor remained tethered to government oversight and was folded into the new state apparatus founded by Calles in 1929, the Partido Nacional Revolucionario (PNR). Consular intervention continued regardless of the change in players, and the key objectives elaborated during the 1920s continued to shape consular conduct. Within these general parameters, Mexican domestic politics of the teens and twenties took form and were exported by way of consulates positioned within or nearby emigrant settlements.

Criteria for Selecting Revolutionary Consulate Personnel

In February 1933, President Abelardo Rodríguez addressed an "important resolution" to the Secretariat of Foreign Relations that reaffirmed an existing policy relating to the conduct of Mexican foreign affairs: "all measures of a political nature" undertaken by accredited diplomatic agents, including the consular corps, shall be under the strict control of the secretary of foreign relations "in representation of the Executive." [32] As for those responsibilities relating to "political activities . . . [the consular corps] shall obey the instructions issued by the diplomatic mission in the respective country or directly by the Ministry of Foreign Affairs. Honorary consuls are included." [33] Foreign Affairs continued to hone a more precise code of conduct for its officers abroad. Consul Visitor–General Adolfo de la Huerta penned a confidential letter to Raul Castellanos, President Lázaro Cárdenas's personal secretary, detailing his views of the indispensable political and professional qualities necessary for consular service. He wrote that "during my trips throughout the [North] American Union I have come to realize the necessity for well-prepared personnel, with absolute loyalty to our Regime [and] with personal sympathy for President Cárdenas." [34]

Both sets of conditions outlined in the Rodríguez resolution and in the de la Huerta letter demonstrate the sophisticated political nature of the consular service. In the first, consuls were subordinate to the instructions and policy directives from the president via the Secretariat of Foreign Relations. In the second, "absolute loyalty" to the executive power and the policies of the administration provided the sine qua non in selecting the personnel for consular appointments. Moreover, the president personally appointed consuls to the posts of critical importance—San Francisco, San Antonio, El Paso, and Los Angeles—choices made from a sense of largesse and rectitude intended to ensure their "perfect fit with the government policies."[35]

De la Huerta's formula for the selection of the consular officials was a political dance in which the steps were formal and elegant. Place and privilege permeated the selection process. Landing a coveted spot on the consular corps required considerable personal and political connections to the high and mighty within the political structure. Artifice and eloquence refined in the Porfirian era provided a familiar pattern for revolutionary forces to build upon.[36] Good family ties measured up well with those reviewing personnel files and carried great weight. It appears that the consular world comprised the tribe of the elite. Thus, the more exalted a candidate's connection in the political hierarchy, the greater were his chances for a successful review. When a candidate's political allegiances were under consideration, loyalty to the president came first. There is no question that loyalty, socioeconomic factors, and well-placed family connections were the key conditions that influenced who was chosen and who rejected. It follows naturally that consuls were generally picked from the "best" families, the wealthier classes of Mexico. For one thing, only they had the means to send their children abroad for schooling. Time spent in the United States, where English and American cultural skills, values, and behavior were learned, was an essential part of the pedigree. Individuals drawn from this pool were thus well prepared to carry out consular responsibilities with the proper finesse. Further, candidates chosen for the corps generally came from those particular privileged and educated classes that professed support for the victorious faction or coalition that eventually came to power in the postrevolutionary period. Family ties and favors rendered served as chips to be cashed in for a position in the state hierarchy.

The following examples, gleaned from the consulate files of the Archivo de la Secretaría de Relaciones Exteriores (ASRE) in Mexico City, illustrate the powerful role family played in the selection process. First let us take up the case of Consul Carlos Ariza, a prominent figure in Imperial Valley Mexican-labor organizing in the late twenties. Ariza's father, Division General Carlos Víctor Ariza from the state of Morelos, enjoyed close ties with several Obregonistas. Ariza's distinguished family spoke of a privileged upbringing, and like many of his cohorts, the young Ariza was trained and schooled in the United States. After completing secondary education in Pennsylvania schools, Ariza earned a law degree at St. Francis College, also in Pennsylvania. Fluent in English, Ariza returned to Mexico City to teach at the English School. He was soon promoted to subdirector, a position he held until he entered the consular service in 1921.[37]

Using his powerful personal connections to the winning side of the 1910 Revolution, Ariza's father, the general, was able to gain that consulate post for his son, Carlos Jr. To do so, he first tapped the illustrious revolutionary figure, General Genovevo de la O, a former Zapatista chieftain turned Obregonista who had eventually received a distinguished position in the Obregón administration. Upon Ariza's request, de la O wrote personally to President Obregón recommending Ariza Jr.: "I have the pleasure to make this presentation," wrote de la O, "of Mr. Carlos Ariza [Jr.], a person whom, with your permission, I recommend to you in a most special manner, a person who desires to collaborate with the Government over which you preside, as a consul of our nation in the United States of America."[38]

Knowing that more than one letter was needed to sway the president, Ariza then approached another influential family acquaintance, Dr. José G. Parres, the provisional governor of the state of Morelos, appointed by Obregón. Dr. Parres lent his formidable weight to the task. "Permit me to recommend," began Parres's letter, "and present to your fine considerations, my good friend, Mr. Carlos Víctor Ariza, son of my good friend Division General [Ariza]."[39]

With such powerful political leverage, his reputation as a known quantity was secure and Ariza was able to gain an interview with President Obregón. Secretary of the Treasury (and former interim president) Adolfo de la Huerta provided the final letter of introduction to Obregón. "Very Dear Friend," he began, "the bearer, Mr. Professor Carlos V. Ariza, has been especially recommended by Mr. José G. Parres . . . so that I may recommend to your fine considerations . . . that [Ariza] receive the post of Consul of Mexico in a population center of the United States."[40] With such favorable recommendations from important political figures, Ariza received the nod from Obregón and began his service at the Hong Kong legation in 1921. He was later assigned to the U.S. station at Tucson, Arizona, in 1924 and then to the Calexico, California, consulate.

The case of Manuel Ortega, although somewhat more complex than that of Ariza, provides a parallel example. Ortega applied for an appointment during the administration of Cárdenas. Here again we see the use of family as leverage to gain a political appointment. Manuel Ortega came from a family of generals. His deceased father, Anatolio B. Ortega, and his uncle and adoptive father, Brigadier General Manuel Ortega B, joined the Revolution in 1910. Young Manuel's education and upbringing depended upon his well-to-do uncle, who sent him to Texas for secondary school. Following Manuel's graduation, the general supported his engineering studies at the Georgia Institute of Technology. In 1935, however, the general, beleaguered by financial stringencies, withdrew his support, and Manuel was forced to abandon his studies and return to Mexico. Undaunted, he began the process of securing a post in the consular service, with which he, fortunately, had ties: his brother, Anatolio, held a vice-consul position in the San Antonio consul-general's office. Anatolio, in collaboration with Manuel, launched what was to become a letter-writing campaign on Manuel's behalf with a note to President Cárdenas's personal secretary, Luis I. Rodríguez. In this letter he made a request outlining a plan to assist his brother. "Most Esteemed Mr. Rodríguez," wrote Anatolio,

I wish to kindly request that you speak with Mr. President in our name so that my brother may be conceded the post of first or second chancellor in the Foreign Service. . . .

I would appreciate if you would inform General Cárdenas that this is a matter of helping the family of the late Anatolio B. Ortega, our father, who was a revolutionary since 1910. Regarding his service to the Nation, there are documents at the Secretariat of War.[41]

Consul General Hill of the San Antonio consulate, son of the late Obregonista General Benjamin Hill, was also enlisted to support Ortega's supplication. Hill implored President Cárdenas's personal secretary, Rodríguez, to bring the case personally to Cárdenas's attention. "Once again I insist," wrote Hill, that Manuel Ortega "is the son of a true revolutionary."[42] As no action was taking place to appoint Ortega, Hill sent another letter two weeks later urging Rodríguez to nudge his boss. "I believe," advised Hill, "that with only one indication from General Cárdenas, Manuel Ortega will be commissioned in the United States."[43] The Governor of Chihuahua, Rodrigo Quevedo, also joined the campaign with a letter to President Cárdenas that repeated the by then well worn heroic phrases: "The young Ortega is the son of the late General Anatolio B. Ortega, who gave important service to the Revolution. . . . help the son of this soldier of the Revolution," exclaimed Quevedo.[44]

The barrage of petitions had a favorable effect, but not the immediate desired conclusion that was sought. Eduardo Hay, secretary of foreign relations, responded positively to the various recommendations on Ortega's behalf in a memorandum to Rodríguez: "I have been looking for the opportunity to fulfill your estimable recommendations; but that opportunity has not presented itself. . . . I shall continue to attend to this matter."[45] Two years passed. The petitions still circulated but without closure. Finally, an exasperated Brigadier General Ortega laid out his agenda clearly in a private letter to Cárdenas. "I believe," suggested Ortega, "that one of the forms in which he [Manuel] can continue his studies is by naming him chancellor . . . in San Antonio, and commissioning him in Atlanta, so that with his salary he can sustain his studies, as long as he is permitted to reside in Atlanta, which is where his school is located."[46]

Finally, the subject of the long process, Manuel Ortega himself, addressed President Cárdenas directly as well: "I have the hope that you, Mr. President, can help me to finish my studies. Given the fact that the government scholarships are of such short duration, permit me to suggest an idea: name me chancellor in the consular service, so that I may receive my salary and pay my studies; but if you have a better manner of resolving my difficulties I will greatly appreciate it."[47]

After Manuel's letter, the Ortega matter disappears from the files of the Archivo General de la Nación (AGN). No matter that we do not know the final outcome; we have insight into the conventional procedures and criteria that the Mexican political apparatus applied in the selection of its consular corps. Political linkages based upon family, wealth, and class were the structures that closed the circle of influence and power.

Not all requests, as we see, could be fulfilled satisfactorily, but many were. Consider the case of Ricardo Hill, son of General Benjamin Hill, close ally to President Obregón. Like Ariza, Hill advanced his professional cause on the ladder provided by family, as his brother Benjamin had done before him, to become a member of the consular service. After seeking and having been granted a position in the service, Hill wrote to Fernando Torreblanca, personal secretary to President Calles: "Yesterday I had the pleasure to receive your polite message . . . in which you communicate . . . that I will fill the next vacancy. . . . one more time you have attended to my supplication, for which I am very appreciative and only wait that some day I may have the opportunity to serve you as well."[48]

A year passed before Hill received his appointment to the Philadelphia consulate. He went on to serve at various locations before arriving in Los Angeles in the early thirties, where he played a major part in local labor conflicts. Hill rose through the ranks and was appointed consul in 1935. Alejandro Gómez Maganda served under Hill in Los Angeles, and he provides the final example to illustrate the tradition.

At the young age of twenty-six, Gómez Maganda arrived in Los Angeles richly decorated with a strong political pedigree. Simultaneous with his appointment, Gómez Maganda held a congressional seat from the state of Guerrero and previously had served as secretary to the president of the PNR.[49] Widely heralded for his oratorical gifts, he enjoyed close personal friendships with the politically powerful. Gómez Maganda could confidentially address such personages as President Cárdenas's personal secretary, Luis Rodríguez, as "My Fine Friend."[50] Rodríguez responded with the salutation, "I embrace you fraternally on this day," and on another occasion he addressed Gómez as "My Dear Brother."[51] Having the distinction of occupying two divergent positions, those of congressman and vice-consul, did not seem to deter the energetic Gómez. Upon notification of his consular assignment, a pleased Gómez wired President Cárdenas: "Upon taking possession of the position which you delegated to me, I send you my profound appreciation, my subordination, and respectful affection."

A loyal Gómez planned to put his speaking skills to the political purposes expected of him. After the first few days in Los Angeles, he wrote to Rodríguez, "I'm thinking of giving a series of conferences concerning our [Mexico's] situation [and] the direction taken by our Regime [sic] and that of General Cárdenas."[52] Gómez kept his promise, and soon after arriving he informed the secretary that he had given "talks to citrus pickers, today seamstresses, tomorrow in Pacoima, the 21st to the Partido Liberal Benito Juárez, after that to the Club Lázaro Cárdenas and so on it goes."[53] Needless to say, Gómez Maganda gained a prominent stature in the *colonia,* in particular among the established organizations and their leadership.

The consular service functioned as a vital link between the central government and the expatriate community. However, projects which anticipated the effective organization of *México de afuera* were based on the political lineage dominating the revolution's leadership. The consular corps received the nod to organize the Mexican immigrant community into the politics of the revolution. Consuls were not left to themselves as they assumed their assigned tasks; they followed blueprints taken directly from the political architecture shaping the Mexican government.

Consuls and the Politics of Emigration

With labor in Mexico safely under favorable tutelage and labor radicalism in check, threats to U.S. hegemony from the southern republic appeared unlikely. The AFL then moved onto other pressing issues with its international partners. As early as 1919, while Gompers was busy praising Morones and Grupo Acción for standing together with the AFL, the latter's executive council voted to call for the legislative restriction of Mexican immigration. Mexican labor, alleged a number of southwestern state councils, competed with U.S. labor, reduced wages, and was unorganizable. Eventually, the AFL and CROM signed a Memorandum of Agreement that obligated CROM to cooperate and lobby for the "voluntary restriction" of Mexican immigration into the United State (and the exclusion of "oriental" immigration to boot).[54] By way of fliers, broadsides, meetings and exhortations, CROM urged its fellow citizens to remain in Mexico, but this strategy produced little reduction in migration. Quite the opposite occurred as migration continued to climb dramatically into the mid-twenties. The voluntary campaign revived under AFL pressure in 1927, as CROM again agreed to do everything at its disposal to discourage emigration. Further, when CROM members emigrated, they would be under orders to "join the unions of their trades, affiliated with the American Federation of Labor." According to Margaret Clark, CROM stipulated that "a failure to do so shall subject such workers to discipline by the Mexican Federation to the possible extent of expulsion . . . upon their return to Mexico."[55] However meaningless the agreement (few migrants were affiliated with craft unions), the symbolism of the agreement demonstrated the extent to which CROM advanced AFL politics and preferred policies into Mexico.

Diminishing migration, a goal first proposed by Díaz as early as 1910 without success, proved to be just as elusive and complex an objective in the late twenties. From Madero through Calles, Mexico exerted little effort to stem the tide of emigration, although authorities continually voiced concern over the loss of its citizens. Their words, however, were so much rhetoric, more in line with nationalistic appeals than with concrete programs. Moreover, the agreement between CROM and the AFL required no more than publicized exhortations to stay put. Other than the media coverage depicting the trials and turmoils experienced by emigrants, the governments applied little more than words to the effort. The reasons Mexico made little effort to stop, or at least slow, the emigration, are not hard to find. First, emigration provided a safety valve for the disaffected, easing political pressure within Mexico. The rural sections, a focus of political unrest, produced the greatest numbers of emigrants as well as a high degree of political disaffection. Writing in 1933, Paul S. Taylor confirmed this aspect of Mexico's immigration policy, noting that Carranza "provided an outlet for landless laborers, who are potential agraristas," that is, peasant land reformers. Moreover, in the region studied by Taylor, no shortage of labor affected the economy and no one imagined the depletion of the local labor supply through emigration. In rural towns, a new cottage industry boomed: lending pesos to peasants seeking to emigrate. "Anyone with money to lend engaged in the business of assisting persons to emigrate," noted Taylor.[56] Taylor quoted one "informed ranchero" from Jalisco: "The hacendados prefer to let the workers get away so they won't concentrate in pueblos [towns] and ask for land. They would [be willing to] loan money to emigrants. The laborers go from the haciendas here the same as from elsewhere."[57] Conceivably, by allowing emigration to take place, Mexico escaped a fundamental social transformation—in other words, a revolution. Arguably, emigration provided Mexico's "way out."

Secondly, revolutionary pragmatism moved leaders to accept emigration as ultimately beneficial for the economy. According to Lawrence Cardoso, Presidents Carranza, Obregón, Calles, and Portes Gil believed that "it was not in the best interests to halt the labor exodus," and they opposed any measure to effectively obstruct emigration. Cardoso affirms that "Mexican consuls and [Department of] Migration personnel frequently did all they could to keep braceros in the United States or to facilitate their re-entry into [the United States]."[58] In a period of economic difficulty, the large amount of money braceros sent to relatives at home was a great assistance to the economically strapped nation. Manuel Gamio "found that approximately 12,000 braceros sent almost $300,000 to their relatives" in the month of July 1926 alone. During the decade of the twenties, at least $58,000,000 flowed into the Mexican economy. Small amounts arrived in the form of money orders; millions more entered as notes, drafts, and cash. Consuls, meanwhile, were advised to assist unemployed Mexicans in the United States in procuring employment and to "remind authorities of the value of Mexican laborers to the vitality of the local economy."[59]

Mexican leaders found it difficult to reject the benefits of uncontrolled emigration and rested content with symbolic calls to its expatriate sons and daughters, exhorting them not to abandon their beloved country, reminding them that the nation needed their service for national reconstruction. Southwestern U.S. employers required a seemingly inexhaustible supply of cheap Mexican labor, and Mexican authorities matched that requirement with a cooperative emigration policy. Cardoso observed that under the revolutionary leaders' direction "Mexico simply became a larger labor pool" and that "emigration provided a better alternative than restless unemployment at home."[60] Indeed, while Mexico officially expressed nationalistic misgivings, railed against emigration, and proffered repatriation to those who had departed, consuls and Mexican migration personnel worked hand-in-hand with employers and labor recruiters in several ways, assisting migrants in entering the U.S. job market.

Detroit Consul Joaquín Terrazas confirmed that Mexico had a financial interest in emigration. "My government," he stated to an interviewer, "would try to stop it if it were not for the need of money by its people." [61] Consulates cooperated with employers when approached, going so far as to announce job opportunities, thus giving the appearance that the consul looked approvingly upon a particular request for labor. Consul Terrazas's remark that "a great many Mexicans come to me in the winter time. They come mostly to try to get me to secure a job for them" reflected an outlook that directly related to his government's policy. [62] El Paso Spanish-language newspapers, for example, published the local consul general's bulletin notifying readers that "shortly, employment will be available for three thousand Mexican laborers in the upper and lower valleys of El Paso, in the cotton fields." Workers interested in picking cotton were offered free transportation, housing, and fuel and urged to apply at the federal employment agency located in El Paso's city hall basement.

An incident during the tenure of San Antonio Consul General Alejandro Lubbert provides yet another illustration of consular-employer complicity. Lubbert contracted for the transport of several thousand migrants to work at the Bethlehem Steel plant in Pennsylvania. George W. Vary, the superintendent of Bethlehem's welfare department, signed agreements with Lubbert whereby as many as three hundred laborers at a time "will be shipped to Bethlehem as fast as they can be assembled." According to the contract, "only such Mexicans as are selected by Consul General Lubbert shall be employed." Contracts stipulated wages, hours, and cost for room and board. Transportation charges and board while en route to Pennsylvania were to be deducted from wages and reimbursed to Consul Lubbert. Any worker who for any reason became a public charge "at any time after the execution of the contract" would be delivered to Lubbert "at their expense." [63] If the employee remained for a year, all transportation costs would be assumed by the employer.

Enthused by suggestions from the Los Angeles Chamber of Commerce that an employment agency for Mexicans be established, Consul Rafael de la Colina pursued the project diligently. To his superiors, de la Colina described the chamber's proposal as one made in "good faith for the Mexican residents of this district." Representatives of the "principal transportation and agricultural companies" met at the chamber offices to discuss the agency. From the perspective of U.S. employers, the repatriation campaign begun in the early 1930s posed a potential threat to their Mexican labor supply, but establishing an employment agency would ease access to the available supply. Ironically, at the same time de la Colina was moving ahead with these plans to secure Mexican labor (see also

Chapter 2), he was cooperating with the repatriation effort. Although the employment agency never materialized, de la Colina seems to personify the Mexican government's ambiguous and contradictory policy toward *Mexico de afuera.*[64]

Several years later, agents representing the Montana beet industry visited the offices of Los Angeles Consul Ricardo Hill requesting cooperation for securing several hundred laborers. Hill informed the agents "that the Consulate would have no inconvenience whatsoever in recommending the employment to my compatriots at the salary indicated," so long as contracts guaranteed a job in Montana and round-trip transportation and all contracts were reviewed by the consulate. Although the agents from Montana eventually recruited labor for the beet industry via posters and newspaper advertisements, that they sought the cooperation of the consulate reveals the complicity that existed between U.S. employers and Mexican consuls.[65]

The Politics of Repatriation

The matter of emigration segued into repatriation and elicited the attention of government authorities in a parallel fashion. As in the case of departing *hijos de la patria,* repatriation presented an opportunity to generate Mexican revolutionary nationalism. The message that *la patria* awaited and needed its prodigal sons and daughters was repeated endlessly and reverberated through the *colonias* across the United States. But repatriation remained primarily a symbolic expression, a matter of national spirit and faith that the government, as the nation's most powerful *patrón,* protected all *mexicanos* regardless of rank, class, or residence. Repatriation, like emigration restriction, never assumed a priority status on the agenda of Mexican domestic politics until pressured by U.S. demands for the return of unemployed and welfare cases in the late 1920s and 1930s. Bending under the pressure, Mexico then offered repatriation to its citizens in a manner that can only be described as thorough cooperation with U.S. authorities.

Generally, repatriation is explained as a complex project that involved several metropolitan areas of the United States. From a U.S. perspective, it was designed to rid welfare rolls of Mexican recipients, thereby lowering budget costs. However, as will be explained in the chapter that follows, the U.S.–sponsored repatriation campaign would never have succeeded to the extent that it did without the full participation and acknowledgment of the Mexican government. In other words, the repatriation drives of the late 1920s and 1930s begun at the instigation of U.S. authorities quickly gained the participation of Mexico and became an international, bilateral program.

Private groups also played a part in the process and provided a second level of activity. Former Calexico consul Carlos V. Ariza worked as a public relations agent, on behalf of the repatriation drive led by the Los Angeles Chamber of Commerce, to improve the image of the Los Angeles authorities in Mexico. Ariza traveled through Mexico's main cities in 1931 publicizing the claims of the chamber to foster an orderly and humane repatriation procedure. In representing the chamber, Ariza held meetings with top government officials, including the president, and arranged an official agreement with Mexico's Confederated Chambers of Commerce over the repatriation issue. Ariza secured the backing of the confederation to cooperate with the Los Angeles chamber by giving assurances that repatriations would be handled in a just fashion.[66]

Repatriation, as policy extended to emigrants, never garnered the interest of Mexican authorities as some narratives contend. High-ranking officials were known to have looked unfavorably upon repatriates and considered them undesirable, something akin to unwanted aliens. In a memorandum to President Cárdenas and his cabinet, Foreign Relations Subsecretary José Angel Ceniceros depicted repatriates as a risk to the nation. The vast majority, argued Ceniceros, "have grown accustomed to live on public charities and do not attempt to find work beyond that which they are obligated to by state or municipal public works once or twice a week." Ceniceros regretted the return of "a large number of indigents who lack skill training and who have acquired dangerous idle habits over the last years of the economic crisis." Very few, he felt, could contribute to Mexico's economic well-being. He pointed out that there were few skilled among those returning, not enough "artisans—carpenters, plumbers, electricians, shoemakers," those with the skills useful to fill an economic niche. Negative portrayals like those of Ceniceros filtered down into the lower echelons of the government bureaucracy and opened the door to a host of troubles faced by returning citizens and noncitizen dependents.[67]

Migration personnel at the border were reported to have treated repatriates with subtle insults and overt contempt, and some repatriates complained of bribery by migration agents to smooth out "improperly" filled-out papers. A border region journalist described the returnees massed at entries "stationed in waiting rooms and corridors of the customs houses, in front of the Migration office and other public places, awaiting transportation . . . a very sad picture." Burdened with providing for the repatriates, municipal authorities in cities along the main highways reluctantly extended assistance and at times refused to help. The town of Nuevo Laredo, this journalist declared, "could not bear the expense of supporting so many people for the extended length of time. . . ." Nor would the railways make a "sacrifice by adding to one of their trains even a box car . . . to relieve the condition of all the unfortunate countrymen." [68]

Repatriates related stories of hunger, despair, and abandonment by their revolutionary government. Rafael Guzmán left Los Angeles in one of several trains loaded with families. "When I got off at Monterrey," he wrote to the Los Angeles Spanish-language daily, *La Opinión*, "my compatriots asked that I write about all the travails we have suffered." He related that their troubles began when they reached the border: "at El Paso, a consular official gave us a strong scolding, telling us that in repatriating, we were at fault for whatever was to happen to us in Mexico." Guzmán complained bitterly that upon crossing into Ciudad Juárez "everything was a struggle . . . nobody paid any attention to us," except corrupt Migration officials. "At the luggage check the customs agents did everything possible to take our last cent that we carried. They even wanted to charge us duties on our dirty clothes." When the group reached Chihuahua after "thousands of hardships" and without the transportation they were promised, the authorities told them that "they could do nothing for them." At last, Guzmán and his compatriots secured passage to Monterrey, but conditions worsened. After three months in that city, he reported that the remnants of the group "were dying of hunger." [69] The Department of Migration system encountered by the repatriates, observed the journalist, had been "in force for centuries, going back to when Mexico was a Spanish colony." [70]

The American consul at Saltillo, Coahuila, reported a parallel problem in that city. Municipal authorities were "noticeably" eager for the returnees, "dependent upon local charity, to depart from their city." The consul added that "a similar policy exists in Monterrey" and noted that "innumerable demands for aid" had left Monterrey's coffers bankrupt. No level of government, local, state, or federal, expressed a willingness to step in to resolve the crisis. Finally, upon the state governor's urgent plea that, if nothing were done, "the town would be overrun and seriously affected by this increasing contingent of unemployed, hungry people," federal authorities arranged a transport to Mexico City. [71]

Mexico had long spoken about colonization projects for repatriates— land at cheap prices, credit, resources, and implements secured by the government. Unfortunately for the colonists, many of the resettlement projects collapsed for a variety of reasons. The first two "model" colonies, established in the states of Oaxaca and Guerrero, were abandoned when disillusioned colonists walked out in disgust. According to the U.S. consul general in Mexico City, the repatriates at the Guerrero colony "complained particularly of the directors . . . and the unbearable [conditions]." Departing colonists bitterly assailed the managers and claimed that "on the pretext of imposing discipline which was unnecessary, the directors were attended by six armed individuals in whose presence the colonists were insulted by word and deed, being threatened with severe punishment in the event of disobedience. They consequently decided to abandon the colony en masse, making a painful 23-day journey on foot to Acapulco. There they lived on charity of the people, and the authorities demanded that they leave the city."[72] José González Soto, a leader of the colonists, testified that the "colonists worked with all their strengths and enthusiasm but that this was useless in view of the deficient system of administration . . . the rendering of assistance was irregular and insufficient, the machinery was taken away from the colonists and the food was extremely scarce . . . and [the colonists were] left for a long time without resources." President Cárdenas offered free passage to Mexico City for the miserable repatriates. In the capital their plight continued, as "the great majority," wrote the American consul general, were "ill and without medicines and food, [which] has required their departure."[73]

That repatriation on the Mexican side did not succeed might well have been the consequence of the misgivings with which authorities viewed the returning compatriots. Five years into the repatriation movement, the Los Angeles daily *La Opinión* scored repatriation, "which might have been highly beneficial for Mexico," as an abject failure. The editorial of March 1936 offers an insight into the fate of several hundred thousand workers and their families: "They were attracted with promises of colonies endowed with potential and were given some inhospitable lands, lacking water and the basic tools for its exploitation. They were called to their country and once they had crossed the border, those men who carried a fortune in knowledge to offer this country, ended up in charity hospitals, or they constituted a new charge for public welfare."[74]

Some have argued that the repatriates' problems stemmed from Mexico's resource scarcity, but that interpretation is difficult to sustain, particularly when the whole picture of consular intervention is assessed. The Mexican government never prioritized repatriation; consequently, repatriates languished alongside their nonemigrant compatriots. Many regretted their return. One *repatriado,* working as a painter at the National Theatre in Mexico City, expressed a common lament. "I have made a terrible mistake," he said, "I should have stayed in the United States. Opportunities here [Mexico City] are fewer than in the United States."[75] In his sorry predicament, he was not alone. The majority of repatriates had believed that life would be better back in the home country; they were sorely disappointed.

Ironically, conditions reached such critical proportions that many repatriates favored the suspension of repatriations. A group calling itself the Unión de Repatriados formally directed a request to the government to suspend the repatriation campaign. After searching "for work in vain" and without the assistance required, they declared that they were forced to take action.[76] Other repatriates found great difficulty adjusting to their old places of residence; many were forced to sell the belongings they had purchased in the United States in order to begin an exodus back to the country that had expelled them. American consul Stewart E. McMullin reported to Washington that "a large percentage" of repatriates eagerly sought to return "after a few years residence in Mexico." At the Piedras Negras crossing, he observed that "repatriates were anxious to re-enter the United States."[77]

Frustration over the repatriate issue among Mexican authorities moved them to attempt to close the border to their returning compatriots. Federal officials resented that many returnees had received public assistance before deciding not to stay put. Eventually, northern governors received orders from the president to "effectively prevent repatriates in their jurisdiction from trying to return to the United States."[78] Mexican consuls stationed at the border's main ports assisted U.S. immigration officials in preventing "Mexicans from attempting to gain illegal entry."[79] In a sincere gesture, INS officials extended a letter of appreciation "for the whole-hearted cooperation" provided by the El Paso Mexican consulate. The matter prompted U.S. Attorney General Homer Cummings to address the Mexican government and praise "the staff of the Mexican Consul General at El Paso for their assistance in aiding us to convince Mexican citizens that they should desist in their attempts to gain illegal entrance."[80] Bilateral cooperation to stem the return of expatriates seemed the order of the day and continued for several years. The highly regarded partnership drew more effusive comments from Los Angeles County Supervisor Gordon L. McDonough in late 1938. On behalf of the Board of Supervisors, McDonough assured Ignacio García Tellez, Mexican secretary of the interior, of the board's sincere appreciation "of your prompt action prohibiting entry to the United States of unemployed Mexicans."[81] Despite the bilateral actions, and the concurrence by the consulate staffs, the return migration could not be stopped, and many observers concluded that for the most part repatriates were eventually crossing over the same paths traveled years before to their former places of residence.[82]

Although painful, repatriation effected but a momentary pause in the migratory process. Against the backdrop of the revolution and its political aftermath, Mexican immigrants established themselves permanently within the United States. Mexican administrations consistently assisted in the procurement of labor for U.S. employers, and when that labor was rendered superfluous and subject to deportation, Mexican authorities lent a helping hand. Within this political context of mutual cooperation, the consular corps provided invaluable service to both Mexico and the United States. Consuls and Mexican officials contributed in multiple ways: they assisted employers of Mexican labor when called upon, downgraded or limited emigration restrictions to voluntarism, fostered repatriation campaigns when required, and organized the expatriates along lines beneficial to both employers and the revolutionary authorities.

We turn now to the policies administered by the consuls and specifically designed for established expatriate colonies.

CHAPTER 2

Organizing *México de afuera* in Southern California

Mexico's consular corps operated under very clear political criteria that structured their activities. Within prescribed limits consuls and their staff set out to meet two main obligations: protecting their compatriots abroad and promoting commerce between Mexico and the host country. However, in the twenties and thirties the charge to protect encompassed far more than is generally understood by the term. As the migrations of the teens and twenties ascended, the Mexican government broadened its domestic agenda to include *México de afuera,* emigrants settled in the United States. Protecting that community meant more than simply offering legal assistance and such other services as would be normally assumed by any consular corps. In the spectrum of Mexican consular responsibilities, no other activity occupied as much time and effort as that of fomenting and orchestrating loyalty to the Mexican government and adherence to its policies. Implementing that nationalist agenda required community-based organizations under consulate leadership and control. On the other hand, spying—keeping an eye out for subversives, potential and real—within the *colonias* also consumed a substantial portion of consular responsibilities. Under the command of the Secretariat of Foreign Relations, consuls willingly assumed the duty to rally expatriates around the banners of the postrevolutionary administrations.

Mexico's governing administrations well understood the critical importance of popular support. Overcoming any political obstacles to that support was essential for surviving the vicissitudes of the fluid political alliances that characterized Mexican politics during the twenties. To generate that support, the Obregón and Calles administrations (1920–1928) fashioned a nationalistic ideology that identified the chief executive with the nation, the state, and the ruling party. That nationalist program emerged as a staple of postrevolutionary administrations. Excluded from this program were leftist economic and political prescriptions for Mexico.

Within the Obregón and Calles brand of nationalism, leftist organizations' practice of refusing to subordinate to their administration's policies was deemed disloyal and such groups were subjected to persecution. The conservative nature of Mexican ruling politics transferred into the United States via the consulates.

A broad appeal to the nationalist sentiments of the immigrant community, sentiments deepened by the revolution, assumed a number of overt and covert organizational forms developed by and dependent upon the consulates. The most important overt projects included the *comisiones honoríficas* (honorary consulates), honorary consuls, the Los Angeles–based Confederación de Sociedades Mexicanas, and the labor union Confederación de Uniones Obreras Mexicanas (which later evolved into the Confederación de Uniones Campesinos y Obreros Mexicanos). These organizations sponsored such activities as operating Mexican elementary night schools, leading self-help and charity organizations, unionization, and patriotic celebrations. Similar in nature to the pro-Díaz *mutualistas* fostered by regional bosses during the Porfiriato, the various associations served as the grassroots defenders of the Mexican state. As the consular-inspired projects and community organizations formed and established themselves, Mexican domestic policies directly impacted *colonias* across the United States. Let us turn first to the covert operations originating in the consular offices.

Espionage

Expatriate Tomás Mares, of Nogales, Arizona, grieved that the "Mexican consulate here, as it is everywhere, is only a nest of spies, they put me on the list of enemies of the government for no reason. The consulates don't do anything but spy and serve as centers of espionage."[1] In retrospect, Mares's remark carried a great amount of truth. Mares had no inkling, as he observed the surreptitious behavior, that consuls were merely fulfilling their general obligations. Under the authority of the diplomatic corps, consular responsibilities included the reporting of all persons and groups suspected of antigovernment activity in the United States. Although issued in 1933, President Abelardo Rodríguez's diplomatic instructions encapsulated ongoing practice and indicated as well the norms for consular conduct in the 1920s. All diplomatic officers were directed "to follow faithfully and attentively all movements arising abroad which might signify risk of alteration of constituted order of the Mexican Republic, or machinations against its patrimony or good name, and to inform the Secretariat of Foreign Relations without loss of time of all activities in this connection."[2] Consulates, according to the instructions, were obligated to defer to orders from the diplomatic mission and the Secretariat of Foreign Relations, the latter having ultimate authority.

President Rodríguez's instructions drew from a long history of border region intrigues along the course of the revolution, a watershed for such activity. Political exiles were plentiful in the southwest, particularly in the larger cities near the border, such as San Antonio, Los Angeles, and El Paso. Some exiles dreamed of returning home to fight another day; others, despairing of righting old wrongs, blended into their new social landscape. Many exiled themselves voluntarily when their faction lost a political joust, while others fled north after losing an armed skirmish, perhaps an attempt at a barracks insurrection against the ruling government or a politically powerful regional boss. Fearing for their lives, but determined to redress grievances, many organized to do battle again.

Such was the case for Jorge Prieto Laurens, a target of consulate covert actions in the 1920s. A former governor, federal deputy, president of the National Congress, and founder of the Cooperativist Party, Prieto Laurens sided with the Adolfo de la Huerta forces in the failed 1924 coup to topple Alvaro Obregón and prevent the imposition of Plutarco Elías Calles to the presidency. Over the course of the attempted coup, various agents in Houston, New Orleans, and Washington, D.C., served as rebel representatives, and one or two even presented themselves as consuls of the provisional regime and self-styled "true" revolutionary government. Notwithstanding the substantial uprising, the Obregón government rallied its forces and routed the barracks revolt. Leaders and followers trickled into the United States. Prieto Laurens recounted that "the immense majority of my compañeros" immigrated into the U.S. and Cuba. "I was like a wandering Jew," he later recalled in his memoirs, and traveled from city to city, New Orleans, Houston, San Antonio, Kansas City, El Paso, and finally Los Angeles. He called his migrations a "pilgrimage" that took him from Kansas to all the states of the southwest.

Prieto Laurens, along with his political companions, settled in Houston, founded a rebel-in-exile newspaper, *La Tribuna*, in 1924 edited and directed by Prieto Laurens himself. Proceeds from a restaurant, La Azteca, established by the same group, provided funds to manage the journal. With a newspaper and a meeting place for the "numerous group of refugees who arrived from all parts: generals, colonels, sailors, aviators, congressional deputies, etc.," political intrigue seemed imminent. A wide audience "in all the *colonias* in and nearby Houston," recounted Prieto Laurens, read *La Tribuna*, and editions even reached New Orleans and Los Angeles by a kind of informal underground delivery system. With such visible levels of political engagement, U.S. and Mexican authorities reacted as expected. Prieto Laurens noted that the "Calles Obregonista consuls harassed us, and the American authorities kept a constant watch on us." [3]

The newspaper's downfall and the group's dispersion was triggered by *La Tribuna*'s publication of a smuggled official version of the Bucareli Agreements along with a "juicy commentary." Department of Justice agents paid a visit to the newspaper headquarters and summarily closed the offices. In the aftermath, exile politics evolved into dreams of reconquest as the exile community in Houston separated into several locales. Prieto Laurens resettled in San Antonio where rebel remnants regrouped to "formulate fantastic plans." The political noose tightened when an infiltrator, César Farjas, who always seemed to have money "for the cause," began to bore from within. Farjas became a regular at meetings, but he raised suspicions, questions were asked, and his cover was blown. Wrote Prieto Laurens, "Farjas was a bloodhound of the Calles-Obregonista consul in San Antonio . . . commissioned to spy on us and report on our ideas and actions, to his superiors in Mexico City." [4] The unmasking of Farjas abrogated his attempts to kidnap Prieto Laurens and others close to him. However, not all of the targeted exiles escaped unscathed. Ex-general Miguel Ulloa was kidnapped in El Paso and executed in Ciudad Juárez, according to Prieto Laurens's account of events during his exile's journeys.

Threatened with arrest and put to the run again, Prieto Laurens fled to Kansas City and then resurfaced in El Paso in the summer of 1926. There he secured employment as a translator for a Spanish-language daily, *El Continental,* which had a substantial readership across the border in Ciudad Juárez. Tailed by Mexican government agents, persecution continued to dog Prieto Laurens's every step. Shortly after the exile was hired, El Paso Consul General Enrique Liekens notified the owner of *El Continental* that the sale of the newspaper in Mexico would be prohibited unless he dismissed the migrant refugee. That same day Prieto Laurens joined the ranks of the unemployed and renewed his "pilgrimage." [5] And so it went for the former rebel, an experience that was repeated many times through the *colonias* of the southwest as exiles of every political stripe found refuge north of the border.

Rebellions rose and fell with regularity during the twenties, so that political refuge across the border became a component of the larger worker migration from Mexico. Political espionage followed closely, and as with the case of the de la Huerta rebels, U.S. authorities often joined Mexico's efforts to undermine any rebel actions on U.S. territory. When a 1929 revolt against Calles led by General José González Escobar spilled into the United States (as most Mexican political activities did), consuls were called into action, but they in turn called upon American law enforcement for assistance. San Antonio Consul General Enrique Santibáñez addressed several complaints to the Department of Justice Bureau of Investigation regarding "rebel activity." Santibáñez contended that exiled leader General López de Lara, among others, held "meetings with discontented refugees . . . and may possibly organize a military expedition to Mexico." J. Edgar Hoover responded energetically and assigned an agent to launch covert surveillance and investigation. The FBI agent reported that López de Lara's "movements are being kept under close observation by the San Antonio Bureau office and the aid of the Customs and Immigration Border Patrol has been enlisted to also watch his movements." The officer closed, stating that should López de Lara "organize a military expedition . . . he will probably be taken into custody." [6]

Santibáñez's requests for assistance alerted the FBI to follow a number of rebels besides López de Lara. Many exiles had formerly held high-level political or military positions. *Carrancista* General Marciano González, for example, was at one time the provisional governor of the Federal District. He fled Mexico after the failed de la Huerta coup, but in the United States he happily joined with Escobar to topple his old enemy, Calles. Described by the bureau agent assigned to tail him as "a professional revolutionist," the office warned the officer to "Keep this subject under close observation." In the cases of the de la Huerta and Escobar exiles, consulates sometimes collaborated with U.S. authorities and at other times acted independently, relying on their own resources. In retrospect, persecution of exiles displayed the close ties and support proffered by the United States for the administrations of Obregón and Calles.

Keeping an eye out for antigovernment activity involved more than tracking individuals. Consuls consistently scanned Spanish- and English-language journals and newspapers, on the lookout for pieces that were either unflattering to the government or politically suspicious. Authors' names were reported. After careful analysis, problematic editorials and articles were clipped and submitted to superiors along with critical comments on the offending piece. For example, Los Angeles Consul Alejandro Martínez submitted a packet of eleven clippings in November 1934 taken from the *Los Angeles Times,* the *Los Angeles Examiner,* and *La Opinión.* Consul Martínez made special reference to the political tone of *La Opinión,* which he accused of being "controlled by clerical elements." He added that the paper "in its recent editorials attacks socialist education on the same par with the de-fanaticism campaign which our government and the Partido Nacional Revolucionario laudably follows." Martínez concluded that he would faithfully send "daily clippings that refer to the situation in Mexico." If the writer of an allegedly offensive article happened to be a correspondent stationed in Mexico (and a Mexican citizen), a negative report could invite a home or office visit from government authorities. The case of San Antonio Consul Ricardo Hill's report to the Executive Office regarding a series of articles on President Cárdenas offers an example. Hill claimed that the suspect pieces were written by "reactionary elements who wish to sweep a veil of suspicion over the irreproachable person of our First Commander." In a subtle fashion, the articles discussed Cárdenas's various properties and raised questions regarding a recently purchased large hacienda, Cárdenas's third, a highly profitable apple orchard. Although the pieces were not openly political nor notably critical, the topic was sensitive, coming at a time of repatriation and land reform, and did not reflect favorably on the president's personal financial interests. Hill wrote that "the matter should be brought to the attention of the writer, who lives in the Capitol." [7]

Radio's treatment of the Mexican government and its officials received substantial attention as well. Broadcasts were carefully monitored, and consuls were prepared to intervene in a number of ways to ensure favorable publicity for their employer. In one case, a consul went so far as to personally call for the removal of an offensive radio personality. In the fall of 1935, Tucson Consul Efraín G. Domínguez convinced the owner of radio station KVOA to restrict the political content of Father Carmelo Corbella's Sunday program. Domínguez alleged that Corbella had falsely attacked the Mexican government's policy on education and religion. Corbella at first agreed to censure his remarks but then reneged and continued to express his opinions, going so far as to urge the boycott of consulate-sponsored functions. This was too much. The consul again visited the station offices, this time to recommend to the owner that he take the priest off the air. In the consul's presence, the owner phoned Corbella and, according to Domínguez, "expressed his profound disgust . . . and firmly and energetically told [Corbella] that he would not allow him on the radio station when there is risk of defamation . . . and he warned Corbella that if he mentioned the religious in our country again or if he attacked our government and its authorities over the microphone, that he would immediately cancel the program." [8] Corbella resisted the threats and resumed the political line. Domínguez responded by renewing his campaign to remove the offending priest from the airwaves. This time he inquired of the Mexican Embassy as to whether the weight of U.S. federal law could be applied to the matter.

We do not know the final resolution of this particular assault on the media; however, all three cases reported here demonstrate the determination of consuls such as Domínguez, Martínez, and Hill to censure the media when necessary. Their actions serve to reveal the profound appreciation which the Secretariat of Foreign Relations had for public opinion. Not only did the secretariat understand the need to control the media; it valued the work of the consuls in this regard. Eloquent praise from a superior for exceptional consular vigilance was frequently given for effective investigation of suspicious persons. Vice-Consul Ernesto Romero, for example, received high accolades in 1938 from Visitor General de la Huerta for "valiant bulletins. . . . he has maintained vigilance over the work of our enemies in that region." [9]

Mexico's shadowy spy network extended well beyond the radius of the consulates. The PNR informed on "seditious" characters both within Mexico and residing in the United States. Sometimes a particularly patriotic expatriate informed on alleged antigovernment activities. More often, the source of reliable information came from consuls. These materials, together with a variety of other leads, were compiled into lengthy, detailed catalogues of antigovernment operations. Confidential reports, ferreted out through questionable legal and illegal means, originated from several sources. In 1935 the Laredo consul, for example, intercepted letters "related to seditious activities" and relayed them in a report to the Secretariat of Foreign Relations. There the report was carefully appraised, rerouted to the president, and later listed with ninety entries, each with multiple strands of confidential information for the year 1935. [10] Another entry for 1935 summarized a confidence from San Antonio Consul Rafael de la Colina regarding an antigovernment political group known as the Villarrealistas. According to de la Colina, the faction "will not go through with plans to transport considerable arms and munitions, having become aware that vigilance by American authorities is increasing."

In all, a variety of sources disclosed information about clandestine meetings, conspiracies, gunrunning, contraband, antigovernment speeches and writings, disloyal government officials, and even mysterious comings and goings. The heated contention between Ex-President Calles and President Cárdenas, which finally erupted in Calles's forced exile in 1936, had spawned a spy network to report on Calles's movements. In this delicate and potentially explosive case, the highest level of secrecy and sophisticated cryptographic codes were required. Using such a code, Consul Ricardo Hill, reporting from the Los Angeles consulate, informed the Secretariat of Foreign Relations: "General Calles to arrive in this city tomorrow." [11] On occasion, individuals not officially connected with the consulate or the Mexican government voluntarily and independently sent sensitive information. Juan B. Ruiz, a Los Angeles druggist with ties with the consulate, sent a confidential letter to Mexican authorities advising that during Calles's stay in Los Angeles, the general had "installed a direct telegraphic line to the Associated Press, an open line without censure [i.e., without eavesdropping]."[12]

Whether Calles was in exile or vigorously contesting Cárdenas for control of Mexico's political apparatus, his moves always merited attention by the ever-vigilant consuls. On the basis of an informant's collaboration, the fervent Cárdenas loyalist Consul Alejandro Gómez Maganda briefly detailed Calles's exile journeys to the president's personal secretary, Luis I. Rodríguez. "Dear Brother," began Maganda, "Motivated by Calles incursion into Oklahoma, I contacted compañero Novarrio, of San Diego, by telephone. Calles passed through Los Angeles, stayed awhile in Pasadena and later continued his march, in open combat with our regime . . . reflecting on his crooked ways."[13]

When necessary, whether courageously or foolishly, trained consuls personally investigated cabals involving shadowy individuals, automobiles, ships at sea and at harbors, and organizations. Brownsville Consul Raul G. Domínguez, stationed at a particularly busy intersection of exile activities, reported his findings to the president's personal secretary (chief of staff), Raul Castellanos. "My Esteemed and Fine Friend," he began, "Yesterday I made an observation trip through various towns in the Rio Grande Valley, among them McAllen, Mission, and Edinburg, Mercedes, etc., as well as Reynosa, Tamps. [Tamaulipas] with the objective of personally coming to know the activities [in this region] of the enemies of our government."[14] Domínguez tailed members of an anti-Cárdenas faction connected to General Cedillas, a former colonel operating on both sides of the border, and an organizer for the fascist pro-Nazi group known as the Dorados. In beguiling detail the consul laid out the structure of mysterious border intrigue that included clandestine meetings, suspicious movements, and internal dissension.[15] Via informants, Domínguez penetrated the inner circle of both the Cedillistas and the Dorados. He then recommended that a former colonel in the Mexican Army be hired as a counterspy. In a fascinating and revealing letter to Secretary of National Defense (and future President) Manuel Avila Camacho, Domínguez made a suggestion worthy of the best of James Bond:

About the interview which I had with (Maltos) I have concluded that I am dealing with an individual that we may use advantageously in this region to thwart the activities which Nicolás Rodríguez and the Cedillistas are operating along the Río Bravo (Rio Grande). The best way . . . to use the service of Maltos would be to assign him a salary or compensation . . . of 60.00 to 75.00 dollars monthly. . . . I believe, my General, that Maltos can serve by placing him among those disaffected from the government, as he appears to have cultivated a friendship with various Dorados and Cedillistas . . . he can provide information without an outward indication that he has contact with the government.[16]

Domínguez asked for permission to implement his plan only after seeking the advice and signal to proceed from central authorities.

Difficult cases, often those involving arms and munitions shipments, generally encouraged consuls to seek the assistance of federal and local authorities. At times, American "soldiers of fortune" surfaced. Such a moment occurred when Los Angeles Consul Alejandro Martínez made a confidential report to the County Sheriffs and the Department of Justice regarding a San Francisco gun club posing as a front for gunrunning. Martínez mentioned a certain adventurer named Harry C. Braun, who provided "precise information" concerning the "gun club." The confidential report stated that according to Braun, the club "received instructions to store machine guns and equipment along the border, especially on the Sonora and Arizona line, to carry out an armed incursion within our national territory and effect a toppling of our government."[17] Martínez urgently requested authority and the funds to establish effective relations with persons such as Braun. Martínez argued that the costs were necessary "compensations for information which may be of value to the police and to our government." Whether Martínez received the allocation to pay informants is not known, but it is clear that he, like Consul Domínguez, was prepared to elicit the cooperation of paid informants and was confident that his request would receive serious consideration.[18]

The rather extensive volume of confidential correspondence involving clandestine political factions and their plans to smuggle by land and sea testify to the intensity of antigovernment activity and the diligence of consuls to counteract those actions. Galveston Consul Cano del Castillo reported a suspicious character who presented himself to del Castillo as a "confidential agent of the Secretary of National Defense and former captain in the cavalry" assigned to investigate the clandestine importation of armaments somewhere on the coast of the Gulf of Mexico. A doubting Cano del Castillo inquired whether the agent, Enrique Jaime Torres, was legitimate and held the commission that he claimed. Cano described Torres: "30 to 35 years of age, brown skinned, gray eyes, small moles on the face, large nose straight and thin, thin eyebrows, speaks with a Cuban or Veracruz accent . . . travels in a dark blue Plymouth with license number A-74-307."[19] Without hesitation Mexican federal officials and port authorities were alerted "in a most discrete manner" of a possible arrival of gunrunning oil tankers. Authorities took no chances, particularly when it came to contraband shipments of arms, equipment, and ammunition. Consequently, the spy was often the spied upon.

Consul Bernardo Chávez, of the McAllen, Texas, consulate, was the subject of a brutal critique from Division General Juan Andreu Almazán sent directly to President Cárdenas. On an official journey through northern border towns, Almazán had obtained "irrefutable evidence" that Consul Chávez "in bad faith destroys the existing harmony among Mexican authorities, between them and American authorities and between neighbor and neighbor of both countries." [20] Moreover, continued Almazán, the "odious egoist" Chávez had not only spread lies about the general's loyalty to President Cárdenas but was seen in his office "at all times in an improper attitude with women," and more. "With this sort of employee," warned Almazán, "it is impossible to develop an energetic action for the country. . . . permit me to respectfully suggest that you release him from his post."

At times ex-spies, former Mexican intelligence agents, entered into the stream of political intrigues. Tucson Vice-Consul Efraín G. Domínguez queried the Douglas, Arizona, consulate for information regarding an "ex-member of the government's intelligence service who resides in that city and who is engaging in unusually large activity in arms trafficking for Sonoran rebels." [21] Domínguez had apparently encountered a number of smugglers, some of them Americans, involved in running guns to Yaqui tribes in the hope of launching an insurrection. Rebel planning apparently took place on the U.S. side of the border, with agents scurrying incognito into Yaqui territory to recruit adherents. Informed of the conspiracy, authorities on both sides conducted countermeasures. The Mexican military issued printed warnings that were distributed throughout the indigenous region. These fliers advised that the intrigues had been uncovered and to avoid two men, Gilberto Quintero and Macial Gallegos, "who have been attempting to incite you to rebel against the government of Señor Presidente General Cárdenas. . . . USE CAUTION WITH THEM!" [22] Domínguez assured the Douglas consulate of his continuing efforts to gather valuable information concerning overt maneuvers.

As the consuls spied, their government and the U.S. intelligence services on occasion believed they had good reason to spy on the spies. The cases of Consul Juan B. Richer, at Laredo, Texas, and Consul Gustavo Padres Jr., at Calexico, California, provide two examples of intensive intelligence surveillance by the G-2, Military Intelligence for the War Department. Reports emanating from G-2 inevitably reached the FBI and eventually the State Department. (Unfortunately, a substantial trove of confidential G-2 reports on the consulates was destroyed in 1929; this severely limits the reconstruction of these activities. Nevertheless, the extant information serves to offer insight into U.S. monitoring of consuls and the occasional discord between Washington and Mexico City.)

In March 1936, Lieutenant Colonel F. B. Mallon, stationed at Fort Sam Houston, issued a confidential memorandum to G-2 headquarters in Washington, D.C., in reference to "Mexican Radical Activities." Mallon received information that Consul Richer, representing the Mexican government, had addressed a union meeting of 250 agricultural workers in Laredo. According to extracts of Richer's speech, taken down by an informant, he advised the union to "unionize all the laboring elements. . . . The doors of the Mexican consulate are always open to you whenever you need any assistance."[23] Mallon contended that not only did Richer's speech contain stronger language than that indicated in the extract, but that the consul participated in yet a second meeting said to be "under the sponsorship of the consul." Moreover, he stated that a third meeting was planned and that "six representatives from the Mexican Department of Labor were scheduled to arrive in . . . Laredo . . . to organize a strike among Mexican laborers, especially among the union workers."[24]

Cries of communist infiltration from the Texas congressional delegation echoed in the press, a charge that Consul Richer denied, arguing that he had in no way "tried to unionize the Mexican elements in my jurisdiction."[25] Administrative wheels quickly turned as the matter was referred to U.S. Consul Romeyn Wormuth in Nuevo Laredo for review. The Mexican government also received a note of concern regarding the affair. The Mexican Secretariat of Foreign Relations ordered a covert investigation, while U.S. Consul Wormuth reiterated his contention that Richer was guilty of meddling in American affairs and acted "under orders in the matter." The furor forced Richer to separate himself from any union contact and to deny any wrongdoing. Not more than two weeks after the first meeting took place, but after the Mexican government had been apprised of American displeasure, Richer was recalled to Mexico City "to be interrogated concerning his consular activities in organizing labor groups in Laredo." Despite Richer's declaration of innocence, the secretariat made it clear that Richer "would in no event be returned to duty at that place."[26]

A contrite Mexican ambassador, F. Castillo Nájera, assured the U.S. State Department that the Mexican government was already taking the "appropriate measures to prevent the repetition of acts capable of giving rise to difficulties." Further, "all members of the Mexican consular service [were instructed] to abstain from . . . meetings of any kind alien to the consular functions."[27] There the case closed, but similar proceedings surfaced every now and then, generally with a more or less friendly disposition.

The matter of Consul Gustavo Padres Jr., of the Calexico consulate, is an interesting parallel. Shrill alarms went up in Washington over an alleged intention by Padres to organize "the Mexican workers of the Imperial Valley [California]." According to a Naval Intelligence report submitted to the State Department, Padres claimed to enjoy the support of Governor Culbert Olson and that the San Diego consulate was "in complete sympathy [with organizing workers] . . . and will do the same in that city." Intelligence alleged that the consul had organized a *comisión honorífica,* or honorary commission, an organization (discussed in detail below) to assist the consul in carrying out his duties with the intention of "organizing workers into the CIO." Information "intimated that the consul would call out on strike at least four thousand men when they return to work this fall; that the workers have great faith in him." Although the agent pointed to Padres's links with the governor's office and his "great respect of President Roosevelt," there were worrisome signs that Padres entertained "a general hatred of any who oppose the radical or Communist movement."[28] Notwithstanding the substantial contradiction regarding Padres's political orientation, the report found a critically concerned reading at the State Department. One official frankly stated, "I don't like this at all." The real issue seemed to be Padres's alleged sympathy for or leanings toward communist leaders in the labor movement. Fantastic as the allegation may appear in hindsight, the State Department took the matter under serious consideration. Assistant Secretary Sumner Welles's memorandum to the Division of the American Republics pointed out "that the situation presents many dangerous features and if anything is to be done about the matter it should be done promptly."[29] Welles inquired as to the propriety of asking the Mexican Embassy to discuss the matter. Upon discussion, Mexican Charge d'Affairs Fuentes was called to the State Department, told of the serious concerns, and requested to respond. In complete agreement that the matter needed sorting out, Mr. Fuentes answered that his government "would ascertain whether the Mexican consular officers in question were engaging in the alleged activities."[30] Three weeks later the State Department received a note: "Mr. Padres has been transferred to Miami, Florida."[31]

As can be seen, consuls assumed significant responsibilities relating to monitoring and reporting of the political activities of the expatriate community. These actions, in turn, were carefully supervised not only by Mexican authorities, but by U.S. intelligence agencies as well. More often, cooperation and collaboration between U.S. and Mexican authorities distinguished border intrigues. Neither the Richer nor Padres cases resulted in serious repercussions, demonstrating that the desire for harmony between the two governments in U.S. territory, though politically motivated, was mutual.

Comisiones Honoríficas Mexicanas

A number of organizations sponsored by the consulates sought to establish the primacy of the Mexican government within the political activities of the expatriate community. One such type of organization, the *comisión honorífica,* effectively served that political purpose in numerous ways, beginning in 1921 when President Obregón ordered the consuls to begin organizing *comisiones* in their districts. Consul Renato Cantú Lara founded the first *comisión* in San Marcos, Texas. From Texas, *comisiones* soon spread throughout the United States.[32] George T. Edson, commissioned to research Mexican labor for the U.S. Department of Labor in 1927, reported that in the string of Mexican villages across the beet fields of the Arkansas River Valley of Kansas, "in every settlement there is a *comisión honorífica* to retain a national contact and allegiance."[33] In step with consulates around the country, the Los Angeles consulate launched a mid-twenties campaign to establish *comisiones* within its jurisdiction and by 1926 had sponsored the formation of thirty *comisiones.* The momentum carried forward into the 1930s as forty *comisiones* functioned at the end of the decade. Indeed, the officials of the approximately fifty-five consulates across the United States assumed the organizational task of establishing a *comisión* within their districts and generally met with success. Distant *colonias* in cities and towns like Yuma (Arizona), Oxnard (California), Pocatello (Idaho), Moline (Illinois), Des Moines (Iowa), Detroit (Michigan), St. Louis (Missouri), Lorain (Ohio), and Pittsburgh (Pennsylvania) each hosted a *comisión honorífica.*[34]

Given the widespread distribution of the *comisiones,* one must assume that the Mexican government considered the *comisión* an extremely important component of its general consular policies. Consulates consistently claimed that the *comisiones'* prime function was the extension of consular protection into the dispersed *colonias.* The *comisiones,* in effect, extended the powers of the consuls to offer protection to their nationals. Additionally, each *comisión,* and particularly its president, by virtue of his position, acted as an agent of the Mexican government and as such embraced the full range of the central administration's politics.

Delegated duties of the *comisiones* fell into three categories: first, "maintaining alive and constant the memory and love of Mexico"; second, "remind Mexicans of their duty to the Fatherland"; and third, "serve as a connector between Mexicans in each of the small localities and consulate." Their endeavors included (1) sponsoring and administering voluntary primary schools for the Mexicanization of children of immigrant parents, (2) taking up charitable collections for the *colonia* needy, (3) organizing Mexican Independence Day celebrations, (4) registering births to Mexican citizens, (5) issuing documents attesting to legal status and citizenship, and (6) taking an annual census of *colonia* residents. In general, the *comisión* president represented the consul in local matters where authority was granted. In at least fifteen locales the *comisión* president was also given the title *cónsul honorífico,* or honorary consul, a position which carried much prestige and added weight to the *comisión.*

Within the small scattered *colonias* of Orange County, in southern California, Cónsul Honorario Lucas Lucio, president of the Santa Ana *comisión honorífica,* carried out his official obligations and acted in a variety of contexts. Frequently, the *colonia* turned to him to resolve myriad problems that afflicted the immigrant community. When agricultural workers lodged formal grievances against their employers, Lucio represented the workers and negotiated for them. In cases where his constituents felt they had been cheated in a business transaction, Lucio assisted them to seek redress. Lucio also published a local Spanish-language newspaper that presented the Mexican government's position on a variety of matters, always in accord with the consulate. Through the *cónsul honorífico* the Mexican government secured its presence in ways that would have been physically impossible given the wide geographic placement of the *colonias.* Moreover, the *colonia* residents knew precisely the political purpose of the *cónsul honorífico:* consuls made it clear that their chosen surrogates represented the Mexican government.

Although *comisión* members were often connected to the traditional self-help organizations, or *mutualistas,* that voluntarily rose from within the *colonia,* the *comisión* was a fundamentally different organizational type. *Comisiones* were not voluntary societies in the sense that the members independently came together to found the group; rather, the organizational impetus invariably came from the consulates. Consequently, the *comisión* held the distinction of a semi-official government body under the supervision and control of the local consulate office. Each *comisión,* presided over by a *comité* comprising a president, vice-president, secretary, and treasurer, was vested by the consul with limited powers. According to the Los Angeles Spanish-language newspaper *La Opinión,* the local consul "named the respective presidents and provides them with the proper interpretations to be given to the regulations." [35] A Chicago president of a local *comisión* described the consulate-*comisión* connection for an investigator working for Manuel Gamio's research project on Mexican immigrants. The investigator, paraphrasing Dr. Juan B. Medina, wrote: "The Dr. *[sic]* is the president of the *Comisión Honorífica* that supports the labor groups that are here. Every year representatives of those groups that have unified elect seven persons; the Consulate names another who has the title of president and together these constitute the *Comisión Honorífica*. These persons receive no salary, and are a group that serves as intermediary between the Consul and the individual." [36]

In some locales the consul exercised near-absolute authority. Anthropologist Norman Humphrey observed that in the late 1920s the Detroit *comisión* operated "under the direct supervision and control of the consul" and that the consul's "decision in any controversy was final and no appeal could be made above it." Humphrey described the authority of the consul within the *comisión* as "more or less autocratic." [37] According to a *La Opinión* editorial, only one in ten *comisiones* acted independently of governmental authority, and although many endured internal conflicts, some of a serious nature, they nevertheless acted as effective consulate agents.

Forming a *comisión honorífica,* the very act of selecting a *colonia* for founding a *comisión,* required the imprimatur of the local consulate. Before naming a *colonia,* the consul made careful analysis of the possible sites and, upon weighing the most advantageous placement, selected the locale for the *comisión.* In early 1928 Consul F. Alfonso Pesqueira announced a project to establish *comisiones* throughout southern California based on the size of the *colonia.* The Santa Barbara *colonia* received the nod "to endow it with a *comisión*" because, he claimed, "it holds a dense Mexican *colonia.*" [38] Consul Rafael de la Colina, who succeeded Pesqueira, continued that policy by "intending to found a *comisión honorífica* in each town or agricultural zone . . . where an established nucleus of compatriots reside." [39] It was an honor for a *colonia* to be selected as a site for a *comisión; a comisión* conferred a sense of importance and commanded respect.

Solemn proceedings, presided over by the consul, invested the *comisión* with the powers to act, in certain instances, in the stead of the consulate. Consul Edmundo Aragón speaks of a typical convocation in his official report to the Secretariat of Foreign Relations on the installation of the Brawley (California) *comisión.* First, Aragón reports, he completed the preliminary requisites and procedures in the proper order. Then, with over three hundred persons in attendance, he presided over "the installation of the first *comisión honorífica.*" The *comisión*'s central committee was elected by popular vote of the members, excepting the president, who "had been named previously [by Consul Aragón] in accord with the established bases and respective regulations."[40]

Should a consul, vice-consul, or representative be unable to attend a *comisión* installation of officers, other means, usually letters, stood to officiate the inauguration. For example, upon the selection of the Chino (California) *comisión*, the outgoing president immediately communicated with the district consul. Consul Alatorre thereupon responded with an official endorsement to the *comisión*, requesting that it "labor entirely for the welfare and betterment of the *colonia* Mexicana of that town. . . . in due time the name of the new President to be chosen will be made known."[41]

Unilateral selection of the *comisión* president by the consul made it "imprudent to ask that they [the *comisión*] separate themselves from the [Mexican] government to resolve the *colonia*'s problems," or so stated a *La Opinión* editorial which candidly and accurately reflected upon the *comisiones*.[42] Speeches delivered at the swearing-in ceremony for the Casa Blanca (Riverside, California) *comisión* attested to the political lineage of the organization. Consul Hermolao Torres "exhorted those present to cooperate with the consulate and with the resplendent *Comisión Honorífica* . . . so that the *colonia* Mexicana may depend upon genuine and active representatives easily able to fulfill their commitments and protect the interests of the community."[43]

The *comisión* linked the *colonia* with the consular officials and, in the bargain, joined the *colonia* with Mexico's domestic politics and foreign policies. Mexico's politics shadowed the *colonia;* thus, when a military rebellion threatened the administration of Interim President Portes Gil, the *comisiones* provided a wide network for orchestrating government support. In a show of allegiance, Consul Pesqueira directed a bulletin to all *colonia* organizations in his Los Angeles–based jurisdiction (which covered most of southern California), advising that allegiance to the government remained undiminished, and pointed to the *comisiones* as exemplary manifestations of support. "All the *Comisiones* in California," exclaimed Pesqueira, "have sent delegations or have written letters or sent messages, affirming their adherence to the constituted government."[44] The very nature of the organizations made for particularly close relations with consular officials.

Members were advised of their obligations and their subordinate position to the consular office. Hierarchical power relations were well understood by all parties. *Comisiones* reported to the consul, who then reported either directly to the consul general or to the Secretariat of Foreign Relations. The secretariat regularly received reports concerning *comisión* activities, membership, officers, and other related information. Consul Joaquín Terrazas of the Calexico, California, office submitted a routine report dated June 30, 1933, to the Secretaría de Relaciones Públicas (SRP) that included the local commission's report to him. "I have the honor to report to you," stated *comisión* president Arballo to Terrazas, "on the actions undertaken by this *Comisión Honorífica* which I preside over, corresponding to the month of June."[45] Arballo then proceeded to list and describe the *comisión* affairs for the month; several illustrate the various assigned and assumed tasks. On June 12, "a credential was extended to Mrs. María V. de Montano permitting her to gather a public collection on account of her husband who is now in a hospital having suffered injuries in an automobile accident, she collected $16.95." On June 20, the *comisión* represented an agricultural laborer who complained that a labor contractor had failed to pay his wage (a common occurrence) and did the same for another worker on June 26.

Mexican Schools for the Children of Expatriates

In the 1920s the Los Angeles consulate announced a plan to Mexicanize *colonia* children by establishing Mexican schools. The consulate assumed the responsibility for administering the enterprise and all similar educational ventures in the future. The first school established during this campaign was the Eastside Escuela México. It opened its doors in the spring of 1926. Los Angeles *colonia* merchants cooperatively founded the school with the assistance and cooperation of Consul Pesqueira. Eventually, the school building was ceded to the consulate by an Eastside merchant formally placing "the school under the direction of the [Mexican] Secretary of Public Education."[46] The Mexican Secretariat of Public Education donated texts, maps, and blackboards and even credentialed the school and sent a teacher to run the daily program. Nevertheless, in effect, the Escuela México and several more schools founded over the next several years remained the bailiwick of the Los Angeles consulate.

Eventually, the southern California *comisiones* were vested with the authority and the obligation to establish and administer such schools. In 1929, Consul Pesqueira issued a set of regulations for the operation of Mexican schools in his jurisdiction. These rules stated that each school be administered by a board composed of a vice-consul representing the consulate's Department of Education, selected parents of school children, and the local, or nearest, *comisión* president. Consonant with the pattern of keeping a taut rein on *colonia* organizations under consulate sponsorship, Pesqueira further declared that the *comisión* president would also serve as the local school board president. Boards selected the school sites and teachers and managed the schools in accordance with the general guidelines handed down from the consulate.[47] According to consulate briefings, bylaws governing the operation of the schools under consulate supervision required the coordination of the *comisión honorífica* with the school program. In effect, the *comisión* and the consulate held power over the schooling projects.[48] As would be expected, the Mexican government dominated the campaign to Mexicanize the *colonia* children via its own network of *comisiones*.

The following examples are typical of the school-related activities of the *comisiones* in several *colonias*. "The compatriots of Clearwater [California] should be proud of their truly patriotic labor," announced an August 1927 *La Opinión* article. "The children of Clearwater have a school that their parents constructed with their own hands." Directed by the president of the local *comisión*, this school, an example of Mexicanization, was constructed upon a lot donated by the previous *comisión* president.[49] "The compatriots of Clearwater," continued the article, "do not spend their time in useless controversies, instead work intensely so that the school continues operating, their way of demonstrating their patriotism."

Like their counterparts in Clearwater, members of the Watts *comisión honorífica* led the drive to establish their school, which they named Escuela Manuel Doblado. When a financial crisis threatened to close the school, the Watts *comisión* collected $260 through a local fund-raising drive to keep its doors open and secure the continuation of the school.[50] "Due to the combined efforts of the *colonia mexicana* of San Bernardino and the members of the *Comisión Honorífica*," read a January 1928 *La Opinión* piece, "the Mexican school has begun to function."[51] An effort to infuse a nationalist culture "within the children and youth of *México de afuera*, who ran the risk of losing their nationality," guided the coursework, which consisted of the Spanish language, Mexican history and geography, as well as "songs, popular games, manual skills, and social education."[52] Seventy children attended on opening day.

In Van Nuys (California), Consul Pesqueira personally initiated a schooling campaign in close cooperation with and aided by the local *comisión honorífica*. At the inaugural ceremonies, musical renditions and spirited discourses entertained *colonia* parents. In the name of Mexico's secretary of public education, Pesqueira donated books and other school items. Later, the *comisión honorífica* "with the collaboration of parents hosted a banquet for Consul Pesqueira."[53] Similar *comisión* projects appeared in Palos Verdes, Santa Monica, Long Beach, Burbank, El Monte, and other towns.

Perhaps it was inevitable, under the shadow of the Great Depression, that the grandiose plans to establish fifty schools announced by Consul Pesqueira in the late twenties would prove extremely difficult to put into practice. Those schools that actually operated suffered severe financial crises as they struggled to survive. Not more than a dozen schools functioned at any one time. Even the first school, founded in East Los Angeles, underwent a financial crisis only months after opening its doors. The Depression that bore down upon the Mexican community was without pity, and it brought scarcity and hardship to all. By the Depression's end, only remnants of the schooling campaign survived.

Pressured by editorials in *La Opinión,* Los Angeles Consul Ricardo Hill attempted to lead a revival of this idealistic schooling enterprise. Plans drawn up by Consul Pesqueira in the late twenties were dusted off by Hill in his much-publicized decision to organize Mexican schools under consulate supervision. At least three schools functioned; one was managed by the Partido Liberal Mexicano (PLM), descendant of the anarchistic Flores Magón movement turned *mutualista,* and an organization with a history of cordial relations with the consulate. However, the *La Opinión* journalist who had spurred the revival found Hill's effort insufficient, though he nevertheless lauded his proposal as visionary.[54]

It is not clear whether all *comisiones* sponsored or assisted in the operation of schools. However, all responded to consular directives or to government initiatives and reported their activities directly to the consul. When challenged by a nationalist call for support, the *comisiones* stood ready to display their patriotism. Mexico's nationalization of the petroleum industry in 1935 provided the clarion call for Mexicanization to burst forth and propelled the *comisiones* into fervent action. In the *colonias,* the international oil crisis dominated daily discourse. Such widespread attention to this situation established propitious conditions for the consulate to gather expatriate support, both moral and financial, for the Mexicanization of the oil industry. The *comisiones* provided an established network for orchestrating the campaign in southern California. During the drive in Mexico City to nationalize oil, a circular was issued by Consul Ricardo Hill urging the *colonias* to cooperate with the *comisiones:*

It is the duty of the *Comisiones Honoríficas Mexicanas* to not allow for one moment the disappearance of the enthusiasm which reigns among our nationals, and with this motive, I desire that it become publicly known to all during the Cinco de Mayo festivities . . . that the government (of Mexico) has given full recognition with satisfaction of the attitude of the *colonias* Mexicanas established in this country, and the government appreciates it. It is also the duty of the *Comisiones Honorí-ficas* to organize that overflowing enthusiasm of Mexicanos so that it may be better availed by our Fatherland, and to that end, there should be studied the manner to systematically receive the contributions that our countrymen spontaneously desire to give to help solve the petroleum question. That should help those persons wishing to send their donation. . . .[55]

Consul Hill advised the *colonia* residents to either send their monetary contribution directly to Mexico City or deliver it to the *comisión* closest to their residence.

Patriotic Festivals

To foster loyalty and patriotism for the patria, the *colonias* were apprised of the directive urging them to develop special plans for Mexican Independence Day celebrations and other national holidays. Under the *La Opinión* headline "Orders to the Consuls in the United States," an article sent from Mexico City noted the nature of the order: "Consuls . . . have received instructions . . . to initiate a general program to stimulate the loyalty of Mexicans toward their country [thereby] strengthening the ties between thousands of emigrants who live in the U.S. and their own Fatherland. . . . at least the love of the Fatherland burning in the hearts of the emigrants will be maintained."[56]

Observing the national patriotic holidays, an important medium for maintaining "love of the Fatherland" and a sense of duty, required considerable effort, time, and, of course, money. Accordingly, the consuls were authorized to "delegate this obligation to the . . . *comisiones honoríficas,* where they exist."[57] The *comisiones* responded energetically. Alongside the protection they extended to the expatriates, *comisiones* dedicated themselves to "guard with great devotion the high respect and dignity of the Mexican nation."[58]

An editor for *La Opinión* commented that the "enthusiasm and sincerity of numerous *Comisiones Honoríficas*" distinguished the celebration of Mexican national holidays. In the central Valley town of Hanford (California), the heart of the state's agriculture, the farmworker *colonia* heartily partook of the 1927 *Dieciséis de Septiembre* (Sixteenth of September) celebration, Mexican Independence Day, organized and directed by the Hanford *comisión*. A correspondent participating in the overflowing display of patriotism drew a sketch of the event in an article for *La Opinión*. Celebrants from the nearby towns of Selma, Porterville, and other rural centers converged on Hanford to honor the 117th anniversary of the proclamation of Mexico's independence. Following tradition, the festival began on the morning of the fifteenth. It was held at the Hanford *colonia* hall, where the flags of Mexico were unfurled to the sounds of national hymns played by the local orchestra. At eight that evening, the national anthem stirred the audience into "prolonged applause." Later, music, recitations, poems, and nostalgic songs greeted with shouts of "more, more!" brought forth "warm reminders of their absent land." [59] The reporter noted approvingly that "there were great demonstrations of admiration . . . for a group of youngsters who sang the Mexican national anthem, their effort rewarded with a collection from the audience." As the hours passed, Señor Juan Fierro, president of the Comisión Honorífica Mexicana, rose to the podium and recapitulated the history of the Hidalgo's Cry of Independence. Then the memorable ceremonies closed as the band played the national anthem, the throng stirred to a patriotic enthusiasm with "loud applause and happy, sonorous 'vivas' to the Fatherland, as well to the men who sacrificed themselves in search of liberty."

On the sixteenth, an ebullient daylong celebration was staged. A crowd of six hundred enjoyed a sumptuous barbecue, listened to songs, poems, skits, plays, guest speakers, and the national anthem. The featured speakers included *comisión* vice-president Ignacio L. Martínez, whose words brought an "avalanche of enthusiasm, [and] demonstrations of patriotism." Culminating the festivities, the celebrants later gathered for an evening dance to the sounds of waltzes and polkas until midnight. A reporter noted that upon the closure, [the assembled] "manifested a great respect, which demonstrated the *colonia*'s sympathy, and affection, which it assigns to the Comisión Honorífica Mexicana." [60]

In southern California, *comisiones* regularly assumed the charge of organizing and hosting the Independence Day activities. In all of these celebrations, a keen but friendly competition arose over which *comisión* would have its festival honored by the presence of the consul or vice-consul. Only a fortunate few were so rewarded. The competition had sharpened by 1927, creating a virtual "downpour" of invitations from the "different ceremonies organized by the *Comisiones Honoríficas*." A flustered Consul Pesqueira called upon the *comisiones* to organize cooperative celebrations and "concentrate their festivities in a central locale." [61] Only in Los Angeles did that centralization occur, and then only through the auspices of the Confederación de Sociedades Mexicanas, which acted as the Los Angeles *comisión* (discussed in detail later in this chapter).

The Role of Charity

Various charitable acts also occupied *comisiones* from time to time and were mentioned often enough for almsgiving to be thought of as one of the *comisiones'* key responsibilities. When a family fell below the minimal standard for subsistence (usually because of unemployment), when a breadwinner fell ill or was injured, or in the aftermath of an earthquake, flood, or other natural disasters, the local *comisión* often went door-to-door soliciting donations to defray expenses for hospitalization, medicine, food, and clothing. *Comisiones* also had the authority to grant a sort of license to an individual to solicit contributions for a worthy cause in the name of the *comisión*.

The deadly Long Beach earthquake of 1933 spurred the local *comisión* to action. A special committee was formed to help those affected by the tremor, an act of compassion that exemplified the charitable works shouldered by *comisiones*. So moved was the Los Angeles consul by what the Long Beach *comisión* was doing to relieve victims of the disaster that the consul issued a bulletin praising the *comisión*. "The Comisión Honorífica Mexicana of Long Beach, California," he exclaimed, "has proceeded with total involvement in the investigations to know the exact consequences of the earthquake within the *colonia* mexicana. . . . there was only one death . . . and one injured." [62]

Comisiones not only raised money for local causes; they also contributed to funds for victims of natural disasters in Mexico. In 1931 a major earthquake in the state of Colima motivated the Santa Paula *comisión* to make a door-to-door appeal for aid. Members collected $17.40 for the Colima victims. Santa Paulans made the same rounds a year later, successfully collecting for flood victims in the state of Oaxaca. [63]

More often it was a personal misfortune that motivated a collection. When Dolores de Reyes, a penniless widow, died, the Irwindale *comisión* raised $87 for her burial. [64] Three years later the same *comisión* felt the obligation to assist José Jiménez and his impoverished family, who had been forced to subsist solely on oranges stolen from local groves. According to a reporter, "The *comisión honorífica*, in accord with the consulate, proceeded to raise a fund in the Mexican neighborhood, and with the collection, passage to Mexico has been purchased for them." [65] The Pacoima *comisión* issued a report upon completing a collection for a local compatriot. It read: "A new act of solidarity has been completed by the Comisión Honorífica Mexicana moved by the illness of Teodocio Ramírez, who remained in bed in serious condition, the above mentioned organization completed a public fund drive. . . . This, gentlemen, is very appreciative to the *comisión honorífica* and to the *colonia* as well."[66]

Legal defense funds for accused Mexican citizens were also collected. On behalf of Juan Reyna, an expatriate who stood charged with the murder of Los Angeles police officer Verne Brindley, $4,400 was raised within the Los Angeles *colonia* to pay his lawyers. After two trials, Reyna received one to ten years in San Quentin. This light sentence was considered a victory for the defense. Consul de la Colina reported the affair to the Foreign Relations office: "Various *comisiones honoríficas* and numerous persons contributed their monetary help equally, gathering together in this way a considerable quantity of money that covered the honorarium of the defense lawyer and the defense expenses, leaving, moreover, a considerable sum [$773.00] for the Reyna family."[67]

Though large sums were coming in and out of the *comisiones*, surprisingly few instances of corruption occurred. One such incident took place in San Bernardino, where a dishonest *comisión* treasurer, Angel del Castillo, "stole monies from the *Comisión Honorífica*, the Mexican school, and the patriotic committee." When discovered, del Castillo fled but was captured in El Paso and returned to San Bernardino for trial. Consul Pesqueira immediately set in motion an investigation of the embezzlement of *comisión* funds to determine whether others in the *comisión* had been involved.[68] No other examples of theft figure in the materials examined for this study.

Building a Network

Comisiones operated within a wide network well beyond the geographic limits of the communities they served. Not only did they report to the consul; they also interacted with each other, thereby constructing a larger organizational culture. However, in 1927 cooperation between *comisiones* was often sporadic, problematic, or nonexistent. It was this disconnection that the consulate sought to remedy. Utilizing its power to convene local and even statewide meetings, the Los Angeles consulate announced in the spring of 1927 the first convention of all the *comisiones* throughout the state.[69]

This preliminary conference set the agenda for a second conference, to be held a year later. Every *comisión* in the state of California was invited to attend this second conference. "This meeting," stated the invitation, "has as its objective the development of interaction and closer association of the *[comisiones]* to strengthen the task of cooperation with the consular offices and in that way make our work more effective." Representatives of the respective *comisiones* also discussed plans to host a national convention of *comisiones* from across the United States.[70] Plans for a national convention never materialized; however, over the years many less ambitious conventions were held.

"Grand Convention of *Comisiones Honoríficas*," announced the *La Opinión* headline of December 9, 1932. President Enrique Holmes of the South Fontana *comisión* petitioned Consul Hermolao Torres to convene a meeting of *comisiones* from San Bernardino and Riverside counties "to treat matters of the highest transcendental importance . . . with the goal of resolving many problems of vital importance that can only be handled through a convention."[71] Two weeks passed and a second call went out for a large-scale conference. Consul Hill and six *comisiones* from East Los Angeles county proposed that meetings be held to bring southern California *comisiones* "to work together for the same ends." Hill, in concert with the *comisiones* at the meeting, and much like his predecessor, Pesqueira, recommended "frequent meetings like the present one . . . to reach improved efficiency in the work of the various groupings."[72] *Comisiones* in other areas beyond California also sounded similar calls. In Laredo, Texas, Consul Efraín G. Domínguez initiated a project to "reorganize the *comisiones honoríficas mexicanas* established in Dolores, Cotulla, and Hebronville." Domínguez and a designated review committee visited each site looking for effective ways for *comisiones* to work together for the greater good.[73]

The value of the *comisiones* to the Secretariat of Foreign Relations was recognized and rewarded when, in 1931, a separate department of the Los Angeles consulate office was created to carry the administrative responsibilities related to the thirty-nine *comisiones* under its jurisdiction. Consulates had previously paid considerable attention to the *comisiones*, but it was seen as insufficient. With the new department a greater coordination and supervision of activities was expected. Several tasks were immediately assigned to the new department: to "increase the number of *comisiones*[,] . . . regularize their tasks[,] . . . carry out methodical inspections of the *comisiones*," and supervise "directly in the elections of the *comisión* central committee."[74]

Weaving a tighter organization brought with it stronger ties to the consulate that the *comisiones* seemed to accept, even sponsor. The Secretariat of Foreign Relations well understood the political benefits that would come from closer interaction between the consul and the *comisiones*. It was to that end that the secretariat strived in the spring of 1933. Subsequently, Secretary Puig Causaranc commissioned Visitor General of the Consulates Luis Lupian to tour the United States to "unify the consulate system" and "unify the actions of the *comisiones honoríficas.*" "During my stay," Lupian was heard to say, "I will visit as many communities as possible where there are organized groups." [75] Upon arriving in Los Angeles Lupian met with Consul Alejandro Martínez, and together they visited a number of nearby communities.

Comisiones issued periodic informational bulletins to the consul describing their major tasks, accomplishments, plans, and objectives. They also made special requests. In all of these communications the *comisiones* recognized the authority of the consul in all matters undertaken by the organization, and consuls exercised that authority. When in the fall of 1932 the Santa Maria and Guadalupe (California) *comisión* submitted a formal request to the consulate seeking permission to form a labor union, Vice-Consul Juan Richer responded warily that "it is of course worthy of support and applause." "Nevertheless," he cautioned, "to grant your wishes I kindly request that you send me a copy of the premises supporting the project, or a copy of your bylaws, if any, or at least an outline of the objectives, tendencies, etc., of the society which you plan to organize for our study and opinion regarding it." [76]

The large number of *comisiones* involved a continual flow of information to the consulate. At times, the volume overwhelmed its resources. It was this situation that prompted Consul Pesqueira to petition his superiors to grant him franking privileges for *comisión* correspondence, "since everything dealt with . . . has an official character, and the said correspondence is very copious and at times voluminous." [77] Pesqueira commented further that he "maintained a constant communication, issuing instructions, forms for the dispatching of documents, circulars, etc." with the thirty *comisiones* within his Los Angeles jurisdiction. A decade passed, 1929 to 1939, but the communication problem persisted. Overwhelmed by the waves of letters, the consulate felt compelled to address the matter publicly through the columns of *La Opinión.* "The consulate maintains," stated the harried consul, "an extremely active correspondence with the *comisiones honoríficas,*" which in turn made the archiving difficult. He cited that 107 *comisión* letters were received in January 1939. Since each letter usually included several official matters, filing them in some order made it necessary to make a copy of each letter for multiple files, a bureaucratic nightmare for any office, especially one with a small staff. The consul requested that to simplify the filing, *comisiones* send one letter for each matter under consideration. "If done in this fashion," continued the statement, "the *comisiones honoríficas* can be assured of better attention to their correspondence." [78]

The masses of information continued to flow to the secretariat via the consul general in San Francisco. Two examples illustrate the nature of the information and suggest why such information was so important to the secretariat. In a routine routing of information, Consul Rodolfo Salazar of the Calexico (California) consulate submitted to the consul general "a list of *comisiones* and Mexican organizations within the jurisdiction of this office." [79] Salazar included the addresses of the five organizations and their key officers. This kind of reporting was not uncommon; consuls routinely informed their superiors of the organizational activity in their areas. When desired information appeared to be lacking, the secretariat called upon its consuls to supply the required report. Thus, in an effort to compile a comprehensive registry of *comisiones,* Foreign Relations directed Consul Martínez in Los Angeles to supply a listing of each *comisión* "specifying the members of the executive committee." [80]

Embarking on any significant project or change in *comisión* objectives without prior approval from Foreign Relations was a risky undertaking for the consuls. Los Angeles Consul de la Colina well understood the chain of command when he sought approval for a planned reorganization of the *comisiones* operating under his authority. Before engaging his plans, he first solicited authorization from Foreign Relations. In his petition he gave a detailed explanation for his project and listed the *comisiones* and the members by branch. In effect, de la Colina sought to remove *comisiones* from less populous *colonias* and reestablish them in larger ones. His simple plan proposed situating the *colonias* closer together. Proximity would make it easier for *comisiones* to communicate and interact with each other and with the consulate.[81] Regardless of the desirability and efficacy of the plan, de la Colina, like consuls before and after him, was granted only limited authority to make such alterations in existing projects, and de la Colina's plan was never fully implemented. Ultimately, the secretariat controlled the general policies governing the *comisiones.*

The Confederación de Sociedades Mexicanas

Growth of the Mexican community in the southern California region was spectacular and brought with it the full range of Mexican cultural practices. By the mid-twenties a large number of independent self-help organizations, or *mutualistas,* had formed in and around Los Angeles. Some served as social support; others had a cultural, labor, or recreational function. Sensing a political opportunity, then consul Rafael Avelyra issued a call for a meeting of the officers of all the *mutualista* recreational, cultural, and labor groups in Los Angeles to form an umbrella organization with official ties to the consulate. His invitation caused much excitement in the *colonia* and resulted in the founding in 1925 of the Confederación de Sociedades Mexicanas (CSM), chartered with the task of "coordinating and controlling" a single city-wide observance of the two main Mexican patriotic celebrations, Cinco de Mayo and Independence Day.[82]

Unlike the *comisiones,* which held a quasi-official consular status and were established across the United States, the Confederación held less "official" but nonetheless close ties to the consulate and functioned entirely within the Los Angeles *colonia* and orbit of the Los Angeles consulate. Indeed, the consul traditionally served as the honorary president and presided over CSM activities, particularly the patriotic celebrations, which were recognized as the official consulate celebrations in the city. Even though the CSM and the *comisiones* functioned independently of each other, their respective members and leaders often had a foot in a third organization as well, thus constructing a wide social network, with the consulate serving as the hub. Moreover, given the responsibility to conduct the official (that is, the consulate's) Independence Day celebration, the CSM, managed by an executive committee, was held in high esteem in the Los Angeles *colonia* and effectively controlled the activities. Among the responsibilities of the organization, the defense of the "good name of the *colonia*" was considered fundamental.[83] Although they were primarily assigned to organize the patriotic festivals, the consul occasionally called upon the CSM to assume other, often unrelated, duties, such as charity collections and, later, the issuing of documents certifying Mexican citizenship and registration of births to compatriots.

In all of its endeavors, the CSM always acted under the consul's watchful eye, seldom, if ever, branching out into independent projects. In preparing for Independence Day, the most important of Mexico's national holidays, the CSM convened meetings with its affiliates, respected professional leaders, East Los Angeles merchants, small publishers, and others to form a Comité de Festejos Patrios "backed by the Confederación," which then proceeded to orchestrate the festival.[84] Observers noted that the planning required "constant meetings for discussing the festival program" over a number of months.[85] Effectively centralized under consulate oversight, the national patriotic observances, held at the large municipal Lincoln Park, expressed the general political philosophy of the Mexican government. Carrying the message with appropriate fervor were the consuls, visiting Mexican government dignitaries, CSM or *comisión* leaders, and representatives of local pro-government groups who delivered the featured addresses.

To attract a large audience, the program for the 1928 Independence Day celebration was publicized in *La Opinión.* The panoply of entertainments—music, speeches, poetry recitals, songs, and skits—was described. CSM president Francisco Gurrola was to serve as master of ceremonies and deliver the main address, Consul Pesqueira to preside, and the Mexico City Police Band to provide uplifting national marches.[86]

Traditionally various Los Angeles officials, including the mayor and council members, partook in the proceedings. At the 1929 ceremony, Mayor John C. Porter officially welcomed a throng of several thousand and took a seat "on the side of the Consul of Mexico." President Gurrola then took the podium and in the name of the "Confederación de Socie-dades Mexicanas [presented the mayor] with a small gift: a small encased flag of Mexico."[87] On the final day of the festivities, traditional music was played, songs were sung, and the poetry of Mexico recited. In addition, patriotic speeches were delivered and the national anthems of both countries sounded. The grand finale, a dance at Lincoln Park's skating rink, provided the social centerpiece to the nationalist undertaking.

There are obvious parallels between the Confederación ceremonies and those hosted by the *comisiones*. Like so many of the activities of both organizations, the celebrations were fueled by political considerations conceived and directed by the consuls. Other ceremonies also became op-portunities for stirring national feeling. When Consul Pesqueira made his official departure from the Los Angeles Consulate, the CSM hosted a fare-well banquet and extended a warm welcome to his replacement, Rafael de la Colina. The CSM officers called "an extraordinary assembly of all the affiliated organizations" to invest de la Colina with the position of Honorary President.[88] One of de la Colina's first acts was to take an active role in planning upcoming festivities, as his predecessors had done before him. In his consular bulletin announcing the festival dates, he also clari-fied the link between the consulate and the CSM. Picked up by *La Opi-nión*, the bulletin assured his constituents that "[t]he Confederación de Sociedades Mexicanas of this city has organized, as in previous years, a series of festivals for the 14th, 15th, and 16th of September . . . to com-memorate the anniversary of our Independence. The Confederación . . . can depend upon the moral support of the consulate just as it has in the past."[89]

The high profile reserved for the consul reflected in each of the central activities of the CSM. The yearly convention of the organization's affili-ates highlighted the assumption of duties by the newly elected board of directors. As honorary president, the consul traditionally inaugurated the convention and officiated at the ritual transfer of the CSM's banner to the new board, symbolizing the transfer of power. As he passed the banner at the 1930 conclave, de la Colina "counseled all the members to dutifully honor it."[90] Following the installation of the new board, awards were pre-sented for meritorious service, to a loud round of applause for the recipients. Consul de la Colina then closed the convention with solemn words, urging the CSM to "proceed ahead along the road traveled [and] assured them that his complete support . . . will continue into the future." [91]

The Founding of the Confederación de Uniones Obreras Mexicanas (CUOM)

In 1926, Clemente Idar, a special AFL organizer from Texas, spent two months in Los Angeles conducting a "survey of the conditions of the Mexican working people" in that city in order to determine whether the "possibility of organizing them existed." Idar returned to Texas and reported that an "active campaign in this direction was not opportune." [92] Although the AFL had sent an organizer to make this survey, the negative result was predictable. The AFL had its own political agenda, as I will show. However, the AFL had no objections to the consulate organizing that labor. In fact, the AFL encouraged it, but for reasons other than securing the welfare of Mexican workers in California. It was the CSM that carried the cause forward.

The CSM made the momentous decision in 1927 to organize the first Mexican labor union in the United States, the Confederación de Uniones Obreras Mexicanas, or CUOM. In that year the CSM convened a special September meeting of the affiliated societies to discuss the "cause of organizing labor unions of Mexican workers." [93] The members immediately rallied to the cause. Consul Pesqueira played a major role at each level of the proceedings. However, Pesqueira, owner of the 45,000-acre Hacienda Cuchuta and family to the wealthy Sonora clan allied to former President Alvaro Obregón, was not the principal motivating force behind the formation of CUOM. That initiative came directly from President Plutarco Calles.

Three years after the CSM's founding, its general secretary, Ampelio González, recollected that "General Plutarco Elías Calles, serving as President of the Republic, recommended to the Mexican consul [Pesqueira] in this city the advantages to organizing into unions. . . . the Confederación de Sociedades Mexicanas received the ideas [as] a means to economically improve the *colonia*." [94] Calles had several other reasons for ordering the consul to organize the union. A sensitive political situation was developing. This was a season of harsh rhetoric from both the U.S. Congress and the American Federation of Labor. Each was calling for a quota restricting Mexican immigration. Delegates at the AFL's forty-seventh national convention, in particular those from California, were highly vocal in support of this restrictive quota. Delegates made incendiary statements, accusing Mexican immigrants of competing with better-paid U.S. labor and forcing wages down.

Calles had several concerns. First, he was worried about a unilateral quota and the potential injury to the Mexican economy that would ensue when the large yearly cash flow (via money orders and other means) from immigrants dried up. Secondly, he saw that the large mass of unorganized Mexican workers provided a fertile field for radical and leftist leaders in the United States to plant their dangerous political ideas. This could undermine Mexicanization and create opposition to the Mexican government's policies regarding the immigrant community. In other words, such organizing could spill south across the border. Calles hoped to placate the AFL, which still held official ties with the government union, the Confederación Regional Obrera Mexicana (CROM), and in the bargain, carry his Mexicanization policy into the ranks of organized labor.

Calles also expected the new CUOM to officially affiliate with CROM and to collaborate with the AFL. Consequently, a considerable number of CUOM's first published statements and actions clearly indicated that it favored the voluntary restriction of Mexican emigration, a task most pleasing to the AFL. Calles cleverly realized several objectives through one organization. That organization, CUOM, eventually played a significant, albeit short-lived, role in the labor movement of that immigrant community.

Within a month of the call to form the union, a representative of the AFL appeared at the CSM offices "with the expectation of exchanging impressions with leaders regarding the new direction given to the [Confederación]."[95] A *La Opinión* journalist noted the significance of the AFL-CUOM connection. *Colonia* "Leaders," began the article, "know that the American Federation of Labor's position is that they cannot equalize salary levels between the East coast and the West coast when Mexican workers are not organized, and that they are therefore poised to help the Confederación."[96]

At the very moment that the consulate lofted Mexicanization via *comisiones honoríficas* and Mexican schools throughout the widely distributed *colonia* complex, a debate surged within the CSM and throughout the *colonia* regarding the appropriateness of a Mexican labor union. Some in the *colonia* claimed that the CSM should have been involved even earlier in unionization, and they questioned why such a move took so long. Others feared the loss of the CSM's popular patriotic observances. Certainly, other issues, particularly Mexicanization, were paramount at the time. At the session that gave final approval to the formation of CUOM, traditional agenda items were taken up, including Mexican schools, the Casa del Mexicano (a Mexican cultural center with the consulate as the centerpiece, a device still practiced by various consulates) among other Mexicanization projects. Finally, the last item on the evening's agenda was articulated: that "the Confederación de Sociedades transform itself into a society of unions." After a formal presentation on the merits of the proposal, discussion was opened by a select review committee (which included Consul Pesqueira). The committee strongly endorsed the motion and urged members to ratify it.[97]

A spirited but harmonious discussion followed in which a number of issues were directly addressed. The debate focused on the lack of organized protection, low salaries, the AFL's critique of Mexican immigration, the inspiration of CROM and the AFL for modeling the new union, and lastly, the contention that the CSM's affiliates, with their sizable memberships, ensured a reservoir of union members. Speakers signified that "the respective contingents [can] generate a large component of great utility for the crystallization of the labor unification following the model of the CROM in Mexico and the AFL." Six resolutions were drafted at the meeting and presented in the official CSM report. This report then went out to the affiliates for general discussion and approval. Four are of interest to this analysis: first, that the CSM "declare itself a party to unionization"; second, that each affiliate form a union; third, that the CSM keep its separate organizational identity; and fourth, that the new union seek official affiliation with CROM and that a call go out for a general convention to formalize the proposed union.

The various affiliates approved the resolutions overwhelmingly, and at the November 1927 meeting the CSM voted the funds to implement plans for a general convention. They gave authority to initiate the organizing drive to a committee which they named Grupo Acción, a politically astute step that paid homage to CROM and made CROM influence more explicit. "Grupo Acción" was the popular name of CROM's highly secretive executive body. Dominated by Luis Morones and his henchmen, Grupo Acción served as CROM's centralized and authoritarian decision-making body. By choosing this copy-cat symbol, the fledgling union identified itself with CROM and could expect to benefit from the affiliation. In fact, within days of the installation of the local Grupo Acción, a gift from Morones and his inner circle arrived. Included in the sizable package were "more than fifty publications including books and pamphlets on syndicalism, cooperativism, labor organizing, worker's banks, and labor, federation, and *confederación* statutes." Even as the local Grupo Acción underscored the centrality of the CSM in the unionization plan and reiterated that the organization "will assume the direction of the nascent organization," the new union declared itself the Los Angeles branch of CROM at the regular CSM meeting later that month.[98]

Working alongside the Grupo Acción, the first executive committee chosen by the CSM administered the fledgling union. By then CROM already had its fingerprints all over the new enterprise. But so did the Mexican government. "Consul Pesqueira Has Delivered an Organized Branch of the CROM in Los Angeles," ran the *La Opinión* headline over the article which informed of the formal affiliation, broadcasting an insight into the rapidly transpiring process.[99] The membership not only acknowledged CROM as its parent; it also recognized the consulate as a partner to the project. As in the case of the *comisiones* and the CSM, the rank and file voted to expand the CUOM executive committee to include the position of honorary president reserved for the consul. Pesqueira, by virtue of his consular position, assumed his third honorary presidency.

Once formally vested, the new fifteen-member executive committee took charge. Influences from CROM and Calles went hand in hand with those of the AFL. As its initial official action, the committee authorized Consul Pesqueira, who was about to leave for Mexico City, to lobby the Mexican government, especially "President don Plutarco Elías Calles" so that he might take steps "to limit Mexican immigration to this country."[100] The executive committee consequently recommended a contract labor system, arguing that employers should have "the opportunity to bring as many workers as needed, but under a firm contract and with round trip passage."[101]

Simultaneous with Pesqueira's departure for Mexico City, the CUOM executive committee "issued a manifesto setting forth the principles of the Confederación."[102] Accumulated ad hoc declarations were incorporated into the statement, and several more were added. The preamble reviewed the political orientation of the new union and the conditions making the organization of Mexican labor under the leadership of the CSM a necessity. "It must be understood," read the preamble, "that this movement's aim is not to agitate, nor to spread or instigate dissolvent ideas."[103] In theory, CUOM promised to follow the politically conservative path laid down by CROM and the AFL.

With its political orientation defined, the manifesto then elaborated eight principles "that the Federation of Mexican Labor will uphold." Again, CUOM promised to "establish solid relations with CROM and to try to stop the immigration of unorganized labor into the U.S." The manifesto also declared a need to "study and resolve in accord with the Mexican government the best systems of repatriation."[104] Following the eight major principles, the document recommended four avenues for improving "the good reputation of the Mexican *colonias*." These four referred directly to the active Mexicanization efforts in practice throughout the region. The recommendations included strengthening patriotism, promoting a "cultural campaign giving preference to the education of our children," providing charitable help for the indigent and a defense committee to "defend Mexicans who are put in jail . . . because of [their] ignorance of the law." Each of the latter efforts borrowed heavily from the normal assignments handed to the *comisiones honoríficas* and the CSM and demonstrated how dominant political networking in the expatriate community had become.

In response to threats of mass deportation of unemployed Mexican immigrants by the Los Angeles Bureau of Charities, CUOM Secretary General Francisco Gurrola sent a personal message to President Calles urging the restriction of Mexican emigration to the United States. The Bureau of Charities had joined the deportation furor then swirling through Los Angeles County and "invited" unemployed Mexicans to return to Mexico and all other unemployed to leave the city. Gurrola reported the bureau's threat almost verbatim in his message to Calles. Further, he requested of Calles that Mexican authorities stop immigrants from entering the United States at key border-crossing points, thereby impeding the flow of alleged excess labor into Los Angeles and at the same time smoothing a contentious local situation.[105] Calles replied, indicating that the note had been passed on to the appropriate government department. Gurrola, having alerted Calles, felt satisfied that "Mexican emigration would be regulated very soon, avoiding the excess of Mexican workers."[106] The next year, 1929, Gurrola was elected president of the CSM.

Mexico's repatriation policy seemed to fit the exigencies of the hour. As the U.S. economy slid into decline in the late 1920s, unemployment among Mexican workers increased apace. With the increase, Mexico stepped up its repatriation campaign. The two drives, deportation and repatriation, dovetailed, giving each added force. All this while Mexicanization flowered and Mexico's campaign of repatriation was launched with promises of good land at cheap prices, provided the repatriates pay their way. The effort meshed well with the rising tide of anti-Mexican sentiment that was then taking the form of raids on areas frequented by Mexican laborers, attacks allegedly made to detain vagrants and deportables. In fact, anyone who appeared to be Mexican posed a target for a police dragnet.

Rather than organizing laborers to protect their rights, Mexico organized its nationals to consider repatriation. This tactic played into the hands of U.S. authorities, who sought "repatriation," in other words, voluntary departure under duress, and deportation, as the solutions to budgetary constraints caused by an economy beginning a nose dive.

Mexican immigration policy essentially mirrored the logic of the repatriation drives that had ebbed and flowed for years until concretized in the massive removal of Mexicans and Mexican Americans from the United States between 1931 and 1935. Mexican administration officials looked very favorably upon repatriations. However, the repatriated were not always treated as equals by Mexicans who had never left home. Secretary of Agriculture and Development Francisco S. Elías, owner of "a great cattle ranch in Sonora" and cousin to former President Plutarco Elías Calles, praised the repatriates for bringing with them valuable resources, in particular a "broadened outlook." Elías contended that, as emigrants, they had experienced "travel and contact with life among such alert and progressive people as those of Southern California" and acquired "a taste for the things of a world where life is speeded up." Having learned the "American ways," returned workers brought modern methods of production to Mexico. Elías found little to criticize regarding repatriation; in fact, he believed it had much to recommend it. As he put it, the mass return provided "a tremendous civic and social asset to the social structure" of Mexico.[107] Notwithstanding Elías's positive evaluation of returned compatriots, both nations' policies were in agreement that immigrants created the problem that repatriation attempted to correct. Consider the following statement by Ignacio Dávila Sánchez, labor attaché (that is, a CROM official) at the Mexican Embassy in Washington, D.C. After a 1928 investigation of the unemployment problem in El Paso, San Antonio, Nogales, and Los Angeles, Dávila Sánchez concluded that "the excess of Mexican immigrants significantly harms, not only the two million compatriots now living in the United States, but even more, the native sons of this country by virtue of the fact that as each day that passes, salaries diminish more and more by the competition brought by the Mexican immigrant."[108] The AFL could not have been more pleased with Dávila Sánchez's findings.

Dávila Sánchez acknowledged that Mexico looked favorably upon a temporary contract labor policy that the AFL proposed as a restrictive device. The AFL intended to lobby for a contract labor law in Congress, provided Mexico agreed to the policy in principle. By recommending restrictions CUOM, in retrospect, appeared to have represented the interests of the AFL and of the restrictionists rather than those of the Mexican immigrant community. (However, as the Depression bore down, the need for such a proposal evaporated, and the idea went no further than discussion.)

Regulating immigration via the contracting of Mexican labor, hardly a novel suggestion, also made the rounds within the ranks of U.S. employers. An emergency contract program lasted three years, from the war years of 1917 to 1920. Thereafter a more or less open border policy "regulated" the entrance of Mexican immigrants. The expired policy continued to attract the interest of authorities, particularly those who feared the loss of Mexican labor via restrictions.

Dr. George P. Clements, manager of the Agricultural Department of the Los Angeles Chamber of Commerce, voiced the need for a contract system in a 1926 address before the annual Friends of the Mexican conference held at Pomona College. Clements contended that the question was "entirely economic" and that "[t]o make the best use of him [the Mexican laborer] we must devise some means to make his service possible to agriculture and industry when needed . . . then return him to his home." Furthermore, with such a policy, "the present question concerning the indigent Mexican will be no more." [109] Clements was certainly not alone in recommending seasonal labor importation. S. Parker Frisselle, representing the California Farm Bureau Federation, testified before a House Committee on Immigration and Naturalization that "we in California would greatly prefer some set-up in which our peak labor demands might be met and upon the completion of the harvest these laborers returned to their country." [110]

Joining a rising chorus, Consul Pesqueira regretted unrestricted Mexican immigration and candidly expressed the same restrictionist argument proffered by Clements and Frisselle. "One difficulty in organizing Mexicans," contended the consul in an interview with Paul S. Taylor, "is the continued flow. We wish this stopped, but would prefer to have it checked by a joint understanding between the governments, rather than by applying a quota to Mexico. It would be all right to admit Mexicans seasonally. The American government could request a number, and we could send them from the parts of our country where we did not need them." [111]

As that message made the rounds of the executive office in Mexico City, CUOM made public its first constitution, crafted at its convention on March 23, 1928. The constitution's radical rhetoric contrasted sharply with its published conservative principles and many of the previous statements that had come from the spokespersons. Phrases like "exploited class," "class struggle," "complete freedom from the capitalist tyranny," and "the exploited class must organize" must have sounded alarms among some. However, the disingenuous language remained tethered to key principles: "the exploited class must organize . . . in accord with the rights which the laws of this country concede to native and foreign workers." [112] Moreover, affiliation with CROM signified the incorporation of staunch antileftist principles as well as acquiescence to the political realities that faced Mexican labor north of the border. CUOM assured its members, and the local authorities, that it would not stray beyond the laws regulating union conduct.

Delegates to the first convention represented mutual aid associations and twenty-four incipient unions formed from the CSM affiliates. After active discussion over immigration restriction, Mexican schools, and cooperation with the AFL, among other issues, the delegates voted to approve the constitution. Apparently, neither major nor minor changes altered the original proposed version presented by the executive committee. CROM managed to contribute directly to the proceedings. Among the delegates sat a fraternal CROM representative, Emilio Mujica, who provided more than fraternal greetings. Mujica stayed "for about a month after the adjournment . . . and helped organize unions in southern California."[113]

In the months following the CUOM convention, regularly scheduled meetings managed to concentrate their focus upon the immigration question. When the Orange County contingent joined in March 1928, the newly elected president requested authority from the executive committee to address yet another resolution to President Calles. He recommended that Calles enjoin measures "to impede the importation of twenty thousand Mexicans who have been contracted [by employers] when there exists unemployed without the slightest hope of finding employment."[114] Although no such proposal was ever planned or implemented, the statement exposed the seriousness with which CUOM embraced the campaign to restrict, or at least regulate, emigration. Meanwhile, Consul Pesqueira completed his journey to Mexico City, having delivered an earlier CUOM memorial personally to Calles, requesting that the Mexican government commit to the "restriction and regulation of Mexican emigration."[115]

The following year a second constitution reiterated much the same material found in the original; any changes seemed to fine-tune rather than alter direction. Again, immigration restriction and repatriation "in accordance with the Mexican government" found its way into the new constitution alongside the familiar lofty, but toothless, rhetoric of "class struggle." The fine print, however, laid bare the union's fundamental political nature: "industries must be in the hands of those who are capable of maintaining said industries in production." That somewhat ambivalent phrase assured that the union did not wish to interfere with their employers' capital. In an official report on the union, a state investigator for the California governor's office wrote that CUOM underscored the importance of respecting "the laws of the United States." Clearly, the second constitution stipulated that the union proceed "always with tact and diplomacy" in the pursuit of its principal objectives: "wages in proportion to the necessities," and the prosecution of unscrupulous employers and cheating labor contractors.[116]

Notwithstanding the large mass of Mexican laborers in the area, the union managed to sign up only about two or three thousand dues-paying members. Due to the transiency of the labor force in southern California, comprised largely of agricultural workers, members experienced difficulty in maintaining their cards. A year after CUOM's founding, approximately two hundred dues-paying members remained on the books, indicating that the promise that CUOM once held had evaporated. Although a few locals survived into the early years of the Depression, CUOM never became an important Mexican labor union.

We can only speculate as to why it languished until it was revived during the 1933 Los Angeles County strike (see Chapter 3). Perhaps CUOM fulfilled its obligations when it lobbied for voluntary restrictions, an obligation that CROM had promised the AFL to honor at the 1927 Pan American Federation of Labor convention. We do know, however, that the Mexican government, via the consulate, significantly influenced the founding and political orientation assumed by CUOM. Despite the union's demise, the general orientation guiding the Confederación de Sociedades Mexicanas did not change, nor did its active presence decline. The same could be said about the *comisiones honoríficas mexicanas,* the Mexican schools, and lesser organizations like the Cruz Azul, a female charity organization sponsored by the consulate. While the CUOM fell into decline, the Mexican electoral politics of 1929 reverberated in Los Angeles and led to a political fervor never seen before in the *colonias.* Many of the prominent leaders active in the CSM, the *comisiones,* and the CUOM surfaced in government-candidate support groups formed for the election. Quite possibly, it was the electioneering effort exercised by *colonia* leaders that weakened CUOM at the very moment that required strong leadership.

The Election of 1929

The spectrum of Mexican politics carried by migrants, political exiles, and, of course, the Mexican government spread throughout the major immigrant settlements. The elections of 1929, held after the July 1928 assassination of President Alvaro Obregón and the yearlong interim presidency of Emilio Portes Gil, drew the well-organized pro-government elements and their less numerous but active opponents, to the fray. Even a group of Los Angeles–based political exiles who had taken a turn of political heart were numerous enough to form a support group in favor of the government candidate hand-picked by Calles, Pasqual Ortiz Rubio. Political agitation like that of 1929 had never affected the *colonia* before, and it attested to the determination, if not the sagacity, demonstrated by the central government in its efforts to shape the politics of the peripheral expatriate community.

Organizations allied to the consulate through the comisiones honorí-ficas, the CSM, and CUOM, as well as other overtly independent but pro-government groups, swung into a determined campaign in favor of Ortiz Rubio. Pro-Ortiz Rubio groups dedicated a good part of their activities during the summer of 1929 to thwarting any opportunity the independent party candidate, José Vasconcelos (who had been secretary of education in the first Obregón administration), may have had to develop a local following. Unfortunately for Vasconcelos, sentiment in the Los Angeles consular district overwhelmingly sided with Pasqual Ortiz Rubio, the candidate of the newly established government political party, the Partido Nacional Revolucionario (PNR), the forerunner of today's Partido Revo-lucionario Institucional (PRI). Crowned with the title "Jefe Máximo de la Revolución," Calles held the reins of government for the six years following his presidency and would do so until after the election of Lázaro Cárdenas in 1934. Prompted by Calles, the PNR nominated Ortiz Rubio at its first convention in the summer of 1929. A group calling itself the Antireelectionists formed a party around José Vasconcelos and named it, appropriately, the Antireelectionist Party. Both candidates launched campaigns across Mexico that reached into the United States.

In California, particularly southern California, that campaign consumed the energy of *colonia* activists and revealed the extent to which the Mexican government influenced the political discourse. Even the generally non–politically active Partido Liberal Mexicano emerged as a stronghold for Ortiz Rubio. As the summer campaign began, PLM's eleven thousand members strayed from the familiar *mutualista* program and focused their energies upon the election. By way of a printed manifesto openly critical of Vasconcelos, the PLM introduced itself to the election-eering tumult. The PLM, according to a *La Opinión* article, "hurled concrete accusations against the candidacy of Licenciado Vasconcelos and simultaneously announced the candidacy of Ingeniero Pasqual Ortiz Rubio." [117] Twenty thousand copies were distributed among members in California and other states and reached their friends in Mexico as well.

The PLM scheduled public campaign meetings from San Diego to as far north as San Francisco, attracting audiences drawn by guest speakers known for their oratorical skills. Frequently meetings were held in conjunction with other pro–Ortiz Rubio groups. The major Ortiz Rubio organization, the Club Reforma Pro–Ortiz Rubio, acted as an umbrella group for a number of Club Reforma branches in the Los Angeles area. Led by Francisco Gurrola, who served as the first CUOM secretary general and the then president of the CSM, the Club Reforma dedicated itself to "intense propaganda in all the centers where labor resides in the American Union in favor of the candidacy of Ortiz Rubio." [118] In the company of the Club Reforma and the PLM, the Partido Laborista Mexicana, the U.S. branch of the CROM's political arm by the same name, carried out community meetings, including mass city-wide gatherings, calling upon the *colonias* up and down the state to support Ortiz Rubio.[119] The Mexico City office of the Partido Laborista sent representatives to the Los Angeles branch and according to *La Opinión,* "they propose to visit the worker neighborhoods where strong organized *mutualistas* are active . . . including those organizations supporting Ortiz Rubio."[120] As the election date neared, the intensity level increased. Sunday, August 17, was especially memorable as the PLM sponsored meetings at *colonias* across the country, including San Francisco, New York, Chicago, Oakland, Santa Ana [California], Pasadena, and Los Angeles.

Various forms of linkage connected the pro–Ortiz Rubio groups with organizations in Mexico. The Club Reforma Pro–Ortiz Rubio, for example, held quasi-official ties with the then recently formed PNR, which was controlled by the Calles machine. To hold ties with a major organization conferred status and legitimacy to a local group. Thus, the Club Reforma held an extraordinary session, as part of its election activities, to proudly announce that the statutes and bylaws of the Partido Nacional Revolucionario paralleled a basic principle of the Confederación de Sociedades Mexicanas, namely, the need to resolve "the diverse problems facing the vast Mexican *colonia* established in this country." The assembly discussed and passed a motion that all Club Reformas up and down the state adhere to the Partido Liberal Mexicano. The motion was greeted with applause from the Santa Ana delegation, led by Lucas Lucio, president of the local *comisión honorífica* and honorary consul.[121]

The overlapping of the CSM's, CUOM's, and *comisiones'* leadership with that of the various Ortiz Rubio groups illustrates the high profile displayed by the Mexican political apparatus at that time. Francisco Gurrola, CSM president and former first secretary general to the CUOM, served as the Club Reforma president and was an officer in the Partido Liberal Mexicano. Lucas Lucio, president of the Santa Ana *comisión honorífica,* served as the local Club Reforma president. CSM Pro-Secretary Armando Flores, who signed the resolution that initiated the formation of CUOM and served on its first executive committee, not only played an active role as guest speaker at PLM campaign functions but also served as the party's secretary of the exterior (and two years later, was elected president). Luciano Falcón, another pro–Ortiz Rubio activist, served as the party's secretary of the interior. The CSM secretary at the time, Leandro Venegas, one of CUOM's founders and a member of the first executive committee, worked diligently for the Club Reforma. He and Gurrola "were commissioned [by the Club] to give a series of conferences in Los

Angeles and nearby towns, where Mexican compatriots reside in large numbers."[122] Another key CUOM organizer, Pedro Salinas, then CSM treasurer (and elected to the post of secretary of education and culture in 1933) led the East Los Angeles branch of the Club Reforma.[123] Antonio M. Villarreal, acknowledged as the most popular speaker in the *colonia* and chancellor at the Los Angeles consulate, served as president of the PLM.[124] The link with the PLM was more than coincidental. The consulate, through Villarreal, bound the two entities into a single political purpose.[125]

With such favorable conditions, the pro–Ortiz Rubio forces picked up the tempo and carried the campaign into the 1929 Independence Day celebrations, an event over which they already exercised a good degree of control. This commemoration, more notable for its strong election-year overtones than for its patriotic ceremonialism, carried the campaign to its nadir. Among the groups officially participating in the event, the Partido Liberal Mexicano enjoyed a high profile. Obviously, the government candidate held the inside track: Villarreal, Luis Medrano, and Francisco Gurrola gave keynote addresses. The Club Reforma lost no opportunity to advertise its objectives by sponsoring a decorated motor vehicle at the traditional Independence Day parade that wound its way from downtown Los Angeles to Lincoln Park. Following suit, all the local Ortiz Rubio organizations placed decorated vehicles in the parade proudly proclaiming their agenda.

Finding that the Mexican Independence Day offered a wonderful opportunity to advance their cause, the Club Reforma held its own celebration on the fifteenth (scheduled so as not to interfere with the official observances) at the Teatro México in the downtown area. Speakers' topics mirrored that of the official CSM activities: Club Reforma Secretary Luis Falcón and notables like Gurrola and Armando Flores gave the traditional patriotic speeches.[126]

Meanwhile, the pro-Vasconcelos groups worked on the fringes, denied the advantages of the political machine related either officially or informally with the Mexican government. Nevertheless, Clubes Pro-Vasconcelos managed to create something of an opposition voice, albeit one overwhelmed by the sizable Ortiz Rubio organizational apparatus. If the number and size of the articles devoted to each group that appeared on the pages of *La Opinión* are any indication of strength, than it can be said that the Pro-Ortiz Rubio crowd won handily. Whereas the Vasconcelistas appeared in fourteen articles, the Ortizrubistas were featured in twenty-six. And of these, most of the latter pieces were much longer articles than those focused on the Vasconcelos campaign. Vasconcelos simply had no chance in southern California. Moreover, none of the Vasconcelos activists whose names appeared in the columns of *La Opinión* during the elections were mentioned in any way in articles dealing with consulate-inspired organizations published before and after the elections.

These examples of political networking around electoral politics conformed to the traditional patterns extant within Mexico at the time. Fluid alliances around individuals, rather than with an identifiable political agenda or ideology, a trademark in Mexican political culture, buttressed institutional practice. Thus, for example, group identifiers in most cases were cast in personal terms, such as *Callistas, Obregonistas, Vasconcelistas, Ortizrubistas,* and later *Cardenistas,* rather than with a distinctive ideological frame of reference, such as *socialist, Liberal,* or *Republican.* Like pieces of an interlocking mechanism, the sundry groupings that circulated about the consulate rallied to the government party candidate, partially out of political convictions, but primarily because of the political culture of Mexico, in which elections brought forth groupings around specific candidates. And if one worked for the winning side, rewards in the form of sinecures might well be expected. Certainly, a sense of nationalist duty to the Patria must also have influenced the decision to participate in the election campaign.

The several chapters of the Partido Liberal Mexicano in California consistently expressed support for the regimes in power. Several years later, Ampelio González, president of the CSM, refreshed the memory of the secretary of foreign relations when he proudly exclaimed, "This worker organization has invariably backed the constituted government in cases of rebellion, and in the [1929] electoral campaign, we were the group that carried it in this country for the actual President of the Republic, Pascual Ortiz Rubio." [127] Moreover, whenever a new executive committee took over a chapter's reins, tradition held that the new directors informed the president of Mexico of the change of personnel while reaffirming the group's loyalty. Armando Flores and Antonio Villarreal fulfilled their official obligation in notifying the Secretariat of Foreign Relations of the election of the new PLM governing body for 1930. The "PLM comprising 11,000 Mexican laborers residing in California," wrote Flores and Villarreal, "sends warm greetings in anticipation of an era of progress and reconstruction of the fatherland." [128] Another letter to President Abelardo Rodríguez from a Los Angeles PLM chapter affirmed that "this group has the honor to address you manifesting its firm adhesion to the Revolutionary principles and to the Government over which you worthily preside. . . . We are pleased to offer our modest but enthusiastic cooperation in all that we can be of service to our Fatherland." [129]

The Rise of Leftist Politics

What is perhaps most striking in the four examples of political organizing discussed above is their distinctive conservative and nationalistic character. What may appear on the surface as internally contradictory, that is, the combining of nationalism (Mexicanization) with conservative corporatist politics, upon deeper examination appears to have been meshed and interrelated quite well. Nationalist propaganda seldom strayed from its politically conservative moorings. Thus, while Mexicanization reached its highest levels during the late 1920s, communists and other leftists were threatened, jailed, tortured, and murdered by government agents in Mexico. Lest any gain surreptitious entry, Mexican immigration authorities were ordered to deny entry to any suspected leftists. Although consuls could not engage in the same level of antileftist action, they nonetheless made every effort to carefully monitor the situation and to isolate leftists from the *colonia* if possible.

The Depression presented the consulates with their first determined challenge from the left. The Communist Party sought to organize within the Mexican community and apparently was meeting with some success. Consular reports and news articles noted the alarming rise in leftist activities, and instructions from Foreign Relations went forward to deal with the situation. On January 5, 1930, the Communist Party held a large rally in the old center of the early Mexican community in Los Angeles, the Plaza, to protest the Mexican government's oppression against leftist labor unions and the "arrests and deportations of various communist leaders." (Consul Pesqueira described the demonstrators as "Russians, Jews, and women.") When the speeches ended, three hundred demonstrators marched to the nearby consulate building and blocked entrances while chanting antigovernment slogans. Consul Pesqueira deplored the rally but praised the police for restoring order and arresting thirteen, none of them Mexicans, although he lamented that "numerous Mexicans took part in the demonstration." [130] In August of that year the newly formed labor union arm of the Communist Party, the Trade Union Unity League, with headquarters in the Los Angeles Eastside, organized another rally in the Plaza to commemorate Labor Day. The purpose of the afternoon manifestation, described as a "Monster meeting" in the pages of *La Opinión*, protested against "unemployment in factories and construction which has left thousands of workers without occupation." [131]

In early January 1931, M. F. Obalora, a major official in the Secretariat of Foreign Relations, sent a worried letter to Consul de la Colina regarding "a communist tumult" in the Mexican section of Los Angeles that "resulted in injuries to some Mexican citizens." He asked de la Colina to inform him "concerning the help and protection that his office has given to our nationals." [132] After a thorough examination and analysis of the problem, de la Colina sent his informational note with the requested data. "During the last weeks," wrote de la Colina, "there have appeared in this city tumults of a communist character around City Hall, caused by individuals affiliated with distinctive radical societies in this locality. Disgracefully, Mexican citizens have participated in these [manifestations] and who have, naturally, suffered the consequences; but these have not requested help nor protection [from this office] of any nature. Those Mexican citizens have refused whatever protection offered . . . from a government, which according to them represents capitalist interests, and is an enemy of the proletariat." [133] De la Colina blamed the "difficult economic situation" for causing the discontent in the *colonia* and warned that "disgracefully the communist propaganda is attracting Mexican workers in a more or less active way . . . and undoubtedly more such conflicts will occur with more or less frequency." Obalora replied without hesitation: "This secretariat recommends that you give your fullest attention to the development of the activities of these elements; you should prevent all friction which can harm . . . the Mexican *colonia*." [134]

While the consulate kept a watchful eye out for communists and others of a similar ideology, an organized campaign sponsored by the consulate and managed by the CSM took shape. Its purpose was to establish a new organization, the Beneficencia Mexicana, dedicated to charity and repatriations. Originally the Beneficencia was charged with raising funds for food and return to Mexico for the families of deported fathers.[135] Deportation drives grew more intense and assumed large-scale proportions in 1931, and the Beneficencia's task broadened to include general assistance to anyone who wished to return voluntarily and who could demonstrate indigence. Consul de la Colina, reported *La Opinión*, asked "all the *Comisiones Honoríficas* which function within the jurisdiction of the consulate . . . to organize Comités de Beneficencia, financing themselves with bazaars, and applying these funds to the purchase of foodstuffs and the repatriation of compatriots." [136] In engaging the Depression-era program of repatriations, the consulate cooperated with local authorities intent upon returning Mexicans to Mexico. Consul de la Colina frankly summed up his government's policies in a 1931 interview with a *La Opinión* reporter, stating, "The Mexican consulate, in cooperation with the Mexican and American charities, has sent compatriots to Mexico in three convoys." [137]

The editor of the Douglas, Arizona, *Daily Dispatch* found much to appreciate in Mexico's efforts. In a 1931 editorial he wrote, "It is a grati-fying fact that the Mexican government has accepted the situation pre-sented in a friendly spirit and has joined the U.S. government and railway companies in providing means to get Mexican families back to their na-tive surroundings." [138] A year later, A. G. Arnoll, the secretary of the Los Angeles Chamber of Commerce, lauded Consul de la Colina and the Mexican government for their "cooperation in distributing these people." A pleased Arnoll observed that de la Colina "has been helpful in every way possible in respect to returning his fellow citizens to Mexico, both through volunteer deportation and direct return." [139] F. W. Berkshire, Los Angeles Director of the Bureau of Charities, corroborated de la Co-lina's testimony. "It is a well known fact," he stated to Consul Alejandro Martínez, "that the Bureau of Charities of Los Angeles County has closely cooperated and consulted with the Mexican consul in Los Angeles. . . . The plan to cause large numbers of Mexicans to be returned to their na-tive country [was] worked out with the full knowledge and consent of the Mexican consul and it is understood that in each instance a representative of the Mexican consulate has been familiar with the details as have the Mexican authorities in Mexico City." [140]

Consul de la Colina absolved the chamber of responsibility for initiat-ing repatriation and put the blame on Filipino farmworkers for rendering Mexican workers superfluous and, therefore, subject to repatriation. Fili-pinos, he claimed, were "controlling more and more the jobs formerly held by compatriots." In contrast, de la Colina and the Chamber of Com-merce enjoyed cordial relations throughout the crisis. The consul and chamber officials met on various occasions over lunch to discuss courses of action for effective repatriation. All of de la Colina's requests from the chamber were promised: an orderly, fair, and legal repatriation free of coercion. Consul de la Colina considered the unfortunate affair a matter of free choice, a voluntary repatriation brought on by circumstances be-yond the control of the compatriots. [141]

In the spring of 1931, the Beneficencia proudly boasted that it was in the process of completing "a gigantic task," the repatriation of 250 com-patriots, offering meals in its newly opened soup kitchen, and "handing out groceries to 200 Mexican families." [142] Nine months later the *comité* had raised a total of $5,700 for relief and repatriations. [143] Leaders in the *comité* readily acknowledged a desire to rid the community of excess hu-manity. Dr. Manual Servin, the stalwart *comité* activist and its president, defended the organization's reasoning for sponsoring repatriations. "My countrymen can be helped by any of the following," he told an audience at an immigration conference. "First, with money, which is the costliest but the least recommended; second, better opportunities to find work and

make him feel desirable. . . . Third, Repatriation . . . this is the measure
that serves a double purpose by thinning the ranks of the unemployed and
giving an opportunity to the Mexican nation to receive their prodigal
sons."[144] Servin, de la Colina, the Los Angeles Chamber of Commerce,
and the Los Angeles County Bureau of Charities agreed that the third
approach held the most to recommend under the circumstances.

The logic behind the founding of the Comité de Beneficencia can be
discerned against the backdrop of the rising discontent and leftist outlook
among the working class. The consulate dropped its unionization drive
(but only for the time being, as we shall see in Chapters 3, 4, and 5) and
instead proposed charity and repatriation as the solution to the economic
woes of the *colonia* that daily grew worse. Meanwhile, *colonia* organizations traditionally aligned with the consul rallied to the cause. The Partido
Liberal Mexicano and the Partido Laborista joined the repatriation campaign and sponsored neighborhood meetings featuring noted speakers
who urged the compatriots to consider repatriation as an alternative solution to their difficulties.[145] On the other hand, communists and others on
the left proposed a political union of the working class, regardless of
nationality or race, based on their class interests, dismissing charity and repatriation (and Mexicanization) as political acquiescence to the domination of capital and the host country's racial oppression. The left, particularly the Communist Party, advocated the empowerment of the working
class via unions, regardless of race and nationality, and a working-class
party. Consulates espoused charity giving to its nationals based upon the
traditional Christian paternalistic ethic combined with the concept of repatriation. The two ideological positions presented the *colonia* with a set
of polarizing and difficult choices. We shall see that even though the thinking of the Left ran counter to the strong nationalist consciousness and the
tradition of charity, its radical agenda provided a fundamental alternative
which many in the *colonia* found meaningful. The 1930s presented the
first large-scale challenge to the political objectives of the Mexican government, and Mexico once again responded to that challenge by involving itself in union organizing.

CHAPTER 3

The Los Angeles County Strike of 1933

The harvest season began in spring with the repetition of a familiar pattern. Fed by costly irrigation projects, acres of fruits, vegetables, nuts, and grains were now ripe for the picking. Summoned to the fields by the rising labor requirements, thousands of farmworkers and their families gathered to bring in these crops. As always, aside from the laborers, growers, and business interests directly involved in this enormous and urgent undertaking, few paid much attention to the cyclic social and economic drama that unfolded each season. But this year would be different. The farm laborers were walking off the fields. A guarded discontent had burst forth as growers tightened their grip and set the lowest hourly wage in a decade. Finally, the workers were resisting this latest imposition on lives that were already living a borderline existence.

The break occurred on June 1, 1933. Six hundred farmworkers assembled at a meeting at Hicks Camp in El Monte, some twenty miles from downtown Los Angeles. Here they spoke out, angrily expressing their sense of injustice. A strike was called that was to be the largest in the history of California agriculture up to that time. The Cannery and Agricultural Worker Industrial Union (CAWIU; a creation of the Communist Party's Trade Union Unity League) served as organizers at this first meeting. Ultimately, five thousand workers joined the rebellion, waging a protracted struggle through June and July. In the end, a settlement was signed and workers returned to the fields. They had been promised just a few cents more for their labor.

Compared with the deadly San Joaquin cotton strike or to the state violence in the Imperial Valley strike, the Los Angeles county strike was relatively peaceful. Yet the strike merits our attention for several important reasons. It was this countywide strike that first brought the Mexican government into the Mexican farmworkers' struggle. As we will show, the consul, the vice-consul, and his associate, acting under the direction of the Mexican president and other high officials, waged a powerful offensive against leftist organizations involved in the El Monte strike and subsequently intervened against those same militant elements that would become central to several strikes that took place in California later in the decade. Significantly, it was an almost entirely unpublic intervention. Secondly, the Los Angeles County strike demonstrates that, at that time, local authorities facing a farm labor conflict would identify its instigators as leftist "agitators" or as leaders in the CAWIU, rather than grant the underpaid laborers the legitimacy of their grievances. Lastly, the El Monte strike witnessed the rebirth of CUOM, renamed the Confederación de Uniones Campesinos y Obreros Mexicanos—or CUCOM, as it was popularly referred to by workers. As in the case of the moribund CUOM, the Mexican consul assumed the position of treasurer in the new organization and held that post until the consul-CUCOM connection was severed in a heated controversy during the Orange County citrus pickers' strike of 1936.

Relegated to the margins of the historical record, the strike has never garnered much attention from labor historians; it occupies but a minor niche within labor historiography. Neither the several journal articles nor the few book chapters that examine the event satisfactorily analyze the political substance of the Mexico–U.S. connection or that of the Mexico–*México de afuera* connection.[1] Whereas most of the previously published articles consider the roots of the conflict as local in origin, the work of Abraham Hoffman touches upon the international factors that surfaced during the El Monte strike. However, Hoffman limits the analysis to events in El Monte and to the polite exchange of notes between Washington and Mexico City. Beyond this problematic and sketchy treatment looms the near silence regarding the questionable, critical actions of the consulate and of Vice-Consul Ricardo Hill and his associate Armando Flores. This chapter extends Hoffman's research by incorporating new data and interpreting it within a broader perspective that analyzes the decisive interventions of consular officials and the Mexican government into strikes of the period involving Mexican workers. This approach has the potential to convey a more profound understanding not only of the El Monte strike (and other southern California strikes I will examine) but also of the role of the Mexican state within U.S. labor history. At the consulate, two officials, Armando Flores and Ricardo Hill, played particularly significant roles in this strike. Consul Alejandro Martínez also wielded his considerable influence, but it was Hill and Flores who interacted with the *colonia* and camps and responded personally to the particulars of the strike's daily unfolding drama.

Armando Flores

As one of the key figures involved in the strike, Armando Flores had an impressive government background. His presence in Los Angeles *colonia* activities dates back at least to 1926 and tied him to a militant pro-government, pro-consul, and pro-CROM past. Flores first appears in the Confederación de Sociedades Mexicanas (CSM), where he held the position of pro-secretario in the executive committee. The CSM, as discussed earlier, spawned the effort in 1927 to establish the Confederación de Uniones Obreras Mexicanas (CUOM). His name also appeared on the roster of the founding convention of CUOM, and he was elected secretario de actas (secretary of the acts) in the first CUOM executive committee.[2] He also served as secretary of the exterior in the Los Angeles chapter of the Partido Liberal Mexicano (PLM).[3] The PLM had long before retired its anarchistic ideology and, like Flores and the remnants of the CUOM, actively supported the government party of Mexico.

Through his participation in these and other highly visible consulate-generated organizations, among them the Comité de Beneficencia Mexicana and the Cruz Azul, Flores gained a favorable reputation among *México de afuera*.[4] Recognized as an experienced labor leader, he delivered addresses at *Dieciseís de septiembre* celebrations hosted by the Comisiones Honoríficas and the CSMs. He was also an avid supporter of the Partido Nacional Revolucionario (PNR); Flores organized the Club Pro-Ortiz Rubio during the 1929 elections and campaigned tirelessly for Pascual Ortiz Rubio, the government candidate, hand-picked by former President Plutarco Calles, Mexico's ruling power.[5] The club held innumerable community meetings during the campaign and added to Flores's stature as an activist, albeit one closely associated with the consulate.[6] Through his past connection to CUOM, the PLM, the Club Ortiz Rubio, and other organizations, Flores had established a wide network in *colonia*s throughout the Los Angeles region. In addition, Flores owned a print shop, which, as will be seen, he used for meetings and for printing strike materials.

Ricardo Hill

Vice-Consul Ricardo Hill, Flores's mentor during the strike and the preeminent consulate figure in the strike, began his service for the Mexican government in 1923 as a member of the Mexican legation in Tokyo. His first consulate assignment placed him in St. Louis, Missouri, in 1927. After several subsequent assignments, Hill was posted to the Los Angeles Consulate around 1933 and named vice-consul in charge of the Department of Protection under the supervision of Consul Alejandro Martínez. This responsibility put Hill into almost daily contact with *colonia* residents, particularly those seeking legal help from the consulate.

Born into a distinguished Sonoran revolutionary family, Hill was immersed in the world of politics from his earliest years. His father, General Benjamin Hill, served as a trusted ally to General Alvaro Obregón, whose forces later triumphed and ensured the presidency for Obregón in 1920. Hill's brother Benjamin Jr. served as consul general in San Antonio during the mid-thirties. Cousin to Plutarco Elías Calles, Hill moved into the foreign service with impeccable family connections that tied him to the fortunes of the ruling revolutionary government. His marriage to Esperanza Pesqueira of the landed Pesqueira family and owners of the Hacienda Cuchuta in Sonora, further strengthened his ties to the militaristic Calles-Obregón machine of northern Mexico, which was to rule Mexico from 1918 to 1934.[7] With the election of Lázaro Cárdenas in 1934, Hill pledged his loyalty to the new regime.

As we have seen, wealth and family connections served as calling cards for sinecures, evident in the process that led to the hiring of Hill in 1923. Political alliances also played a role. Documents in the Abelardo Rodríguez file at the Archivo General de la Nación (AGN) in Mexico City demonstrate that Hill received his post largely due to his father's loyalties to Obregón. Yet Hill had other qualities that made him an ideal candidate for consulate responsibilities. Like many children of the Mexican wealthy, Hill had been groomed for such service through private schooling in Mexico City and the United States. He finished his preparatory schooling at the New York Military Academy, Cornwall-on-Hudson, where he undoubtedly learned English.[8]

As was true of all who served in government posts, loyalty to the president and to the administration's policies was considered paramount, essential to the smooth operation of the consular corps. Hill's conduct during and after the strike demonstrates his full and complete allegiance to Mexico's ruling party. Conventional interpretations misconstrue the roles taken by the Vice-Consul and Flores in relation to the growers and local authorities, portraying the growers as successfully maneuvering Hill and Flores to fit their labor strategy. In his classic work, *Bitter Harvest: A History of California Farmworkers, 1870–1941,* Clete Daniel, for example, contends that "local authorities . . . seized the opportunity to remove Communist organizers . . . in order to permit full control of the strike to fall to presumably less clever and more malleable Mexican strike leaders."[9] Daniel depicts the move against the CAWIU as one primarily driven by local authorities and posits that the consul merely responded to their urging.

Two crucial factors omitted from Daniel's analysis provide the analytic paradigm for this study. First, the removal of "Communist organizers" was paramount to all parties involved in the conflict, save, of course, the CAWIU. We will show that local authorities, Japanese farmers, and the Mexican government shared the same watchful anxiety regarding communists or leftists in labor organizations and were almost as apprehensive about independent labor union movements. Vice-Consul Hill required no prodding when it came to contesting the CAWIU for leadership of the strike. Anticommunist politics was not a novel undertaking for him. Only a few weeks before the June 1 strike meeting, Mexican federal police, acting to prevent leftists from speaking at the May Day rally, arrested over twenty-one suspected communists on trumped-up charges of "appearing to intend to perform" terrorist acts. Like the faithful government servant he was, Hill carried out Mexico's political policy toward labor unions and communists. Hill's consular duties and his family loyalties committed him to this course, and he pursued it with zeal.

Second, Professor Daniel, like other scholars, overlooks the political drives organized by the Mexican government, beginning in the early 1920s, in an effort to channel expatriate political activism onto conservative ground. The nationalistic political spadework performed by the government through CROM and CUOM has sometimes been mistaken as evidence of IWW-style anarchism, if not revolutionary radicalism. The confusion arises from a misinterpretation of CROM's use of rhetoric that skillfully mimicked leftist theory and language but in action had little to do with Marxism or even anarchism. Both CROM and the consulate were, in fact, rooted in a highly conservative ethic that rejected Marxist principles. Indeed, in Los Angeles the consulate had long cultivated a tradition of *mexicanismo*, a Mexican conservative political consciousness consonant with the ruling party. Hill and Flores were well schooled to carry the conservative banner that had been passed to them. In attempting to subvert radical tendencies and build a conservative union movement, the two men invoked a narrow nationalistic *mexicanismo* that was antithetic to the Marxist principles of class politics espoused by the CAWIU. This conservative consulate perspective, born of elitest privilege, stopped far short of the working-class politics that formed the bread and butter of the CAWIU.

The strike scenario presented a labor conflict unparalleled in California history. Three nations were represented: two foreign consulates (those of Japan and Mexico) acting on behalf of their largely foreign-born nationals, and the host country's mediators, business interests, and local authorities. At the strike's end, the respective consuls represented each of the antagonists in the negotiations that led to a temporary settlement of the strike, with Mexican consular intervention most notable in bringing closure to the conflict. Consular intervention receded from the scene in the late thirties; however, a decade of conservative consular activism in the Mexican labor movement seriously impeded the CAWIU from making inroads into Mexican labor. The farm labor movement, pulled in opposite directions by the conservative nationalist charms of the consulate on the one hand and the appeal of the CAWIU's union militancy on the other, never composed itself long enough to establish its own union agenda.

The Economic and Social Context in Los Angeles County

By the second decade of the century, industrial and manufacturing interests in the Los Angeles region were well on their way to transforming the economy from one rooted in agriculture to one based largely on urban industry. However, before agriculture vanished, several decades of a bifurcated economy had characterized Los Angeles County. Unlike its rural neighbors to the north and south, the four-thousand-square-mile area straddled both an industrial and an agricultural base. The city of Los Angeles contained the manufacturing and industrial sectors; the county held the agriculture and stock-raising areas. In 1925, for example, agriculture and stock raising production totaled $86 million. Two hundred fifty thousand acres of agricultural fields produced a variety of crops, predominantly citrus, grains, vegetables, and berries. Manufacturing outlets in the city of Los Angeles produced $417 million in goods. Although always a lesser player in the overall economy, agriculture remained a vital and successful component. Boosters proudly advertised that Los Angeles County held more citrus acreage than any other county in the state, and only Imperial County grew more field and truck crops than Los Angeles. U.S. Census reports show that each year, beginning in 1909, Los Angeles County outperformed all others in the nation in the value of farm products. Carey McWilliams, the keen social critic of California, did not exaggerate when he named Los Angeles County the "richest agricultural county in the U.S." [10]

Nevertheless, industrial inroads into agricultural zones created social and economic conditions that directly affected farmworkers. Oil production increased from 4 million barrels a day in 1900 to 105 million in 1920, stimulating the development of port facilities, refining plants, road and building construction, and, of course, real estate. During the boom years of the 1920s, oil, real estate, construction, tourism, entertainment, and exports expanded phenomenally. Construction in the city of Los Angeles expanded seven times, reaching $500 million in value and placing Los Angeles third in the nation in terms of new construction. In the county, eight new cities were created in that fabled but short-lived era. During the 1920s migrants from across the nation poured into the region at the rate of 100,000 per year. Within the decade the county's population had increased by 1 million, reaching 2.2 million on the eve of the Depression. This rapid spiral set two simultaneous and apparently contradictory forces in motion. On the one side, industrialization and urbanization eroded the existing agricultural bases; on the other, an increased market demand stimulated the production of local agricultural products. The balance ultimately leaned toward urbanization, but not without some beneficial consequences for maintaining agricultural production.

The Japanese Farmers

The transition in land use from rural farming to urban sprawl led to a system of temporary marginal farming areas that would soon give way to industrial development. Eager real estate developers, ready to gain lucrative properties, aimed their sights at these rich agricultural areas while the landowners held on, waiting for property values to rise. Retaining their lands in the interim proved profitable in itself through leasing arrangements with local farmers, in particular with Japanese farmers, who were skilled in methods that elicited optimum results from limited land areas. The owners, rather than improve their properties, rented to these experienced farmers who had established a tradition of successful truck farming on just such marginal tenant parcels. The practice had begun about 1900 and continued during the rapid urban growth period of the first two decades. This business arrangement worked for both parties, as shall be seen during the strike, when white landowners and Japanese farmers, ironically, landed on the same side, arrayed against the farmworkers. Subsequently, at least two types of economic formation—small-scale truck farming, averaging approximately seventeen acres per parcel, and a variety of urban systems—interacted and expanded side by side.[11]

At the turn of the century, the Japanese population in the state stood at 1,200, but by the end of the Depression decade it had reached 100,000 residents, of whom nearly 37,000 lived in Los Angeles County. The vast majority were engaged in small-scale tenant farming, as is reflected in the statistics on Japanese land ownership. By 1920, statewide, the Japanese owned only 8 percent of the farm acreage under their operation, amounting to 30,306 acres out of a total of 390,635. In Southern California, a paltry 3.5 percent of Japanese-run farms were owned outright.[12] These numbers confirm that substantial numbers of Los Angeles County white landowners, banks, and industrial and real estate interests held contracts with Japanese agriculturists. Thus the landowner, as noted, held a strong business interest in maintaining the Japanese as tenant farmers.

Japanese farmers cultivated 44,000 acres in Los Angeles County during the heyday of Japanese agriculture in southern California, using a variety of resourceful strategies.[13] For example, they turned large tracts of unused properties into productive farms; even land under electric power lines was cultivated. Farmers would move with the seasons from one location to another as land became available for leasing, or from one soil type to another as demand for a particular crop increased.

During the Depression many Japanese farmers, to facilitate marketing, organized into grower cooperatives called associations. By 1940 farmers associations controlled 90 percent of the county's truck farms, growing crops like asparagus, lima beans, carrots, and cauliflower, and they supplied nearly 100 percent of the strawberry crop for the region. In the rural Gardena area, south of the city of Los Angeles, approximately seven hundred Japanese farms cultivated "bunch vegetables" in addition to strawberries and other berry fruits. Japanese farmers controlled 50 percent of the produce market in central Los Angeles.

Despite the bankers' and industrialists' sword hanging overhead, the Japanese engaged in intensive capitalist enterprises linked inextricably to the larger economy. These enterprising outfits may have appeared to be marginal because of their relatively small acreage, but the business world considered them substantial contributors to the expanding market economy.[14] Significant, in terms of the strike, is the fact that extensive truck farming requires masses of laborers, young or old, regardless of gender, and requires them to be ready to work on call, on a day-to-day, hourly basis. And because many, many pickers must be hired, the Japanese, like most growers in California, were strongly motivated to maintain the lowest possible per-hour wages for these individuals. To that end they used, and depended upon, the widely available cheap labor of Mexican families and, to a lesser extent, that of single Filipino and Japanese workers. As the economic atmosphere darkened and prices fell precipitously, farmers attempted to cut their labor costs, sparking a crisis for the workers who could not accept this assault on themselves and their families.

The Mexican Workers

Responding to this regional thirst for labor and stimulated by Mexico's open-door investment policies and the the upheaval of the 1910 Revolution, Mexican migration increased enormously during the first three decades of the century, swelling the population figures by as many as one-and-a-half million across the Southwest. In the city of Los Angeles the Mexican population rose from 33,644 in 1920 to well over 100,000 in 1930. The county census placed the number of Mexican residents at nearly 200,000, but reliable observers estimated 250,000.

These rapid population increases inevitably led to the development of new settlements. Approximately thirty small enclaves outside of the huge Los Angeles *colonia* were scattered throughout the county at the end of the boom twenties. Popularly known as camps, and subjected to the practice of restrictive covenants, many were tucked away on the fringes of towns. Segregation affected the *colonia* residents in almost every phase of their lives and extended beyond the community—to work, public education, recreation, residence, and religious practice. Children attended segregated schools, if at all, when not in the fields with their parents. And adults were denied equal access to public and private venues. Effectively segregated from Anglo neighborhoods, these families lived "across the tracks," a popular (and often literally correct) referent for the "Mexican quarter."

Often camps were set up on bits of land that owners had parceled out as rental areas exclusively for Mexican tenants. Described by one observer as "Patches of ground . . . as small as twenty by thirty feet," these plots rented for one to ten dollars a month. Given the scanty resources at their disposal, renters then built their own homes using inexpensive, secondhand, or discarded materials. Amenities were not provided. Extraordinary revenue thus accrued to landowners, at no expense, from otherwise unproductive lands. County welfare and health officials investigating several local camps reported that "the annual return to the owner amounted to over a thousand dollars per acre, in return for which the owner had made no investment whatever in sanitation or road improvements."[15] Such a revenue stream would be sufficient incentive for landowners to favor the status quo and to favor the Japanese rather than the Mexican strikers; a landowner's personal prejudices against Asians, if any, would not be a factor. Further, landowners, as a capitalist class, were, by and large, automatically opposed to unionization. A strike would be insupportable.

Most Mexican laborers were employed primarily as common labor, and nearly eight out of every ten—children, men, and women—worked in agriculture. One study, by Professor James Batten of Pomona College, of 788 randomly selected Mexican homes, surveyed among other things the occupational pattern. Batten reported that "the largest number of Mexicans visited were unskilled laborers engaged in agricultural pursuits." Batten's study also found that 75 percent of the families earned less than $100 monthly and that one third reported their children working part- or full-time to help support the family.[16] Even in relatively good times, poverty stalked the largely immigrant Mexican communities as they began the process of establishing roots in a new and often alarmingly hostile society. And as the Depression deepened, the trappings of poverty began to seem insurmountable.

As I have noted, county truck farmers were also hit hard by falling prices. They countered their dwindling returns by cutting wages for farm laborers by as much as one half. Wages that had been as high as 25 cents an hour the previous year were cut to 10 and 15 cents an hour in 1933. Apparently, it was not an easy call, but after heated debate, the powerful central Japanese Grower Association won over a majority of its members to agree to these steep wage cuts. Reducing wages made business sense to the farmers, but to the farmworkers it was the bitterest of pills, impossible to swallow in silence. In the face of this blow, a strike appeared to offer workers a realistic opportunity to reverse the decline. A strike would be a visible signal to the world of the pickers' plight and would force growers to authorize a decent raise in the per-hour wage, county wide. In any case, the laborers had little to lose since the wages offered were insufficient for survival, even if help from the county relief agency were counted in. The strike was all they had.

The Strike

The Los Angeles County strike, sometimes mistitled the El Monte Berry Strike, pitted the two largest minority communities in the county against one another. It is true that two ethnic groups collided. However, placing the emphasis on the ethnicity of the two adversaries, rather than on their places in the division of labor, results in a superficial understanding of the struggle. More accurately, the strike constituted a conflict between small-sized profitable business operators and their poorly paid labor force. While ethnicity was a component, the fundamental issues propelling the strike emanated from a labor-capital relation. A study that gives primacy to the ethnicity of the antagonists merely skims the surface of the conflict. Wages were always the fundamental issue from the perspectives of both workers and growers.

The CAWUI organizers arrived in the El Monte area sometime in the spring of 1933. They encountered a potentially explosive situation in the *colonias* and camps: laborers rife with discontent were without resources to resist the wage cuts. The cadre began its work and soon attracted enough followers with sufficient energy to mount a challenge to the growers. A petition was hammered out, asking for an increase in wages to 35 cents an hour. In late May a contingent of farmworkers representing the San Gabriel Valley area and led by the CAWIU delivered this demand to the home of the secretary of the San Gabriel Valley Japanese Association.[17] There was no reply. It was in reaction to this affront that the general meeting of workers was called for June 1 at Hicks Camp in El Monte.

Hicks Camp bordered the sandy banks of the usually dry Rio Hondo and agricultural fields. The hamlet-like community of rented rustic homes and dusty lanes housed some one thousand residents in the off-season and expanded to about fifteen hundred during the harvest. Like the many dispersed Mexican settlements throughout southern California, Hicks Camp had no other reason for existence than to provide a modicum of shelter for the labor required to work the surrounding farms.

By the end of the first day of June, the six hundred farmworkers who had assembled for this meeting, carried on a wave of optimism, had voted a strike unanimously. They had come with their anger and despair to confront the crisis. They had talked and listened to the CAWIU organizers. And finally they had moved to redress the miserable wages by their own actions. Hicks Camp was transformed that night from a quiet, isolated *colonia* to the vital control center of a countywide strike movement.

Before the boisterous meeting ended, an immediate halt to all work in the area had been declared. There would be no return to the fields until the workers' demands were met. In the fervor of the evening, a strike committee, comprising fifty Mexican, Filipino, and Japanese workers representing the area work sites, took on the task of coordinating and organizing the strike. In a deliberate attempt to widen the participation of other workers, the CAWIU leadership had stepped back and assigned only two of its members, Lino Chacón and J. Ruiz, to the committee. This strategy (to pull workers into the planning process) was ultimately disadvantageous to the CAWIU; it was, in fact, a fateful decision that would significantly stifle the union voice during the first week. The two men were, however, elected to the posts of treasurer and organizing secretary, and with other members they swung into action the next morning, issuing leaflets, flyers, and bulletins, as reported two weeks later in the *Western Worker,* the organ of the Communist Party's West Coast branch.[18] The strike action spread like wildfire, and work stopped in many sections throughout the county.

Pickets were assigned to various work sites, and, according to the *Western Worker,* within a few days "over one hundred of the workers joined the CAWIU."[19] Daily meetings at Hicks Camp, designated as strike headquarters, brought workers together for briefings on the strike's progress. Mass demonstrations were held to rally support from settlement dwellers. Informational leaflets bearing the logo of the CAWIU, printed in Spanish, English, and Japanese, spread news of the strike throughout the county and urged workers to join the movement. From the very beginning, a powerful conservative faction in the strike committee challenged the CAWIU for control and, in fact, threatened the union's very presence in the strike. A disruptive internecine fight for control of the strike ensued. Unknown to union representatives at the time, the strike committee included old-line CUOM leaders, one of whom, Armando Flores, was soon to dominate the committee. Although Flores was a print shop owner and not a farmworker, his consular connection conferred power and prestige. He used both to contest the CAWIU and its followers among the strikers; in this effort he was joined by Vice-Consul Hill, with whom he had already established a political partnership. The Flores-Hill partnership was destined to play a leading role in thwarting the union.

In the initial days, after El Monte and Venice, the strike had spread to San Gabriel, Belvedere, and Santa Monica and soon encompassed several thousand workers in widely separated areas of the county. The lines of power were clearly drawn, with the consular coupling of Hill and Flores on one side, and the CAWIU on the other. As events unfolded, the consular emissaries would prove the more formidable foe. Influenced by consular prestige and the establishment's antiunion sentiment, newspaper reports scarcely referred to the union. *La Opinión* covered the strike intensively, but not one article focused on the union to any extent beyond mere mention. The silence must be interpreted as deliberate. Frequent and lengthy articles closely followed the actions and statements of Hill and Flores and subtly slanted the news in their favor. An example of this bias can be found in a *La Opinión* report on a strike meeting held on June 3. One hundred twenty-five workers had gathered at the Venice Celery Growers fields to demand an increase to 30 cents an hour. These strikers then assigned a small delegation to seek out the consul for support. The news story gives prominence to the consul and implies that he would deliver "justice." The account reports that workers "abandoned their jobs and immediately sought out the Mexican consul in Los Angeles, so that the case may be investigated and justice done." [20] In spite of the lack of CAWIU news coverage, the union's presence is undeniable, and it continued to exercise its influence among the workers. If the strength of the forces brought against the union is any measure, Hill and Flores must have seen the CAWIU as formidable. Or perhaps it is that kind of overkill that emerges when an enemy arouses a powerful, almost personal animosity, as did the leftist leaders of the strike. In any case, the consulate, using every resource at its disposal, set out to destroy the Cannery Union and its influence.

News coverage, as we have seen, favored Hill and Flores with numerous mentions, heightening their visibility and importance. The very opposite held true for the CAWIU. The union was made to seem isolated from the daily intercourse of the *colonia*. Whenever an article did cite the CAWIU, it was often done in a disparaging manner, for example, using a gross misspelling or making errors in identification. One *La Opinión* item reported that strike circulars handed out in the affected sites were printed under the logo of the "Comité de Acción de la Unión Industrial de Obreros de Agricultura y Ganadería." The exact translation, "Committee of Action of the Industrial Union of Workers in Agriculture and Cattle Farms," seems a caricature, a studied insult.[21]

As the strike spread and as incipient labor unions in the form of local committees were established, the tension caused by the two contradictory political orientations at the center of the movement threatened the cohesiveness of the endeavor. However, Vice-Consul Hill and Armando Flores steadfastly pushed their agenda, gaining ground, inch by inch. With consular as well as other conservative powers behind them, the consul emissaries had the advantage, and with the support of their followers on the strike committee, they began to coordinate the dispersed actions and bring all factions—except the CAWIU—together into one single movement.

Hicks Camp remained the strike headquarters, and by the end of the first week Hill and Flores had taken a central position. On June 5 the strike committee sent an official delegation, consisting of the conservative faction, to consulate offices, where they were assured that consular intervention would take their cause directly to the president of the Japanese Association. According to *La Opinión*, Vice-Consul Hill also "offered to make a personal visit to Venice and other nearby centers with the purpose of personally learning about the situation of Mexican workers in the region, and to take necessary steps in the name of the Consulate's Department of Protection to help the strikers."[22] Hill then addressed himself to the urgent neediness of the strikers' families, leading delegates on a walk of several blocks to the offices of Adele Callahan, the head of the county welfare bureau, to inform her of the plight facing worker families and to request aid. Callahan assured the group that she would authorize relief supplies to be sent to the needy.

Later that same day, at a meeting at Flores's print shop, presumably of the strike committee, new directives were drafted. With no CAWIU present, these more conservative actions, reflecting the Mexican government's agenda (to maintain the existing order) rather than the union's defiant militancy, were carried forward. First, the committee formed several co-ordinating subcommittees; second, and more importantly, the committee decided to send an informational memorandum to Mexico's secretary of foreign relations and secretary of industry, commerce, and labor. In addition to informing the Mexican government concerning the strike, the group resolved to seek the solidarity of "labor organizations in Mex-ico."[23] Finally, they agreed to communicate strike information to Mexican newspapers, especially Mexican labor journals. It is significant that the strikers turned to their government and, it seems, turned their backs on the CAWIU cadre who had been the instruments of action on June 1.

Within days of the strike call, the consulate, the administration of President Abelardo Rodríguez, and Mexican labor organizations were all pulled into the conflict initially led by the very antithesis of Mexican offi-cial politics, the CAWIU. At the same time, formal leadership was swing-ing inexorably to Flores and Hill. At a June 6 rally in Santa Monica, where both men addressed the crowd, Flores distributed strike bulletins without the CAWIU logo, a power play that made it appear that the CAWIU had been shut out. Significantly, the bulletins had been composed by Flores and printed in his shop.[24] News reports had, as we have shown, placed Flores and Hill at the center of the labor crisis. Still, a militant faction continued picketing, attended meetings, and made their voices heard, urging strong tactics to discourage scabs.[25] In spite of their de-termination, and by their own reckoning, the CAWIU continually lost ground within the strike committee and was relegated to working in the wings rather than at center stage. The union's understandable confidence during the first few days of the strike had proved unwarranted. With nei-ther a firm grasp of the conditions affecting labor in the area, nor with the time to effectively build a union, the organizers, outsiders themselves, would soon be on the outside. In the meantime, the CAWIU managed to enlist members into the Young Communist League, and, together with seasoned members, they distributed food and supplies in the laborer settlements, among other activities. The CAWIU, being too few and too inexperienced, had occupied a precarious position from the start. But Hill and Flores, recognizing CAWIU influence, determined to fight it tooth and nail. In spite of the fractious infighting that roiled within the strike com-mittee, the strike's rampant energies had pulled in more than five thou-sand workers, and by the second week the work stoppage extended across the county.

Hill realized that even a weakened CAWIU would continue to pre-sent obstacles against negotiating a swift settlement, a complication that growers and local officials also feared. According to the local Japanese newspaper, *Rafu Shimpo,* the growers asserted that if "the radical element [were] weeded out of the union movement[,] the farmers [would] have a better chance to cooperate with labor."[26] Another cause of anxiety for the vice-consul and local officials was the prospect that a communist-led organization would extend its control over the political organizing of Mexicans throughout the region and beyond. This fear impelled Hill and Flores to act with all speed before the CAWIU could recover, and they pushed hard during the early days to get workers to negotiate. In spite of their efforts, the CAWIU retained enough influence to thwart the early-negotiation drive. This failure apparently taught Hill and Flores that in order to get what they wanted, the CAWIU must be brought down once and for all. The consulate and the growers were focused on a *quick* settlement. Extrapolating from that, one could predict that Hill would push unrelentingly toward that end, whether or not the settlement arrived at would do justice to the workers' demands. The consulate had never concerned itself with significantly bettering conditions for the laborers. The CAWIU had seemed to do that. And in spite of the fact that the consulate had ignored the injustice of the wage scale applied to Mexican labor, the workers, it seems, gratefully accepted as genuine the efforts the consulate made "on their behalf." Empowering the workers was clearly not the reason behind the consulate's involvement, although its rhetoric (and even actions) sent a different message to the laborer compatriots, one that, as will be shown, even the growers misconstrued.

It took just nine days for the inevitable and final rupture between the two factions to take place. During that period the consulate, through the strike committee, had reached out to the consul-friendly Los Angeles Police Department (LAPD), in particular to its notorious Red Squad, the main intelligence-gathering agency in the Los Angeles area. Dedicated to subverting and destroying leftist, and even liberal, organizations, especially militant labor unions, the Red Squad had naturally directed its attention to the strike and, in particular, the suspect leaders. With the consul's tacit approval, the squad had assigned several undercover agents, including one described as a Mexican, to infiltrate and investigate the ranks. A stream of reports kept the Police Department, and presumably the consul (and thus Mexico City) informed of the strike's progress. The dossiers on the leftist strike leaders gathered covertly by the Red Squad present clear evidence of the LAPD's alliance with the Hill faction. The squad's surveillance and intelligence reports demonstrate support for Hill and foreshadow an even more direct involvement in events that led to the ousting of CAWIU leaders and paved the way for a takeover by Hill and Flores.

Among the Red Squad's stream of reports, the one dated June 7 stands out. It offers irrefutable evidence of complicity between Hill and the squad. This report was sent directly to Captain William F. Hynes, the Red Squad's commanding officer, and describes the anticommunist interventions of squad agents surveilling a strike meeting held in the Venice area. The agents first observed "the Mexican consul . . . advising and directing the Mexican field workers" and then proceeded to continue their investigation. Testimony at a congressional hearing fills in details of this crucial event:

We went to 4065 Ocean Park Ave. and there found sixty or seventy Mexicans gathered, and in the midst of their group were two white fellows and a Jewish woman. We listened to their conversation and gathered therefrom that these three were communist organizers. . . .

After questioning these three subjects, I informed them that we knew their purpose in being among the field workers was not to lend aid and food as they had stated to the group, but that they really were there to create dissension and unrest among them. I warned them to stay away, owing to their affiliation (with) the Communist Subsidiary *(sic)* organization — Agricultural Workers Ind. Union (the CAWIU). I then went to the group of Mexicans assembled there in the meeting and informed them that these three people were communist agitators. I asked if they wanted to be led or influenced by any such organizations and they immediately answered they did not and were not aware that the communists were taking part in the strike movement. I spoke to them regarding a raise in pay, saying they must also take in consideration that the grower himself was receiving very little for his product and therefore was unable to pay a very high scale of wages; *told them that if their consul was advising and directing them, I was sure they would not get into any trouble, but if they were communist led and directed, it might lead to trouble for them, such as deportation, etc.* (emphasis mine)[27]

Well informed of the battle for leadership, Red Squad strategy aimed at steering the strike into the hands of the consul and eliminating the dangerous CAWIU. The intervention, reflected in the Venice incident described above, was at first merely persuasive. But to knock out the CAWIU completely, the squad would require the participation of the consul as well as the Hill and Flores faction in the strike committee — plus a specific moment to stage the event. Chosen for the coup was a meeting to be held at the Hicks Camp headquarters on June 9, and a careful plan was developed under the direction of Mexican Secretary of Foreign Relations Puig Casauranc. With the support of the local police (and presumably the growers), the plan went forward. The ambush, orchestrated by Vice-

Consul Hill, engineered the expulsion of CAWIU members from the strike committee and from the movement. "The expulsion," read a *La Opinión* article, "made in public, was taken at the very moment that Señor Ricardo Hill, chief of the Consulate's Department of Protection, exhorted a large gathering of workers." [28]

As previously noted, there were just two CAWIU members on the strike committee, Lino Chacón and J. Ruiz. Both were thrown out and charged by Hill with distributing communist literature and with "frequently urging militant measures against scabs." Those acts, which had indeed taken place, were tantamount to a crime in the eyes of Hill. [29] Many in the rank and file, but certainly not all, appeared to accept the abrupt action and generally followed Hill's lead. When eyewitnesses described the tense meeting, they showed an almost worshipful respect for their consul. One laborer was quoted as saying, "Today in the afternoon Señor Ricardo Hill, in whom we have placed all of our confidence, came by Hicks Camp to help us. We told him of the presence of those elements . . . and since Señor Hill discovered that these men were communists, he expelled them in the presence of all our compañeros." [30]

Although news reports portray the expulsion as a spontaneous decision, research shows that the action was preplanned and had wide ramifications. At least two agencies, the Mexican government and the local police, were integral to the affair. The evidence just presented exposes police involvement in pro-consul tactics some two days before the Hicks Camp meeting. There is other clear evidence that further implicates the police as participants in the June 9 scheme to effect the expulsion of the CAWIU.

The CAWIU's version of events alleges (accurately) that some form of collusion between the police and Hill was instrumental. According to the union, the "police posed as friends of the strikers," and the coup began when "on the pretext that the bosses wanted to talk terms, the police lured the settlement committee into the police station and held them there for several hours." [31] In the absence of the strike leaders, the *Western Worker* continued, "the consul called a meeting, denouncing our comrades as 'reds' . . . and warned them to keep away from the CAWIU. The workers were turned against us." The CAWIU further alleged that Hill promised strikers the protection of the Mexican government on condition that CAWIU members be expelled. [32] The *Los Angeles Times* supported the CAWIU view of the affair. A *Times* reporter wrote that the meeting "was addressed by a representative [Hill] of the Mexican consulate in Los Angeles. The strikers were urged to run the agitators out and were told that when this was done an earnest effort will be made to obtain a settlement." [33] Hill made it clear to the strikers that the promise of government protection was contingent upon kicking out the CAWIU; in other words, the rank and file were threatened with their government's abandonment if they did not fall in line behind Hill. (Later events in the San Joaquin Valley cotton strike demonstrated the same consular strategy: again the government promised material support in exchange for following the consul's lead. See Chapter 4.) Note that the CAWIU version cited above verifies that a militant faction continued to operate (albeit with very diminished strength) in the strike movement; and its small disruptive presence serves to explain why Hill and Flores would continue their wary watch.

The day after the expulsion of Chacón and Ruiz, as CAWIU forces struggled to regain lost ground at a Hicks Camp meeting, their comeback attempt was suddenly terminated, as police intervened. Some two months later, the *Western Worker* reviewed the raid that had routed the Cannery Union and landed members in jail: "[Union organizers] were gathered in the [Hicks Camp] hall when the police raided it, arrested eight of them and jailed them. Soon after the Mexican consul again came on the scene. . . . This time our comrades couldn't counteract his fakery since those not arrested were being kept away from El Monte by the police. The consul then formed his own organization of workers. . . . Ten days later a so-called 'liberal' union was formed." [34]

A different perspective was reflected in *La Opinión*. Immediately after the June 9 meeting, a commission of strikers, led by Hill, appeared at the newspaper's offices "to give an accounting of the expulsion of the two individuals considered communists." As told to *La Opinión*, the strikers praised Hill for his leadership and joined their voices to his. In an article titled "Ya tienen esperanzas de arreglo" [They Now Have Hope for a Settlement], their comments revealed, once again, the alliance between the local authorities and the consul: "Now that we have expelled those two 'leaders' the authorities have lent us all their support, indicating to us, in addition, that the movement we have initiated is totally justified." [35] Mexico's Secretariat of Foreign Relations also made marked reference to a notable improvement in "the attitude of the local authorities towards the strikers . . . probably due to the fact that Communist agitators" were eliminated. [36]

Despite the absence of their key organizers, the remaining Cannery Union militants and their followers carried on. They appeared at the picket lines, they ran scabs out of the fields, and on an old mimeograph machine they printed strategic and tactical directives and leaflets denouncing Hill. Hill's response was to tighten his hold. Backed up by the police, Hill's powers appeared unassailable. Whenever "agitators" came on the scene, the police were curiously near at hand, ready to give chase or arrest them. Evidence supports the CAWIU's charge that Hill, with the assistance of growers and police, compiled a "blacklist" of all activists and organized patrols "to keep [the CAWIU] out of the fields." [37] The *Los Angeles Times* reported that at one gathering of peaceful pickets, all suspected CAWIU members were "placed under arrest . . . as soon as they made their appearance." [38] Predictably, the level of militancy decreased upon the official departure of the union from top posts, and the more "peaceful" non-CAWIU pickets were left alone. [39]

Without the CAWIU's feistiness, volatile incidents on the picket lines were less common. Credit for pacifying the movement is given to Consul Alejandro Martínez, who had seized the moment following the expulsion by "appealing to them [the strikers] to return to their work at once and settle their difficulties peacefully." [40] Martínez's personal plea failed to ignite a general move back to work, and the strike dragged on, stirred up occasionally by the CAWIU. One day in late June, for example, CAWIU militants created an "incident" by urging pickets to forcibly remove scabs from the fields. Martínez responded to this alarming news with "instructions to the Mexican workers to disperse and not to congregate in the zones where the Japanese fields are located." [41] Responding to Consul Martínez's authority, most strikers dutifully went back to their settlements. In his optimistic July 1 strike update to President Rodríguez, Martínez stressed that "for the moment alarming characters have disappeared" and that "strikers have retired to their respective camps to await the results of the negotiations." [42]

Police protection arranged between the sheriff, Hill, and Flores also helped hold picket lines within bounds. The June 25 edition of the *Times* reported that an "Announcement of [a peaceful picketing] plan was made . . . after a conference between strike leaders . . . the Mexican consulate, and Sheriff's officials." [43] Thus twenty-five days after the strike began, the Mexican consulate had stepped in and taken charge. The prestige of the consulate had been brought to bear in the persons of Hill and Flores, whose class and manner commanded the respect of their farmworker compatriots and whose dedication to the cause of the workers filled them with hope. Further, the strikers had placed their trust in a president who had shown them that he cared. He would help redress their grievances. Even picket lines became calmer, for now as strikers marched, the police maintained a distant presence. And finally, the "agitators" had been consigned to a minor role.

Before the strike events, Consul Martínez had rarely interacted directly with the *colonia;* such contact was Hill's responsibility. But with a major strike to deal with, Martínez and Hill, in spite of some tensions between them, began to work together more closely, coordinating the consulate's efforts to end the strike as quickly as possible. To that end Martínez reached to the higher echelons of power. Martínez, who like Hill had no stomach for unions and strikes, had applied to President Rodríguez and Secretary Puig Casauranc for help, and he kept these lofty officials up to date on strike developments. Martínez was to reach to even greater heights as he addressed his requests for intervention to California Governor James Rolph and finally to President Franklin D. Roosevelt.

Although an event such as the expulsion would appear to have been authorized by local authorities, a deeper review of the evidence uncovers the specific policy directives emanating from former President Calles and Secretary Puig in Mexico City. Puig's July 1 memorandum to President Abelardo Rodríguez in which he summarizes strike events refers explicitly to Mexico City's direct involvement in the consulate's decisions and actions leading to the CAWIU expulsion.

Consul Martínez (in Los Angeles) explained that the presence of elements connoted as communists among the strikers made the work of the consul difficult, and for that reason the authorities refused to support those elements (the strikers), and the employers rejected any negotiations. *The consulate received instructions to correctly organize the striking elements and procure the elimination of the communist leaders* (emphasis mine). On the 12th the consul communicated that the definite committee was formed, the existing conflict settled, and the agitating elements of communist affiliation eliminated. These satisfactory results were communicated to CROM.[44]

June 14 was a crucial point in the strike. It was then that the consulate, invoking its full consular powers, stepped up its involvement and moved from behind the curtain that had cloaked the agency's intense interest and involvement. The first move was to form a new strike committee of nonmilitant members under consul supervision. The consulate offices were designated as new strike headquarters, replacing Hicks Camp, and all strike activities would now be coordinated by the consulate. Further, the consul ordered that henceforth no transactions other than those of the new strike committee would be recognized as authoritative.[45] Thus, by June 14, five days after the CAWIU rout, the consul, in consultation with Mexico City, had taken control; Martínez's official approval would henceforth be required before the new committee's directives could be acted upon. As for the strikers, their journey from Hicks Camp to the impressive building housing the consulate was to take them from their humble community to a proud chamber of power. Federal mediators assigned to the strike observed the change in headquarters that further isolated the more militant workers and symbolized the change in leadership: "All leaders of the striking Mexicans and their activities had been transferred to the Union League Building . . . in the offices of the Mexican consul and the Mexican government was represented by a Mr. Hill, Mexican vice-consul, and a Mr. Marcus, attorney for the Mexican consul who acted as the spokesmen for all Mexicans involved in this dispute."[46]

"For the first time since the strike began," announced an article in *La Opinión* titled "El consulado unifica a los huelgistas" [The Consulate Unifies the Strikers], "the Mexican consulate and the strike committee, the two forces in the strike, are working together to gain the triumph of the movement."[47] Both consulate and strike committee looked toward Mexico City, particularly to CROM and General Calles, as well as to Washington, for legal, moral, and monetary support. With the CAWIU apparently out of the picture, the strike now became an overt political dependency of the Mexican government.

In spite of the consulate takeover, with neither side moving toward settlement, the strike stalled. Growers nervously sat on their hands, apparently hoping to outlast the workers, whose suffering was severe. It was at this juncture that Hill and the strike committee called upon Mexico as a lever to force the growers to the bargaining table to negotiate under U.S. federal arbitration. The consulate generated a flurry of strike messages to Mexico and Washington, enlarging the scope of the outreach movement. In telegrams to the White House, Flores made an urgent request for a "full investigation as soon as possible."[48] Two days later the U.S. Department of Labor's Conciliation and Mediation Service directed commissioner E. H. Fitzgerald to "take up the situation affecting Mexican laborers . . . in southern California."[49] Fitzgerald interceded, orchestrating over seven meetings with the strike committee and Hill between June 21 and June 25. A formal negotiating session was set for June 26. At last the two sides would face each other as they sat down together at the same table.

At this lone negotiating session, Hill, Flores, Attorney Marcus, and the fifty members of the strike committee represented striking workers, and Japanese Consul Satow and the Grower Association secretary, S. Fukami, represented the growers. The association had in a prior move offered 15 cents an hour but, after two days of lobbying by the Los Angeles County Chamber of Commerce, had finally upped it to 20 cents, which was put on the table on the 26th. The strike committee balked and would not go along with the offer, bringing negotiations to a halt. Pressure to accept the offer was applied from all sides, with Hill pushing hard, but the committee was adamant. Three hours of parleying produced no signs that the committee would capitulate. They dug in their heels; "the Mexican group refused to sign."[50]

Acting independently and in opposition to their consulate mentors, a majority of the strike committee had insisted that a "minimum wage for all Mexican workers in California" be part of the deal. Thinking they had the growers "on the run," they tried to push their advantage by asking that a general expanded wage gain for workers beyond the county region be included in the settlement. They were mistaken in judging that the growers would capitulate in order to get the strike settled. The Growers Association representatives said no. Although they had agreed to increase the wage to 20 cents an hour for this specific venue, the Japanese Association refused a general pay demand that went beyond it. It was a standoff. Hill's efforts to pull the committee back in line had failed. The strike was on.[51] Los Angeles Chamber of Commerce staff member Ross Gast commented in an interoffice memo to Dr. George Clements, head of the chamber's Agriculture Bureau, that "he [Hill] told me privately that he wanted to sign but could not control the group." Hill was especially frustrated because he had worked tirelessly in back rooms to hammer out the agreement with "the strike leaders, the El Monte Chamber of Commerce, and the Los Angeles Chamber of Commerce," and the growers.[52]

In reality, members of the strike committee had refused suddenly to give full responsibility to Hill and Flores. Such independence suggests that militant members, though few, still had real power, enough to swing votes. Hill and Flores had apparently been overconfident, expecting to pull off the settlement without opposition, but they had underestimated the activist faction. It was still in business, most surely led by Guillermo Velarde, an IWW sympathizer. The strikers had for weeks pinned their hopes on Hill as the embodiment of the Mexico City connection. They had invited the intercessions of President Abelardo Rodríguez, of former President Plutarco Calles, and of CROM. Their grand expectations were not to be easily extinguished, especially not by Hill, whom many of the strikers evidently had trusted. In mid-June communications to CROM headquarters had urgently requested "funds to purchase provisions to sustain the movement." Apparently, such gestures led workers to believe that outside assistance would lead them to the victory for which they had sacrificed.[53] In an instance of seeming solidarity with the strikers' plight, the consulate had sent a message earlier to Mexico's Secretariat of Commerce, Industry, and Labor requesting that the Secretary sponsor a boycott of all Japanese goods imported or manufactured in factories owned by Japanese. A similar appeal had already been made to the local Mexican *colonia,* and merchants were asked to donate groceries for distribution to strikers' families.

Eucario León, CROM's secretary general, assured Flores that the organization stood solidly behind the strike movement. "For your information," he wrote, "we have given instructions to all CROM federations and confederations to declare a boycott of all articles of Japanese origin . . . we also request that our Government join in solidarity with this decision . . . we have also asked the unions to send monetary support as soon as possible."[54] Pleased with León's reply, Flores answered in the pages of *La Opinión* that "the institutions of Mexico continue cooperating to obtain the triumph. The triumph will not be that of the Mexican pickers, but of all Mexicans."[55] The voices of the pickers themselves were strangely silent. As Mexico City's power brokers assumed the central place in the conflict, the pickers seemed to recede to the background, and the governing institutions could move as they pleased in order to assure an outcome favorable to their interests. The pickers themselves could hardly be expected to be aware of this underlying agenda, especially when all signs pointed the other way.

The positive news, from the pickers' perspective, was that CROM had responded to their pleas. Following the receipt of that response, *La Opinión* headlines broadcast "CROM Supports the Strikers" and reported that a CROM commission had scheduled a meeting with President Rodríguez to request "rapid measures to back the movement."[56] Flores also petitioned Former President Plutarco Calles, the power behind the administration of President Abelardo Rodríguez. Flores wrote, "Taking into consideration your undeniable sympathy for the agricultural laborers, we respectfully implore whatever help possible to sustain the strike."[57] The message assured Calles of "our gratitude for material and moral support."[58] Calles responded favorably to Flores's petition and the next day wired $150 by way of the consulate. Two days later he sent another $600. From El Sauzal, his resort-like hacienda in Ensenada, Calles began to orchestrate Mexican activities linked to the strike, and even the strike itself, no matter that it was unfolding in the United States.

Word of Calles's support reached deep into the *colonias* and camps, and Calles emerged a hero among the strikers and in the worker settlements, where shouts of "Viva el General Calles" reverberated through the streets and dirt paths of these strife-torn places. One leader described Calles as "a great friend and defender of the working class" and "high protector of the working class."[59] Others were so moved they had "no words to express their gratitude to General Calles."[60] A representative of the strike committee, heartened by Calles's monetary donations, exclaimed that "The moral support from Mexico is sufficient to take us to victory."[61] Grateful feelings of appreciation buoyed the movement throughout the county. Calles had not only boosted the strikers' morale; he was seen as a savior, rescuing the strike from collapse.

Actions and messages from Secretary Puig had further encouraged the pickers. Puig expressed his government's interest in the strike to U.S. Ambassador Josephus Daniels, thoughtfully pointing out that all radicals had been expelled and requesting that Washington intervene on behalf of the strikers. A *La Opinión* article reported that Puig not only declared the Mexican government's support but added that $1,000 was to be sent to the Los Angeles consulate as a demonstration of the president's cooperation.[62] A CROM statement followed Puig's message, assuring that the "boycott operates with full vigor in the Republic" and that CROM affiliates in Baja California "are prepared to raise a fund . . . to help the Los Angeles workers."[63] In total, the monies originating in Mexico and sent to the consulate for disbursement to the strike committee came to more than $4,000; Calles personally sent more than $1,000. All this activity took place prior to the negotiations on June 26. It might be assumed that such impressive high-level maneuvering would have raised the hopes of the strikers and thus would have been a factor in their decision to reject the growers' wage offer.

It is commonly assumed in political circles in and out of Mexico that Calles openly pulled the strings at the President's Office and at the Secretariat of Foreign Relations. Certainly, the stream of strike information flowing back and forth between Mexico City and Los Angeles always reached Calles's headquarters, and this personal involvement strongly implicates him in decisions and activities that affected the strike's outcome. A special memorandum on the state of the strike prepared by Puig for President Rodríguez reflected on Calles's role in the support movement. In that memo Puig quotes from his previous wire to Calles: "With pleasure I write, my General, that from the beginning of the strike this Secretariat has been in constant contact with the striker's committee, and the CROM Executive Committee has given absolute support to the movement."[64] In a later telegram sent from the President's Office to Consul Martínez, Puig acts as go-between, passing on Calles's enthusiastic evaluation as well as congratulations on following the president's "orders": "Señor General Calles congratulates the Secretariat [of Foreign Relations] and you for your efficacious and patriotic labor undertaken in the strike of Mexican workers, *thus complying with the orders transmitted from the President via this Secretariat*" [emphasis mine].[65]

Upon the unexpected breakdown of the June 26 negotiating session, U.S. Commissioner Fitzgerald prepared a preliminary report for Director of Conciliation H. L. Kerwin. Meanwhile, the strike committee continued to seek outside support by sending telegrams to the Mexican ambassador in Washington, the Department of Labor, and the AFL "soliciting their aid for the movement." Recognizing where the power lay, the committee voted to send two delegations to Mexico. The first would go to Baja California to meet with General Calles, express their appreciation for his help, and provide information on the status of the strike. "Our principal object," stated Flores, "is to give Señor General Calles our personal thanks for his moral and material support . . . and to inform him of the course of our negotiations with the Japanese growers." [66] The second delegation would journey to Mexico City to confer with "leaders of the principal labor organizations, including CROM, to request assistance and support for emancipating the Mexican workers in California." [67]

Thus, shortly after the negotiations had failed, nine delegates led by Flores traveled to Enseñada and met with Calles at El Sauzal. After receiving their expressions of gratitude, Calles offered his "counsel and recommendations regarding the orientations that the strike should assume." [68] The next day Calles sent an additional $600, compelling the consulate to issue a bulletin stating that Calles "has demonstrated that he is truly concerned for all the problems of Mexicans, whether residing in the Fatherland or in a foreign country." [69] Calles's next move was to wire Governor James Rolph requesting state intervention. Playing on the racial issue to support his argument, Calles noted the "duty to strike given the miserable wages received from the Japanese bosses, who even while living in a country of high culture are shorn of all human sentiment and deny their workers those rights enjoyed in the modern world." [70] Again the appreciative strikers shouted "Viva el General Calles!" as Governor Rolph called upon the State Department of Labor Statistics to investigate the conflict.

Technically, the evidence available—letters, memoranda, telegrams, news coverage—leaves no doubt as to the involvement and direct intervention in the strike of the Mexican government. Calles, the government of Mexico, and the ruling party (the PNR) can be seen as one political entity, and it was Calles's support that made him into the hero the strikers needed. So strong were the feelings Calles aroused among the striking pickers that they informally honored him with the title "Father of the Movement." [71] Nevertheless, in spite of Calles's support, the hot summer month of July began without a settlement on the horizon. In Mexico, Calles, the PNR, President Rodríguez, and CROM forged ahead, organizing nationalist propaganda in defense of the strike. Calles issued telegrams in late June to Luis L. León, the editor of the official government (and PNR) newspaper, *El Nacional,* and to the PNR president, General Manuel Pérez Treviño, urging their collaboration with the support campaign. CROM responded to the strikers' pleas by directing that all affiliates back the strike.

From across Mexico, CROM unions responded, sending their messages to President Rodríguez. Calles continued to outdistance his compatriots in the support campaign when he wired President Roosevelt, again invoking the race issue, "begging attention to the wretched and painful economic situation of our Mexican laborers . . . owing to the ill treatment which they receive from these Orientals."[72] *El Nacional* thoroughly supported Calles's call for "justice," repeating the claim that the strike was merely the "legitimate defense for our workmen suffering under the oppression of cruel Japanese," and later referred to "miserable salaries which [Mexicans] received from these Orientals." Mexican government authorities apparently found it useful to invoke Japanese racial imagery in their communications. Even Flores and Hill were inclined to place more responsibility for the strike on the Japanese as a looked-down-upon ethnic group than on the growers in general or white landowners. By playing on the distrust of the Japanese that existed, Hill and Flores could undermine the credibility of the growers.

Among the local authorities, the Los Angeles County Chamber of Commerce had had the greatest impact on the outcome of the strike. The police and sheriffs were active partners, but much of the credit for bringing the growers and laborers together for the negotiating sessions in June and later in July belongs to the chamber. Its interest in the situation was political, devolving partially from the highly questionable leases held by Japanese farmers. As noted previously, the Asiatic Exclusion Act placed a three-year limit on land leases to Japanese citizens, and most of these leases, at the time of the strike, had been allowed to go into violation. The chamber was well aware that Japanese-run farms produced a multitude of crops that entered the Los Angeles market and contributed to the economic health of the area. Dr. George C. Clements, director of the chamber's Agricultural Bureau, acknowledged that most of the Japanese growers were "illegally on the land" and that this fact "would unquestionably be reflected back on the landowner," a revelation Clements, in protecting his constituency, wished to avoid. He finessed the dilemma with a policy recommending that every effort be made to "squelch" violent confrontations that might lead to publicizing any infractions of the Asiatic Exclusion Act.[73]

Anxious to prevent these problematic land leases from coming to light where they most certainly would be used by the other side, chamber members urged a negotiated end to the strike. As the strike moved toward negotiation, Clements expressed relief that the Chamber of Commerce was "able to get the Sheriff's office to use diplomacy rather than force in preserving the peace."[74] Chamber staff member Ross Gast was of the opinion that in spite of one incident of police intemperance, over the course of the strike "police authorities on the whole tended towards favoring the Mexicans."[75] Gast forgot to mention that "agitators," militants, and communists had been selected for arrests and physical violence.

In sharp contrast to the later Imperial Valley and San Joaquin Valley strikes, surprisingly few arrests and episodes of violence occurred in this first smaller strike, and no strike leaders (other than CAWIU members) were ever arrested. Except for occasional minor articles, the antiunion *Los Angeles Times* paid surprisingly little attention to the conflict. A columnist for the *Times* humorously summed up the reasons why so little space was devoted to the strike: "Sheriff Biscaluz's men and the county constabulary certainly know their berries. They have handled the ticklish berry strike situation with tact and finesse. Hundreds of men ready to cause strife . . . have been kept well in hand with only a few instances of actual physical violence."[76]

The friendly relations that existed between the Mexican consulate and the Los Angeles County law enforcement agency may also have worked to tamp any impulse to violence against the largely Mexican strikers. In 1931 Consul de la Colina had presented Sheriff Frank Dewar, Deputy Sheriff Edward Duran Ayres, and County Supervisor Henry W. Wright with honorary badges of the Mexico City police force. Inspector General Jaime Carillo gave out the handcrafted, gold-embossed emblems, and Consul de la Colina spoke briefly of "the cordial relations which exist between Mexico and the United States and the effective cooperation of the police in both countries."[77] Such speeches were standard diplomatic fare. In this case, the honor and ceremony may have reaped its reward. Sheriff Ayres answered de la Colina's warm salute in kind during the conviviality (as the journalist covering the affair described it) by referring specifically to his official visit to Mexico City earlier in the year as a guest of the metropolitan police chief. While in Mexico, Ayres had visited each precinct station and gained a close view of the technical and judicial branches of Mexico's police. [It is highly probable that Deputy Sheriff Ayres's trip was taken as a consultant.]

Five months before the strike flared, Mexico's emissaries had again honored Los Angeles law-enforcement officials. In response to Consul Martínez's recommendation to Mexico City's Inspector General, honorary police badges were awarded to Sheriff Eugene Biscailuz and Los Angeles Police Chief James E. Davis by the Mexico City Police Department. Martínez's recommendation rested on his conviction that the awards would "provide more effective ties in the already good relations that happily exist between the Mexican and American authorities." Martínez further suggested that a friendly pistol-shooting match between Los Angeles and Mexico City police departments would do well to cement "happy relations."[78] These focused efforts on the part of the Mexican consulate to ingratiate the local authorities may have had a subtle quieting effect on police officers so honored and thus may have determined the much less violent tenor of the strike, as compared with the San Joaquin Valley and Imperial Valley conflicts.

Race and ethnicity also played a role in the El Monte strike. Racial discrimination, a shadow that fell equally on both the Mexican pickers and the Japanese farmers, affected each group politically and economically in different ways. In spite of their economic success, for example, the Japanese suffered from limitations on land use and ownership and castelike restrictions that circumscribed any political power that their economic standing would otherwise have warranted. Not one Japanese served on the sheriff or police forces, joined the County Chamber of Commerce, or served on a city council. The Mexican laborers were even more removed from the centers of political power in Los Angeles, and they were held in as much disregard as were the Japanese. Such racist attitudes directed toward both groups were significant in determining the almost aloof position taken by the Chamber of Commerce, sheriff, and police during most of the conflict. Thus authorities appeared to be equally distanced from both Japanese growers and Mexican laborers. One chamber official expressed this neutrality perfectly in a blunt memo to Clements: "I note your memo regarding the Mexican and Japanese trouble. I am inclined to agree with you that both of these groups are playing against the American interests here. . . . Personally, I am not very much in sympathy with playing much with either the Mexicans or the Japanese." [79]

Notwithstanding the comments cited above, the Chamber of Commerce generally took the side of the growers. Clements would summarize several years later that the chamber had "done a good deal of work for the Japanese in order to save ourselves." [80] At the same time they did not advocate the use of force to destroy the incipient union. Given the racial tenor of the time, had the growers been of the white majority, a drastically different and more violent outcome might very well have occurred.

By any measure, agriculture was an important commercial entity in Los Angeles County, although not as great as in the San Joaquin and Imperial Valley regions, where strikes would follow within a few months. Racial issues aside, what was seen as key to County Chamber officials was the necessity to the fresh produce industry (and thus to the city) of maintaining a large, tractable, cheap labor force of pickers. Mexican immigrant labor had fulfilled this requirement for many years. As noted, the border was open to facilitate the entry of this essential human resource, deemed indispensable to the harvest process. That essentiality required that the recalcitrant laborers be mollified rather than destroyed. Further, the chamber had reason to fear that a violent confrontation might also fuel sentiment to raise barriers against this flow of irreplaceable workers. So while Clements and the Chamber of Commerce may have wished in their hearts to hasten the end of the strike by using police action, they refrained.

Looking for a way out of the dilemma, the chamber, with the cooperation of Sheriff Biscailuz, hit upon a strategy to undercut the union by peaceful means, divide the ranks, and settle the strike. First, Clements arranged that "the Mexicans be fed," for in his opinion, "a full-bellied Mexican rarely fights and is more tractable." Clements launched his program by asking that the county welfare office distribute relief supplies, and this was done. However, he was to go much further than full bellies. His next move was to recommend that all able-bodied citizens of "Mexican stem" be transported as soon as possible to wherever their labor was needed in the state. Sheriff Biscailuz agreed to the plan but added that he "thought the finer thing to do . . . would be to scatter them through the San Joaquin Valley as needed." Clements then urged that every effort be made to encourage Mexican nationals to accept the Mexican government's offer to situate them in California colonization projects. At the same time, undercover agents (probably from the sheriff's office) were assigned to the labor camps to encourage repatriation, a strategy that, if successful, would remove the recalcitrant and more militant workers, whose places would be taken by a new wave of hopeful Mexicans fleeing Mexico, where even harsher economic conditions prevailed. Apparently, only the offer of relief was taken up by the strikers, as proposals for repatriation and migration failed to have their intended effect.[81]

In seeming contradiction to Clements's proposal that repatriation be encouraged were statements in which Clements "deeply regretted" the loss of Mexican labor through the mass deportation campaign that the offices of the county welfare department had been running for some time. Embedded in Clements's remarks were the chamber's political concerns regarding the welfare department's repatriation policy (even though he himself had toyed with such an approach as a tactic). Clements now lamented "the loss of 150,000 Mexicans from California in the last three years" and felt that "a marked shortage of this type of labor" was bound to "create [a] bidding [war] by the employers for the few remaining Mexicans in the state."[82] Further restrictions in the availability of Mexican labor spelled possible ruin for some employers by running up the cost of labor at a time when state policy had actually committed to Draconian cost-cutting. Clements warned that such a shortage would create a tempting situation for labor organizers among Mexican workers.

Clearly the chamber's interests lay in a rapid and peaceful solution to the strike. But as July began the strike lingered on, perhaps, in part, because pickers continued to believe that their government would lead them to victory. For those in authority, the time had come to close off the strike;

patience had run out. From Mexico City came the word, a directive that would resolve the impasse. On July 4 Consul Martínez received his instructions from President Rodríguez: "I deem it advisable," stated the president, "that you actively resolve the strike at the earliest." [83] Martínez immediately responded, informing President Rodríguez via phone that "in his estimation a 20 cents per hour offer was satisfactory." This response, with an exact per-hour figure, makes it clear that Consul Martínez had conferred privately with the growers to discuss a wage settlement agreeable to them before convening a new negotiating session with the strikers. Since Martínez made no mention of the opinion of the strikers as to the wage offer, we can assume that either their known views did not enter into his calculations or the strike committee was not consulted. [84]

The new negotiating session took place on July 6. But the preselected 20-cent figure was not used in the final arbitration. The two sides agreed to 16.5 cents per hour (or $1.50 per nine-hour day) for "steady workers" and 20 cents per hour overtime; temporary workers were to receive 20 cents per hour. It was an interim settlement whose terms would be in effect for thirty days and renegotiated on August 15. The signing, witnessed by Japanese Consul Satow and Consul Martínez, increased salaries by a few cents but, ironically, was lower (by 3.5 cents) than the amount offered by the growers' associations at the failed June 26 negotiating session. Nevertheless, workers went back to the fields—under a new union. On July 15, the CROM-affiliated Confederación de Uniones Campesinas y Obreras Mexicanas (CUCOM), which had been born during the confrontation with the CAWIU, as cited earlier, celebrated its organizing convention. The Cannery Union moved on.

In spite of the minimal gains, Armando Flores, the first secretary general of CUCOM, praised the settlement. *La Opinión* reported that "don Armando Flores, who since the beginning of the strike became its leader[,] . . . considers yesterday's agreement Mexican labor's biggest triumph in the strike movements of the United States." [85] Although previous news articles had referred to him only by name, with the settlement Flores's stature rose, and the traditional title of honor and status, *don*, now preceded his name. Consul Martínez also received favorable comments for his role. Deputy Thomas Barker of the State Division of Labor and Law Enforcement praised Martínez for having provided "splendid aid and cooperation" during the negotiations. [86] Hill also received his measure of accolades. A *La Opinión* journalist revisited the strike a year later and in his report reminded readers that among the consulate officials, Hill enjoyed the highest regard and affection among industrial labor and agricultural workers in the state of California. In the journalist's opinion, "the most salient person among the Mexican representatives in this city, Hill worked tirelessly among those in continuous contact with him, [and] his prestige would come to have unanimous recognition, when eighteen thousand *[sic]* pickers declared the largest strike by Mexican citizens in California."[87]

In its congratulatory message, Mexico's government laid to rest any doubts regarding the lines of authority. The Official Bulletin of the Secretariat of Foreign Relations announced: "Upon the termination of the strike movement, General Calles, through the Ministry of Foreign Relations, congratulated Consul Martínez and Vice-Consul Hill. The Ministry of Foreign Relations pointed out that the effective and patriotic labors of these men had been carried on in compliance with orders from the President of the Republic."[88]

General sentiment placed responsibility for defeating the Japanese growers on the shoulders of the Mexican government. "The victory," stated a journalist in *La Opinión*, "without doubt was reached thanks to the decided cooperation offered by the Mexican government, the labor associations of the country, and in particular General Plutarco Elías Calles who, from his residence in El Sauzal, sent large donations of money for sustaining the movement."[89] As was to be expected, the CAWIU viewed the government's role with disdain and attacked the agreement as traitorous and one that gained the workers little for their sacrifices. One defiant faction on the strike committee, led by Guillermo Velarde, an IWW sympathizer and CUCOM undersecretary, bitterly assailed the settlement, charging that it was a "sellout." So angered did Velarde become that he turned with finality against Hill and "stopped coming to the [consulate] office."[90] Flores lauded the agreement, and, adding his voice to others', proclaimed that Mexican institutions and leaders had saved the strike from defeat. Flores emphatically declared the wage agreement a victory and credited the triumph to the Mexican government. The workers were not mentioned, much less thanked for their sacrifices. "If General Calles had not intervened in our favor," Flores exclaimed, "sending money to help the strikers' families, the movement unequivocally would have failed."[91]

Thus credit was given where credit was due. But was it? Calles's motives give us pause and deserve closer scrutiny. The Los Angeles Chamber of Commerce contended that the Machiavellian Calles saw an opportunity to recoup political ground vis-à-vis his contenders by posing as a defender of Mexico and its working class. His political fortunes most surely motivated Calles, and little evidence exists that he ever distinguished himself as a defender of working-class interests. Less than noble reasons for Calles's show of interest in the strike were proffered by Secretary Puig during candid conversations with Ambassador Daniels and

Japanese Ambassador Hori on the subject of Calles's intentions. Daniels's July 5 dispatch to the secretary of state passes on Puig's perspective on the matter: "In reply to a question by Mr. Hori as to whether General Calles was 'very much interested' in this situation, Secretary Puig replied that the General's interest was due chiefly to 'his geographical propinquity.'" Daniels accepted at face value Puig's statement implying that Calles had no deep interest in the strike other than his own driving political ambition.[92]

Although the CAWIU had been eliminated, in large measure as a result of consular directives, the Chamber of Commerce nonetheless misconstrued the roles played by Hill and Flores in the strike and expressed grave doubts about the two officials. Clements failed to appreciate that without Hill at the helm, the Cannery Union would surely have exacerbated the labor struggle. Hill and Martínez were determined to end the strike through arbitration and appeals to Mexican patriotism. However, the strike was like a monster with two heads: it was impossible to lead in a single direction. The level of militancy forced Hill, correctly as it turned out, to ride out the storm, until he could rid the strike of leftist influence and bring the workers to settle with the growers. The chamber misread Hill's pragmatic approach, which took time, and viewed it instead as evidence of Hill's desire to continue the strike. Clements and the chamber, in blaming Hill and Flores for prolonging the strike, may have been creating a smoke screen to cover up their own poor handling of the strike; but in any case they were, of course, wide of the mark in faulting the two consulate officials. Hill's alliance with the strikers and his cheerleader rhetoric may have been interpreted as an incitement to worker belligerence, but his motives were as antiunionist as those of Clements; only their methods as to reaching a settlement differed.

Soon the ever-present communist bogey loomed as the Chamber of Commerce launched direct attacks on the consulate officials. In interoffice memos, some chamber officials went so far as to charge Flores with vague allegations of undercover communist connections. Other equally fantastic charges were brought against David Marcus, the American lawyer who assisted the consulate in legal matters, alleging that he worked as a labor organizer. But it was on Hill that they heaped the greatest abuse, accusing him of "questionable" activities, especially criticizing his penchant for bringing the Mexican government into what the chamber considered a purely local matter. These issues were actually contradictory. On one hand, to the consul's credit, Hill had eliminated the "agitators," and on the other, he appeared to have prolonged the strike, making it more than possible that the illegal land leases would come to light and have serious repercussions on the landowners.

Notwithstanding the complexity and ambiguity of these issues, the

Chamber of Commerce decided to address a grievance to Washington, requesting a Department of Justice investigation of Hill's involvement. Clements spelled out the complaint to his superior, Mr. Arnoll, the Chamber's secretary and general manager. He alleged that CROM and the Mexican government had directed "Mexican consular offices" to interfere and "organize the Mexican people and agitate." He pressured Arnoll to "[c]all the attention of Washington and request that the Department of Justice" make an investigation.[93]

The complaint went to the Department of State with the request that the matter be forwarded to the Department of Justice. Rather than involving Justice, State chose to keep the issue as quiet as possible and maintain the matter under its purview. State's Division of Mexican Affairs reviewed the charge, and its preliminary evaluation found that "little actual evidence" of "improper intervention" had been submitted.[94] In further discreet investigation, officials concluded that no action should be taken "without more conclusive evidence than we now have that Mexican intervention in the dispute was of a character which might be held either unlawful, unfriendly, or improper."[95]

Several months after the strike reached a closure, a communiqué issued by Ambassador Daniels to Secretary of State Hull commented on a Mexican Foreign Office bulletin reviewing in detail the actions taken by the Mexican government in the strike. Daniels's comment reflected what appeared to be the State Department's official opinion regarding Mexico's (and Hill's) conduct. The communiqué dismissed any basis for charges of misconduct by suggesting that the [Mexican Foreign Office] bulletin "need not be read unless you are interested in the matter." Daniels continued: "The dispute appears to have been settled. . . . The bulletin describes in great detail the various steps taken by the Mexican Foreign Office to support its nationals in California. . . . My impression is that its principal purpose was to demonstrate to the Mexican people the efficiency and vigor with which the Mexican government protects its nationals living in even so powerful a country as the U.S."[96]

The U.S. State Department accepted the Mexican government's narrow and disingenuous view that the conflict was a simple case of Mexican laborers against Japanese farmers and posed no immediate threat to U.S. interests. Mexico's proud insistence that its actions were directed solely at protecting the interests of its citizens living abroad was found acceptable.

The State Department recognized the difference between hostile nationalism harmful to U.S. interests and that benevolent nationalism exhibited by the Mexican state. Mexico's skillful manipulation of nationalist rhetoric barely concealed a corporatism adapted to U.S. economic and political hegemony. Mexico, in its subordinate role, had bowed to U.S. policy, foreign and domestic. The State Department could afford to uphold the larger view that as long as conservative objectives grounded consular activities, the strike and its nationalist appeals merited minor attention. State Department officialdom had no reason to bother penetrating the veneer of Mexican "nationalism" to see the condition it masked. As for the members of the Mexican hierarchy in thrall to the United States, perhaps they could defer to the saying, "so close to the United States and so far from God." And so when it came to their compatriots abroad, they were indifferent. Perhaps their "sellout" of the Mexican workers, or at the least Mexico's refusal to stand by them, can be seen on the very deepest plane as a sellout of their own nation.

Postscript: The 1936 Citrus Pickers' Strike

Within a few months of the July settlement, Ricardo Hill had left the Los Angeles consulate as a result of his involvement in a widely publicized verbal altercation with a Los Angeles police officer over an incident unrelated to the strike or labor matters. Hill's superiors considered that his conduct and the surrounding controversy necessitated a transfer, without prejudice, to New Orleans. Armando Flores also faltered. After internal reshuffling and a dispute, he lost the leadership of CUCOM to his opponent, Guillermo Velarde, the new CUCOM secretary general. The union counted nearly two thousand dues-paying members and about an equal number of non-dues-paying members enlisted in forty-two locals.[97] Under Velarde, CUCOM embarked on an independent course. Although formally affiliated with CROM and the consulate, CUCOM stepped away from these ties and initiated a period of cooperation with CAWIU. Between 1934 and 1936 CUCOM launched several important agricultural strikes in the southern California region in a united front with other national unions and the CAWIU. After the Communist Party embarked on the United Front in 1935, the communist-led unions disappeared and the activists merged into the trade union movement. Subsequently, the CUCOM opened its ranks to absorb known leftists and communists without questions.

However, CUCOM's independent course was not without challenge. Promoted to consul in 1935, Hill returned to Los Angeles with written instructions from the Ministry of Foreign Relations to "take charge of Mexican labor problems in the United States."[98] Hill's first opportunity to engage in labor-problem solving in his new venue appeared in 1935, with stirrings of a strike among citrus pickers in neighboring Orange

County. CUCOM was organizing the pickers and preparing for the possibility for a strike. Again, as before, Hill made frequent appearances at worker meetings. Velarde certainly would have retained vivid memories of their clash during the 1933 strike. Once again, labor tensions overflowed, and as the 1936 picking season opened, the largest and costliest strike to affect the citrus industry to that date was called. This strike of over 2,500 pickers has been described elsewhere; a summary, underscoring the significant details, follows.[99]

As in the 1933 strike, and perhaps even more so here, Consul Hill's ambitions went beyond the duties of assisting his compatriots: he sought leadership of the movement. At his side was Lucas Lucio, founding member of CUOM and an honorary consul by virtue of his activity in the Santa Ana Comisión Honorífica. Again, Hill's mandate was to steer the strike away from radicals, in this instance, separating the rank and file from union leader Velarde. In the midst of the strike, Hill's grab for power would bring him into a fierce struggle with Velarde.

As in past strikes, Hill chose a nationalistic strategy that divided pickers into factions by separating out only Mexican laborers to represent and ignoring the Filipino and American pickers. Velarde and his comrades had a more all-encompassing approach and organized pickers as a class, regardless of nationality. Hill's exclusively pro-Mexican practices did not go unnoticed. One critic, AFL organizer J. B. Nathan, reported: "According to members of the strike committee . . . Consul Ricardo Hill's activity has tended to split the unity of the strikers composed . . . of Mexican citizens . . . American-born Mexicans, Filipinos, and Americans."[100]

From the start, Hill led the drive to oust Velarde. Again we see, as in the events of the 1933 agricultural strike, Hill's penchant for establishing bonds with local authorities in order to develop a consensus on what authorities would tolerate as politically appropriate activities for the CUCOM. Los Angeles County Chamber of Commerce official Arthur E. Clark met with Hill in the turbulent two months prior to the strike call and told him "very firmly" that Hill needed to "do a big job of housecleaning in that alleged Mexican union." Hill assured Clark that a partial "housecleaning" had already been accomplished. However, the growers apparently insisted that a more thorough cleansing was necessary and that Velarde must go.[101] President J. A. Prizer of the Orange County Protective Association, the local organization of growers spearheading the antiunion drive, declared to the membership that Hill had given his word "that the radical element which had brought about the strike would be out of the picture."[102] Hill kept his promise, according to Maxwell Burke, a Santa Ana lawyer and Lucio's employer. Burke wrote that Hill and Lucio had advised workers to "deliberately [keep] themselves free from any radical group." Burke further remarked that he had known Hill "for a number of years . . . [and] he has never used his office or his personal influence for any radical movement."[103]

Once the strike had erupted, the simmering militancy of the workers could not be easily harnessed, and after four weeks of picketing unrest, the first violence erupted as the police and vigilantes attacked the picket lines. Such episodes of extreme physical confrontations became daily occurrences. Inside the strike, Velarde and Hill continued to clash. In the sixth week, Hill set in motion the events that would topple Velarde. Hill was aided by the police and sheriffs, who attempted several times to arrest Velarde, compelling him to go underground. Again, true to his word, Hill followed through for the economically and politically powerful. Under the protection of authorities, and accompanied by sheriff deputies, he and his partner Lucio made the rounds of picker communities throughout the county, urging the formal expulsion of Velarde (now in hiding) and all radicals on the strike committee. Velarde fought back in a fierce declaration of independence, charging that "Hill and Lucio have no authority," that they were attempting to "trick the Mexicans into a settlement," and further, that "only the union can negotiate union matters, not the consulate."[104] But it was too late. Velarde was overwhelmed by the forces pitted against him. The police soon arrested Velarde on incredible, trumped-up charges of "vagrancy" and driving on the wrong side of the road. With Velarde safely out of the picture, the union came fully under Hill's command at the sixth week of the strike. Assisted by Inspector General of Consulates Adolfo de la Huerta, Hill then proceeded with all haste to negotiate an end to the strike—on growers' terms. Growers had demanded, and received, a commitment from Hill and de la Huerta "to use their best efforts to clean out radical and red elements, particularly Velarde and his union group, from the ranks of the Mexican pickers." This had been done. Now, with the approval of Hill, growers "blacklisted" sixty alleged radicals. Union recognition, the single demand that union militants regarded as nonnegotiable, was absent from the agreement.[105]

Long before the agreement was signed, regional political power brokers had joined the fray, unnoticed. Representing the elitist Harrison Chandler, publisher of the *Los Angeles Times,* was his personal secretary, John F. Dolan. Dolan was also legal adviser to the Mexican Consulate (for which he received a handsome fee). His impeccable credentials earned Dolan a seat at the negotiation table, and he acted on behalf of his mentors in bringing a swift end to the strike. According to one labor journalist, Dolan had a hand in arranging concessions that would be agreeable to the consulate and growers and also participated in discussions in Chandler's stead.[106] As is not unusual in such a politically fraught event, a colossal network of social, business, and governmental interests in effect appropriated the strike and decided its fate. The editor of the *Pacific Rural Press,* a conservative growers' journal, reported that Inspector General de la Huerta "offered to call off the strike if the farmers would agree to a bit of 'face saving.'" What was meant by "face saving" was not clear. The editor further alleged that de la Huerta had put rebellious Mexicans on notice to return "to work . . . quietly warning them that the Mexican government would not stand behind them if they refused to accept the terms of the agreement." [107]

Angry union militants charged Hill, Lucio, and de la Huerta with subverting the union by turning workers against Velarde and challenged their right to negotiate for the union. One leader, Bernardo Lucero, attacked Hill and Lucio at a CUCOM meeting, where it was reported that "he told the workers of the treachery of Lucas Lucio" and Consul Hill. Lucero accused Hill of "splitting the workers with fine words and promises." A battered CUCOM, like the CAWIU in 1933 and 1934, gathered itself and issued a statement regarding Hill's coup. The consul was vilified by CUCOM for "traitorous" and "contemptible acts" that "undermined the unity of the workers." The statement summarily dismissed Hill's justifications, reading in part, "All the explanations that . . . Consul Hill may make . . . will never wipe [the] disgrace from the records of the labor movement." [108] With this definitive pronouncement, the CUCOM's executive committee, by unanimous agreement, repudiated the consul and announced the severance of all relations between CUCOM and the Mexican Consulate.

In an ironic twist, growers were also dissatisfied with Hill's performance. Despite Hill's cooperation in excluding radicals from the strike movement, growers felt that Hill had failed them by leading the union rather than calling an immediate end to the strike. The ultra-conservative county branch of the California Associated Farmers, a group that had dedicated its efforts to the cause of eradicating agricultural unions, sent a complaint regarding Hill to the State Department. The complaint cited Hill for having gone "far afield of his duties as a consular representative" and demanded that his consular privileges be recalled. Just as the Los Angeles County Chamber of Commerce had done three years previously, the Associated Farmers disregarded the service performed by the consul. Hill responded in a written defense, stating, "I have not been very active [in] organizing Mexican labor, except in cooperation with the local police, Federal officers, and the National Labor Relations Board . . . so that there would be no disorder among our people." Hill reaffirmed his unwavering antiunion stance by pointing out that the radicals opposed him: "any radical group will let it be known that they are against me." [109]

No one could accuse Hill of "coddling" radicals; one pro-consul lawyer contended that due to Hill's efforts, "when certain . . . radical people appeared . . . they had been told that they were not needed nor wanted." [110]

It is not difficult to identify the factors that led to the growers' misunderstanding of Hill's role in the strike. What they saw was that Hill had deliberately involved himself in the workers' cause, he spoke at strike meetings, and he had taken control of the strike committee (and thus became a strike leader). He had a legitimized consular role in relation to the Mexican laborers, and he possessed the authority and the power to end the strike. So why didn't he snap his fingers and send the pickers back to the fields? Like all such organizations, the Associated Farmers were so blinded by self-interest that they were unable to see the workers as anything but pawns to be placed where one wanted them. What was Hill up to, the growers could ask themselves, what was he waiting for? It was but a short hop from that question to the suspicion that Hill was a pro-union leftist himself.

Apparently, such suspicions were not unanimous; there is evidence that many growers in the association, even certain leaders, had read Hill's actions accurately. Notwithstanding the members who disagreed, the Farmers Association fired off its denunciation of Hill to Secretary of Labor Frances Perkins. Perkins, in turn, passed it on to Secretary of State Cordell Hull, along with a message suggesting a certain degree of caution in regard to the association's complaints, pointing out "that pressure has been brought to bear upon Mr. Strathman to file complaints against the Mexican officials." [111] Perkins was cognizant of Hill's distaste for strikes, and according to federal mediator E. H. Fitzgerald, Hill had stated on "more than one occasion" that he was "not in favor of strikes." Indeed, Fitzgerald was well informed of Hill's battle to expel Velarde and his group from the union. In a strike update written to his superior, H. L. Kerwin, Fitzgerald had vehemently defended Hill: "Radical and communistic leaders will step in and trouble is bound to come [and] Mexican officials will lose control." Employers, he continued, "will find that they would have been better off" with Hill as union leader. Upon hearing of the charge brought against Hill by the growers, Fitzgerald expressed his profound disagreement. The charge against "Council [sic] Hill," he wrote, "was based on reports that were not reliable and not in keeping with the facts." [112]

John F. Dolan, the private secretary to *Los Angeles Times* publisher Harrison Chandler and his representative during the negotiations that brought the strike to an end, also steadfastly supported Hill during the furor. In a letter to California Congressman John S. McGroarty, Dolan argued that Hill was "wrongly attacked" and that the charges from grower interests "are absolutely without foundation." Dolan named Hill as a victim of a "travesty of justice" who was "crucified on the cross of unfounded rumors." Dolan added praise that Hill "has done much to promote friendly relations between the two countries."[113]

The growers' complaint, as we have seen, reached Secretary of State Cordell Hull. After taking the charges under consideration, Hull's staff was advised to evaluate the allegations. Subsequent to that investigation, Hull absolved the consul in his report to Labor Secretary Frances Perkins: "It does not appear that the difficulty is due to the activities of the Mexican consular officials."[114] Notwithstanding the confidentiality of the State Department's report, this document fell into the hands of the Mexican Embassy. Now it was the turn of Edward L. Reed, chief of the Division of Mexican Affairs, to meet with Luis Quintanilla, charge d'affairs in the embassy. From there, Quintanilla sent the report on, with his evaluation, to the president's secretary in Mexico City. In glowing terms, Quintanilla absolved Hill of any improprieties and described Hill as a model consul and a defender of exploited Mexican expatriates. "In my humble opinion," wrote Quintanilla, "the conduct of Consul Hill merits applause from those who know perfectly well the difficulties inherent in the charge of Consul of Mexico in regions of the U.S. where a tradition exists of systematically exploiting Mexican labor." Furthermore, Quintanilla goes on, "there is no complaint at all against Hill from the American government. Mr. Reed as well as the American functionaries responsible for this matter have the highest regard for Hill, and profoundly respect him and perfectly comprehend his position."[115] Hill, whose case had gone all the way to the seats of governmental power of both the United States and Mexico, had been absolved of wrongdoing at the very highest levels and earned a measure of respect as well.

So ends this phase of Ricardo Hill's consular activities. But we may briefly follow Hill's path as he pursued his career in the service of the Mexican government. Archival papers reveal that a few weeks into the 1936 strike, Hill had inquired of President Cárdenas's personal secretary Luis I. Rodríguez as to the possibility of securing a government party seat in the National Chamber of Deputies from his home state of Sonora. In support of this request, Secretary Rodríguez had suggested that Hill meet with the "leaders of our Party, who with a more precise insight than I can give you, can answer what is best for you."[116] That reply confirmed an initial positive appraisal of Hill and was a signal for him to proceed further. In later correspondence with Rodríguez, Hill presented himself as a faithful guardian of the people who would "guarantee order, progress, and the well-being of Sonora" (the *científicos* under Porfirio Díaz would have appreciated such a claim). Avowing his conviction that the people of Sonora needed a government that was "honorable and patriotic," Hill went on to assure the president that he "identified entirely with the sincere and truly revolutionary policies of Señor Presidente Cárdenas." [117] In closing his application for support, Hill was careful to say that the fulfillment of his plans would require the "sympathy of the President of the Republic."

A year after his departure from the Los Angeles consulate, Consul Hill was awarded a deputy seat in the government-controlled Federal Chamber of Deputies from the state of Sonora.

In the San Joaquin Valley, hundred-pound cotton sacks were first weighed and then loaded onto wagons for transport to railroad cars.
COURTESY OF THE BANCROFT LIBRARY.

Abode for migrant lettuce worker(s) and family on the east side of Brawley, the Imperial Valley. COURTESY OF THE DEPARTMENT OF SPECIAL COLLECTIONS, UNIVERSITY RESEARCH LIBRARY, UNIVERSITY OF CALIFORNIA, LOS ANGELES.

Living quarters reserved for Mexican agricultural workers in the Imperial Valley. These shacks in the Brawley east side were rented for $4 to $6 depending on size. COURTESY OF THE DEPARTMENT OF SPECIAL COLLECTIONS, UNIVERSITY RESEARCH LIBRARY, UNIVERSITY OF CALIFORNIA, LOS ANGELES.

A not untypical living quarters for Mexican field workers and family in the Mexican section of El Centro, in the Imperial Valley. COURTESY OF THE DEPARTMENT OF SPECIAL COLLECTIONS, UNIVERSITY RESEARCH LIBRARY, UNIVERSITY OF CALIFORNIA, LOS ANGELES.

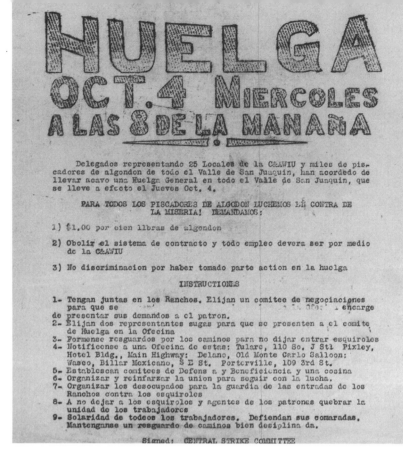

Flyer in Spanish distributed throughout the San Joaquin Valley's labor camps announcing the cotton strike to begin October 4 at eight in the morning. The CAWIU handout listed the union demands and instructions and urged solidarity. COURTESY OF THE BANCROFT LIBRARY.

Corcoran Camp, in the San Joaquin Valley. Striking workers were evicted from grower-owned housing and made camp at Corcoran, union headquarters and site of many a union meeting. The traveling circus at left offered nightly respite from official repression. COURTESY OF THE BANCROFT LIBRARY.

PEA-PICKERS

PISCADORES DE CHICHAROS

STRIKE

HUELGA

A STRIKE has been called in all PEA FIELDS by the CANNERY AND AGRICULTURAL WORKERS INDUSTRIAL UNION:-- We cannot live on the ONE CENT per POUND now paid. We are DEMANDING TWO CENTS per POUND. DO THIS IMMEDIATELY:-- Elect a WORKER from your field to our STRIKE COMMITTEE.

Refuse to return to work until notified to do so by the CENTRAL STRIKE COMMITTEE. Join the PICKET LINE.

---DONT SCAB---

To the WORKERS of IMPERIAL VALLEY. SUPPORT the STRIKE of 3000 PEA PICKERS at CALIPATRIA by refusing to work in the fields on STRIKE.

Dont believe the NEWSPAPERS CONTROLLED by the GROWERS, that the STRIKE is over. Hold MEETINGS in your town, COLLECT FOOD FOR THE STRIKERS.

A VICTORY in this STRIKE means BETTER CONDITIONS for all of US.

La HUELGA Biene ablande en TODOS las CAMPOS del producto, por la UNION INDUSTRIAL DE AGRICULTURA Y CANERIA. Nostros no podemos Vivir con 1¢ en la livra que se nos paga. Mejores Condiciones de Vida. Como agua limpia, y reconosimiento de La Union, hun director por cada 100 trabajadores. Guieremos aser esto en este momento ,elijan hun trabajador de su campo que occura al Comite de Huelga, no Bayon a trabajar esta que dicho Comite finalise sus trabajos, y lo aga del cano similiente de Uds.

---NO SEAN ESQUIROLES---

Trabajadores del Valle Imperial, sos 3000 trabajadores en HUELGA en los Campos, no se crean de los patrones, ni de los que disen lo Periodicos que la Huelga termino. "Es todos falso" agan juntas en su Pueblo, colecten probison para pos Huelgistas.

Que la VICTORIA de mejores Condisiones de VIDA es para TODOS.

DONT SCAB!

NO SEAN ESCIROLES!

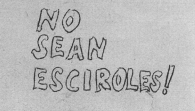

Bilingual CAWIU flyer announcing the strike of pea pickers in the Imperial Valley, spring of 1934. COURTESY OF THE IMPERIAL COUNTY HISTORICAL SOCIETY.

To The Workers of

IMPERIAL VALLEY

MASS MEETING

Under Protection United States Government

THE POLICE WILL NOT INTERFERE

AZTECA HALL

10th and H Streets, Brawley

Tonight 7:00   MAR 11 1934   Tonight 7:00

—Auspices Civil Liberties Union—

Los Trabajadores del

VALLE IMPERIAL

GRAN MITING

Esta Noche a las
7:00
En el Salon Azteca

Bajo la Protection del Gobierno de Estados Unidos

LA POLICIA NO INTERVENDRA

Auspicios de la UNION de LIBETADES CIVILES

Su ASISTENCIA es NECESARIA

Bilingual flyer urging workers to attend a meeting sponsored by the ACLU to discuss Constitutional rights. The meeting was disrupted when vigilantes kidnapped A. L. Wirin, organizer of the meeting. COURTESY OF THE IMPERIAL COUNTY HISTORICAL SOCIETY.

THE
LETTUCE
PEA & MELON
STRIKES
VIGILANTES - TEAR
GAS - SHOTGUNS - KID-
NAPPINGS - ASSAULTS - IN-
JUNCTIONS - REDS - COURT TRIALS
TERROR -- CLASS WARFARE -- FASCISM!

FIGHT AGAINST TERROR + FASCISM IN IMPERIAL VALLEY

COME AND HEAR THE TRUTH !

About General Pelham (Sell'em) Glassford -- TERRAZAS' union
-- the facts about the Melon strike -- the latest arrests--
the frame-up of Stanley Hancock and Dorothy Ray

MASS PROTEST MEETING
SUNDAY — MAY 13 — 8 PM
852 8th Ave

JOIN THE UNITED FRONT FIGHT AGAINST TERROR, FASCISM, AND WAR !

A U S P I C E S

UNITED FRONT COMMITTEE FOR ACTION AGAINST FASCISM AND WAR
(International Labor Defense, Young Pioneers, Communist Party,
Young Communist League, International Workers Order, I C O R,
County Emergency Relief Association, Fishermen and Cannery
Workers Industrial Union, Women's Council, Construction
Workers Industrial Union, Unemployed Council, A.F. of L. Rank
and File Group, Cannery and Agricultural Workers Industrial
Union, Relief Workers Union.)

Flyer distributed by the United Front against Terror urging workers to protest official violence in the Imperial Valley. Note the reference to Consul Terrazas and General Pelham Glassford. COURTESY OF THE BANCROFT LIBRARY.

Pat Chambers speaking to anxious strikers at the Pixley union hall as growers quietly prepared to fire into the crowd; they killed two and wounded nine.
COURTESY OF THE BANCROFT LIBRARY.

Strikers on their way to the picket line in the San Joaquin Valley.
COURTESY OF THE BANCROFT LIBRARY.

Funeral march for the men slain by growers during the cotton strike. Placard declares, "Mexican Consul represents Mexican bosses." Photograph taken from the film Century of Progress, *produced by the Film and Photo League.*
COURTESY OF THE ARCHIVES OF LABOR AND URBAN AFFAIRS, WAYNE STATE UNIVERSITY.

Banner carried by funeral marchers stating: "Our compañeros died but we promise to continue until death or victory." Photograph taken from the film Century of Progress, *produced by the Film and Photo League.*
COURTESY OF THE ARCHIVES OF LABOR AND URBAN AFFAIRS, WAYNE STATE UNIVERSITY.

Mary Decker, organizer and leader of the CAWIU in the San Joaquin strike, speaking to striking rank and file. Photograph taken from the film Century of Progress, *produced by the Film and Photo League.*
COURTESY OF THE ARCHIVES OF LABOR AND URBAN AFFAIRS, WAYNE STATE UNIVERSITY.

State Labor Commissioner Frank MacDonald and Leonsio Acosta appealing to workers at Corcoran Camp to abandon the strike. Their entreaties were for naught.
COURTESY OF THE BANCROFT LIBRARY.

MEXICAN CONSUL TEAMS UP WITH BOSSES TO BREAK OUR UNION.

vide and Conquer, the slogan of the bosses. To this they have plenty of stool-pigeons, plenty paid agents. In the cotton strike we found — all working to break the unity of 12,000 Negro and White workers, the UNITY THAT N THE STRIKE! The Mexican Consul is an example. He came to Mexican workers and used this — "be patriotic Mexicans, you don't belong in — country. Don't cause international complications. Organize your own Mexican Union. Go — to work for 60¢".

— he had the nerve to get up at the Fact Finding Hearing in Visalia and pretend to speak "for Mexican country-men". At the hearing when — was asked if he thought the police had given Mexican workers sufficient protection — he — "I'd rather not answer, I'm supposed to — erate with the officials and Law of this country." Oh, yes, Mr. Bravo, we sure do know how — cooperated with them against the strikers. — further, after telling the Mexican workers — this WAS NOT their country, he said at the — ing: "The Mexican workers have always been — riotic workers. If this country should go to — the Mexicans will fight for them." At the — time, Mr. Elliot, an American, supervisor of —

Tulare County, said to some American Union members — "Why do you belong to that Red Union, why don't you organize into your own union?" Sounds like the Mexican Consul, doesn't it? And if there had been any Negro bosses in the valley, they would have told the Negro workers to organize their own union.

The Mexican Consul forgot to tell the workers that he's getting a good salary from the Mexican bosses who are exploiting the Mexican workers in Mexico. He forgot to tell them that 7 years ago the rich growers went to Washington to get more Mexicans in California, in order to lower the wage standard. He forgot too, that HE DOESN'T REPRESENT THE MEXICAN WORKERS, BUT REPRESENTS THE MEXICAN BOSSES WHO ARE CONTROLLED BY THE SAME AMERICAN FINANCE-CAPITAL THAT CUTS OUR WAGES IN THE U.S.!

And who does Mr. Elliot represent? And who does Chief of Police Springer of Corcoran represent when he tells the comrades in Corcoran they can belong to the AFofL but not to the C&AWIU? Whenever workers of all races get together in a militant union to fight for decent wages, the bosses always have their lackeys to do their bidding.

****

ACOSTA, MEXICAN CONSUL REPRESENTATIVE, CAUGHT RED-HANDED !

tor, "Agricultural Worker": Dec. 4th, 1933.

— Comrades: On the morning of November 29th, a representative of the Mexican Consulate, represent — Mr. Acosta in Fresno, called at my home saying that the Consul wished to talk to me concerning my — icipation in the Cotton Strike and Union. I accepted the invitation and departed to Fresno with the — resentative who tried to tell me in many ways that I was wrong in participating in a "red union" (to — ch I agreed to prevent quarrel on the road.)

— arrived at Fresno about 11 A.M. and immediately went to the Consul's office where many things were — cussed and to which I disagreed. Some of the points discussed were: — that I should urge my people to abandon the C&AWIU, and — this way prevent international difficulties between Mexico and U.S. and help to bring a better relation between — two countries. 2—That he would give me authority to — anize a Mexican Labor Union in the Valley and would finance me in my efforts, (money and car), just so we would — away from the Reds and their C&AWIU. 3—That this — ican Labor Union could affiliate to the A.F.of L. — that if I didn't accept his offer my people were in danger of being deported. 5—That since we were not American — izens we had no right to protest because our actions would — make us "Reds". 6—That solidarity with Reds was a — y bad step to take both to Mexico and U.S.

— as able to answer his questions and refused his offer. — told him that modern capital was responsible for our — ion and that it's necessary for us to act that way in — er to live. That it was time for us to appreciate what — cola and Hidalgo were supposed to have done for us, — that we were now the slaves of capital. That the — ves before the Civil War were better provided with food, — thing and shelter then we are. That if it was the reds — anizing the workers to put up such a good fight like — cotton strike, then I am a Red. Seeing that his threats — e not working the way he desired, he lost hope and that — s the end of a happy day.

Very comradely yours,
Salvador Olmedo
Portersville, Calif.

EVERY C&AWIU MEMBER SHOULD BE AN ORGANIZER!
THE COST OF LIVING GOES UP EVERY DAY!
PREPARE TO FIGHT FOR HIGHER WAGES!

Acosta

EL CONSUL MEXICANO REPRESENTA A LOS CAPITALISTAS

Divide y triunfaras, la consigna de los patrones. Para llevar cabo esto consigna, ellos tienen muchos instrumentos pagados entre los trabajadores. En la huelga del algodon los encontramos trabajando para quebrar la solidaridad de 12000 obreros de todas nacionalidades la solidaridad que gano la huelga! Como ejemplo esta, el consul Mexicano. El dijo a los trabajadores Mexicanos: "Mexicanos sean Uds. patriotas! Uds. no pertenecen a este pais. No sean Uds. causa de una complicacion internacional. Porque no se organizan en su propia Union de Mexicanos, vuelvan Uds. al trabajo por los 60¢ el 100 lbs.?

Este sinverguenza tuvo el descaro todavia de levantarse ante la comision investigadora de la situacion en Visalia y pretender hablar en defensa de los "trabajadores Mexicanos." En la audiencia cuando se le pregunto que si la policia dava a los Mexicanos suficiente proteccion, el dijo: "Prefiero callarme y no contestar. Mi deber es el de cooperar con los oficiales y las leyes del este Estado." Claro, Mr. Bravo, nosotros sabemos cual fue su cooperacion. Ademas despues de decir a los Mexicanos que este no era su pais, el dijo despues que: "Los trabajadores Mexicanos han sido siempre buenos patriotas. Si este pais alguna vez se encontara en otra guerra, los Mexicanos lucharan por el."

Al mismo tiempo que esto pasaba, un supervisor del Condado de Tulare decia a unos trabajadores americanos, miembros de la C&AWIU: "Por que se han hecho Uds. miembros de esa Union roja, porque no se organizan Uds. en una Union de Uds., Anglo-sajones?"

No les parece, compañeros, que esto suena lo mismo que el consul de Mexico? Si hubiera havido algunos amos negros en el Valle, por seguro ellos hubieran dicho lo mismo a los obreros negros, que formaran su propia Union.

El consul olvido decir a los trabajadores que el reciva un buen salario. Olvido decirles que 7 años hace que los ricos rancheros del Valle fueron a Washington a pedir que se dijera entrar mas Mexicanos en el Estado, para de este modo rebajar el nivel de vida y salarios.

Olvido decir que el no representa a los trabajadores Mexicanos, sino a los capitalistas Mexicanos los cuales estan controlados por el Capital financiero Americano.

A quien representa el supervisor Mr. Elliott? A quien representa el jefe de policia, Springer de Corcoran, cuando este les dijo a unos compañeros que ellos podrian pertenecer a la A.F.ofL. pero no a la C&AWIU?

RECORDAMOS AL CABALLO EN EL HOCICO!

EL CONSUL MEXICANO SE UNE CON LOS PATRONES

EDITOR - EL TRABAJADOR AGRICOLO
Dec. 4, 1933

Queridos camaradas: Por la mañana del 29 de noviembre de 1933 un representante del consulado Mexicano, del señor Acosta en Fresno, vino a mi casa diciendo que el consul deseo hablar a me de mi participacion en el huelga del algodon y en la Union. Acepti la invitacion y parti para Fresno con su hombre que me informo que no tenia razon participar en una "union comunista."

Acosta

Llegamos a Fresno cerca de las once y inmediatamente fuimos a la oficina del consul donde discutimos muchas cosas, por ejemplo: 1-Que deben incitar a mis compatriotas dejar de mantener el C&AWIU y de este modo prohibir dificultades internacionales entre los Mexicanos y los Estados Unidos. 2-Que me dara la autoridad de organizar una union Mexicano el Valle y me equipara con dinero y un carro. 3-Que al no aceptara sus ofertas sera posible que mis compatriotas a deportarian. 4-Que los Mexicanos en esta union no podran afiliarse con la Union. 5-desde que no eramos cuidadanos de los Estados Unidos no teniamos el derecho de protestar porque todos creeran que eramos "comunistas". 6-Que una solidaridad con esta union era un gran error por Mexico, tambien como por los Estados Unidos.

Pude contestar a sus preguntas y rehuse sus ofertas y le dije que el capital moderno era responsable que era necesario que nos conducimos de este modo para vivir; que debiamos apremir lo que hizieron Lincoln y Hidalgo, pero ahora eramos los esclavos del capital. Dijo que las condiciones de los esclavos en los Estados Unidos delante alla Guerra civil eran mejores que las nuestras ahora. Que si los rojos son los que organizaban el trabajador para mejorar sus condiciones y vida, yo soy un rojo.

Viendo que sus amenazas no valieran nada, abandono sus esfuerzos.

Su compañero
SALVADOR OLMEDA
Porterville, Calif.

****

Pages from the English and Spanish editions of the CAWIU newsletter
Trabajador Agrícolo/The Agricultural Worker, *December 5, 1933, accusing Consul Enrique Bravo and his assistant Leonsio Acosta of collusion with the growers.*

CHAPTER 4

■

The San Joaquin Valley Strike of 1933

The year 1933 would be a historic one for the Cannery Union. The union would lead thousands of disenfranchised agricultural workers in a series of bitterly contested battles against powerful grower consortiums in the rich agricultural regions of California. By August of that year, the CAWIU would have survived three failed strike actions, at Los Angeles, Lodi, and Fresno, and three successes, at San Jose pear ranches, the Tagus Ranch at Fresno, and the Oxnard beet fields. Now a Cannery Union cadre would enter the San Joaquin Valley, this time to organize workers laboring in the vast cotton fields. The army of laborers coming into the Valley for the immense cotton harvest would include Mexican, Black, white, and Filipino workers, making up a picking force numbering as many as 15,000. The greatest contingent, about 75 percent, would be Mexican. About 90 percent of the entire force would labor within a family unit.

The strike, the largest agricultural strike in U.S. history, would be called on October 4 and last just three weeks, but it would rock the Valley to its core as furious growers hurled themselves into the conflict. In their rage against workers who had dared insist on their rights, ranchers would trample on the Constitution, backed by a compliant legal system. In the turbulent clashes that would characterize the strike, growers would wade into unarmed strikers, causing three deaths and scores of injuries. None of the men participating in these operations would be held accountable. Summary evictions would empty labor camps and leave hundreds of men, women, and children homeless. In spite of these depredations, the strikers would persevere and win a major wage gain.

Their triumph against immense odds will stand as a symbol for the determination of working people to band together in defense of their class interests. Together these pickers overcame the unyielding refusal of growers to grant "their" labor the right to freely organize and bargain collectively. It was toward the end of 1933 when the thousands of workers in the Valley rose up as a body under the stewardship of the communist-led Cannery Union and insisted upon exercising those rights. In so doing they cracked open the repressive system of social stratification that allowed inhumane agricultural labor practices to flourish in the United States. As the strike unfolds in this retelling of events, we will also see the results of CAWIU's learning curve as the union honed the art of organizing among the agricultural proletariat. The CAWIU's leaders were now skilled in this task, and they maneuvered into the new territory with high hopes, unflinchingly confronting the issues raised by the conflicting class interests that prevailed in the cotton-rich San Joaquin Valley.

The previous organizing campaigns had been smaller in every respect. They had involved fewer workers, anywhere from several hundred to a few thousand strikers, and the extent of the agricultural base was smaller too. The San Joaquin Valley's cotton zone was vast, stretching one hundred miles in one direction and thirty to forty miles in the other, flowing across six counties and encompassing hundreds of widely distributed picker settlements.

After reviewing the specific circumstances that had led to the labor crisis in the Valley, the CAWIU's organizers developed an approach and a strategy. They had been badly punished in other strike venues, but they had learned tough, valuable lessons. They knew now, for instance, that they must neither trust, or tolerate, the participation of the Mexican consulate. This time the CAWIU came prepared for the manipulations and duplicity of consular officials. They had seen and heard these representatives of the Mexican government twisting their Mexican compatriots to their antiunion political ends. Cannery Union leaders had been thrown in jail in actions emanating from growers in alliance with the consulate and local authorities, and leaders had watched as emissaries of the Mexican government attempted repeatedly to undermine the union's influence and create a consul-run union (in league with the growers). This time, too, the Cannery Union recognized as fundamental to winning the necessity of forging as tight a bond as possible between themselves and the rank and file.

Organizing Plans

Organizing workers, the first step in a strike action, may be the most crucial exercise. The Cannery Union strategists respected the force of racial and national divisions and tensions running deep in U.S. society, particularly in the working class, and were aware of their presence among the workers in the Valley. Further, they believed that elements of a racialized culture within the working class could be overcome by the proper approach. They therefore made plans to deal with race as a factor in organizing the mix of workers in the Valley. (The strike itself, one might note, represented an example of racial animosity, as white landowners lined up against mostly nonwhite pickers.)

Several union leaders, among them Sam Darcy, designed a plan that would undercut the potential for racism and narrow nationalism, attitudes that could hinder the creation of a single, solid union. The approach would be to establish union leadership in each of the four communities that formed the picking force. It was recognized that through shared experiences in the fields and in the labor camps, and being well known to one another, certain natural and trusted leaders would emerge from such groups. The union's leaders would urge the active recruitment of these local leaders from each of the main workforce groups, with their different racial and ethnic mixes. With these particular leaders representing the rank and file of the core communities, it was hoped that racial tensions would ameliorate, and perhaps even dissipate entirely as a decisive element. In this way the CAWIU planned to integrate the leaders who would be guiding the rank and file, and eventually such a cadre would be capable of taking charge of the strike that was planned.

In addition to divisive racial issues, organizers had to overcome problems of old rivalries and antagonisms that would always be present but that were exacerbated by the harsh conditions of the settlements and camps. In this they were helped by the first combative skirmish at Woodville. It was a turning point, just four days after the strike was called, that brought strikers together. As Clete Daniel has shown, "separate groups of strikers quickly put aside their differences to defend themselves and their allies against a common foe." [1] That fierce but brief encounter not only strengthened the union but brought forward a charismatic leader. Bill Hammet, a displaced Oklahoma preacher they called Big Bill, became the leader and spokesperson for the strikers. Prodded by CAWIU leaders, Hammet organized and presided over a strike committee comprising Mexicans, Blacks, whites, and Filipinos. Supporting the strike committee and the rank and file were CAWIU organizers Darcy, Pat Callahan, Pat Chambers, Leroy Gordon, and Caroline Decker, who remained the force driving the union forward in the Valley.

Also working in the union's favor were the many workers who were familiar with the organizing process and the sacrifices to be made in a strike. Paul S. Taylor observed that during the San Joaquin cotton strike, the CAWIU had "organized many of the same people in other harvests" and that an experienced core "formed the nucleus of union leadership." [2]

Land Tenure in the Valley

To understand the genesis of the strike and its tortured path, we must examine the social disequilibrium that led inexorably to this event. One first recognizes that the poor, landless, agricultural proletariat in California worked under the strictures of a system based on a land oligopoly. That foundation differentiated California's land tenure pattern from those found in other states, particularly in the Midwest, and remained unchanged into the Depression era. This difference rested on the presence of a stream of cheap labor flowing from the country just the other side of California's southern border. It was Mexican workers who crossed over that border by the thousands to find work in the fields that made possible enormously profitable capitalist agriculture.

Ever since capitalist agriculture came into prominence in the Southwest in the second half of the nineteenth century, cheap labor has remained the indispensable component of production. Without that plentiful human resource, economic development over the first decade of this century would surely have been delayed and would have had a very different complexion. California's agricultural dominion, tantamount to a giant industrialized plantation, existed and flourished by virtue of the availability of this cheap, abundant, mobile, legally disenfranchised labor. This mass, made up largely of immigrants, was the essential harvesting mechanism that drove the monumental agricultural machine. Nonetheless, these workers had no political power, no "rights" as we know them. Growers had gathered all such power unto themselves, dominating state politics, local city councils, sheriffs, boards of supervisors, and the press. The vast financial interests of the agriculturalists allowed them to manipulate laws through legislative interventions, to subvert judges, and to affect decisions even at the federal level, including those of members of Congress at home and in Washington. All were seemingly at the beck and call of the growers.

In 1933 cotton was king in the Valley, but it had not always been so. In 1916, this crop was nearly nonexistent; only 3,000 bales of cotton, produced on a paltry 5,500 acres, were marketed. As the second decade came to a close, however, the state's cotton region began to shift from the Imperial Valley in the south to the northern San Joaquin Valley, and by the mid-twenties a nearly complete transition had taken place. As a result of the move to the vast, fertile San Joaquin Valley, cotton underwent a spectacular expansion that brought an unprecedented and continually increasing demand for labor. Ten years of steady growth overwhelmed the region with such bounty that by 1925 the 258,000 acres under cotton cultivation produced 233,308 bales. An expansion on this scale required capital, infrastructure, scientific methods, and, as has been shown, a large supply of cheap labor capable of maneuvering over the three-thousand-square-mile cotton zone. To preserve their hold over this gigantic enterprise, it was imperative that labor remain a "tool" in their hands rather than be acknowledged as politically independent workers. At all costs, outsiders would not be allowed to organize them.

Over the years, Valley acreage under cotton had become concentrated in the hands of a few colossal consortiums. Land expansion meant consolidation as the powerful land companies appropriated smaller plots, and by the end of the twenties, monopolistic enterprises virtually controlled the land and the industry. By 1930, only four ginners marketed the Valley's cotton, down from forty in 1910, and these giant enterprises controlled much of cotton financing as well. It was then that banks, large growers, and ginning companies joined forces to form the California Cotton Cooperative Association, consolidating their wealth and power into a social and political monolith that held dominion over the life of the Valley.

The Cooperative Association, together with railroads, trucking companies, and other ancillary industries, comprised a network of interlocking business interests that dominated the economic affairs of the Valley on the eve of the Depression. Such associations possessed enormous cash reserves for lending purposes. Valley banks and ginners financed most of the farms, and one gin company, Anderson Clayton, made available $6.5 million to growers in California and Arizona. The Bank of America held the lion's share of cotton loans, so that by 1929 the bank financed more than half the cotton supply through $10 million funneled primarily to the four gin companies.

Significantly, these four gin companies, in turn, redirected that financing in the form of small loans to cash-strapped farmers forced to mortgage crops and personal property. Guided by their combined and overlapping self-interests, these banks, monolithic farms, and ginning companies utilized the California Cooperative Cotton Association to control every factor of production.

In 1933 the Boston Land Company owned forty thousand acres, and the King's County Development Company owned thirty-four thousand. About half the cotton ranches, however, measured less than fifty acres, and some farms were as small as a few acres. The smaller growers who had bought in the early years before the rapid expansion of the twenties found they could not survive without borrowing. They were unable to cope with the higher costs of irrigation, technology, and rising land values (which led to higher taxes). As a result, many small outfits were forced into tenant farming, sharecropping, or wage labor on the larger ranches.

According to Devra Weber, some "moved back and forth on the lower rungs of the economic structure, between sharecropping, tenant farming, and wage work." Those who remained to eke out a precarious existence faced the combined power of the "large growers and ginners who ruled the economic, political, and social life of Valley towns."[3]

Having taken power, ginners used it to enforce loan agreements drawn up to favor their interests. What's more, such restrictive loan agreements became standard, industrywide practices. Finance contracts covered pricing and wages. They established prearranged sales prices and labor costs, which, in turn, forced smaller ranchers to pass on these set wage levels to their workforces. The immense resources of the larger enterprises conferred financial independence, but the smaller farmers were not so fortunate and soon found themselves in thrall to banks and ginners. Mortgaged "on nearly everything the grower has," farmers then passed on the financial burden embedded in the contracts to the picking force.[4] The discrepancy between large and small growers was a significant factor in shaping the organizational strategies of the CAWIU and leading the union to attempt an alliance with small farmers.

Labor and Community in the Valley

So much acreage was put under cotton during the twenties that it soon outstripped the available labor supply for picking. To build an adequate workforce, growers assigned recruiting agents to urban centers and ran newspaper ads and circulated flyers publicizing the availability of work in the fields. These efforts, initially pursued by individual landowners on a trial-and-error basis, soon evolved into a more organized approach, and a consortium of Valley cotton growers formed the San Joaquin Valley Agricultural Labor Bureau. The bureau's purpose was to recruit labor and organize it during the peak season and, not incidentally, to prevent the possibility of labor unionization.[5] Comprised of nine elected representatives engaged in supplying labor for producing the key agricultural crops from six counties, the bureau also set wage scales for harvesting various crops to forestall any upward swing. Wages were adjusted in a cooperative manner as the labor supply was threatened. A key figure in the process was bureau manager Frank Palomares; he exercised the broadest authority in securing the necessary laborers. Known up and down the state, the bilingual Palomares concentrated his efforts within the Mexican communities. Traveling frequently to urban centers in search of workers, he often negotiated with public charity bureaus and state employment offices.

From the perspective of large agricultural enterprises, Mexicans were an essential resource. S. Parker Frisselle, owner of the Kearney Ranch in northern California, candidly framed his colleagues' anxieties over cotton labor in testimony before a U.S. Congressional committee in 1926: "We must have labor, the Mexican seems to be the only available source."[6] An editorial in the *San Francisco Examiner,* sensitive to agricultural interests, addressed the growers' second question that Palomares sought to resolve: "The problem is to move the labor supply about rapidly as they are needed in each locality."[7]

In the early years of cotton development, laborers were secured from southern California, primarily the Los Angeles area, which came to be known as the "principal reservoir of California agricultural labor"; the Imperial Valley was a lesser source.[8] Paul S. Taylor had identified a considerable seasonal north-south migration of workers, numbering roughly thirteen thousand, that began with the spring and summer fruit harvests and carried into the fall cotton picking, which lasted until January or February, depending on conditions. Taylor also found, on the basis of rather informal research, that as the cotton acreage increased in the late twenties, the southbound migrations began to slow apace, "an indication," he concluded, "of permanent accretion of the Mexican population to the [San Joaquin] Valley of California."[9] In other words, Mexican laborers and their families remained.

Indeed, in response to the expanding Valley economy, the Mexican immigrants began to form communities wherever they could settle. The edges of the larger towns were probably the more desirable places, but many moved into private rented spaces or labor camps provided by growers and, when traveling, into camps alongside the roads and irrigation ditches. A tentative promise of employment through most of the year provided the incentive that made settlement, however rudimentary, a compelling choice to these workers. Understandably, since it served their objectives, the Agricultural Labor Bureau sought to encourage the establishment of these settlements. It showed no social or moral concerns, however, for the unspeakable conditions that prevailed.

As the agricultural labor force became a permanent presence, these settlements outside towns up and down the Valley multiplied, and within them was established, in spite of the poorest living conditions imaginable, a complex and rich social life. Ethnic and class transformation followed. *Colonias* in Selma, Hanford, Arvin, Tulare, Corcoran, Kingsburg, and the largest center, Fresno, became a series of hubs to which the laboring crews returned after temporary work migrations. On patches of land provided by the growers on the periphery of their fields and often remote from towns, laborers threw up their shanty camps and, against great odds, created a sense of community.

The California Division of Immigration and Housing studied camps in three Valley counties, 126 of them in Madera, Fresno, and Merced counties alone. In Madera, where 41 grower camps existed, workers lived in cabins and tents. One thousand cabins were counted. Of the approximately 500 tents that were counted, 116 had wooden floors and 300 to 400 did not. Extrapolating, it is probable that in the remaining 85 camps distributed throughout Fresno and Merced counties, more than six thousand persons accepted these deplorable accommodations as home and made of them their unique communities.[10]

Within those settlements populated by Mexican immigrant families, we find a variety of social organizations. Central to the building of community was the family, out of which grew mutual self-help societies, consulate-inspired patriotic committees, small businesses, organized recreation, and labor associations that, all in all, constituted a complex cultural life. The contemporary stereotype of Mexican laborers and their families as roaming the countryside without a home is mistaken. Permanent residence was the rule for most of the Valley's Mexican population; migrations were but temporary deviations. One study of fourteen cotton camps in three Valley counties found that 82 percent of all Mexican families "have either definite county residence or probable county residence" and that a "considerable group of people classified as 'migratory' are living year around under labor-camp conditions and do not migrate, but have continuous residence over a period of years."[11] The study also substantiates periods of flow: cotton pickers entered the annual job market in September and stayed until February or March, when they migrated to "the coast for peas and other early vegetables, and then to the coastal valleys for the fruit crop, and inland for the grapes and hops."[12] Worker migration, then, must more accurately be seen as a temporary move radiating from a base community (their homes), to which laborers returned when their stints of picking in distant fields had ended.

Creative forms of family and social structures developed, as Devra Weber points out, undergirding a network of communities that stretched across the Valley and beyond, extending as far as other regions of California and even Mexico. As was the case in Mexican communities throughout the United States, each Valley community developed a personality based upon a number of interacting factors. Central were the intimate Mexican traditions of self-help, *compadrazgo,* and family sharing that helped diminish the impoverished conditions that weighed heavily on the people. Nevertheless, the burden of subhuman wages that consigned these laborers and their families to such abject poverty could not have been easily borne, with or without the vitality of the community.

Growers preferred to hire Mexican workers with families for reasons associated with production costs. The family that was available in almost unlimited numbers ensured the grower a steadiness that a single worker was less likely to supply; and, as we have seen, wives and children brought their labor into the bargain. And a bargain it was: growers paid less per hour for the labor of women, and children cost the rancher nothing. Thus growers from Texas to California depended heavily upon these families to keep production costs down.[13] There was still another advantage for the grower of hiring families instead of solo laborers. When looking to hire a crew of pickers, contractors needed only seek out the head of a family to secure a platoon of laborers. Once again, we see demonstrated how closely hiring practices in the Valley resembled slavery, with its dependence on the family (as labor). But it must be pointed out that at least slaves were known to their owners, having been personally bought and paid for. Perhaps, unfortunately from the grower's viewpoint, the Mexicans were not actual slaves and must be paid—but paid as little as possible, it seems, for growers held wages at the lowest possible levels they could set.

Assembled by contractors under assignment by the grower or the ranch manager, pickers were anonymous hands because a picker seldom met face to face with the landowner. Contractors delivered crews to specified ranches to work at a per-pound piece rate, already set by the bureau (or individual owner) for so many hours, perhaps days. Most contracted workers gathered at a prearranged meeting place. If freelancing, however, they searched for work by car through the rural road network that cut across the vast verdant fields. Arriving at the picking place, whole families and single laborers filed into the fields. Individuals then separated as they entered the rows and began the arduous task of picking the cotton bolls off the rough, thorny bushes. Adults strapped a twelve-foot-long bag to one shoulder and either dragged it between their legs or draped it over their backs, where it trailed behind as, picking with both hands, they bent over the dark green cotton plants. Children picked nearby, following behind their parents or another relative. When filled, the bags were extremely heavy. A big man could carry as much as one hundred pounds. The best pickers could fill their bags three times a day if working a full day (from dawn to sunset).

Contractors recruited from the camps and *colonias* (and ghettoes), often assembling the same crew year after year. To land and keep a spot on a crew often required a kickback or a portion of the wage—an abuse pickers coped with in exchange for keeping their jobs. Contractors would also extend loans to their crews, provide a personal favor, or supply a needed good, practices that, though they led to personal ties, fitted into the scheme of the existing power relations and worked to the benefit of the grower, keeping work crews intact, bound by their debts to stay. These personalistic practices resembled, in some ways, the *patronismo* found in the haciendas of rural Mexico. By extending protection reminiscent of feudal class relations in rural Mexico, the *patrón*, in the form of the contractor, served to maintain the capitalist class relations in the Valley and the domination of growers over the workforce. Eventually, as the Depression deepened, the practice of loans and kickbacks was heavily abused as contractors began to exact ever-greater tribute without balancing the returns to the pickers. All the while, wages set by the Labor Bureau were falling far below subsistence levels. Additional costs to the picker also accrued from having to pay for as many as two picking sacks each season, at $1.50 and up, plus gasoline for their old and battered second-hand Fords and Chevys that were essential when searching for work along the migratory route.

Wages for cotton pickers varied depending upon skill and speed. Men could generally pick 200 to 300 pounds per day, women averaged only 150 pounds, and children dropped mere handfuls into their parents' sacks. In the mid-twenties, growers paid $1.00 to $1.65 per hundred pounds, but soon after the Depression hit, wages sank to rock bottom. Wages that had fallen to 20 cents per hundred pounds in 1932 rose to 40 cents in 1933. This was still far below the standard levels of the twenties. Assuming an excellent day's picking is 300 pounds at 40 cents per hundred pounds, the skilled picker could earn $1.20, his maximum for a day in the fields. By adding the contributions of his wife and children, the family earnings for one day's work could reach as high as $3.00. However, field conditions such as rain and small crop sizes often cut into the workday and the length of the season. Rarely, if ever, could workers count on a six-day week or the course of a full season. These, then, were the circumstances that prevailed on the eve of the great strike of 1933, and it seems evident that even the smallest increment of deterioration of the laborer's plight would be sufficient to disrupt the nervous equilibrium that existed between workers and growers.

What income was required for a family to survive during the Depression years? An independent estimate placed the "minimum subsistence budget" at $972 per year, while the Relief Administration considered $780 to be the lowest possible subsistence budget. One study by the California State Relief Administration undertaken in the mid-thirties showed that the median family income per year for California's agricultural workers stood at $574, far below the accepted standard for meeting the elementary needs of the average family.[14] Another survey conducted in 1935 by the State Relief Administration tracked 775 migratory families, averaging 4.5 family members, and found that "the average yearly earnings per family was only $289." Data demonstrates that a family could earn between $2 and $5 per day if picking conditions were at their best. However, according to one official report, in the course of an entire season, weekly earnings could be so seriously affected by the inevitable slack periods that "family incomes [could] average less than $2 per day."[15] A health nurse with seven years' experience in the cotton camps had tallied weeks worked and noted the breakdown as "about four weeks in October, three weeks in November, two weeks in December, a week or less in January [and February] and possibly a week in March."[16] After a careful study, an official with the California Department of Social Welfare concluded: "It is certainly safe to say that in the majority of cases the pickers do not earn enough throughout the year to provide more than minimum subsistence, and are far below the standard of a 'health and decency budget.' There is certainly no margin for medical care."[17]

Segregated from the community at large, pickers threw up their camps beside rail tracks, highways, and irrigation ditches. The town *colonias,* somewhat less crude, did offer the benefit of more stability. Yet agricultural laborers in general and Mexican pickers in particular could find some comfort in their sense of community. For those living in the camps, however, a community so rudimentary could offer little relief. Children, as noted, were contributors to the family income and, when making the migratory loop, attended mobile schools if they went to school at all. Schools let out early, at noon, so the children could begin working in the fields. In these segregated schools, teachers found that migratory children were "over-tired . . . restless and inattentive." Children were "so inadequately fed and clothed" that, as one teacher said, "about all we can do is to keep the stoves going so that the children will be warm until they have to go home again"[18] (or back to work beside their parents in the fields).

Camps were made up of usually self-segregated minorities, either Mexican or Black families. In one case, a camp with twenty-one cabins was managed by a Black laborer. Although the large southern California Mexican population supplied the greatest numbers of migrants, Blacks, although in lesser numbers, followed the same route. Paul S. Taylor estimated that more than three thousand entered the Valley during the 1927 and 1928 seasons. As in the case of Mexican migrants, Blacks settled into separate quarters in towns and in the labor camps.[19] Soon the two groups were joined by a third migrant stream made up of displaced white farmers and their families from the Dust Bowl states, Arkansas, Oklahoma, and

Texas. Together, the three groups, plus a modicum of Filipinos, comprised the entire cotton labor force in the Valley. Most camps, as stated, were self-segregated, but some were biethnic. One example, the Bonita camp, had opened its doors to white and Mexican families, and both groups shared in the community, picking side by side in the fields. In the absence of proper sanitary conditions, children were often sick and health problems were prevalent. According to the study of cotton migrants at the Bonita camp, "of the twenty-six children examined, only three were without defects." Four children suffered malnutrition and five others had rickets. Other children had tonsillitis, badly decayed teeth, and sundry health problems. The income of one white family, reported a health official, did not allow for much needed "dentistry, medical supervision, clothing, and milk." [20] Down the dusty alley, "which turned to deep mud . . . after a light rain," lived a typical Mexican family. The State Welfare Department reported: "One young Mexican . . . says he can earn only $2.50 a day picking cotton as he is not a fast picker. He and his wife, together, earn about $4.00 a day in the peas, each working ten hours. This is only for a short period of time and involves traveling a long distance. The children are malnourished and need cod liver oil, but the father, who seems devoted to them, says he cannot afford to buy it." [21]

The trials of camp living affected all families—Mexican, Black, white, and Filipino—equally. All children suffered malnutrition equally, and parents endured miserable wages together. According to the California Social Welfare Department study, camp families "are living under housing conditions which in general are very bad, and at best inadequate. They have irregular employment, and insufficient income to provide for periods of unemployment. Their children are growing up without an opportunity for normal education and recreation. . . . The medical care which they need is not available to them." The report made a further judgment regarding these migrants, alleging that "they cannot form community ties." [22] In fact, the Mexicans who had congregated in these tattered communities along the migratory routes were able to establish linkages with distant friends and family; they interacted with town dwellers and participated in the activities of the Mexican *colonia*. In Bertha Underhill's study of fourteen labor camps in three Valley counties, one typical camp "made up entirely of Mexicans" stationed ten miles from the nearest town consisted of thirteen cabins "in very bad repair" with extremely poor sanitation. Yet, Underhill observes that "an atmosphere of contentment and well-being in the camp blossomed among the thorns." [23] Shared experience and the productive process itself lent themselves to broader community culture. All pickers suffered under the same crushing poverty. The shared experience of picking and living together had, in forging a sense of community and connection, created the political base that could, and did, generate the impetus and energy for a strike movement, and this helps explain the high level of unity achieved over the course of the struggle.

The Mexican Connection: Consul Enrique Bravo

By the end of July, the fires of the Los Angeles County strike had turned to smoldering embers. Meanwhile, the strikes that had flared in other locales before reaching the San Joaquin Valley had ended. The tumultuous early thirties had drawn the consulates into the strike arena, and the San Joaquin strike provided the second opportunity for significant consular intervention. The strike involved a rather simple dialectic: on the one side, the CAWIU and the rank and file, and facing them, the combined front of growers; local, state, and federal authorities; and the Mexican consulate. Although several accounts of the event offer a vivid impression of that deadly yet successful strike, none has provided an adequate analysis which portrays and explains the central role played by the Mexican consul, Enrique Bravo, and his assistant, Fresno *Comisión Honorífica* President Leonsio Acosta. Bravo and Acosta were to earn the very highest praise from growers, local and federal officials, and their superiors in Mexico City, leaving no doubt as to whom the two men would pledge their loyalties. In efforts reminiscent of those of Ricardo Hill and Armando Flores in the Los Angeles County strike, Bravo and Acosta joined with state and federal mediators and campaigned to separate Mexican strikers from their affiliation with the Cannery Union. What's more, they attempted to represent the pickers themselves. Bravo's vigorous efforts were less successful than those of Vice-Consul Hill, and he failed to draw Mexican strikers away from "red" leaders. The strike force remained unified under the Cannery Union's leadership throughout the three-week offensive. Notably, sensing the strength of the CAWIU behind them, workers felt empowered to withstand the aggressions of grower vigilantism.

Just who was this man, Enrique Bravo? As were many of his colleagues, Bravo was schooled in the United States. After completing his course of study at the elite Escuela Nacional Preparatoria in Mexico City, Bravo was personally awarded a monthly stipend by President Obregón to study finance at the University of Texas at Austin. After earning a bachelor's degree, Bravo attended Columbia University for one year, taking courses in finance and earning unimpressive grades (he failed English composition). Before entering the consular service in 1925, he held a number of positions in the United States, including that of translator in

Austin, Texas, and as correspondent for the Brentano Bookstore in New York City.

In 1925 Bravo entered the foreign service and was first posted to the New York consulate. He was promoted to vice-consul in 1926 and later transferred to Detroit, Michigan, where he served under Consul Joaquín Terrazas. (Terrazas figured prominently in the Imperial Valley strikes of 1933 and 1934, as we shall see in the next chapter.) From Detroit, Bravo traveled officially to Lyons, France, and then in 1929 to Los Angeles. In 1931, owing to the growth of the Mexican community in the expanding agricultural districts, and after careful review, superiors in Mexico City declared their intentions of founding a new consulate in the San Joaquin Valley in the city of Fresno.[24] Up to that time, Fresno had been under the administration of the Los Angeles consulate. The planned consulate was scheduled to hold jurisdiction over fifteen counties, stretching from the Sierra Nevada mountain range in the east across the low coastal mountains to the counties lined along the Pacific.

It was Vice-Consul Bravo who received instructions and the honor of establishing this new consulate in the San Joaquin Valley town. Bravo would be overseeing well-developed and highly organized communities. *Comisiones honoríficas* functioned at Hanford, Pinedale, Tulare, and Fresno; lodges and self-help societies operated in Madera, Fresno, and Selma. A Mexican school, the Escuela Mexicano Benito Juárez, taught *mexicanidad* to the children of the Fresno *colonia*. As is evident, Bravo had led a very uncommon and privileged life, one far removed from the socializing experiences of the masses of compatriots whom he would be representing before the varied institutions of the United States. Nevertheless, within the month, Enrique Bravo was elevated to consul, taking full charge of the Mexican consulate. He immediately moved center stage amid joyous greetings from Fresno's surrounding *colonias* at a reception in his honor.

Over one thousand compatriots, including the most prominent leaders, filled the hall to overflowing to welcome Bravo and his wife. They were, it is reported, "warmly applauded" as they proceeded into the hall, while the local orchestra played a "march of reception." Upon ascending the dais, and after the Mexican National Anthem had been rendered, the audience rose in a "frenetic applause that lasted for some minutes."[25] Bravo would have been well pleased. All of the *colonia* societies, including the *comisiones,* sent their representatives. Hosting the reception was Leonsio Acosta, president of the Fresno *comisión honorífica* and a veteran of the Mexican Revolution in Chihuahua. It was Acosta who made the solemn official introduction that welcomed Bravo to the Valley and officially introduced him to the hundreds of celebrants. Bravo was regaled with poetry recitations, youth chorus renditions, and a roster of speakers and salutes. He then delivered his inaugural address, which *La Opinión* described as "an extensive and judicious peroration upon topics of interest to all Mexicans."[26] The public ceremony, which had begun at three o'clock in the afternoon, lasted until six. At eight in the evening the festivities continued as the Bravos were fêted at a private banquet held at the "elegant restaurant Morelos." Leonsio Acosta served as toastmaster at the elaborate party hosted by a select group of forty prominent *colonia* leaders. The traditional ceremonies were described by one reporter as "characterized by cordiality and grand enthusiasm," and it was not until close to midnight that the Bravos, the guests of honor, and the invited dignitaries departed, "taking with them the most pure and honorable memories of a brilliant and sumptuous fest."[27]

As their respected consul, Bravo commanded the allegiance of the Mexican *colonia* in the region from the start. This allegiance was useful, and Bravo took full advantage of his position to forge stronger links with the *colonia* and establish and extend the new consulate's influence. He was successful. Just eight months after his brilliant reception, Bravo was able to report to the Secretariat of Foreign Relations that he had established a Confederación de Sociedades Mexicanas and fourteen *comisiones honoríficas* and was in the process of setting up eleven more of the latter.[28]

Bravo was welcomed, as we have seen, with open arms. But his future was not to be perfectly smooth despite the initial red-carpet treatment. Bravo's aggressive campaign to extend his jurisdiction and power had created resentment and opposition. Soon he was complaining to his superiors concerning the "petty town politicking" among the societies, alleging "abuses, fraud, and exploitation," in particular during the Independence Day celebrations. Bravo's enemies in the *colonia* responded in kind, accusing Bravo of public drunkenness and other acts of misconduct. Bravo, not to be outdone, hurled epithets at his accusers, calling them cowards and "pochos" (an insulting term for Americanized Mexicans). Bravo, a member of society's elite class, did not hesitate to characterize the president of one self-help lodge, the Alianza Hispano Americana, as having "the worst ancestors." Unsurprisingly, Bravo was finding the Fresno *colonia* too stressful and turbulent a neighborhood. Thus, within his first year as consul, Bravo expressed his desire to move his residence to another locale and further requested that the consulate be removed to a "better area." He whined that his compatriots came at all hours of the night with petty problems that he could not possibly resolve. Again expressing his sense of place and privilege, he justified his request to remove the consulate office, in part, on the claim that it was rare, particularly in Fresno's Mexican *colonia* of six thousand, to find "three people who have the fifth year of instruction, the majority are manual laborers."[29] Bravo's pious superiority to the oppressed people he had been sent to represent served to isolate him in the tough environs of the Valley. In spite of his elitist demeanor, Bravo had managed to forge a significant bond with a key *colonia* leader, Leonsio Acosta. Together, two years after the consulate was established, they formed a tight partnership that would prove formidable as they joined the ensuing strike action with the intention of subverting it and became a major obstacle in the path of the Cannery Union and the strikers.

The Strike

The wide distribution of picker communities and their cultural and social structures shaped the organizational design of the union. Twenty-five locals were established in widely separated picker quarters. Living rooms, pool halls, saloons, and other community gathering spots served as union meeting halls. In Delano, union members met at the Old Monte Carlo Saloon; in the Wasco area, the Salón Mexicana de Billares alternated as the union hall; the Porterville local met in a room at 109 Third Street.[30] And so it went throughout the Valley floor during the organizing months of August and September.

By the fall of 1933, the union had begun a pragmatic organizing strategy based on preexisting community culture and structures. It was a lucky break for the few Cannery Union organizers that an intricate web of work relations and cultural practices, particularly among Mexicans, already existed and would facilitate organizing. Moreover, many pickers had prior union experience: some had participated in labor strikes in Mexico, and others had taken part in one of the strikes in Oxnard, Lodi, Fresno, or San Jose, among other places. The Cannery Union's reputation had preceded it. Workers had heard the news of the Cannery Union's winning some strikes against growers by the time the organizers first entered the cotton region in August. In any case, after years of starvation wages, the picking force was bound to respond to anyone or any institution that would hear their grievances, and fight for them. Thus they needed little prodding to join a strike. After years of starvation wages, a strike seemed reasonable, even necessary.

Two weeks before the start of the picking season, and after only six weeks of union organizing in the Valley, representatives from each of the locals that had been established met and announced, as reported, that "a cotton strike will be called in ten days unless their demands were met," according to the *Berkeley Daily Gazette*.[31] Pickers asked for one dollar per hundred pounds of cotton, abolition of the contractor system, a union hiring hall, and most important, union recognition. On the following day, Pat Callahan attended a growers' meeting and officially placed the union demands before the bosses. The growers stonewalled; no discussion took place. They refused to address the proposals and dismissed Callahan from the meeting. A strike now loomed in the immediate future. A few days later, the San Joaquin Agricultural Labor Bureau formally announced the season's wage scale at 60 cents per hundred pounds, up from 40 cents the year before but well below the union demand. Adamant in its position, the union stood firm at one dollar and made preparations to strike.

On October 2, Callahan announced the locals' decision to strike in two days throughout the San Joaquin Valley cotton fields. Thousands had already walked out, and numbers grew to five thousand by the date of the walkout. On October 4, picking came to a near halt as somewhere between twelve thousand and eighteen thousand walked out of the fields to engage in what Sam Darcy would describe as "the toughest strike I ever knew."[32] Whenever the Cannery Union entered an area, shrill political alarms sounded, directing growers to prepare for battle against the "invasion" of "reds" and "agitators." Arrayed against the union stood a formidable phalanx: the growers, the political and economic force in the Valley, and their chief allies, the banks and ginning companies. Lined up behind the dominant groups stood a parade of dependencies: the police, sheriffs, courts, chambers of commerce, local elected public officials, and state and federal authorities. Also wedded to the growers' cause was the Mexican consulate (which had played a prominent part in the Los Angeles, Oxnard, and Guadalupe strikes). Consul Enrique Bravo and his associate Cónsul Honorífico Leonsio Acosta, as we shall see, represented the interests of the Mexican government (but not the Mexican strikers) over the duration of the three-week conflict. Those interests, in strongly opposing the union, were identical to those of the political and economic establishment. Ultimately, the consulate and the growers fought side by side against the union.

The enormous social and political chasm which cut across California's agricultural society (and which originated in the state's industrialized agricultural system) was laid bare when the two classes collided in the picking fields. Historically a subordinate and powerless class, farmworkers threatened to take back unto themselves power held exclusively by the dominant classes in the Valley. At once, growers and other forces tradi-tionally aligned with the growers, either because of self-interest or be-cause of a shared political ideology, coalesced into a united front. Facing these combined powers was a union of cotton pickers. The two forces, their antagonisms rooted in the productive process, prepared for battle. It would be a bitter, violent, even deadly one.

As the "walkout spread from town to town" and camp to camp, thirty elected delegates comprising the union's central strike committee voted immediately to begin "strong militant picket lines." Meanwhile, calls went out throughout the state for support, particularly food supplies, which began to arrive and allowed families to subsist. In order to forestall scabbing, the union organized unemployed councils in the larger towns.[33] Organizing continued as new locals formed. Delegations were assigned to invite workers at various camps and communities to join the movement. Appeals went out to poor farmers "to join them in their fight against their common enemy, the finance corporations," although without much suc-cess as smaller farmers found it difficult to break away from the domina-tion of the economic giants.[34]

In the little Valley towns affected by the strike, not every shopkeeper was unsympathetic to the pickers. Some knew many of the strikers as regular customers and would extend credit or donate money and food. Growers reacted to such kindly acts by taking out newspaper ads that warned store owners to cease cooperating with the unionists or face dire consequences.

Demonstrations, mass meetings, and marches down main streets car-ried the union message to the Valley towns. But newspapers thumped the drums for the other side, showing their pro-grower bias in supportive headlines. "Growers Plan to Break Valley Cotton Strike" was the headline that ran on the front page of the *Visalia Times-Gazette* early in the strike. Protective leagues and other associations of growers sprang up through-out the Valley, in the words of one news article, in order to "resist wage increase demands of striking pickers" and "rid the district of all strikers and strike leaders."[35] Their superior power and position naturally fed growers' confidence. An October 6 offer by state officials to mediate the strike was abruptly rejected. Instead, the growers began a campaign of harassment, even terrorism, that would have serious effects on workers' lives. Without notice, families were evicted from the labor camps by armed growers who marched into the camps and forcibly removed pick-ers and their belongings from the cabins, sending people and things spill-ing out onto the highways. It is well documented that at a Wasco camp "an army of between 200 and 300 armed farmers . . . demanded evacuation." While at the Peterson ranch, "75 growers . . . gave the occupants of the cotton camp five minutes to get their sacks and start for the field. Those who did not wish to work were instructed to leave the camp immediately. The proposition . . . was received with derision." An entire community of 150 Mexican pickers and their families was sent onto the highways, and the camps were deserted by the evening.[36]

By the end of the first week, the power of the growers appeared unassailable. Many workers had been reduced to roadside wanderers: with no place to turn, they must settle. Still they persevered. It was then that the first physical violence flared. Described as a "free for all fight," seventy growers attempted to break up a strike meeting being held in the town of Woodville. The growers "were repulsed by a large band of strikers who had assembled for a mass meeting," according to one journalist. The same reporter noted that the incident, which led to greater solidarity among the workers, "occurred when the ranchers drove up to the mass meeting with the intention of breaking up and sending the agitators on their way. The two groups clashed and the ranchers, out-numbered by the strikers, were forced to retire." One rancher's arm was broken, another badly beaten, while strikers endured cuts and traumas.[37]

The outcome of the Woodville "free for all," in which the growers suffered a defeat, merely served to increase their determination to destroy the union. They were now armed and dangerous as they prepared to use extralegal force. Law enforcement agencies, in league with the growers, patrolled roads, molesting caravans of pickets and arresting pickets for minor infractions when possible, often ironically, on charges of blocking highways. As one highway patrolman said, their job was to "keep the strikers moving" to prevent picketing.

Two months before the strike began, law officials, already reacting to the unrest in the camps, had developed tactical plans to contain a possible strike; in this they were guided by their own county sheriff, George J. Overholt. It was at the annual August convention of the California Peace Officers, held in Fresno, that Overholt declared his support for the growers. Overholt also suggested measures officers could use to override laws that he worried were too restrictive and might thereby weaken or eliminate the range of tactics available to officers when confronted with a strike. Los Angeles Police Chief James J. Davis also spoke at the convention, sympathetically noting that Overholt was "suffering from what we are all suffering." He went on to outline specific strategies: "with all that you now have, I would suggest that you use it through your local judges to give every agitator the limit for disturbing the peace or inciting a riot or destruction of property or any other charge you can put against them." Chief Davis's advice received a round of applause and in effect gave law enforcement in the Valley the go-ahead to use all force necessary to bring the pickers around.[38]

It was a mandate for vigilantism. Now fully protected by local and state law enforcement agencies, armed growers roared down the dusty roads intimidating caravans of strikers on their way to picket lines. The *San Francisco Examiner* described one encounter in Tulare County: "Accompanied by 40 deputies, Sheriff Hill caught up with a caravan of strikers headed toward Earlimart from Corcoran. He halted the trucks, ordered all of the occupants onto the road, then arrested the drivers and confiscated the 10 vehicles. The arrested men and the machines were sent to the County Jail here under an escort of armed deputies. The strikers were left to make their way back to their camps on foot." [39]

Forced evacuations had removed thousands of pickers and their families to five concentrated settlements. The largest tent camp, a shanty town, sprouted overnight in Corcoran. It was named "Little Mexico" by its three thousand or so inhabitants who pitched their makeshift homes under the surveillance of police, sheriffs, and highway patrol. Ironically, the punishing chaos of dispossession merely served to strengthen the strikers' resolve to fight the growers who were responsible for their relocation, and in their new proximity the workers found themselves bound ever more tightly together by the same goals. So it was that these evictions, these armed intimidations, had failed to weaken the strike; like metal tempered by fire, the growers' deprivations only made the strikers' resolve more steely.

The stubborn willfulness of the strike force seemed to inflame the growers' minds. Who did these bands of pickers think they were? No strangers to guns, the growers had been arming themselves steadily with the help of the sheriff's office. And now, finally, a self-righteous anger, fueled by an arrogance that class superiority confers, reached the danger point. Already skating on the very edges of the law, growers were about to go beyond the point at which murder could be committed and justified afterwards. On October 9, C. H. Earnest, head of the McFarland local, wired President Roosevelt to warn him of impending violence and to make an urgent appeal for protection. "Esteemed Sir," began Earnest's wire,

Thousands of people are out on strike in the cotton fields in the San Joaquin Valley(.) our local union has observed the law(,) we have resorted to no violence we shall not resort to any(.) there has been gun play by our opponents(.) the gin and finance companies are active against us(.) having little money we have little influence(.) the forces of law have permitted the ranchers to be armed(.) we are being threatened to be mobbed and our camps raided by gunmen and our women and children murdered(.) we are advised this violence is to occur tomorrow morning(.) we are only asking for a living wage(.) we trust and believe you will take action to protect our families against violence(.)[40]

The next day, October 10, three men were murdered and nine more people suffered gunshot wounds, including a woman. In the worst incident, a strike demonstration in Pixley, where women, men, and children had gathered for a mass meeting, ranchers carrying shotguns ambushed the crowd and fired directly into the unarmed workers and their families. Two men were shot and killed. One was president of a *comisión honorífica* investigating the strike for Consul Bravo. The other man was a striking picker. In addition to the murdered men, almost a dozen people suffered gunshot wounds. As the first shots rang out, frightened people ran across the street seeking the protection of their union hall. The growers continued to shoot volley after volley into the retreating crowd. The dead and wounded littered the street and sidewalk. Eyewitness testimonies captured the slaughter. "The cotton fields of Tulare are stained with strikers' blood today," wrote a journalist for the *San Francisco News*.

Two short-torn flags droop over the doorways that framed the brutal shooting of unarmed strikers as they peacefully entered their headquarters. . . . I saw eleven unarmed persons shot down in cold blood. One was a women. Two were killed. . . . The slaughter had been sudden almost like an ambush. . . . The strikers broke, ran into their red brick, two storied headquarters building. All but a few. They lay on their own tracks where the farmers' bullets had dropped them. Some lay very still. Others weakly pulled themselves up by their elbows, tried to crawl to safety. . . . For several minutes the farmers kept their sniping attack with their guns. The flags over the doorways danced a grotesque jig as shots ripped through their stars and stripes.[41]

When the firing stopped, a nearby State Highway Patrol car moved up. The officers stood by for several minutes but did nothing. The growers sped off in their automobiles, still pointing their weapons out through the open windows. After hesitating and seeming to mull over a course of action, the patrolmen then moved forward, stopped the caravan, and confiscated the growers' weapons. No arrests were made.

Later that afternoon Pedro Subia died from eleven gunshot wounds. He had been shot by growers breaking up a mass demonstration taking place in the town of Arvin. Paul S. Taylor summarized the testimony at the inquest hearing, which, he wrote, "indicated that only the growers were armed and the consensus of opinion was that all the shots, variously estimated at from five to 100 [sic] came from . . . the growers' side of the road." [42]

Eight growers were eventually charged with the Pixley slayings. Nine strikers were arrested for the Arvin death. Pat Chambers, the Cannery Union leader, was indicted and jailed on "criminal syndicalism" charges. All arrested ranchers were released on bail, and several months after the hostilities had ended, a jury declared them innocent of all charges. The crimes went unpunished. Law enforcement agencies responded to overtures to undermine the CAWIU and openly sided with the growers. As one sheriff put it, "We protect our farmers here in Kern County. They are our best people. They keep the country going . . . we serve them. But the Mexicans are trash. They have no standard of living. We herd them like pigs." [43] Thus, it speaks to the power of the growers and the ruling class that in the aftermath of the violence against unarmed people there was complete amnesty and a general justification for the armed ranchers who had fired the bullets.

The state's efforts to act as mediators and settle the strike by arbitration had failed, the growers having refused to go along. Later, the federal government tried to bring the growers to the bargaining table but with the same results. Growers might have gone along in perfect safety in view of the pro-grower bias in evidence among state and federal authorities.

The union, meanwhile, maintained a well-organized strike in spite of the growers' escalation of force. Furthermore, strikers stuck to the original demands they had laid out in early October. But to the growers, the tenacity with which the laborers met the harassment and violence used against them was hard to believe. It belied the contemporary racial stereotypes of "peon Mexican labor," "white trash," and "colored folk." The mobs' attacks failed to move their "natural inferiors" to their knees and, in an unforeseen side effect, had created some public opinion sympathetic to the farmworkers.

The final phase of the strike began on October 13 when Deputy Commissioner Edward H. Fitzgerald of the Department of Labor's United States Conciliation Service convinced leading growers to defer to an independent mediation commission that would investigate the claims of both sides as a step toward settlement. Fitzgerald expected that the proposed commission would act as an arbitration board and that during the arbitration process all strikers would be expected to "return to work immediately." [44] According to Taylor, the commissioner "conferred with the growers and attempted to secure a commission satisfactory to them, and he refused to treat with the communist leaders, dealing only with the Mexican consul and individual strikers." [45]

As these maneuvers aimed at bringing the sides to agree on procedure went forward, Consul Bravo and his associate stepped up their activities. Bravo and Acosta remained on the sidelines during much of the first week of the strike. However, after the shootings at Pixley and Arvin, Bravo made a dramatic plea to Governor Rolph to order the disarmament of the growers. According to Bravo, growers emboldened by "radical tendencies" were "using force" although pickers were "in perfect spirit to abide by the laws." Concurrent with his urgent telegram to the governor, Bravo embarked on a parallel mediation effort with Federal Labor Commissioner Edward Fitzgerald. Bravo now took his place among the high-profile players: Fitzgerald; George Creel, director of the Western District office of the National Recovery Administration; Governor James Rolph Jr.; Frank MacDonald, state labor commissioner; and the San Joaquin Cotton Growers Committee of the California Farm Bureau Federation.

Labor Commissioner MacDonald reported that an organized campaign involving state and Mexican government authorities operating early on sought to end the strike. "Owing to the tense, dangerous situation maintaining in the strike area," wrote MacDonald, "the deputy labor commissioners in the district and I, assisted by the Mexican Consuls E. Brava [sic] and J. L. D. Acosta [sic], redoubled our efforts to bring about a termination of the strike."[46] According to MacDonald, formal conferences between himself, Fitzgerald, Bravo, and Acosta with "a committee representing cotton growers, the cotton gin owners, representatives of financial interests and others in the Farm Bureau Headquarters in Visalia" held discussions relating to ending the strike through mediation. It might be presumed that Bravo's participation in those critical meetings would be as a de facto representative of the Mexican workers and their interests. However, the consul had not supported the strike action, and would, without hesitation, ratify the mediators' plan to end the strike immediately without meeting the union's demands.

Once federal officials had decided the form the mediation process should take, a fact-finding commission was established on October 13, whereupon Bravo expanded his role further by formally joining that effort. Fitzgerald hoped to achieve a strike amnesty pending the outcome of mediation by ignoring union leadership and dealing only with "individual pickers . . . to represent the strikers during negotiations." Bravo allied himself with Fitzgerald in this maneuver. A newspaper reported that Bravo "agreed to cooperate with the movement for arbitration and said he would urge his countrymen to return to work pending negotiations." Fitzgerald and Bravo journeyed together through the countryside on a mission to "select two representatives from each of the cotton camps, who will meet with the arbitration board [i.e., the fact-finding commission]."[47] Bravo also toured the camps alone and even attended Cannery

Union meetings carrying his urgent appeals to the workers. One newspaper was prompted to proclaim, "The San Joaquin Cotton Strike is over. Pickers will be on the fields on Monday." [48]

The union mounted its own counter-campaign to help workers stand up to Bravo's attempts to roll back the strike. But it was Bravo who received news coverage. "I am very glad to have a chance to help in settling this matter," he said to a reporter, and promised that he would "try to convince the Mexican pickers to accept the price set by the arbitration board, but they tell me that they cannot live on 60 cents per hundred." Bravo's endeavors relieved growers, and in one article a rancher was said to be optimistic that "the situation appeared . . . well on its way to settlement and expressed belief that the strike would be abandoned." [49]

At this time, sheriffs and police were in the process of deputizing growers (a way of authorizing them to carry arms and use them if necessary). Bravo was making the rounds of camps and *colonias* in Tulare and Kings Counties on October 12 and presented strong appeals to the strikers "not to take part in any parade to Visalia or other communities." Bravo claimed that "he had talked to most of the Mexican leaders and that they had promised not to participate in marches proposed by the union."

Newspapers looked favorably upon Bravo's sudden jump into the conflict and made a point of presenting his optimistic political perspective on the union and the strike. [50] The October 13 front-page headline in the *Visalia Times-Delta,* "Mexican Consul Says Nationals Ready to Go Back to Work," repeating Bravo's claim, was followed by an editorial in the Visalia newspaper describing Bravo as the "authority for the statement that his nationals are ready to return to work at the 60 cents per hundred pounds which the growers had been paying." [51] The next day the same newspaper again praised Bravo in an editorial for "urging strikers to return to work" and for "aiding, not hindering, the cotton harvest." [52]

Growers found a faithful ally in Bravo and an extremely valuable one. As an official of the Mexican government, Bravo had close political and cultural relations to the picking force, but he was quite willing to work for the growers' side. Media reports showed Bravo urging strikers to refrain from violence, demonstrations, and picketing. He continued to apply himself diligently to convincing pickers to return to work pending arbitration, and would always tell workers that the Mexican government stood ready to protect its nationals. This message must have had considerable appeal, but the true meaning of these statements is not clear. Bravo and Acosta adapted quickly to the escalating affair with an ambitious plan to exercise leadership among their compatriots. Consul Bravo's claim that he now spoke for all Mexican pickers was accepted by the growers and greatly appreciated. The consul was their man.

With federally sponsored mediation looming, Governor Rolph and Fitzgerald announced their confidence in an early settlement. According to the *San Francisco Examiner,* Rolph "based his optimism on communications with Enrique Bravo . . . who has been investigating the trouble in the San Joaquin Valley. . . . Bravo assured the Governor that 95 percent of the strikers were Mexicans, that they will abide by the law, and will return to work if given assurances their differences with the farmers will be submitted to fair arbitration."

When strike leader Big Bill Hammet heard that Bravo was presenting himself as a spokesman for the Mexican pickers and was reporting their willingness to abandon picket lines and return to work, Hammett responded sharply. "This Mexican consul is trying to split us up into two groups, Mexicans and Americans. We are not going to let him do it. We are going to stick together." [53] In fact, attempts by Bravo to turn Mexican pickers against their leadership, particularly the Cannery Union's white cadre, had been witnessed by the press. On October 17, news reporters observed Bravo at an early morning McFarland gathering where he addressed "a large band of strikers [and] urged them to join for arbitration," avoid violence, and observe the laws. He ended his talk by suggesting that sharp differences distinguished the strikers from their leaders, and he asked of his primarily Mexican audience, "Show me a single leader or agitator who has ever picked a stalk of cotton." [54] While Bravo and the growers entered into a formal strategic alliance, the union campaigned to expose Bravo's complicity with its avowed enemies.

During burial ceremonies held at St. Aloysius Catholic Church for two of the three Mexicans killed on October 10, some 1,500 unionist marchers carried a variety of placards. One announced, "The Mexican Consul Represents Mexican Bosses." [55] By then, the focus of the ten-day-old strike had devolved upon mediation and Consul Bravo. The Cannery Union took on Consul Bravo without hesitation, targeting him for a barrage of sharp attacks in Spanish and English via mass flyers as well as articles in its regular union newsletter. One Spanish-language flyer with the subtitle "Patrol the Consul" labeled Bravo the "agent of the growers." In the words printed on the mimeographed flyer, "The consul appeals to our patriotism knowing that that is his principal weapon, and saying that he had nothing against the union, but we know that he supports a Mexican union which would cause divisions among the people. The consul and his representative [Acosta] are agents of Mexican financiers controlled by American capital. . . . Compañeros, do not allow the consul and his lackeys to break our strike. . . ." [56] Another flyer commissioned by the strike committee three weeks into the strike, declared that "we had the consul and his agents on the scene trying to divide the Mexicans and whites. And he failed! In a few locals, for example, in Wasco, Shafter, provocateurs were brought in and some discontent was created among the workers."[57]

Based on information from both union literature and the pro-grower press, the consul actively and openly engaged the grower cause, a participation that accelerated after the Pixley and Arvin shootings. Paul S. Taylor concluded, on the basis of his firsthand observations, that "[e]fforts were . . . made on behalf of the growers, and through the Mexican consul, to undermine the confidence of the strikers in their communist leaders, to induce the formation of separate unions on the basis of nationality groups, and to invite direct dealings between strikers' representatives and growers, which would ignore the communist dominated leadership."[58]

The Cannery Union allowed Bravo to enter its camps to address meetings and rallies, a tactical decision based on respect, common language, culture, and nationality that tied the Mexican laborers, in particular the elderly pickers, to the consul. Steeped in the tradition of rural Mexico, the older pickers revered the authority of the central government and "wanted to rise and bow when the consul came in."[59] The leaders acknowledged the consul's attraction, and as one commented, "But the workers did not know him . . . so we had to tell the workers about Bravo. He went around to the camps and spoke to the Mexicans. We had to permit him to enter the camp," but we "also had to tell the workers about Bravo . . . we thought it was better to let him speak and let him expose himself." In spite of the opening, Bravo failed to deliver. At the Corcoran camp, Bravo made his usual pitch, urging strikers to "form their own union." The *Fresno Bee* alleged that the consul acted in concert with growers when he addressed the Corcoran strikers:

After his meeting with the growers and gin men, Bravo went to the strikers' camp in Corcoran where he addressed some 2,000 workers. He told them a straight-forward story of the attitude of the growers and suggested that they deal directly with the growers through their own committee of workers rather than through the white strike agitators. . . . His address did not meet with the approval of strike leaders. . . . At Pixley last night, a Mexican consular representative (Acosta?) was reported to have attempted to break up the strike union by trying to get Mexican strikers to separate and form their own union.[60]

A *La Opinión* correspondent described a similar maneuver, and fate, at an October 14 Tulare strike meeting: "In the afternoon, the Cannery and Agricultural Workers Industrial Union that directs the strike convened a meeting at the International Pool Hall attended only by union members. The meeting was in progress when Señor Enrique Bravo, Mexican consul in Fresno, arrived and was received with applause by the Mexican strikers. Consul Bravo spoke to the compatriots and, according to the information I could gather, the consul's words went contrary to their expectations and unfavorable for the strikers."[61] Again, Bravo made little headway in that foray, but he announced that he would attend an open-air mass meeting in a public park to deliver yet another appeal to return to work. However, the consul never even appeared at that, having apparently been unnerved by the cold reception from his compatriots on the previous night. A strike leader commented with obvious satisfaction that "Bravo spoke only once in each camp. He never went back. The Mexicans understood him. They knew he wanted to break the strike—divide the ranks. They saw the whites and Negroes and Mexicans all working together . . . they wanted to go on that way."[62]

Bravo served growers and federal efforts at mediation and also fulfilled independent instructions from his superiors "to the letter." Stationed in San Francisco, Consul General Alejandro Lubbert maintained contact with the State Department of Industrial Relations and Fitzgerald. In a strike report to Mexico City, Lubbert wrote that he "occupied himself in finding a solution to the conflict." On October 14, shortly after Bravo began his strategic campaign, Lubbert wired Mexico City: "Consul Bravo has received instructions as indicated to me [by the Secretariat of Foreign Relations]."[63] One newspaper commented that Bravo's pleas with strikers—to accept the 60 cent rate until the arbitration decision was made—had been put forth "upon instructions from his actual government."[64]

One probable motivating factor in the sudden intervention by Mexico City was a lengthy telegram sent by L. D. Ellet, chairman of the San Joaquin Cotton Growers Committee, to President Abelardo Rodríguez. Warning of radical agitators and American communists intimidating some "six to eight thousand of your nationals," Ellet presented the growers' case and made a thinly veiled request for Mexican intervention in the strike. The Executive Office relayed the memorandum to Foreign Relations with the request that they respond directly to Ellet. A noncommittal letter politely indicated that the matter would be taken under consideration.

Upon the news that growers had agreed to the formation of a fact-finding commission to investigate the claims of both sides in the dispute, Fitzgerald announced that the "strike is over." Fitzgerald's claim was premature. Not only did the strike continue during the commission's preparations and formal hearings in spite of Bravo's exhortations to the strikers to resume work, but strikers refused to participate in the proceedings independently of their leaders. Further, the Cannery Union, having learned from experience that arbitration was a means of undercutting independent union actions, agreed to participate only on condition that the commission's conclusions would not be legally binding upon the strikers. The union hoped the hearings would work in its favor by becoming a forum to publicize its cause. Federal mediators, however, had one single objective in mind: end the strike immediately. And to achieve that end, they sought to separate the rank and file from the Cannery Union leadership. That hope and expectation brought together all interested parties at the hearings.

A flyer printed in both Spanish and English, "Aviso oficial a todos los coscheros [sic] y pizcadores de algodón"/"Official Notice to All Cotton Growers and Cotton Pickers," officially announcing the establishment of the fact-finding commission, carried appeals by seven officials (including Bravo) to the protagonists to arbitrate in good faith and abide by the decision of the commission. In his brief, encouraging statement (printed in bold type, unlike the other statements), Bravo not only advised that arbitration would settle the conflict but made a strong appeal to the Mexican strikers to return to the fields immediately pending the hearings. Bravo exclaimed that the "[s]pirit of friendship between Mexico and the United States in mutual accord to solve the present situation of the cotton picking has decided to submit the problem to an arbitration board of experts. . . . This accord urges the immediate work of the pickers. . . . Countrymen return to your work with the full assurance that the Mexican government is watching your interests."[65] In effect, Bravo attempted to do what Fitzgerald had been unable to do: end the strike prior to arbitration. None of the remaining six pronouncements made such a direct appeal to the Mexican strikers, and not one mentioned the CAWIU. All were directed at the "cotton pickers and cotton growers." Fitzgerald also made a statement reiterating his stance, which coincided with Bravo's: "It is urged," he remarked, "that the cotton pickers return to the fields in a 'status quo' position"[66]—in other words, at the same wages, with no gain.

Three days before the flyer was distributed, the Spanish-language daily *La Opinión* reported that "Consul Bravo . . . continues making overtures [to arbitrate] and today announced that Mexican workers are ready to return to work immediately."[67] The "Official Notice" merely crystallized the mediation strategy undertaken by Creel, Fitzgerald, and MacDonald. However, Bravo held the keys to a successful outcome, since he allegedly had the power to influence the majority of the pickers. The strategy of the growers thereupon swung away from outright confrontation to dividing the workers into separate groups and then isolating the Cannery Union from the rank and file. Bravo, it seemed, had the most advantageous position for achieving that end. Nevertheless, bad luck or just poor leadership plagued Bravo. On October 16, the day the flyer was distributed, it was reported that Bravo "has taken a very active part seeking a solution. On Friday he appeared at a Visalia strikers meeting with his representative Acosta." Copies of the "Official Notice" were simultaneously distributed throughout the camps and *colonias*. The strikers were not so easily manipulated this time, and the notice was greeted with jeers, hoots, and shouts of "Viva la huelga" as strikers tore up the announcement.[68] Bravo, undaunted by this incident, continued to plead with the strikers to end the strike.

Despite official optimism that the strike would soon be over, the strikers maintained their resolve and strengthened their movement. While Bravo made the rounds of the camps, a police officer observing an October 17 rally at Pixley noted that "the speeches delivered last night were the most defiant he has heard thus far. Speakers called upon the strikers to keep every worker out of the field." Charges that Mexican pickers were duped by "red" agitators also failed to interest the strikers. As one Mexican striker attending a rally put it, "We will continue the strike even if all the white strikers are put in jail." One speaker angrily charged that "Enrique Bravo, the Mexican consul, did not represent the strikers."[69]

Rebuffs from the strikers failed to deter the local pro-grower press from acclaiming Bravo for his service to end the strike. One editorial observed "that Enrique Bravo . . . is correct when he says that a majority of his people in this district are satisfied with the 60 cent wage and would return to work were it not for the communistic tactics of 'strike' leaders to prevent them from doing so."[70] The growers' faith in Bravo held in spite of his inability to persuade strikers to go back to work. He was a staunch and valuable ally. However, his failure to split the union left Creel with no choice but to bow to the determination of the strikers as to their representatives at the hearings.

Thus the hearings began on October 20 with the CAWIU representing the rank and file. Growers, led by Edson Abel, attorney for the California Farm Bureau Federation, called their expert witnesses, all large growers, starring L. D. Ellet. The strikers, represented by Caroline Decker, selected their witnesses from the union rank and file. The growers testified that they could not afford more than 60 cents per hundred pounds; the pickers stuck to their original list of demands.

During the push and pull of questions and statements, Bravo rose and requested the opportunity to speak independently. As Bravo prepared to present records regarding pickers' cost-of-living estimates, Decker interrupted, protesting that "Consul Bravo does not represent either the Mexican or the American cotton pickers, only the Mexican government." Decker's protest was valid. Bravo had earlier testified that in his capacity as consul, he represented only the "non-striking" Mexican pickers. The *Visalia Times Delta* backed up that claim, reporting that "Consul Enrique Bravo presented the commission with data stating that he was representing Mexican workers not affiliated with the union now conducting the strike."[71] So Bravo and Acosta declared themselves representatives of a pro-consul, pro-grower rump group within the striking force. Nonetheless, Commission Chairman Ira B. Cross, a University of California economist, requested to hear the consul, and Bravo gave his statement, a surprising argument for 60 cents per 60 pounds, a figure equal to the union demand of one dollar per hundred. The growers did not flinch. [They must have realized Bravo's mistake.] Then Bravo continued, "The Mexican has been an honest, just, and loyal worker, he is liked by the grower, he is easy to handle." He then implicitly defended the growers' use of violence during questioning.

Cross: Have you ever asked local authorities to give the Mexicans in these camps or in these meetings protection?
    Bravo: Yes.
    Cross: Have they been given that protection?
    Bravo: Yes.
    Wirin (Attorney for the CAWIU): In what way have Mexicans been protected?
    Bravo: We are in communication everyday with the Governor's office in Sacramento with regard to things happening in this State.
    Cross: But what protection has been given?
    Bravo: I cannot make that statement. I am not in a position to criticize local authorities. The two countries are friendly and are trying to cooperate with each other.

Edson Abel then turned the questioning toward the earning differential between Mexico and the United States, attempting to show that pickers are better off in the Valley than in Mexico. Bravo cooperated in answering Abel's query, prompting Caroline Decker to declare, "In the opinion of the union it makes no difference how Mexicans get along in Mexico." Bravo retorted that "The young lady has never been to Mexico, and knows nothing about the country." There the matter rested. Bravo's reticence concerning protection confirmed to the growers that he was a friendly witness for them.[72]

After two days of testimony, the hearings ended amid rising tensions that threatened to escalate into violence. Paul S. Taylor's description of the atmosphere as "tense with feeling" captured the moment: "The audience of a few growers and officers, and some hundreds of Mexican, Negro, and 'poor white' pickers left their chairs as they crowded closer and closer in a ring of intent faces encircling the table. . . . A reporter of the *Fresno Bee* told me afterwards that he expected violence to break out. Norman Thomas . . . declared it the most dramatic strike scene he has witnessed."[73]

The Fact-Finding Commission's Report

After two days of deliberations, the fact-finding commission issued its recommendations, which urged growers to accept a wage scale of 75 cents per hundred pounds and included statements deploring violations of the Constitution. State and federal officials endorsed the wage increase; growers, though upset at the wage increase and the hand slap over their legal transgressions, nevertheless followed suit on October 25. However, the striking pickers refused the settlement and continued to hold out for one dollar per hundred. As the offer wound its way through the camp grapevine, the Mexican secretary of foreign relations reviewed its labor policy and reiterated standing instructions to its consuls. In a message circulated through the consulates, the Secretariat emphasized that it was prepared to "offer necessary help and support" for the Mexican strikers, but nevertheless, the Secretariat warned, "it is recommended that the consulates make investigations to determine whether the strikers' demands are just and that consuls are prohibited from leading a strike." Former president Calles also expressed his impressions on the strike situation and promised to "help the strikers not only through intercessions on their behalf, but also with personal pecuniary support if necessary."[74] Until then, neither Calles nor the Mexican government had publicly or privately offered material or moral support for the strike, nor did any actual support arrive from either party. This hands-off approach to the strike demonstrated a marked reluctance to intervene with charitable donations as long as the Cannery Union held leadership. Instead of outright support, Mexico's government sought to alter the organization of cotton pickers with promises of support as an enticement. Effectively neutralized by an uncompromising opposition, Bravo wielded another weapon: the carrot and the stick, a traditional ploy of governments, and in Mexico it went back at least to the Porfiriato. Well before before the fact-finding commission's hearings, Bravo had dangled government aid to leverage Mexican strikers back to the fields. The *San Francisco Chronicle* noted that Bravo and Acosta

incurred the antagonism of many of the strikers . . . after making a tour of the strike area. . . . Bravo and . . . Acosta . . . intimated dissatisfaction at the attitude of some of their nationals who might want to come to them later for some redress or protection during the progress of the strike. Observers said that if Bravo is repudiated by the Mexicans among the strikers, his hands will be tied if they expect aid from the Mexican government. It is possible, said the observers, that the Mexican government may ex-patriate those of its nationals who disregard the wishes of the consul.[75]

After the commission's decision, Bravo revived the threat, reminding strikers that they ran the risk of losing government assistance if they refused to accept the compromise agreement. "Mexican pickers," stated a news article, "were told by the Mexican consulate that they need expect no aid from Mexico if they refuse to return to work."[76] They refused to return to work. They had never, apparently, expected aid from the Mexican government.

Ignoring threats of evictions from the resettlement camps and the loss of any possibility of government aid, caravans of strikers continued their treks to the fields for mass picketing. As one headline put it, strikers "Refuse to Pick Cotton or Evacuate Camp." In retaliation, Kings County sheriff Van Buckner ordered the Corcoran camp evacuated by 3 P.M. on October 26. A showdown followed as strikers refused the order. Hoping to avoid more violence, Frank MacDonald rushed to the scene to lift the order. Acosta accompanied MacDonald, not only translating for the state labor commissioner but addressing the crowd, recommending that they end the strike. As the strikers milled at the guarded entrance to the camp shouting "Viva la huelga," MacDonald "pointed out that it was foolish to prolong the strike." The strikers stood their ground and retorted that the fact-finding commission "ignored our arbitration proposal" of a lower 80 cents per hundred pounds.[77] In the union's view, a good-faith arbitration had never occurred, an argument sustained by the available evidence. Information leaked during the strike suggested that the 75-cent wage recommendation had been arranged prior to the commission's deliberations.[78]

Persuasive tactics by Bravo and MacDonald were broadened to include threats of possible deportation. MacDonald suggested that a "bluff at [mass] deportation or even deportation of 10 or 20 Mexicans will save the situation" by forcing a return to work. Creel expressed interest in the return of recalcitrant Mexicans to their homeland but found, after he had conducted "a very thorough investigation," that "almost every Mexican has been in this country for a much longer period than the three years during which they are subject to deportation."[79] Deportation seemed not to be an available option. Talk of importing strikebreakers from Los Angeles never materialized, nor did calls by the San Joaquin Agricultural Labor Bureau for terminating state relief to feed camp dwellers in order to starve them into submission.[80]

Federal and state mediation strategy focused on getting the two sides into a negotiating session to resolve not only this dispute but to institutionalize a mechanism to avoid strikes by harmonizing labor relations. Explicitly, the long-term objectives of Creel and his colleagues focused on forging an organic unity between capital and labor, an old progressive goal. But Creel was not against using a wide spectrum of methods to bring the union to mediate under federal supervision. Proposals from farming companies in the region in support of the growers' efforts to dislodge the strikers were sent to Creel. One came from the San Diego Fruit and Produce Company, which offered to send Creel "Two Mexican labor leaders, Ramirez and Sanchez, who have organized Mexican labor here in [the] Salinas Valley and peacefully settled all labor disputes." The two were described as potential undercover men available for "immediate service," who, according to the company representative, "could do a great good in that district."[81] Creel considered the possibility of using the two, and in his response to the company official, he put the offer on hold rather than decline it. "Will have to wait on the report of the Cotton Strike Commission before deciding further steps," he answered.[82] Such shenanigans proved unnecessary.

On October 25 the growers accepted the commission's decision on the new wage level. The growers had become convinced by Creel that the commission's decision to raise wages held the only useful approach for ending the strike and eliminating those conditions leading to radicalism and communist activity among working people. The following day the Cannery Union's central committee also voted to end the strike. The strike was over. The union's decision was a difficult one. The strikers had been adamant; they had held their ground and refused to cede any measure of their independence to an arbitration board. However, the pragmatic unionists recognized their measure of success and deemed it unlikely that they could better it by extending the strike and its hardships any further. Morale was high, and the Cannery Union would continue to build the union and to work toward those demands that had not been realized.

Now that the strike was over, Corcoran Camp, the dynamic symbol of the pickers' struggle, returned to an expanse of dry scrub brush. The remaining temporary makeshift communities followed suit. Striker families packed their meager belongings—tents, bedding, and portable stoves—piled them onto their automobiles and trucks, and caravaned onto the rural roads. Down the highways where once they paraded as pickets, they now sought employment at the new rate—but in protest, they refused to work in the Corcoran area. Leaders found it difficult to find work. Some, like Bill Hammet, had to travel a hundred miles before finding employment.

Peace had been restored, but only after the Valley had been rocked by the largest labor strike in the history of United States agriculture. With the '33 strike etched deeply in their psyches, the pickers and growers returned to their places in the division of labor of the cotton industry. The Cannery Union considered the struggle a victorious achievement that proved that even a disenfranchised agricultural labor force could, if organized, hold the growers and their allies at bay—and make them pay.

Critical to that achievement was the union's success in countering and preventing Bravo's message of nationalistic unionization and ethnic isolation from ever taking root. There is little doubt that Bravo's concerted attempts to steer the strikers into a separate organization had struck a chord with many Mexican workers. Even the CAWIU had recognized the dangers posed by Bravo's entreaties and they were, of course, aware that he had made some small gains. Growers were extremely satisfied with all that Bravo did on their behalf. He had earned effusive accolades from the Valley's growers, law enforcement agencies, politicians, and the press and had emerged a shining example of a loyal and trusted ally, a key player in an ultimately successful partnership.

Lest Mexican officials unwittingly misinterpret Bravo's actions, Corcoran Chief of Police R. E. Springer and Kings County Sheriff W. V. Buckner wired President Abelardo Rodríguez soon after the settlement. "Honorable Sir," began the telegram,

A very extensive strike among Mexican cotton pickers which has waged *(sic)* for three weeks has just terminated in this county and without bloodshed(!!) largely through the untiring efforts of your honorable consul Enrique Bravo(.) A small handful of Communist agitators were successful in withdrawing cotton pickers from the fields(.) Approximately four thousand of them and parked them on a ten acre lot just outside of the small city of Corcoran which made a very delicate situation(.) *This is to express our gratitude to you and through you to him for the wise and unstinted efforts put forth to divorce the Mexican people from the communistic influences which resulted mutually beneficial to the growers as well as pickers*(.) Señor Bravo has been a valuable factor in settling the strike and we thank you for having him with us. . . . (emphasis mine.) [83]

Springer sent a separate wire to Calles, the power behind the throne in Mexico City, shortly after the settlement to express his gratitude for Bravo's contributions. "We feel highly complimented," he wrote, "in having had the pleasure of working with your representative, Consul Enrique Bravo. He was always a gentleman and was untiring in his efforts in behalf of the welfare of his countrymen." [84]

Governor Rolph received State Labor Commissioner Frank C. MacDonald's strike report, which, in addition to congratulating law enforcement for its "exceptionally able and impartial handling of the strike," summarized the main engagements in the conflict. Numerous references to Bravo's and Acosta's involvement bore testimony to the importance given to the two by the authorities. MacDonald identified several personages for special tribute, and a glowing accolade was handed to Bravo and Acosta. "I deem it my duty," stated the commissioner, "to report that Mexican consular representative, L. J. Acosta, rendered every possible assistance . . . in urging them [the strikers] to accept the decision of the Fact Finding Commission. Mexican Consul Enrique Bravo also rendered valuable assistance in these efforts." [85]

Finally, Consul General Lubbert added his voice to the chorus of praise in a dispatch to Mexico City reporting on the strike. Obviously, Lubbert appreciated the contributions from the federal and state authorities as well as those from Bravo and Acosta. His version of the event indicated that all worked in concert. "I consider it just to inform your authority that Consul Enrique Bravo followed instructions to the letter in the course of the [strike] movement." Moreover, continued Lubbert, Bravo "labored tirelessly, having remained in the region for more than 24 days." The report mentioned that Bravo made lengthy trips visiting strikers' camps in the strike zone. So extensive were the distances traveled that Bravo and Acosta shared a $300 reimbursement from the Mexican government to cover the costs for gas and room-and-board during the strike. Lubbert gracefully noted that the $300 Bravo spent while conducting consular duties during the strike "can be considered quite low as it is understood that Señor Leonsio Acosta accompanied him during that time, with the purpose of cooperating with him."

As for Acosta, Lubbert found much to congratulate. He effectively "helped Consul Bravo, abandoned his work and family temporarily" so as to complete their task. "I should also point out," finished Lubbert, "that during the course of the entire strike movement, I was in constant

personal contact with [Governor] Rolph[,] . . . George Creel[,] . . .
Frank C. MacDonald[,] . . . and [Edward] Fitzgerald[,] . . . who actively
intervened in the matter and, as I understand it, offered everything at their
disposal to resolve the strike in a just and favorable manner for the
strikers."[86] In a private letter to Javier Gaxiola, personal secretary to
President Rodríguez, Lubbert depicted a harmonious working relationship among the authorities. "The consulate received effective help and
cooperation," he wrote, from state and federal authorities, "particularly
from Mr. George Creel . . . a personal friend of mine."[87]

Bravo did not shrink from heaping similar praise on himself, and in
doing so he crowned his record with heroic feats. In his report to his superiors, he depicted himself as the central figure who had maneuvered all
sides into the settlement. "After innumerable conferences," he wrote, "between myself and the authorities who took part in the matter, as well with
the leaders of the strikers and representatives of the growers, an end to
the strike was reached."[88] The flurry of public officials' statements regarding his role in the settlement made his assertions seem plausible, although
it is highly doubtful that Bravo alone had carried the day, as he claimed.

Compliments flowed long after the strike. When the Mexican government made plans to transfer the Calexico consulate office to the coastal
city of Monterey in 1935, the move was opposed throughout the Valley.
Telegrams requesting that Bravo remain descended upon the Secretariat
of Foreign Relations from the Fresno County sheriff, the Fresno chief of
police, the mayors of Bakersfield and Watsonville, and the chambers of
commerce of Pacific Grove, San Benito, and Watsonville. A telegram from
the Fresno County labor commissioner to the Secretariat of Foreign Relations exemplifies the reaction: " . . . press reports that your government
is considering the elimination of the Mexican consulate in this district[.]
earnestly request that Enrique Bravo . . . be retained."[89]

Some in the Mexican *colonias* voiced the same regret at the proposed
move, but these were from the *comisiones honoríficas* and other organizations established by Bravo. The *comisión honorífica*, Comité de Beneficencia, and Sociedad Juárez of Bakersfield added their expressions of
support for retaining the consulate in the Valley. Juan Briones and Andres
Saavedra wrote directly to Foreign Relations, stating, "This Comisión
Honorífica has the pleasure to recommend the return of Consul Bravo so
that he can be at the front of the chain of Comisiones Honoríficas and
Cruz Azules which he organized."[90] Despite these pleas, Bravo removed
the consulate to Monterey. The change no doubt pleased him, since he
had earlier expressed regret at having the consulate amid so many untu-
tored compatriots who arrived at all hours of the night seeking redress for
a long list of problems.

On the other side, striker condemnation was swift. They criticized Bravo for trying to divide the ethnic groups, a ploy that had pleased the growers and authorities. One Black leader from the Pixley area recalled the design in Bravo's strategy: "Many Negroes live in Pixley. More in that neighborhood than elsewhere. Negroes and whites struck as well as Mexicans. There were no differences between them. They all stuck together. Bravo tried to break the strike by getting the Mexicans to quit the union. They tried the same with my people too . . . white, Mexicans, and colored people all worked together. Just like brothers. They tried to split us apart like they always do but we wouldn't." [91] Because of that strategy, bitterness remained among many strikers. A memorandum in Bravo's file at the Archivo de la Secretaría de Relaciones Exteriores in Mexico City noted that alongside official letters "praising his work of protection given to the Mexican workers" were found "various attacks and accusations." Some, like Baltazar Estrada and Herculano Ramos, filed complaints with the Secretariat of Foreign Relations written in the simple language of men without much formal schooling. In disgust, they asked for justice, demanding that "Bravo either comply with his responsibilities or undergo a review of his actions." [92]

Several months later, a lengthy memorial to President Rodríguez signed by eighty Mexican citizens lamented Bravo's service in the interests of cotton growers. The signatories, according to the *La Opinión* article reporting on the complaint, accused Consul Bravo of having failed to deliver "the requisite attention, and abandoned the workers to their own fate." Our motive, wrote the complainants, "is that . . . during the San Joaquin cotton strike in which various compatriots lost their lives, Consul Enrique Bravo failed to act according to his official position. Instead, he operated arbitrarily and with extreme timidity. Not only did he allow the situation to stagnate, but he also helped to make those crimes committed against our people go unpunished." [93]

Claiming victory, the CAWIU surveyed the strike experience: "The workers know that they won by defeating not only the finance companies and rich ranchers, the local sheriffs and their deputies, but the entire capitalistic government including the state police, the U.S. state and so-called mediation boards, and the treacherous Mexican consul." [94]

As those words were spoken, labor tensions in the Imperial Valley to the south were heating up.

CHAPTER 5

The Imperial Valley Strikes of 1933–1934

With the culmination of the violence-torn San Joaquin strike, the CAWIU, buoyed by workers' confidence, turned south to the Imperial Valley, where the term "farm fascism" fitted grower politics better than in any previous strike. In both events the Constitution became a scrap of paper and local authorities enforced laws as they pleased and violated or suspended legal rights in their furious efforts to defeat the CAWIU. Of the three strikes, however, it is the Imperial Valley strike in which we witness the most cynical dismissal of democratic principles. Again, the Mexican government, acting through its consulate, joined with growers and the county's political infrastructure to oppose the CAWIU and, indeed, any independent labor organization. The actions of Consul Bravo in the San Joaquin strike seem rather guarded in comparison with those of Consul Terrazas. Terrazas openly and enthusiastically embraced the growers' cause, reestablished the pro-grower union (originally founded in 1928), and, with the help of the ruling government in Mexico City, ultimately contributed to the defeat of the CAWIU.

In this chapter I again examine the political right's direct interference in labor-grower conflicts and reveal the continuing pattern of U.S./Mexico complicity in depriving field workers of their rights to organize, negotiate, and strike. In reviewing and analyzing the events surrounding the Imperial Valley strikes of 1928 through 1934, we once again observe consular officials striding into the strike conflict, taking center stage, maneuvering, even plotting, to carry out their political agenda.

The Setting

The Colorado Desert, a desolate land in the southeast corner of California bordered by Mexico and Arizona, was for hundreds of years a vast dry lake bed that had grown nothing but "cactus, sagebrush, greasewood, and mesquite." At the turn of the century speculators set out to transform that arid landscape. Financing the construction of an efficient system of irrigation canals, they diverted water from the Colorado River into the lake bed and its fertile alluvial soil, and almost overnight this desert depression, appropriately renamed the Imperial Valley, emerged as "one of the richest agricultural areas of the world."[1] Since its initial development in the early 1900s to the present time, the Valley has remained an agricultural Garden of Eden. Without an appreciable economy at the turn of the century, "the largest irrigation area in the world" blossomed. It was in 1920 that the Valley was first called "The Inland Empire" and even "America's Winter Garden." Irrigation, excellent soils, and sufficient capital, combined with an ideal desert climate, ensured that at least one crop could be harvested every month of the year. But it was cheap labor that made harvesting possible and profitable. Ten years after the first ditches were cut through the barren lakebed, 242,110 irrigated acres produced citrus, field crops, truck crops and dairy products and pastured 83,000 head of livestock. By the beginning of the 1930s, the "fabulously rich" irrigated zone had increased to 525,000 acres and supplied a quarter of the nation's lettuce and nearly a fourth of its melons and cantaloupes.

Imperial Valley agriculture generated immense profits as it adhered to the pattern of large-scale agribusiness prevalent throughout the state. In the beginning stages of development, small farms existed side by side with the larger parcels, always in their shadow. But the shadows got longer and longer as the process of land concentration picked up speed and began absorbing the smaller farms one by one, until within a few decades a handful of giants controlled the Valley. These giant producers relied on a relatively easy process of land acquisition based on their capacity to "market locally and in the east . . . at virtually monopoly prices." The advantage this gave them made it virtually impossible for small farmers to compete, obliging them, in turn, to abandon their holdings at bargain prices to these large-scale competitors.[2]

In 1934 a special committee charged by the statewide Associated Farmers to investigate the Valley's strikes reported that "the corporate type of farming is of greatest importance from the standpoint of acreage farmed and value of outputs."[3] Statistics taken in the mid-thirties verify the centralization of land ownership under the control of a handful of landowners: 11.5 percent of the farms held 49 percent of farm acreage; these figures represent the big landowners. On the other hand, 50 percent of farms held only 21 percent of acreage. Profits accrued accordingly. In 1929, 10.5 percent of farms (numbering 299) received nearly 60 percent of the county's farm income, and 37 percent of farms (or 1,068) received

4.1 percent of farm income.[4] Seventy-four enterprises (owned by individuals or companies) controlled 48,000 acres of lettuce, peas, and carrots, the region's "luxury crops." Data for 1936 showed that 51 large grower-shippers operated or leased 84 percent of the melon acreage and earned $9 million, almost half of the gross agricultural income for the county, about $22 million. Since these same grower-shippers farmed or leased other crop acreage, their portion of the total earnings increased in step. "On a very conservative basis . . . it can be estimated that these 51 concerns received between two-fifths to one-half of the total agricultural income of the county."[5]

These large enterprises seldom managed their lands directly; instead they based their operations on a widespread system of leasing contracts.[6] A system controlled by absentee landlords was the norm in the Valley economy. In 1935 owners operated only 25.2 percent "of all land in farms in the county," while 71 percent of the county farm acreage was "assessed against owners living outside the district."[7] The practice of absentee ownership by "large scale corporations who lease much of the land . . . hire all the labor, and operate with paid managers and superintendents" became the typical practice.[8] "The system," observed Paul S. Taylor, "is, in effect, large-scale agriculture upon a leasing rather than an ownership basis, for the majority of growers do not own much land."[9] Land corporations basically controlled the "inputs and outputs," including field, crop, acreage, type of labor, wages, and costs of production. Managers carried out the specifications according to the contract drawn by the landowner. The average farmer (the one who actually farmed) was for all practical purposes a variation of the hired hand (he had a manager). Although growers and shippers sentimentally eulogized the farmer at every opportunity, small-scale farming (by individual farmers) had been completely marginalized by the large economic enterprises that dominated the marketplace.

The sheer size of Imperial Valley and the numbers of acres under cultivation required a massive supply of labor. But not until the introduction of cotton in the second decade of agricultural development were Mexicans a significant sector of the laboring force. Arrangements to import labor were made by Valley growers to temporarily satisfy their needs. Most Mexican workers found their way into the region through a borrowing system established by local growers who tapped into Arizona and Texas cotton labor pools. In the early years, Mexican labor migrated in and out of the Valley rather than forming permanent settlements or camps. Then in 1931 acreage under cotton fell to less than three thousand acres from a high of fifty-eight thousand in 1918. Several factors influenced this drop, among them poor productivity in the Imperial area compared with that in the San Joaquin Valley, and the expansion of truck-crop acreage. This shift in crops now created a need for a permanent labor supply and attracted Mexican workers by the thousands. By the late twenties, Mexicans dominated this market, comprising 90 percent of the approximately 15,000 laborers needed to perform the ranch work, clean the irrigation canals, and harvest the crops. So it was that before the end of the twenties the Mexican population in the Valley had swelled to an estimated 20,000, comprising over one third of the county's total population of 54,500.

The remaining labor force included Filipinos, Asian Indians, Blacks, whites, and a sprinkling of Japanese, Chinese, and Koreans. During harvests growers selected individual groups for particular tasks. In general, white labor performed shed and machine labor. Mexicans were favored for the spring and summer cantaloupe gathering. Considered too diminutive for the melon and cantaloupe work, Filipinos found themselves shuttled into the winter lettuce and asparagus harvests. For other crops, such as peas, tomatoes, and carrots, usually a broad selection of laborers, dominated by Mexicans, assembled for the picking.

Resident labor never satisfied the labor requirements at peak harvests, and for the lettuce cutting as many as three thousand Filipinos and five thousand Mexicans migrated into the Valley. As the Depression deepened, displaced white labor stepped into the migrant stream and, like their minority classmates, signed on to perform the back-breaking work. The unavoidable commingling of nationalities at winter and spring picking threatened a class dynamism that challenged the effectiveness of growers and the consulate to control farm labor. Consequently, splitting the ranks assumed a prominent goal on the growers' antiunion agenda.

Many county boosters proudly referred to the Valley as the "richest farming area in the world," and the evidence supported their claim. Yet, as in most of California's profit-driven agriculture, farmworkers and their families endured low wages, poor working conditions, harsh living conditions, and social ostracism. Lush fields belied the intense desert heat that often reached 120 degrees in the summer and hovered at the 100-degree mark during harvests. Heat strokes plagued workers when laboring during the harvest months of May through September. Deaths occurred periodically and underscored the dangers of working the desert "garden." [10] On the last day of June 1929, with desert temperatures soaring, tragedy struck. All eight members of the Armenta family died of the heat when their car broke down while they were searching for work on an isolated stretch of highway outside of Brawley. [11] In June and July of that year, a total of eleven laborers died of heat exhaustion while working in the fields.

The State Bureau of Labor Statistics report for 1926 states that "the growers of the Imperial Valley heretofore made no effort to protect the health and decency of their Mexican workers." These same growers, continues the report, have "made no provision for the housing of Mexican families," encouraging instead the construction of "squatty and filthy shacks on their ranches." [12] While conducting his research in the Valley, Paul S. Taylor observed that the "location of rural Mexican populations is almost entirely determined by the crop conditions of the moment." [13] Over the years Mexicans workers often lived in temporary camps that could relocate in response to the system of land lease and crop rotation which required shifts from one place to another. Permanent housing remained the exception. Taylor added, "In some cases, his housing is furnished, or he can construct his own, rent free, on a ditch bank, or he may rent a small 'shack' in town, or during the course of a single year he may live in all of these ways." [14] Campbell MacCulloch, the secretary of the Los Angeles Regional Labor Board, noted that "because of the methods of cultivation, diversion of crops, and instances of tenant farming, permanent construction on the ranches is not usual." [15]

That was one side of the housing situation but not the only one. Permanent *colonias* were established in Brawley, El Centro, Calipatria, and other towns when the intensification of a particular crop required year-round worker availability. The Brawley "Mexican quarter" was built up during the expansion of melon, cantaloupe, and vegetable production. El Centro's *colonia* owed its existence to lettuce, while Calipatria's was anchored in the cotton fields. Perhaps because of its status as a border town, Calexico's *colonia* sheltered a sizable number of day laborers. Growers referred to these town dwellers as "house Mexicans" or the "better class of Mexicans" to distinguish them from the ranch camp residents.

Thus we see two types of Mexican settlements, transitory and permanent, situated in a variety of settings. In fact, the largest numbers of workers, about 75 percent, occupied permanent quarters they either rented or purchased. "Villages almost entirely of tents, with the most primitive facilities" housed both permanent and migratory workers and families. Houses "built of boards, weeds, or anything that was found at hand" offered a "pitiful semblance of a home." A federal commission assigned to investigate the Valley's labor troubles in 1934 reported that "words cannot describe some of the conditions we saw." In the towns with permanent *colonias,* the commissioners found "shacks that are disgraceful and a lack of sanitation in all its aspects." [16] Often these camps, particularly the migratory camps, were called "ditch bank" camps, referring to their placement alongside the irrigation canals. The water in these canals was used by families for drinking, cooking, washing, and bathing. The appalling absence of basic sanitary provisions in the camps and on the ranches "provided the necessary conditions for a considerable percentage of typhoid." [17] Even U.S. Secretary of Labor Frances Perkins considered the Valley's health problem "one of the most serious aspects of the Imperial Valley situation." [18] County health officials acknowledged, somewhat reluctantly, that there "was much to be desired." [19] County and state authorities ignored these infractions of basic health regulations. When the State Division of Immigration and Housing inspected 303 laborer camps throughout the state, the Valley camps received the worst ratings. Only 56 camps in the state were found "good," and 118 were rated "bad" and subject to prosecution. Of these "bad" camps, 79 were located in Imperial County. Oblivious to the report, growers did nothing to improve conditions.[20] Wages ranging from 12 to 15 cents an hour, a lack of health-code enforcement, and the total absence of concern on the part of county officials and growers led inexorably to "deplorable living conditions of the mass of workers."

Working conditions in the fields were equally inhumane, and hiring had its own devious protocols. Ninety percent of the operators or tenants used the contractor system when hiring their labor force, a system of hiring that all but guaranteed an unorganized labor market. The system worked in a hierarchy of capital relations starting with the landowner, descending to the operator (or tenant), then to the contractor, and finally to the workers. The landowner demanded a prearranged dollar figure from his operator for a particular harvest. The operator then met with the contractor to give his specifications for the numbers of laborers required, the hourly rate, and the hours to be worked. The operator handed over the wages to the contractor to be paid out when the day's work was done (workers seldom met face to face with an operator). Wages, working conditions, hours, and so on having been set by the operator, the contractor assumed full responsibility for the completion of the harvest and the disbursement of pay to the work crew. On the surface the contractor system appears to have been a more or less conventional business arrangement. However, the contractor (usually himself a farmworker or former farmworker) acted as a "middleman"; and like all middleman arrangements, it lent itself to severe abuses. In the venue of this agricultural setting, and with wages in his possession, a contractor would often fail to pay the wage agreed upon. Commonly he would take off a percentage for himself, called skimming, or even worse, he would abscond with the entire crew's wages.

Another common business practice, the bonus system, was perhaps even more problematic. In this arrangement, the operator would hold back a portion of a worker's pay, usually 25 percent, to be paid at the end of the season on condition that the worker remain the entire season. The bonus was used as a control device (a kind of blackmail) that forced laborers to work the season or lose a sizable portion of their wages. Workers thus tended to stick to the job even when another operator promised higher wages. In this volatile work environment, where families lived so tenuously, steadiness and predictability were difficult to achieve. The operator thus stood a good chance of keeping the so-called bonus. Workers endured intense desert temperatures, the lack of fresh drinking water, the absence of toilet facilities, and an overbearing contractor who acted as a foreman, but they felt compelled to work the season so as not to lose the bonus that, even so, scarcely brought the wage to subsistence level.[21] Wages in 1933 ranged from 12 to 15 cents an hour, about $400 a year. Wages, the bonus system, working conditions in the fields, numerous instances of contractors stealing their pay or paying wages below that stipulated by the operator: all were the focus of workers' discontent, but not a single one of these issues was being addressed. Growers and operators insisted that wages were adequate for Mexican labor, winked at the "skimming," defended the practice of bonuses, and never attempted to correct the abuses or conditions of work.

The majority of growers, especially those in truck farming, depended on Mexicans as an irreplaceable class of workers. One company executive remarked that "Large scale production would be impossible without Mexican field labor" and added that using Mexican labor reduced costs by ".50 percent." A foreman for a large grower agreed, stating that "Mexicans are very satisfactory" even if, as he said, they required "constant supervision." Another observed that a "small gift, and recognition of their national holidays" increased the reliability of Mexican labor. Such paternalistic practices, along with extreme notions of individualism, sheltered growers from any sense of responsibility for the welfare and standard of living of their labor force. A county police judge and justice of the peace, H. B. Griffen, put it this way: "a dollar a day is enough for a Mexican field worker."[22]

Prelude to 1933–1934

The Strike of 1928

A study of earlier conflicts broadens our understanding of the unrest that would eventually lead to the large Imperial Valley strikes. As far back as 1917, attempts at organizing farmworkers in the Imperial Valley had occurred. The formation of La Unión de Trabajadores del Valle Imperial (the Imperial Valley Workers Union) in April 1928 was the first successful effort.[23] Shortly after its founding, and after an aborted strike, the union assumed the name Asociación Mutual del Valle Imperial (Mexican Mutual Aid Society of the Imperial Valley). The name seemed fitting in that the leaders were closely connected to existing Mexican mutual-benefit societies. The union held its meetings in the Benito Juárez Mutual Benefit Society Hall, and many union members belonged to the society as well. Consul Carlos V. Ariza, as was the case with later consuls, played a significant role in the Imperial Valley Cantaloupe Workers' Strike of 1928. Ariza had arrived in Calexico in 1927 but was abruptly dismissed from the service in 1928 for allegedly extorting $500 from a widow who had sought consul help in securing a $4,000 indemnity. Consulate services in these matters were considered gratis, so any remuneration would be inappropriate. However, Ariza was never formally charged with this abuse of office. In 1931 Ariza resurfaced as the Mexican representative for the Los Angeles Chamber of Commerce on matters relating to the "repatriation" drive promoted by the chamber. Ariza handled the chamber's public relations mission to reassure Mexico's people and government that the "Los Angeles Chamber was prepared to help all Mexicans who are resident in the United States."[24]

In Calexico in 1927 Consul Ariza was continually approached to settle charges against contractors through the Benito Juárez Mutual Benefit Society. The society itself, as noted, had been formed to address grievances held by workers against labor contractors who "skimmed" or absconded with the crew's wages. Ariza proposed the organization of a unionlike association for redressing and remedying wage claims. The structure and leadership of the existing society were retained in the new labor organization; however, the consul, a main force in the organizational drive, was to hold and wield the greatest influence in its subsequent actions and political orientation. Organizational goals were clearly stated in its articles of incorporation, and set forth as its prime objective was the "collection of moneys and wages due the members."[25] The union, however, did not challenge the contractor and bonus systems and merely asked for a guarantee that "the contractor [pay] his men the standard rate."[26]

Known informally as La Unión, the organization gained distinction as "the first local . . . actually formed as a unit" of the Confederación de Uniones Obreras Mexicanas (CUOM) and was, in great measure, the result of Mexican Consul Ariza's efforts.[27] From its inception, La Unión, ostensibly organized as a union of Mexican workers [Filipino workers were considered competitors and were excluded], had a conservative political slant as contractors and "even a few merchants" were included as members.[28] In fact, Filemon González, union head and president of the

Benito Juárez Mutual Benefit Society, was himself a labor contractor. The union espoused limited goals and went to great lengths to dissociate itself from leftists, especially communists. It claimed to employ only legal means to gain its limited objectives.

Within a month of incorporation, the new union signed up twelve hundred members, opened offices in four valley towns, and delivered its first petition for a wage increase in early May. The union first approached the Chamber of Commerce, politely requesting its intercession for a small raise in wages for cantaloupe picking, free ice for drinking water, and free picking sacks. The chamber denied the petition. The union then submitted it to the growers, who refused the request and also refused to negotiate, fearing that doing so would confer de facto union recognition. Many of the organized workers had expected better results from their society and broke with the conciliatory approach favored by the leadership. In mid-May they called a spontaneous strike in two locales.[29]

When the strikers urged their fellow rank and file to follow, the union leadership reacted quickly. Addressing a letter to local newspapers, they disclaimed any connection with the militants and accused them of violating the union's class collaborationist ideals and of harming "the good name of this society and in this way to disorganize us."[30] However, control over members had weakened as the rank and file took matters into their own hands and debated among themselves as to the best course of action. "Recalcitrant workers harangued and argued with willing workers and prevented them from beginning to pick melons." On several ranches workers refused to work until their petition was favorably answered. Workers "gathered in pool rooms and street corners in Brawley and Westmoreland, discussing loudly and vociferously the affairs of the union."[31]

The sheriff moved quickly to prevent meetings, closing down the union hall and going so far as to shut down pool halls to prevent Mexicans from using them as a place of assembly. When Félix Rodríguez refused to close his Westmoreland pool hall, Sheriff Gillette arrested him, his wife, and a customer. Mexicans were arrested in their homes and on the streets and roads without provocation, other than that they were not working. Over sixty strikers and nonstrikers were arrested, and many were threatened with deportation merely for being members of the Sociedad. All arrested were charged with vagrancy or disturbing the peace and held under exorbitant bails, reaching $1,000 in many cases. The harassment, arrests, and threats by authorities had their intended effect: the walkout was stifled.

As noted, Ariza had vacated the consulate in 1928. The new consul, Hermolao Torres, in a report to his superiors in Mexico City requested intervention to end the practice of arbitrary arrests and huge bails. After Torres communicated with Mexico City, action prompted by the U.S. State Department brought an official of the California Bureau of Labor Statistics, Dr. Louis Bloch, to review the situation in the Valley. With the cooperation of Vice-Consul Alcocer, Bloch carried out his investigation and subsequently issued a report calling for reform of the contractor system, but not its termination; a modified bonus system that reduced the 25 percent withholding to a more modest level; and a general amelioration of working conditions.[32] Dr. Bloch's report containing recommendations for reforms was not binding on the growers and required only voluntary enforcement. Thus control remained in the hands of the growers and no wage increase was offered. However, all charges against those arrested were dropped and previous "misunderstandings," as Bloch described the matter, between laborers and growers were allegedly cleared up.

As the disorder of the short-lived strike dissolved into the routine of the cantaloupe harvest, the editor of the *Imperial Valley Press* saw fit to comment on the effect of the militants on the union. "It is unfortunate," he wrote, "that a few radicals within the ranks are likely to subject all the Mexican laborers in Imperial Valley to criticism and censure." The editor maintained that "the better class of Mexican people"[33] did not desire the strike. Based upon the union's communications and actions, one can only assume that strikes were not considered an option, a policy that surely elicited a favorable response from growers. Instead, the union went to some lengths to purify its image. Shortly after the strike, it changed its name to the less offensive Asociación Mutual del Valle Imperial.

The new Asociación, minus "radical" influence, again operated openly, "without trouble," and with the acknowledgment of local authorities. At this time, Consul Torres had been replaced by Consul Rendón Quijano, who attended the first meeting inaugurating the new era of cooperation and reported to the consul general that Brawley officials were also in the audience and that "these men were highly satisfied with the organization." Rendón added, "The Asociación continues functioning in complete harmony."[34]

The Strike of 1930

The second phase of organizing and strike activity in the Valley began in early 1930 with the arrival on the scene of the Communist Party's Trade Union Unity League (TUUL). The Mexican Mutual Society's weak and nonconfrontational leadership faced a substantial challenge from an organization that espoused the overthrow of the capitalist system.

A cadre of TUUL organizers intent on organizing the workers in the Valley formed the Agricultural Workers Industrial League in January 1930.[35] The cadre appeared in the Valley as a spontaneous Mexican and Filipino lettuce pickers' strike erupted and attempted to lead the strikers. The movement had begun in mid-December when a representative of the analogous Filipino association approached the Mexican Asociación to suggest that a coordinated effort at negotiating might be more effective. Within two weeks a *"comité mixto"* was delegated with the authority to negotiate with growers. While the joint committee attempted to enter into bargaining, Calexico Consul Edmundo Aragón announced his first official visit to Brawley. The Asociación leaders convened a large meeting at Brawley's Teatro Estrella to welcome him. Several hundred members cheered the consul, who delivered salutations from the Mexican government and urged that the *colonia* unite under the banners of the *comisión honorífica* and the Cruz Azul. Journalists covering the meeting observed that the consul avoided any reference to the buildup of labor tensions in the Valley. The consul's visit was unproductive, and within a week the two associations, frustrated by grower recalcitrance, called a general strike in the lettuce fields.[36] The AWIL organizers immediately sought out the leadership in the strike committees of the two associations hoping to develop cooperative and friendly relations and eventually affiliation. The Mexican Asociación proved intractable; its leadership refused to allow TUUL organizers to address its gatherings and steadfastly rejected invitations to affiliate.[37]

Early in the strike the U.S. Department of Labor's director of conciliation service wired Charles T. Connell, the field representative, to mediate. Connell assessed the situation and submitted several reports to his superiors in Washington in which he made clear his intentions to support the growers' interests. While maintaining a neutral stance, he would take steps to eliminate the TUUL as a factor in production by gaining control of the labor force and separating the workers from radical influence.

To some extent, eliminating the radicals had already been effected by the *asociación mutual,* first by refusing to deal with the AWIL (or TUUL); secondly, by pursuing a repatriation program in cooperation with the Mexican consul as a solution to worker grievances; and thirdly, by seeking ties with the government-controlled union in Mexicali, the CROM-affiliated Confederación de Sindicatos y Uniones Obreros de Mexicali. At the same time, *The Brawley News* reported, "A suitcase containing radical literature seized by the police . . . has been turned over to the district attorney's office." The story continued, "Officials of the Asociación Mutual del Valle Imperial aver that circulation of this literature, and other representatives of outside societies said to have been operating here, have no relation to the association, which has refused representatives of such assuredly subversive organizations permission to speak in its hall." Referring to the consulate, the story read, "Consular representatives, active against outside organizations, confirm the claim that the Asociación Mutual is not identified with any unlawful practices."[38] The following editions of the Brawley *News* addressed the issue of repatriation as a labor-problem solution. A headline announced: "Repatriation to Farms in Homeland Proposed for Mexicans." The story quoted Asociación president A. S. Mejía: "'We believe that colonization on a Mexican agricultural project will be better than 30 to 35 cents an hour in Imperial Valley,' stated President A. S. Mejía. 'No more labor meetings are to be held in the Asociación Mutual Hall,' he said. 'Last night's meeting was in the interest of the proposed colony in Mexico as will be subsequent meetings.'"[39] With each of these measures the Asociación was further distanced from the TUUL.

According to TUUL organizers, the Asociación leaders constantly fought against the TUUL-led Agricultural Workers Industrial League while collaborating with the Mexican consul, Commissioner of Conciliation Connell, and the local Chamber of Commerce.[40] The Asociación's friendly alliance with the cohorts of the growers must have pleased Connell, for he wrote that from his perspective the key issue was "to keep the Mexicans from listening to the agitators and heeding their propaganda. This is the objective and only solution of a very grave problem."[41] Echoing Connell, the Mexican ambassador in Washington sent instructions to his consul in El Centro that he "recommend to the laborers all moderation in their attitude" toward confronting growers.[42]

The lettuce strike, which had begun in late December, collapsed in early January. On January 16, Commissioner Connell wired to Washington, "Threatened Strike Averted. . . . Workers concluded remain at work under present wage scales."[43] The Asociación, in disarray, hurled accusations at the AWIL and later at the Filipino association, blaming them for the failure. Los Angeles Consul Pesqueira depicted the AWIL organizers as "anarchists, Russians, Jews, and women who provoked a great calamity." Meanwhile, the consul general in San Francisco and Consul Aragón in Calexico offered their assistance to their compatriots provided that they "reject all communist elements."[44] As for the Asociación Mutual, a campaign, in cooperation with the consul, to repatriate its members became the main task of the organization.[45]

The consul general joined the others in blaming the AWIL for the failed strike and further claimed that "the strike was nearly won but because of the intervention of the Moscovites, the Valley growers reacted and the perfectly organized movement . . . took a bad turn."[46] Not to be outdone in red bashing, the Confederación de Sociedades Mexicanas president, Francisco Gurrola, announced in Los Angeles that in "light of the intervention of the Russian communists," the Confederación would reevaluate its previous decision to provide economic aid to the strikers. *La Opinión* also reassessed the strike and published a rash of articles critical of the Filipinos, describing them as low-wage competitors to Mexican labor.[47]

Despite this barrage of opposition and the failure of the January strike, the TUUL mounted a major spring effort. The lines were drawn. On one side was the TUUL, determined to organize Mexicans and Filipinos in preparation for a May cantaloupe strike; on the other was the consulate-led Asociación, equally determined to repulse the militants. The TUUL organizers reported finding the "rank and file very friendly" although the leadership of the Asociación "bitterly opposed" them.[48] TUUL organizers Frank Waldren and Harry Harvey were able to address a meeting of the Asociación, and according to Harvey, "we had to be careful because the cops were after us." The chairman of the meeting protected the two by hiding them behind a hanging blanket on the makeshift stage while the police waited to intercept them at the entrance. Here, Harvey describes one of the few successes for the TUUL during that campaign:

When it was our time to speak the Mexican chairman reached behind the curtain and pulled us out before the audience. The Mexican workers went wild with joy and enthusiasm. The cops tried to work their way up front to arrest us but the Mexican workers, who are very militant, blocked their way and would not let them get at us. When we were through speaking we sneaked out a side door where we arranged to have a car waiting for us. By avoiding arrest we were able to continue, for a little longer, our work of organizing.[49]

Such threats of arrest forced the organizers underground. In attempting to elude the police, TUUL organizers held their meetings at night. "After dark," recalled Harvey, "we would immediately scoot around the shacks and hovels of the workers who were always glad to see us." Workers made sure that guards were posted, and routes for safe departure and escape, if necessary, were prepared in advance.

Within this virtual war zone, Commissioner Connell formulated his strategy for "conciliation." Connell worried about future harvests, particularly the imminent cantaloupe harvest beginning in May. "The radical communist group," he reported to Washington in February, "are bound to stir up trouble . . . the pickers are Mexicans and are easy subjects for the Communistic organizers, then there are several thousand Filipinos in the Valley who are tainted with the propaganda of the Communists. It is a dangerous situation and serious trouble is feared if the Mexicans walk out in May [sic], the shippers are due to lose large profits."[50] Connell, along with local authorities and the consul, had a single objective, and that was to eliminate the communists and their sympathizers. Any means, legal or otherwise, would be permissible. Instructions also came from the office of the consul general in San Francisco to the Imperial Valley consulate "to investigate asserted activities" by the AWIL, "alleged to disseminate objectionable theories."[51]

As April began, the growers and shippers could wait no longer. Plans were made. And on April 14 AWIL headquarters in three Valley towns were raided by the county sheriff, supported by local and state authorities.[52] Literature, posters, and flyers were seized as evidence. Later, on the basis of the testimony of three undercover agents, the County Grand Jury issued an indictment of sixteen AWIL organizers for violations of the California Criminal Syndicalism Law. Thus the cantaloupe strike had been averted, union leadership was in jail facing trials (nine were eventually tried and sentenced to from two to forty-three years in state prison), and the union movement was abruptly halted.

The other side was jubilant. A. N. Jack, president of the Growers and Shippers Association, thanked Connell for his timely intervention and assured him "the active cooperation of all the Imperial Valley growers and shippers in your endeavors."[53] Jack also reiterated an argument that growers broadcast widely: that the responsibility for labor uprisings rested squarely on the shoulders of "agitators." "If I thought," stated Jack, "that this spirit of unrest was created by disagreeable working conditions, insufficient pay, long hours, or some similar cause, I would be working to correct that condition." But, he continued, "the hours are relatively short, those who live on our ranches are better housed than they have been accustomed to in their own country, and the pay is better." Such a denial of reality is hard to countenance. Conveniently, this refusal to look allowed them to deny any notion of grower responsibility for the conditions that led to the labor strife. Connell, in friendly acquiescence with Jack, promised to cooperate "to the best of my ability."[54] In these complacent exchanges we see how Jack and Connell reinforced one another's class attitudes toward working conditions and wages of the farmworkers and exculpated themselves from any accountability. In any case, the cantaloupe strike was over before it began.

Notwithstanding this defeat, the TUUL continued its work of organizing the pickers. And in August the consulate again responded to the AWIL threat with a "most tenacious campaign" that involved establishing "Brigadas de la Cruz Azul Mexicana" and comisiones honoríficas "in those areas meriting their functioning."[55] Eighteen months later Consul

Aragón proudly reported that a *comisión honorífica* executive committee had been installed at Brawley. Three hundred compatriots witnessed the inauguration and heard the consul extol the patriotic tasks of the *comisión*. Several local authorities had been invited to the ceremony, including Lon Cromer, the Brawley Chief of Police, who spoke briefly. According to Consul Aragón's report to his superiors, Cromer sympathized with the nascent Mexican institution and "offered to help it in any way that he could."[56] Moreover, Cromer guaranteed that within his jurisdiction "he treated all Mexicans the same way that he treated any other foreigner, within the established laws." As the ceremonies came to an end, Cromer received "expressions of appreciation from the assembled members of the colonia."

In 1930 the consulate exercised a spurious calming influence on its Mexican compatriots, which served to mask the unrelieved oppression that workers faced every day. The "agitators" were gone, but the restless discontent continued in the settlements and the fields. Small work stoppages involving a few dozen workers were not unusual. Between 1930 and 1933 these eruptions grew to encompass hundreds and eventually thousands of workers. Still, these skirmishes did nothing to change the basic situation. The stage was set for a more massive rebellion. All the more determined in the face of this unrest were the foes of unionization— the federal mediators, the Mexican association led by the Mexican consul, and, of course, the growers. A season of strikes appeared inevitable.

The Strikes of 1933 and 1934

For the three years following the failed strike of 1930, the Communist Party had turned its attention away from agricultural organizing in order to focus on unemployed councils and urban industrial workers. The lull in the Valley was deceptive. It was an uneasy peace soon to be shattered in 1933, when a new agricultural campaign was launched by the CAWIU. The time was right. Wages had dipped to pre-Depression levels, and in the spring of 1933 a wave of walkouts and strikes, led by the CAWIU, had been steadily advancing across the Valley floor.

As had occurred in the Los Angeles County and San Joaquin Valley strikes, the consulate-led Mexican workers association fought off CAWIU incursions in the picking fields. The CAWIU organizers with time had learned from previous strike events, and so perhaps had the consulate. Both consulate and CAWIU began this new battle armed with a sophisticated understanding of the nature of the conflict. The CAWIU understood, for example, that with the wages of the workers at issue and with both the consulate and growers committed to the status quo and opposed to unionization, fear of communism would be used to confuse CAWIU's organizing efforts. The agricultural working class would be blindsided by this convenient bogey and forced into cooperating with the interests of the growers. Growers, police, courts, and the federal mediators (who would come in later) established a solid footing to defeat the efforts of the workers to organize and bargain for a living wage.

However, it was 1933, and the Mexican consulate and the U.S. entities were considering a different strategy. To placate a workforce that was demanding a union, the growers broke with their long-held antiunion policy and conceived of a plan whereby a "union" would be established. But it would be under their control. In effect, what they proposed was an in-house union with leadership in the hands of the Mexican consul, who would act in compliance with growers' agenda. The agreement between the consulate and the growers and the "union" that ensued had the blessing of the U.S. federal government. In the spring of 1934, the investigative reports (of which more later) of two U.S. agencies had urged that in order to stabilize the labor situation a conservative organization of workers be established whereby disputes could be settled through negotiation.

The series of labor struggles that took place in the Imperial Valley between October 1933 and June 1934 were characterized by such high levels of violence that observers were prompted to compare the Valley to regions of the United States made notorious for their volatile class relations. "The blind prejudice," wrote a Protestant minister from Los Angeles, "of a large section of the population exceeds what we have been led to expect in the coal mining areas of Kentucky, Virginia, and Pennsylvania." [57] Another witness to events in the Valley, a United Press reporter, described the Valley as a "Harlan County, with much additional and original elaboration." [58] Joaquín Terrazas, the Mexican consul stationed in Calexico, was instrumental in turning Imperial Valley into a border-style Harlan County in the years 1933 and 1934.

Joaquín Terrazas

Explaining the conflicts and their resolution requires that we single out Consul Terrazas for particular attention. Terrazas was born and raised in the border state of Chihuahua and may have been related to the *latifundista* Terrazas clan, a politically powerful family of Chihuahua, though evidence of that connection is not conclusive. Terrazas left home as a young man to attend the Instituto Científico y Literario in the state capital. After completing his studies, he journeyed to California to take a two-year course in commerce at the Los Angeles Business College. Returning to Mexico, Terrazas found employment in a series of modest jobs as bookkeeper, typist, stenographer, and finally bank cashier in various Chihuahua businesses. Nothing in his education or in his experience indicated that Terrazas held the qualifications, other than speaking English, for the consular service. Lacking such merits, it is quite possible that political connections secured his first assignment in 1921, the consulate in Nogales, Arizona. Later he was posted to Detroit, serving as consul supervising Vice-Consul Enrique Bravo. From there he was sent to Los Angeles. In every jurisdiction Terrazas's tenure was without distinction. He performed the usual duties, made the yearly census, participated in the formation of *comisiones honoríficas,* and, most importantly, kept careful check on the activities of these organizations, dutifully reporting any "seditious" organizations and individuals.[59] Terrazas enjoyed the "perks" that the service offered and preferred living in the United States because, as he once said, "of the opportunity to educate my children and have them learn English as they never could in the schools of Mexico."[60]

The consul had a seamy side, a history of political corruption that had been carefully concealed from public view. In a confidential report to the Department of State, U.S. Consul at Mexicali Howard A. Bowman wrote that bribes had been paid to Terrazas through the Mexican Immigration Service. Terrazas had exacted a personal "fee" of $20 from aliens entering through Mexicali, supposedly to expedite the process of legal entry. Other unidentified forms of bribery were reported as well.[61]

In 1933 Terrazas was posted to Calexico, in the heart of the Imperial Valley, and was almost instantly plunged into the labor maelstrom. In the seventeen years that he would serve the Mexican government, no other assignment would gain him such notoriety as his tenure in Calexico, where amidst controversy he rose from mediocrity to emerge as a central figure in the border county labor rebellion. As the new consul to Calexico, Terrazas would make one of his first acts to insinuate himself into the revived Asociación Mexicana del Valle Imperial. As we will see, although the U.S. federal government was well aware of Terrazas's corrupt practices in Mexicali, he emerged as their key figure within the labor conflict for achieving grower and federal mediation goals in 1933 and 1934.

The Gathering Storm

Terrazas was in place and ready for battle when the first strike occurred in October of 1933. This was a lettuce strike led by workers demanding a wage increase, and it was settled within two days through negotiations with growers. It was Terrazas who represented the five hundred members of the revived Asociación Mexicana del Valle Imperial and who led them to quickly settle the strike.[62] A druggist, R. R. Flores of the Mexican *colonia,* also sat in on the negotiations and, according to the *Brawley News,* acted as "one of the spokesmen for the Mexican organization."[63] A. N. Jack, the head of the Imperial Valley Shippers and Growers Association, represented the growers at the meeting. As reported in the *Brawley News,* Jack was generous in his compliments to Terrazas. "He [Terrazas] was inclined to be eminently fair and just," stated Jack, "in the handling of the local situation and it was a pleasure for the growers to meet with him."[64] The *Brawley News* reported, disingenuously one supposes, that "the growers and workers are now in complete harmony." The *News* continued its coverage, stating that the agreement prevented "professional agitators from flocking into the Valley." The "agitators" referred to were the CAWIU, active in the San Joaquin Valley at the time.[65]

Consul Terrazas emerged from the lettuce strike negotiations as the growers' champion. However, it might have been predicted that a strike that lasted but two days had not gone anywhere. And so the short-lived labor peace broke a few weeks later in mid-November when two thousand pea pickers went out on strike. Again the consul intervened and the brief strike led by the rebellious rank and file was quickly settled. However, this strike alarmed growers because of the appearance of "agitators," the now common euphemism for organizers who challenged the grower hegemony. In fact, a CAWIU cadre had arrived and found a receptive audience in the Valley. But time did not favor the CAWIU; it was too short, and the union was outmaneuvered by Terrazas, who was able to lead association members away from the "reds." The strike ended, announced the *Brawley News* headlines, after "Shippers and Leaders of Mexican Organization Reach Understanding in Brawley Meeting."[66]

Growers were again enormously gratified by Terrazas's performance. The heads of several companies reportedly stated that "through the Mexican consul, Joaquín Terrazas, the Mexican laborers had apologized for the strike."[67] Terrazas explained that the strike had originated in the communist element but that workers, if left alone, preferred to work. In fact, the strike was broken through two astute grower maneuvers: first, strike leaders identified as "reds" were arrested; and secondly, negotiations were conducted with the newly proclaimed "official" union leaders. The *Brawley News* reported on the strategy: "Once the more conservative leaders of the Mexican union were allowed to have control with the alleged agitators and their threats in the event of disobeyance [sic] out of the way, the strike differences were settled at once to the satisfaction of both laborers and shippers."[68] For the moment an interval of uneasy calm returned to the Valley. It was a waiting game, and it would not be a long wait. CAWIU organizers, fresh from the October San Joaquin cotton strike, were gaining a foothold in the Valley, and again workers welcomed them in spite of the Asociación's anti-CAWIU stance. The next confrontation was soon to be.

The pattern of spontaneous strikes in defiance of the Mexican Asociación leaders, a pattern established as far back as 1928, now began to repeat itself in late 1933 and early 1934. The determination of the rank and file to take matters into their own hands from time to time presented difficulties for the growers and consuls. Thus far the growers had been able to manage these problems without a break in production. But with the appearance of experienced and committed union organizers, the balance of power was shifting. Wages continued to be the main issue, and the grower-approved union had done nothing to deal with it. This led to factions and divisions within the Asociación that created a significant opening for the CAWIU.

At the same time, federal mediators had concluded that deplorable conditions and low wages had produced the discontent that led to strikes. These U.S. mediators advised growers to eliminate poor conditions as an effective way of separating workers from communist influence. Growers had historically ignored such appeals, and they did so again. They would win by using strong-arm tactics and dividing the workers. Growers would go on explaining strikes by pointing to "agitators" who allegedly misled contented labor. As members of the dominant class, they could count on police and courts to support their interests; they could also depend on Consul Terrazas, who offered his loyal support.

The CAWIU first set up its headquarters in Brawley in November 1933 and quickly drew in members from the Mexican association. By December the CAWIU had gained the sympathies of the majority of Valley workers—Mexican, white, Black, and Filipino—many of whom joined the renegade union. The stage was set for the events of January and February 1934 with new leadership and a new organization. The consul and growers, though perhaps not yet aware of the shift in loyalties, no longer enjoyed a free hand to settle labor disputes. By January 2, 1934, the CAWIU had so empowered Mexican association members that, at a regularly scheduled meeting between the association and growers, worker representatives demanded a surprisingly sharp wage increase. Taken aback, growers refused to discuss the issue and the meeting broke up, but not before the CAWIU organizer had invited workers to attend a CAWIU meeting scheduled for January 4, two days later. "The invitation was received with loud expressions of sympathy and the majority went to the proceedings."[69]

The *La Opinión* journalist present at the emergency CAWIU meeting on January 4 observed that "a numerous public waited anxiously to hear the purpose of the invitation." An organizer made the announcement. The CAWIU was calling a strike. Asociación members were invited to join in the work stoppage, and sentiment for a strike was overwhelming. After a dialogue among workers, they agreed on a demand of 35 cents per hour, a guaranteed minimum working day of five hours, free transport to the fields, fresh drinking water, abolition of the contractor system, and union recognition. When a call went out to form a strike committee, "at once 25 workers came forward," and soon an order went out to print ten thousand informational leaflets in English and Spanish. The strike of five thousand Valley lettuce and vegetable workers was declared throughout the Valley, to commence January 8. The Mexican association, in effect absorbed by the CAWIU, "went out of existence." [70]

The police and the courts reacted predictably, resisting any threat to their interests. Many key county officials held farmlands and had a direct connection to the labor conflicts. For example, Captain Frank Oswalt, in charge of the Valley's State Highway Patrol unit, owned and farmed four hundred acres of lettuce, melons, and cantaloupes near El Centro. E. H. Harrigan, the "absolutely dishonest and unscrupulous" county agricultural commissioner, "owned and operated four ranches." [71] Other law-enforcement authorities who were farming land included Chief of Police Brawley, Lon Cromer, County Sheriff George Campbell, and Undersheriff Rodney Clark. The Undersheriff was said to "operate a considerable acreage." Within the court system, H. B. Griffin, police judge and justice of the peace, also owned and farmed land. [72]

Trampling on legalities, as the growers referred to civil rights, growers began their strikebreaking campaign with a vengeance. The blatant circumventions of law in the Valley during winter 1933 and spring 1934 being widely known, the ACLU now entered the fray. Famous for its use of constitutional law as a defense, the ACLU now invoked the Bill of Rights in acting to defend the rights of workers to strike and bargain collectively. As we shall see, the consul would vigorously oppose the ACLU as it championed the legal protections that had been stripped from union membership.

A. L. Wirin, the ACLU attorney, reported that "the officials announced that no meetings of any kind, anywhere, would be allowed in the Valley . . . meetings on a private lot, or in a private meeting hall have come under the ban. Half a dozen Mexican workers chatting on a street are a 'public meeting' and dispersed by the police." [73] On January 13, *La Opinión* reported that "All locales where strikers meet were invaded . . . to prevent workers from meeting." [74]

At a meeting of five hundred strikers on January 12 convened to discuss their demands, one of the first violent incidents took place. The assembly was broken up by "fifty deputy sheriffs, police, and highway patrolmen" by tossing tear gas canisters into the hall. Workers fiercely fought back. According to a *La Opinión* reporter on the scene, "the strikers . . . changed the order of things when they returned the canisters" and temporarily repulsed the attack. The lawmen then regrouped and chased the strikers out of the hall and into the street, where a second pitched battle ensued, with strikers defending themselves against the lawmen. The strikers were forcibly dispersed and arrests were made. After the melee, the hall stood in ruins, the kitchen ransacked, doors unhinged, windows broken, and chairs and tables splintered. One infant who had been exposed to the deadly tear gas fumes contracted pneumonia and later died.

Later that week, workers and police engaged in a second battle. The union had called a demonstration in Brawley to demand the release of their jailed comrades, and "over 1000 workers mobilized." Trouble erupted when police rushed forward, surrounded the demonstrators, and hurled tear gas canisters into the crowd. At the onslaught, the crowd fled in every direction.

Not all confrontations resulted in attacks or brawls, as strikers often found themselves too greatly outnumbered and simply did what they were told. As an example, a caravan of strikers on their way to the Calexico picket lines "were corralled by the authorities . . . and compelled to walk ten miles from Calexico to the El Centro jail." [75] Mass arrests, tear-gas raids on peaceful assemblies, prohibitions against picketing, beatings, and other wholesale violations of constitutional guarantees became everyday occurrnces and undermined whatever semblance of law existed. "Reds," "agitators," and strikers were subjected to arbitrary arrests, illegal searches and seizures, kidnappings, and other acts of violence. Anyone in support of the strike, or even critical of the breakdown of law, was treated to similar attacks. In time, residents of the Valley who were sympathetic to the strike felt they could not afford the retaliatory risks involved and remained silent. [76]

Although the arrests of union leaders greatly hindered the strike, they failed to knock it out. Workers continued their fight in the fields without a break. On January 22 a Los Angeles newspaper described the strike as "the most hectic strike here in several years." [77]

As in past labor troubles, growers approached the consul for his services, which he willingly rendered. Even though the Mexican Asociación had been bypassed, Terrazas was able to use his considerable powers as consul to persuade workers to abandon the strike, return to work, and reject the CAWIU. Terrazas also worked directly with growers in coordinating specific actions to break the strike. In one such action, a mass arrest was made of some eighty-seven strikers near the town of Heber. The arrest was led by police and vigilantes comprised of off-duty police, sheriff's deputies, growers, and hired goons. The workers, men and women, were marched together to El Centro, a town six miles away. Just outside the El Centro city limits, Terrazas had been stationed to intercept the terrified families. Terrazas must have appeared as a beacon of safety; they were ready to listen to his words. According to a newspaper report, the workers "were talked to for a few minutes . . . showing them the futility of their stand and exhorting them to return to their work without further trouble. The consul's speech had the desired effect and upon the promise of the strikers that they would return to their homes peacefully and not listen further to agitators, they were released." [78]

The editor of the *Brawley News* used his newspaper as a pulpit, as did editors of other Valley newspapers, warning strikers that deportations might very well be the consequence of their actions and stating in an editorial that "Mexican workers brought across the border to labor in the lettuce and cantaloupe fields have been wisely counseled by Consul Joaquín Terrazas that they have been allowed to come to the American side for a specific purpose and that they are expected to obey the laws of this country. Those who do not accept the advice of their countryman should be made to understand that their place is on the south side of the boundary." [79] The next day a *Calexico Chronicle* headline cheered Terrazas (and the antiunion constituency), proclaiming, "Terrazas Will Help Quell Strike Trouble," and credited him "with stamping out two previous strikes." Terrazas, the article stated, appealed for a one-day truce and arbitration, "hoping for success" among Mexicans, but declared that "Filipinos, Americans, and Negroes will probably not listen to anything I have to say." Terrazas confidently maintained that he could "induce Mexican workers to return to the lettuce fields." [80]

The cowardly assault on the unarmed strikers during the forced march to El Centro followed by the compelling words of Terrazas combined to quell the strikers, who found themselves torn between a wave of violence and a retreat back to the fields. Both the big stick and the soft words were aimed at manipulating the strikers—and the strategy worked. By the last week of January the strike, already in disarray, had ground to a halt. In addition, the arrests of CAWIU leaders Pat Chambers, Dorothy Ray, and Stanley Hancock had seriously weakened the union's ability to continue the strike. Nevertheless, in spite of the army of growers, police, and vigilantes determined to eliminate the CAWIU as an influence in the Valley, the union pushed on with its organizing campaign.

The ACLU was a constant presence. And significantly, it had sought and been granted a federal court injunction to restrain police from breaking up the ACLU meetings for discussion of workers' constitutional rights.[81] The court injunction was ignored. If anything, it appeared to have incited the vigilantes to further violence. In one brutal incident on January 23, ACLU attorney A. L. Wirin, who was about to address an assembly of several hundred defiant Mexican workers, was kidnapped, beaten, robbed, threatened with death, and dumped in the desert miles from the nearest city. His car was then destroyed by the mob of vigilantes comprised of growers and police officers. After some time the ACLU meeting continued, the participants being unaware of the seriousness of their colleague's plight. Several of Wirin's companions addressed the assembly, closely watched by an excited crowd of some two hundred men who had been called out by the American Legion "in case of trouble." Many of these men, acting out of alcohol-induced bravado, were unruly and belligerent.[82] After the ACLU meeting was adjourned, Wirin's companions, still unaware of their colleague's fate, went out in search of him and were set upon by the legionnaires. Men and women were "atrociously treated by the legionnaire vigilantes. . . . They were made to throw up their arms and keep them up for half an hour, while vigilantes searched them, poked guns in their ribs and abused them."[83] One of the victims counted twenty-seven guns pointed at him at one time. Another victim, Helen Marston of the San Diego ACLU, recalled guns run up and down her blouse by men "liquored up" for the evening's proceedings.

The bureaucracy in Sacramento, the state capital, remained silent as to the proceedings in the Imperial Valley. No official statements were made regarding the kidnapping and beating of ACLU representative Wirin or about guns used against unarmed citizens. Timothy A. Reardon, the director of the State Department of Industrial Relations, reported to Governor Rolph that after a visit to the Valley he saw "nothing seriously wrong." Reardon instead criticized Wirin for defending strike leaders and for "provoking dissatisfaction" among laborers. "Outsiders have taken the strike from the hands of the field workers," concluded Director Reardon.[84] The vigilantism of the Imperial Valley growers was not to be reprimanded. Aside from the ACLU, the CAWIU, and scattered friends and supporters, there was no opposition to the lawlessness of the authorities; they enjoyed an unlimited range of power. With no brake, only an accelerator, the conflict escalated. To oppose the union supporters entering the Valley, growers called on their own backup: the police.

In mid-January Captain William Hynes, of the Los Angeles Police Department's "Red Squad," arrived to carry out his own investigation and, like Reardon, blamed the communists and the ACLU for inciting workers to a "campaign of violence . . . a destruction of property." Hynes's under-cover "probe" "uncovered" a secret plan "for a mass attack upon the county jail," fortunately "prevented by the prompt action of the Mexican consul urging his countrymen not to engage in any such attack." [85] Al-though Reardon and Hynes held the communists responsible for the strike and the violence in the valley, the ACLU concluded in a blunt state-ment that a "total collapse of local and state government happened in the Imperial Valley." Wirin, having barely come out alive from the kidnap-ping, stated, "The federal and state constitutions have been suspended. Freedom of speech and freedom of assemblage exists only for legion-naires, vigilantes, and ranchers." [86]

Campbell MacCulloch, executive secretary at the Los Angeles Re-gional Office of the National Labor Board charged with investigating the Valley situation, acknowledged that authorities "went beyond their legal limits" but concluded, "that they were forced to take the action they did is hardly to be questioned." He strengthened his argument by adding that fifteen hundred communists "have been sent into Imperial Valley . . . and the situation is fraught with real danger" (a charge impossible to be-lieve).[87] That the CAWIU posed a major threat to the Valley's peace and economic well-being was agreed upon by all parties—the growers, the Department of Labor, the National Labor Board, the Federal Imperial Valley Commission, and the Mexican consul. But as to fighting this men-ace, two camps existed: one considered any action, legal or illegal, as jus-tified in ousting the CAWIU; the other favored a more subtle, indirect, but generally legal action.

Federal Intervention I

The ACLU's assessment that federal and state constitutions had been vio-lated in the Valley was set forth in a complaint by the ACLU and for-warded to the Department of Justice. This in turn prompted the Depart-ment of Labor and the National Recovery Administration's National Labor Board to dispatch a federal commission to the Valley in late Janu-ary. Simon Lubin, William French, and J. L. Leonard, men of impeccable Progressive liberal beliefs, comprised the commission. Campbell Mac-Culloch's suggestions to the commission members initiating the investi-gation are revealing. MacCulloch's "avenues of inquiry into the Impe-rial Valley" listed brief evaluations of fourteen individuals. First on the list was Consul Joaquín Terrazas, whom MacCulloch described as one "thoroughly informed on the problems and conditions of the Mexican workers in the Valley. Exceptionally fair-minded and anxious to lend every assistance."[88]

The federal commission conducted its investigation between January 29 and February 7. During the survey, the commission witnessed a strike in the pea fields led by the CAWIU that left four thousand pickers in the northern section of the Valley idle for at least a week. The pattern of previous walkouts continued as arrests, mass evictions, beatings, and general harassment prevented the union from fully carrying out its plans. Growers attempted to force strikers to return by interdicting federal relief supplies and by forcing the evacuation of several thousand workers and their families from a pickers' camp (under the guise of enforcing county sanitation regulations).[89] Nevertheless, growers were eventually forced to the negotiating table; at the initial parley the pickers demanded 1.5 cents per hamper, the growers refused, and the meeting ended without closure. It is not clear whether the union realized any gains before the strike ended on or about February 20. The federal commission's investigative report offering a new path for grower-consul cooperation had been issued on February 14, six days prior to the end of the strike.

In the commission's report, the Valley authorities were cited for overstepping legal sanctions in dealing with the strikers. Significantly, the three officials who abhorred the influence of the communists recognized that harsh living and working conditions were significant factors leading to the workers' discontent, factors the CAWIU could manipulate to their advantage. A living wage, a decent house, and the right to organize, they reasoned, would eliminate the threat of communist influence, and this recommendation was included in the commission's report. The report also urged the federal and state governments to "take every necessary step to protect all persons in their constitutional rights." The report went on to warn, "The menace of further disturbance warrants immediate action toward the removal of those conditions, real or fancied, that create and encourage discontent." Making explicit its anti-CAWIU stance, the commission cited a "lack of open and efficient leadership" (due to the presence of the CAWIU) as contributing to labor instability. The report briefly mentions an organization in process of formation (during their investigation) among Mexicans under non-CAWIU influence and appears to present it as a potential alternative.

The evidence is sketchy, but it seems that the Asociación Mexicana formed in late January comprised of merchants, civic clubs, and social and fraternal organizations is the organization referred to in the commission's report. The political character of the group is reflected in its appeal via English-language newspapers asking that the community recognize and respect the "stable" and "proper" Mexican element. Whether or not that Asociación would later be identified in the report as the acceptable and preferred union in process of organizing is not clear. In the *Brawley News,* the officers of the Asociación are quoted as stating: "The actual purpose of the committee is to make disappear the impression that the Mexican residents of Brawley as a whole are a disorderly element and that they are interested in any unlawful activity. This statement is made due to the fact that present circumstances are creating such impressions among many local American residents."[90]

In its final recommendation, the report suggested that the federal government "encourage the organization of workers, in order that collective bargaining may be effective in matters of wages and conditions, both working and living, and that the right to strike and peacefully picket shall be maintained. . . . Specially do we recommend that the United States Department of Labor representatives who can speak Spanish [be available] to organize for the purpose of collective bargaining."[91]

Growers were immediately hostile to the report. Their resentment was directed primarily toward the references to their lawlessness and the unconstitutional tactics of police and vigilantes. They showed no resistance to the recommendation for the development of a cooperative union that had in fact evolved from the commission's deliberations with grower representatives during their investigation. Growers had agreed with the proposal for an organization of labor, even one headed by the AFL. However, a union headed by Consul Terrazas, which they arranged, only sweetened the deal. Growers could conduct business as usual, "agitators" would be checked, and it would all be aboveboard as growers fulfilled a key federal commission recommendation.[92]

There was some anxiety among growers that Terrazas would not remain in the Calexico consulate to see the affair through to a successful conclusion. Shortly before the commission report was issued, A. G. Arnoll, managing secretary of the Los Angeles County Chamber of Commerce, wired President Abelardo Rodríguez in an effort to secure Terrazas's tenure as consul: "controversial matters between workers and employers in the Imperial Valley can reach happy ending if Mr. Terrazas . . . remains in the Valley during the next four months. The Mexican working class is the key . . . and the consul enjoys the confidence of all."[93] Terrazas not only remained the four months but also did not leave the Valley until 1938.

The day after the report was issued, Campbell MacCulloch, sensing urgency, acted immediately by wiring Terrazas: "Please advise by telegraph if you believe any possibility of obtaining truly representative committee Mexican field workers to sit in on conference with growers under our auspices STOP Also if you believe former union of Mexican laborers can be revived and made effective unit and with which growers could sign agreement on hours wages etc."[94] Terrazas wired MacCulloch his reply that same day (with a duplicate to A. N. Jack, representative for the growers): "Yours I am working hard right now organizing new and effective union of Mexican laborers in Valley with view of cementing cordial and permanent relations between workers and growers and thus eliminating outside influence of agitators."[95]

Terrazas's "union" received a sub-rosa official recognition even before it had been established. It had already won backing from the Valley's power base. Growers had by now bowed to the reality that a union in the Valley was inescapable, but with their man Terrazas at the helm, they could relax in the knowledge that a company union would be the result of Terrazas's organizing efforts. In truth, the Asociación as a union of workers would never exist, as it should, as an oppositional entity to the capitalist class. Under Terrazas's leadership, the Asociación would function as a house union and growers could rest assured that "their" workers were not organized. As before, the labor market belonged to the growers, and they could control it. Once again we see evidence, in the growers' strong and overt favoritism toward the consul, that Terrazas was their willing tool rather than a representative of his compatriots, the Mexican workers. Under Terrazas's leadership the Asociación promised the growers the continuation of a disorganized labor market.[96] As one "prominent Valley Shipper" exclaimed at a Rotary Club luncheon, "the conservative wise [sic] efforts of the consul to settle the labor trouble and his fairness to both sides had been of inestimable worth to the Imperial Valley."[97] Playing the consul card had worked again. Thus, Terrazas had the support of growers, local and state authorities, and the Department of Labor's National Labor Board. In an odd and ironic twist, Terrazas, an official of a foreign government, emerges here as an agent of the U.S. government in its campaign against independent unions.

The day following the exchange of wires with MacCulloch, Terrazas met with J. L. Leonard of the commission and a committee of growers to discuss "a union of Mexican laborers in the Valley to prevent further strike troubles."[98] Four days later, newspapers announced plans for an organization limited to Mexican agricultural laborers and headed by Terrazas. Leaflets distributed throughout the Valley invited Mexican workers to the first organizing meeting at the old Calexico boxing arena. In an editorial, the *Brawley News* expressed its approval for the conclave, contending that the "gathering is to form a union not only to protect the workers, but also the growers from further labor trouble." The paper's advocacy continued, "Consul Terrazas not only maintains the highest respect of his countrymen, but also enjoys the confidence of the growers who look upon him as a man who desires to be fair when controversial issues arise." [99]

At the former boxing arena in Calexico on or about March 14, the crowd of workers who had gathered there were addressed by Terrazas and Luis Valdés, secretary of the Mexican government's conciliation and arbitration commission in Mexicali. [100] The presence of Valdés is another example of the official connection between the Mexican pro-government labor central, the corrupt Confederación Regional Obrera Mexicana, (CROM), and the two southern California Mexican unions, the Confederación de Uniones Campesinos y Obreros Mexicanos (CUCOM) and the Confederación de Uniones Obreras Mexicanas (CUOM). Valdés spoke to the audience and explained that "relations with communists do not yield good results" and that workers should "ally with the elements of order and faithful interpreters of the law." He then promised the "cooperation and support of workers on the other side of the border." [101] Valdés's conservative politics coincided with those of Terrazas, and the two officials would collaborate, as we will see, with the growers in the consul's and growers' organizing drives.

There is evidence officially linking Terrazas with CROM as well as with the Mexican police. A Valley politician stated that the association organized by Terrazas in collaboration with Valdés was an affiliate of a Mexican union with 2 million members (referring to CROM). [102] The second organizing meeting bore out this tie. In addition to Valdés and Terrazas, two labor leaders from Mexicali (one a member of the government's arbitration board) addressed the gathering; later, the Mexicali Military Marching Band performed. Meetings addressed by Terrazas and Valdés were held at several Valley towns, and a committee was formed at each site to act as the union local (a CROM affiliate). In addition to CROM's cooperation with Terrazas, the Mexican government also became involved when the Mexican police contributed to the anti-CAWIU campaign. The *Los Angeles Times* reported during the January lettuce strike that "Terrazas and the Mexican police are working in full accord with officers on this side of the line." [103] When CAWIU organizer Stanley Hancock fled to Mexicali to escape threats of physical violence and certain arrest, Mexicali authorities, acting in response to the Calexico police, promptly deported him. [104]

Thus a network of organizations linked together through the institution of the Mexican state had now joined with the growers to establish a union. Not only did the conservative Mexican union CROM and the arbitration board cooperate to establish the grower union, but also local growers reciprocated by rendering "all possible assistance to Consul

Terrazas in his efforts to form a union."[105] Naturally, county politicians publicly backed Terrazas. The Mayor of Brawley, R. L. Baker, for example, wired Terrazas during the organizing campaign: "I wish to take this opportunity of expressing my appreciation for the efforts you are putting forth in promoting industrial peace."[106] Later the same official made a generous offer of a vacant lot and "assistance in the construction of an 'adobe' assembly hall to serve as headquarters for the union."[107] Growers could afford to include Mexican nationalist inducements (an 'adobe' hall) when their purpose was to control labor unionization. The Brawley headquarters planned for the new association, named the Casa Mexicana, was intended to serve as a cultural center, with "auditorium, office, and even living room for workers."[108]

In spite of threats to workers of physical harm, acts of terrorism, and the usual nationalist rhetoric and inducements, Terrazas's unionization drive failed to garner widespread support. An estimated 150 laborers had attended the first meeting; a few more showed up at the second. Apparently, laborers had resisted Terrazas's promises as well as the growers' threats and refused to join the Asociación. An ACLU investigation into civil rights violations revealed "cases where men were given four days by ranch owners to join the association on threat of being discharged unless they did so."[109] Investigator Ernest Besig gathered further evidence verifying that growers had used such threats throughout the Valley. The foreman at the Sears Brothers Ranch in Brawley, for example, "gave 12 workers [a few days] to sign applications for the consul's association" and said that two had been discharged and forced to leave the campgrounds for failing to sign.[110] Besig contended that the "Terrazas union was not very popular and that those who signed the applications were doing so merely to keep their jobs."[111] Only a few were fooled by the nationalist charms. In the *colonias* Terrazas was "subjected to criticism" for his activities, prompting Terrazas to schedule meetings outside of the Mexican neighborhoods.

When queried by Besig in regard to widespread intimidation and threats of violence, Terrazas was patently dishonest, responding that "he knew of no such intimidation."[112] Terrazas maintained that "the Mexican association was not a labor union," and, "In fact, no union existed." He further claimed that in sponsoring organizational meetings "he was merely taking a census of the opinion of his countrymen to ascertain whether or not they wanted to form an association."[113] Incredibly, Terrazas insisted that the ranch managers had handed out the association sign-up cards and that the growers, therefore, were the real organizers! It would seem that telling the truth was not one of Terrazas's strategies.

Generally, noted Besig, the CAWIU was "making little progress" in its organizing campaign in the face of "the anti-Communist agitation ... and the intimidation of workers and organizers by the authorities." [114] "They are forced," concluded Besig, "into the Terrazas shipper-controlled organization." [115] Intimidation tactics (by growers) had stunted CAWIU organizing efforts, and yet the union made some gains. Besig found that even though workers in El Centro feared what would happen if they joined the union, many were willing to attend the secret organizational meetings. His investigation also revealed that many workers realized that the association was in fact "a company union, a union organized and controlled by the growers and shippers." [116] Clearly, the workers wanted a union that would represent them, and when they were able to put their fears of grower retaliation aside, the CAWIU managed to sign them up. Altogether around 800 joined the CAWIU. With 500 members, the Brawley local was the largest; Calexico's local had 150 members. Only 50 or so workers officially joined the Communist Party; just three chapters of the Young Communist League (YCL) were active. The YCL drew its membership "from Mexican boys in schools" who, despite serious consequences, "placed the initials YCL on their jerseys, as well as the communist insignia." [117]

In spite of the fact that the Asociación Mexicana del Valle Imperial had faltered (and was losing members), on March 27 it initiated its first countywide organizational meeting at the *comisión honorífica* headquarters. Presided over by Terrazas and the comisión president, the meeting was attended by the delegates of the Asociación and the Board of Directors of the Imperial Valley Growers and Shippers Protective Association. The purpose of the meeting was to negotiate an agreement. Terrazas and the growers had apparently settled beforehand on the terms of the pact. The Asociación asked for wages of 25 cents an hour for field labor (hoeing, cultivating, irrigation) and 13 cents an hour for picking cantaloupes, without guarantees as to number of hours. The growers readily agreed to this wage scale; there was no negotiation. The CAWIU had demanded more, 35 cents for field labor and 16 cents for picking. Among other terms, the Asociación had agreed that pickers would "exercise more care in the picking of melons and that they will properly follow instructions of their employers." [118] Several of the same promises made in the 1930 agreement reappeared in the 1934 "sweetheart" pact. Growers agreed to provide free ice and water, but picking sacks would be charged, the cost refunded at the end of the season or when the worker was either fired or quit. If workers struck they would, of course, lose the refund. The final clause clearly defined and reinforced the relations of economic and political power in the Valley: all grievances against employers would henceforth be processed and arbitrated exclusively by a committee of four representatives from the Imperial Valley Protective Association, an arrangement undoubtedly worked out with Terrazas's consent.

On March 28 the Asociación distributed its first official *Boletín* informing Mexican workers of the accord reached at the meeting "presided over by the Consul of Mexico, Señor Joaquín Terrazas." As in previous Mexican labor associations, the latest one limited membership to those of "Mexican citizenship or descent." [119] Furthermore, growers refused to offer work to any laborer who did not possess an Asociación membership card. This provision was perhaps the final threat—no card, no work—and in effect provided the growers with an official labor contractor. The *Brawley News* referred to the new association as a "clearing house for all Mexican labor" standing ready "to combat communism." [120] Terrazas boasted that he expected "to dominate the actions" of the Asociación and would thereby "curb the activities of the communist organizers." [121] In fact, the agreement pledged the Asociación to patrol the fields to keep communist organizers from contacting workers. The growers also expressed their intent "to provide protection . . . from interference from communist agitators."

Growers had finally gotten an agreement that gave them everything they asked for. And it was Consul Terrazas who had delivered it to them. To show their appreciation, a reference to a resolution in the agreement included their thanks, "commending Señor Joaquín Terrazas, the consul of Mexico, for his efforts in aiding the preservation of industrial peace in the Imperial Valley and a copy of this resolution is to be mailed to Mr. Terrazas's government in the City of Mexico." [122] Valley newspapers jumped on the bandwagon, saluting Terrazas for his "splendid work in bringing his group together" and "preserving harmony between the growers and workers." [123] Asociación handbills in Spanish were passed out through the Valley to inform all Mexican workers of the terms, warning those who wished to keep their jobs, and who had not yet signed, that they had better join the Asociación. All CAWIU members were now shut out of work in the fields. [124]

Mexico City had, of course, been kept up to date. Consular dispatches had informed the central government of Terrazas's operations in phrases that were careful to indicate that Terrazas had been solely motivated in all his endeavors by his loyalties to the Mexican government rather than by any personal concerns. Terrazas's superior in San Francisco, Alejandro Lubbert, sent a copy of the federal commission's report to Mexico's president, Abelardo Rodríguez, along with a note that read: "This copy of the report was given to me by Mr. George Creel, intimate friend of mine and director of the N.R.A. along the Pacific coast, with whom, as I have informed the President, I am in constant contact." [125] Lubbert's favorable evaluation surely must have caught the attention of the president and the secretary of foreign relations. "The commissioners' recommendations," noted the consul general, "reflect the favorable attitude of the superior American authorities toward the working class, be they foreign or national." Federal intervention, he assured, will "notably improve the conditions of thousands of Mexican workers in the agricultural fields of California." [126] While the report underwent review, Terrazas arrived in Mexico City, where he provided a thorough briefing of his conduct. The Secretariat of Foreign Relations found no problems with Terrazas's performance, and Terrazas returned to the Valley, where he immediately resumed his organizing campaign for the Asociación.

The CAWIU was fully aware that the Asociación, acting as the growers' union, had defined objectives and strategies: to control wages, to prevent strikes by dividing the workers, and to eliminate the CAWIU. It was understood that splitting Mexicans, white Americans, Blacks, and Filipinos into separate factions would make a major strike unlikely. In an effort to preserve the consul's union from any CAWIU infiltration, growers had formed a massive anti-Communist (anti-CAWIU) drive. Vigilantes were primed to assault and harass CAWIU members and sympathizers. The ACLU was also targeted for harassment and was finding it more and more difficult to travel unmolested through the Valley, and even more problematic was conducting the informative meetings to apprise workers of their rights under the U.S. constitution (e.g., the rights to organize, bargain, strike, and picket). In spite of the difficulties, the CAWIU maintained its presence and continued to organize right into May, when the cantaloupe harvest was scheduled to begin.

Federal Intervention II

However, for the second time the federal government, in the guise of putting the national economy on its feet again and of protecting upcoming agricultural harvests, intervened in the Valley. This time it created a new post, that of Special Conciliator in the Imperial Valley, and chose retired Brigadier General Pelham D. Glassford, formerly chief of police in Washington, D.C., to fill the position. Glassford's assignment was announced in the Valley on the same day that the Asociación and the Protective Association signed their agreement (March 27). As would be expected, substantial negative commentary from growers and the press greeted Glassford's arrival on April 4. To allay any fears or mistrust, he quickly declared his intention of helping workers cleanse their ranks of agitators.[127] Glassford was more than willing to acknowledge that he leaned toward the growers. "I'm no reformer," he said with a shrug. "I've got to be reasonable. I've got to show a certain partisanship for the purpose of keeping my influence down here. The growers and shippers control the banks, the press, the police, the American Legion, everything! I can't afford to aggravate them too much." Furthermore, he asserted, the real danger stemmed from the presence of the CAWIU, whom he described, in his colorful way, as a "bunch of skunks." [128]

Glassford's disarming candor in describing power relations in the Valley so accurately and so matter-of-factly shows him to have been the perfect emissary for the investigation. One supposes that Washington knew that one of their own would protect the United States from the leftist scourge. Valley newspapers had long before suspended all pretense of objectivity and reported events, or withheld information, entirely for the benefit of growers. Randall Henderson, editor of the *Calexico Chronicle,* expressed a sense of pride in defending the grower interests, especially as they affected labor. "If you will look back through the files of the Chronicle," he wrote to A. N. Jack, "you will find [that] the Chronicle gave loyal backing to the program of the vigilantes, as well as the growers. . . . The Chronicle is with you 100%." [129]

The day after Glassford arrived, he met with Terrazas for an hour and a half and, at Terrazas's invitation, joined him for dinner at a Mexicali restaurant along with several other guests. One was Howard A. Bowman, the American consul stationed in Mexicali, who had earlier issued a confidential dispatch to the State Department describing Terrazas's corrupt practices and other questionable activities and who had inquired about the legality of a foreign official's organizing labor unions. [130] The State Department, in responding to the dispatch, had brushed aside Bowman's concerns about the consul's integrity and avowed its approval of Terrazas's actions, stating, "If it is true that the Mexican consul formed the 'union' at the request of the Sheriff, I don't see how we can very well take him to task." [131] The State Department may have been misinformed or merely covering up, but although the county sheriff undoubtedly approved of Terrazas's activities, it was not he who had requested that Terrazas organize a labor union; it was, of course, the growers.

Glassford did his job: for six days he listened to testimony from representatives of the Asociación, the CAWIU, the ACLU, the growers, and citizen groups. He then left for his ranch in Phoenix, promising a full report by April 16. Before leaving, however, Glassford issued a preliminary statement that left no doubt as to where his sentiments lay: "There exists a very serious situation in the Valley, created by attempts to organize a local unit of the cannery and agricultural union. My investigation has shown that the union is indisputably though indirectly connected with a widespread Communist program. The situation created by the activities of the outside agitators and threats of a strike to destroy the very important melon crop, have resulted in unlawful interference by officials and organized citizens with constitutional rights of speech and assembly." [132]

Growers were miffed that Glassford had referred to allegations of "unlawful interference by [Valley] officials." [133] However, Glassford was kind enough to rescue the growers from any culpability by blaming the communists. The CAWIU, he implied, was involved in a massive communist program that had so seriously threatened the harvesting of crops that officials had no other choice but to unlawfully interfere with their rights. Glassford granted that under the circumstances constitutional guarantees did not apply. Clearly what mattered was maintaining production in the fields.

Glassford thereupon recommended that a labor organization be established under government supervision—in his words, "a regimentation by the Government—and you might even call it a Government or a Federal labor union." [134] He was candid in stating that he had designed his scheme "in collaboration with a number of shippers and growers" and federal and state authorities. Glassford's recommendations were tainted beyond measure by his theories regarding race and intelligence, attitudes he evidently felt no hesitation about expressing in explaining his reasoning. Ironically, he refers to workers' poverty in respect to their inability to pay dues to a reputable union. Glassford also excuses growers and shippers for refusing to enter into contracts with such farmworkers: "Owing to quite a number of different races and nationalities, generally of a low order of intelligence, of lacking considerably in education, they are very susceptible to being aroused by agitators, unable to pay dues that would attract reputable and experienced labor organizers and consequently, for at least a number of years, it cannot be expected that the growers and shippers would enter into any agreement with such labor." [135]

Glassford offered a simple plan: deport all surplus labor, register and transfer labor "in an organized manner," and establish camps at "points of big harvests." He also recognized the value of the Asociación in promoting his recommendations and explicitly legitimized and justified the Terrazas union. Not more than a month after issuing the recommendations, he called upon the Growers and Shippers Association and the Asociación Mexicana to meet and "expand the agreement of March 27 so that it may constitute a complete basis for the mediation of labor disputes." [136] Apparently, under consulate leadership Mexican workers met the requirements for establishing a labor organization. Once again, we see that federal mediation in the labor disputes was not impartial. The recommendation favored the growers, recognized the Asociación Mexicana as a legitimate worker union, and cited the CAWIU as "agitators." Terrazas was commended for his actions by the Mexican government through the auspices of Secretary of Foreign Relations J. M. Puig Cassauranc, who expressed "[c]omplete approval of his activities in organizing Mexican field laborers." [137]

The bias of the National Labor Relations Board representatives, MacCulloch and Glassford, was so blatant that they behaved like paid agents of the growers and shippers. And the CAWIU could always be invoked as the real problem. When CAWIU delegates argued in testimony before Glassford that free and open elections should be held so that workers could choose their affiliation, Glassford argued that elections would be impractical and "extremely aggravating to the present tense situation." [138] Glassford's arguments against an open election are understandable. It is highly probable that in a contest between the Asociación Mexicana and the CAWIU, the CAWIU would have won. It is a matter of record that at the ACLU meeting the night of Wirin's kidnapping, workers had expressed their preference for the CAWIU. At that meeting, which was attended by hundreds of workers, as well as A. N. Jack and some twenty growers, convener Chester Williams posed several questions to the assembled laborers. Williams first asked whether they earned enough wages to live on decently. The workers sent up an emphatic *no.* Then he asked whether they wanted a union organized by the Mexican consul. The answer was again *no.* Then he asked, "do you prefer the Cannery and Agricultural Workers Industrial Union?" A vigorous thrusting up of hands answered *yes.* [139]

Campbell MacCulloch, of the National Labor Relations Board, like Glassford, was impervious to any arguments impugning the Asociación's connections to Terrazas. Helen Marston, a San Diego ACLU activist who had experienced several harrowing ordeals at the hands of the Valley's organized vigilantes, wrote to MacCulloch expressing her strong criticism of Terrazas. She wrote in part that "it would be impossible for Terrazas to organize anything that was not in the interests of the dominant class, due to his background, training, and mental outlook. . . . That is without doubt the feeling of all the Mexicans with whom he came in contact in the Valley." [140] MacCulloch immediately replied, "I cannot share [your] view of him, as I believe Mr. Terrazas to be entirely sincere and likely to succeed with his organization of the Mexican workers." [141]

Timothy Reardon, the director of the California State Department of Industrial Relations, supported MacCulloch and Glassford in opposing the free election favored by the ACLU. In denying an election, Terrazas's Asociación Mexicana was automatically validated as the workers' union.

In his persuasive wire to Secretary of Labor Frances Perkins, Reardon argued that an election would advance communism. "Growers and resident employees in Imperial Valley have entered into bonafide collective bargaining agreement. . . . Favorable consideration by you of request of American Civil Liberties Union to promote Imperial Valley employees [sic] election will create confusion spread discontent advance communism and injure the workers." [142]

Governor Rolph, in a letter to Perkins, also protested vehemently against the elections and, like Reardon, emphasized an existing "collective bargaining agreement." [143] Perkins responded to Rolph, assuring him that "no such election is being contemplated by General Glassford. . . . Moreover, there are so many difficulties that would exist if a poll of agricultural workers were to be taken that I am sure you would pause for a long time before taking such action." [144]

It is perfectly clear that the growers had no intention of permitting a union election to take place. For one thing, such an election would involve recognizing the right of the CAWIU to appear on the ballot. In Imperial Valley in 1934, that was not to be. But in any case, the truth appears to be that the CAWIU would have emerged victorious and the growers knew it. One and all, growers, shippers, and federal, state, and local authorities stood firm: there would be no election. The Asociación Mexicana was recognized as the official worker organization. In effect, the Glassford commission's recommendation in mid-February that the federal government organize labor materialized in the spring 1934.

The CAWIU correctly assessed Glassford's role and in a mimeographed bulletin accused him of deception. On May 1, Glassford answered, issuing his own bulletin (seven thousand copies printed in Spanish), charging the union with publishing "falsehoods and erroneous quotations . . . for the sole purpose of misleading the Mexican workers into doubting the honesty of the federal government . . . the principal objective of this [CAWIU] bulletin is to incite a strike. Nothing could be more harmful than a strike at this time. The present melon season promises to be a successful one and this is important to the economic welfare of the entire community." [145] Glassford, like mediator Connell in 1930, had one objective, and one he was most anxious to fulfill. In his own words, it was "to prevent a strike." [146] It was the objective shared by growers and Terrazas alike and formed the basis for the united front against the CAWIU. The Asociación, under Terrazas's direction, appeared to fulfill the directives of the federal conciliator for a federally organized union.

Terrazas's devoted efforts on behalf of the Imperial Valley Growers and Shippers Association did not go unrewarded. When the dust settled and with the CAWIU marginalized, Managing Secretary C. B. Moore (who had had past business dealings with Rodríguez) addressed a letter to President Rodríguez extolling Terrazas. (Moore sent a similar letter to Consul General Lubbert). "My Dear Abelardo," Moore wrote: "The agricultural people of California are indeed fortunate they have as a representative of the Mexican government a man of the ability of Consul Terrazas of Calexico. My contacts with Consul Terrazas covered a period of many months and I found him at all times not only a diplomat but a person of great understanding. . . . We have been particularly fortunate in having such a man to deal with in our recent troubles." [147]

Several years after the rebellion, the editor of the El Centro *Morning Post* fondly recalled that Terrazas was "the greatest single stabilizing force in the pea and cantaloupe strike of three seasons ago." Furthermore, "He was a wise leader and Imperial Valley cannot help but remember Consul Terrazas with reverence." [148]

However, not all correspondents gave Terrazas high marks. Mexico City received numerous letters from labor and civil rights organizations and independent writers expressing their strong disapproval of Terrazas. Predictably, Consul General Lubbert sprang to Terrazas's defense, alleging in a letter to the Secretariat of Foreign Relations that the attacks were coming from "recognized communists and agitators, who it is well known, is the group that has been organizing strikes and disturbances." [149] The secretariat may have accepted Lubbert's explanations for the attacks on Terrazas, but most workers well understood the implications of the agreement signed by the Asociación. One letter typical of many notified President Rodríguez that Terrazas had acted in "subordination to the agricultural companies of Imperial Valley." [150] Another group of strikers fearing retaliation wrote anonymously to the secretary of foreign relations stating that the "companies have taken advantage of Consul Joaquín Terrazas, so that he may form a union exclusively of Mexicans, placing us at the mercy of the companies who will pay us what they please." [151]

The CAWIU expressed the greatest contempt for Terrazas, who, they claimed, was a front for a union "organized . . . by the farmers." "Consul Terrazas," read the CAWIU's *Workman's Bulletin* of April 2, "sells his merchandise (the workers) to the farmers and the farmers state the price." [152] The CAWIU's charges against Terrazas, the growers, the police, and Glassford carried the weight of truth, but police intimidation and blacklisting of non-Asociación laborers caused many who preferred the CAWIU to join the Asociación out of fear. An offensive timed for the melon season appeared doomed. [153] In some measure, the Cannery Union's difficulties resulted from the failure to spend sufficient time in organizing the rank and file. Upon reflection, the union leadership acknowledged that organizers, perhaps understandably, were swept up in spontaneous strike eruptions and went along with them.[154] Raids on meetings, arrests of leaders, and harassment of the rank and file also contributed to keeping the union off balance. In addition, the weak union base had allowed Terrazas to exercise his consular authority with the workers effectively, putting the CAWIU organizers (outsiders) at a disadvantage.

It is impossible to say whether a more concentrated effort at organizing would have made a difference in the labor union movement in the Imperial Valley in this period. However, evidence suggests that Consul Terrazas's union, the Asociación Mexicana, affiliated with the CROM of Mexico and supported by the government authorities in Mexico City and across the border in Mexicali, played a major role in the Imperial Valley capitalist offensive against independent agricultural worker unions regardless of communist leadership. Studies of the Los Angeles County Strike, the San Joaquin Valley Strike, and the 1936 citrus picker strike in Orange County support a similar conclusion. In each of these affairs, the consuls sought to lead Mexican workers and offered conservative agendas in alliance with growers and shippers. Consuls in these events also struggled against leftists within union ranks, but the thrust of their policies and operations, as was the case in the Imperial Valley struggle, was to secure a capitalist agenda.[155]

CHAPTER 6

Denouement and Renaissance

As we have seen, during the twenties and thirties of this century a series of agricultural strikes took place in the fertile valleys of southern California in which thousands of Mexican laborers participated. Beyond question, the development and outcomes of these labor conflicts were manipulated by government officials and consuls acting on policy directives from deep within Mexico. Consuls attempted to separate union rank and file from independent and leftist influence and competed for leadership by establishing mutual societies under their control. Consuls entered the political relations of capitalist production as collaborators with powerful grower associations to defeat worker demands for higher wage levels and improved living and work conditions.

Washington addressed these violent agricultural conflicts by authorizing federal investigations. In every case, the reports that emerged from such reviews showed a distinct bias in favor of the U.S. agribusiness interests whose low-wage policies were the object of the Mexican laborers' protest. The reports were sanguine when it came to consular interventions; the investigators, high U.S. officials, had only praise for the Mexican consuls. Invoked again and again as justification for setting aside constitutional guarantees as to rights of assembly and rights to organize was the specter of communism.

Although using the red threat to mask an antiunion stance proved an effective strategy, not every offensive announced itself as a fight against communist agitators. In the Orange County pickers' strike and the San Antonio garment workers' strike of 1938 (which we will review shortly), consular interventions deflected the strike actions by Mexican workers seeking union recognition and a wage raise and protected the business interests involved without allegations of leftist agitation. While a pro-union policy was espoused through rhetoric and the manipulation of workers and events, consuls' underlying agenda was always antiunion, and this true policy was vigorously but covertly pursued. The pickers' strike has already been reviewed, but the garment workers' strike two years later, discussed below, gives us another scenario for consular interference in the affairs of its expatriate working class.

The brief appearance of the Confederación de Trabajadores Mexicanos in Texas in the late thirties and early forties marks the Mexican government's final union-organizing effort among *México de afuera*. But though no longer directly involved with union activities, the Mexican government has continued its interventionist policies in Mexican community affairs across the United States. Providing further contexts for Mexican government involvement in the wake of the Second World War were the Bracero Program and the Chicano Movement, and in the eighties and nineties, the economic and political crises within Mexico. As we move into the new century, the power relation between the United States and Mexico continues its dark historical path. With a debilitated PRI that still maintains power over opposing parties, Mexico shows no evidence of heralded democratic reforms or of altering its exploitative relation to Mexicans living in the United States whether as Mexican citizens, or first-, second-, or third-generation Mexican Americans.

The San Antonio Garment Workers' Strike of 1938

In 1938 the garment industry provided a major source of employment for women in the large Mexican community of San Antonio, Texas. As early as 1932 the International Ladies Garment Workers Union (ILGWU) had laid the groundwork for unionizing this industry and had made significant inroads in several plants in spite of the opposition of employers, the San Antonio authorities, and the local Mexican consulate. One of the ILGWU's successes was with the Texas Infant Manufacturing Company, the second largest employer in the city's garment industry.

At the beginning of 1938 union leaders lodged an official complaint against Texas Infant management, charging the company with unfair labor practices under the National Labor Relations Act. The union alleged that María Martínez, an operator, had been fired for belonging to the ILGWU and for refusing to join the Council of Garment Workers, an employee "union" financed and directed by the company. In a complaint filed with the National Labor Relations Board, the ILGWU demanded that Martínez be reinstated and that Texas Infant's company-sponsored union be dissolved. After an investigation the NLRB judged that the ILGWU case had merit and directed the company to dissolve the Council of Garment Workers and reinstate Martínez. Texas Infant refused to comply. In response to that refusal, the ILGWU declared a strike in

March 1938. All of the strikers were Mexican women, all belonged to the ILGWU, all walked off their jobs.

During the early days of the strike action, strikers angrily accosted workers attempting to cross their picket lines with shouts, exhortations, and even shoving and jostling. The Texas Infant Council instantly charged the ILGWU with assault and lodged complaints with police. Heavy police patrols responded with court orders limiting picketing to one picket per entrance. The strikebreakers were all members of the company council and, like their ILGWU adversaries, were almost all Mexican citizens. Within days of the strike, the president of the council (and plant foreman of Texas Infant Manufacturing) sought the assistance of Consul José Guadalupe Pineda in opposing the ILGWU. Pineda then met with representatives of the Texas Infant Council and local authorities, including the mayor, police commissioner, and the chief of police.

According to Pineda, his mission, taken at the request of the president of the Texas Infant Council, was to protect "the 60 Mexican citizens working at the plant." Pineda made clear that although the Mexican citizens who had joined the strike were beyond the scope of his involvement or protection, he would willingly extend assistance to the organization seeking to break the union's influence. Pineda supported and collaborated with the principals arrayed against the ILGWU, and evidence implicates him in the execution of the company's labor policy. Upon the discovery that Pineda was working directly with Texas Infant to defeat the strike, ILGWU leaders Rebecca Taylor and Barney Egan sent a telegram protesting the consul's actions to Labor Secretary Frances Perkins and Secretary of State Cordell Hull. They wrote: "We desire to emphatically protest the actions of José Guadalupe Pineda Consul General of Mexico stationed in San Antonio Texas Using his office as a strike breaking agency attempting to break a strike of Mexican garment workers at Texas Manufacturing Company here and using his office against the strikers and in favor of outlawed company union which the National Labor Board has ordered dissolved." [1]

News of the ILGWU's complaint to cabinet members of the U.S. government apparently reached the Mexican embassy in Washington. It is not clear, however, whether Pineda was spoken to or counseled to remove himself from overt intervention. We do know that Texas Infant settled the strike and agreed to cease labor code violations and to dissolve its Council of Garment Workers, the illegal company union. In this episode, as in the San Joaquin cotton strike, the consul did not succeed in his efforts to break the strike, nor was he able to prevent Mexican clothing workers in San Antonio from joining the ILGWU. Once more, in the guise of helping the Mexican community, the consulate pursued antilabor and antiunion practices. Wage demands and rights to form or join a union were not defended, constituting an abandonment of the principles of protection of Mexican workers. Consular collaboration with U.S. financial interests in this episode of strikebreaking is not unique. It is a typical incident involving Mexican consuls in antiunion interventions.

The Confederación de Trabajadores Mexicanos del Norte

As the Great Depression with its tumultuous union building and strikes came to an end, Mexican union activity in the Southwest lost much of its earlier energy. Within Mexico CROM had long ago fallen from grace, but as long as it operated, it maintained its ties with the Los Angeles–based Confederación de Uniones Campesinas y Obreras Mexicanos (CUCOM). Finally in 1936, a new union was established as the government bypassed CROM and founded the second official labor central, the Confederación de Trabajadores Mexicanos (CTM), with the blessings of President Lázaro Cárdenas. Appointed to lead the new union was Vicente Lombardo Toledano, a quasi-socialist/populist and former high officer in the CROM hierarchy who had resigned in a dispute over union leadership in 1933. As the designated government union, the CTM would be expected to enjoy the traditional privileges conferred on this officially sanctioned institution.

Historian Hobart Spalding Jr. noted that the CTM "reaped immediate benefits" from the government connection: "Official agencies supplied financial aid, and men favorable to its cause occupied political offices at national, state, and local levels. The government helped finance a CTM university designed to raise the consciousness of workers and train future leaders. . . . Under the leadership of Lombardo Toledano, a close confidant of Cárdenas, the CTM kept growing." [2] However, although Cárdenas appeared to concede extensive powers to the CTM, he retained control through various maneuvers. First, as "a check on the confederation's power," he extended constituencies to other labor organizations. For example, Cárdenas forbid the CTM to organize peasants and instead established another union, the National Peasant Confederation, to cover that venue. He then incorporated that organization into the Partido Revolucionario Mexicano (PRM), the newly reformed and renamed official government party. In effect, the government usurped CTM initiatives and made all decisions critical to labor matters. The CTM had no choice but to bow to government dominance and accept that Cárdenas was the final arbiter, enforcer, and legislator on all questions regarding labor. The Cárdenas era, in furthering the Obregón-Calles labor policies, recycled what had been a staple of the Mexican state since the Porfiriato. As Spalding put it, "the years of 1934 to 1940 fit naturally into the flow of historical events. Cárdenas actually continued trends begun in the 1920s. He kept labor subordinate to the ruling party."[3]

With CROM stripped of power, CTM moved into CROM's territory and began to replicate its rival's former exploits by initiating an organizing campaign among Mexican laborers in the U.S. Southwest. The surviving documents of CTM's organizational drives tell of a fairly sophisticated plan to extend the ranks of the CTM north of the border, creating a "CTM del Norte." Records show organizing campaigns in Texas in 1936, and in California in 1938 or 1939. Only in the Texas case is there material testifying to successes. In a May 1935 memorandum to Cárdenas, the Dallas local denounced alleged "Callista" consuls holding posts along the border and urged their immediate dismissal. Other papers relate to at least two annual congresses of CTM affiliates held in Texas. In late 1939 American Consul General James B. Stewart sent an urgent confidential memorandum from Mexico City to the State Department with information gathered by a Mexico City informant that the CTM planned a second San Antonio convention with its affiliate in that city set for January 1940.[4] The "urgent" matter wound through the government bureaucracy to the desk of FBI head J. Edgar Hoover, and the director was cautioned to handle the matter with diplomatic tact. The State Department memo went on to suggest that the CTM congress might generate a positive political outcome for both countries. As it turned out, this perspective was accurate.

According to documents from the Archivo General de la Nación, the Mexican government had hoped that a second CTM congress would serve to unify and expand CTM del Norte membership. Reports indicate that some degree of organizing had gone on in Texas and California in the mid- to late thirties, although the extent of the organizing is not clear. The summary of the second congress (the only documentation available) indicates that the confederation had established its headquarters in Dallas and that at least two other locals functioned, the second in San Antonio, the third in Austin. The San Antonio local executive committee served as the organizing committee and host for the congress. The two-day meeting opened with an elaborate "literary-musical program" on the evening of January 6, 1940, with a number of dignitaries and delegates in attendance. On the podium sat Mexican Consul Miguel Alvares Acosta alongside local union officers, delegates from the Mexican branch of the CTM, and invited guests, including the president of the San Antonio Confederación de Sociedades Mexicanas. Apparently, only union delegates from the region attended.

The second day's proceedings were occupied with a busy agenda: fifteen resolutions were debated and passed. Topics ranged from dues, new committees, reform of committee structures, duties, new bylaws, and the consulates. Several resolutions dealt with the Mexican government, specifically with the quality and extent of the relations between *México de afuera* and the consulates, and here the resemblance to the 1927 Confederación de Uniones Obreras Mexicanas (CUOM) constitution is remarkable. In proposing and passing Resolution 7, the congress repeated nearly verbatim a principle enunciated in the first CUOM convention. Delegates directed the CTM del Norte officers to "request that the Government of Mexico intensify the repatriation of Mexicans resident in this country . . . [and] that the Government continue to establish Agricultural colonies for the repatriated. . . ."[5] Continuing the pattern, Resolutions 8 and 9 implored the Mexican government to thoroughly investigate the failed colonization projects and recommended actions to eliminate "the abuses and mistreatments victimizing Mexican workers who return to the patria." Resolution 12 addressed ways in which consulates might improve and amplify services and stressed the need to "eliminate subtle discriminations that are at times visited upon expatriates when requesting assistance" and "provide guarantees for the protection and defense of Mexicans" living abroad. Resolution 13 is quoted here in full:

The Mexican consular corps shall be asked for their cooperation, and if it is within their responsibilities, engage the resolution to the Problem of the Unification of Mexicans, guiding them within an orientation of Racial and Patriotic Fraternity, so that the divisions, distances, and intrigues which disgracefully exist in the Mexican colony of this country shall come to an end. Moreover, the Consular corps shall be requested that it, or another body commissioned by the consulate, take charge of directing the Mexican patriotic festivals.

Upon the election of a new executive committee, a seven-point summary of the proceedings went forward with unanimous approval.

The first two summary items referred to labor's political status in Mexico and to the relationship between the CTM del Norte and the Mexican government. Both references underscore official organized labor's traditional subordination to Mexico's ruling party and the regime. The first restated a standard provision of the CTM, an unequivocal "Support for the policies of Señor General Cárdenas, on behalf of the Mexican workers resident in the United States of North America." The second proclaimed the "expressed desire of Mexican workers in the United States that the program of the current Mexican government unfold without interference." In addition, the congress reaffirmed its adhesion to the parent CTM, an organization affiliated with the PRM, "in consideration that the organization [the CTM] represents not only the workers of Mexico, but the popular civic sectors of the country as well." The fifteen resolutions, together with the summary, expressed loyalty to, and support for, the administration of Cárdenas, the ruling party, and the institutions of the state. Several supplications directed at the consulates and requesting their intervention in the social and economic problems facing *México de afuera* are noteworthy. The final summary point, "that the [consulates] act more efficaciously in the interests of the compatriots," indicates a conviction that consulates were not only capable of defending the civil rights of the Mexican community, but should comprise the primary public institution for meeting those responsibilities.

The decade of the forties opened with promises of renewed vigor for Mexican union organizing in the Southwest. Delegates voted to continue their efforts and to convene a third congress in 1941 at Austin, though it is doubtful that that congress ever took place. In any case, it appears that the FBI and the State Department were unconcerned about another CTM congress, apparently concluding that U.S. interests were not at stake. That comfortable response no doubt reflects the State Department's understanding of Mexican-government actions in the affairs of Mexican citizens working in the United States, an involvement that traditionally gave U.S. interests precedence. Mexico's foreign policy had been consistently pro–United States; policy statements favored the U.S. stance in relation to the Americas and often echoed the very language of U.S. policy statements. Taken altogether, the circumstances surrounding the CTM congress caused no alarms to go off in either the State Department or the FBI. Based on past history, both agencies could feel confident that the congress of the CTM, the official Mexican-government union, would cause no problems. The status of Mexican workers in the United States would remain the same.

Three months after the CTM congress, the El Paso, Texas, Junior Chamber of Commerce held a convention of business leaders where the excellent relations between Mexico and the U.S. were reaffirmed. Local consulate officials were invited and, in addressing the assembly, used the occasion to voice their approval of U.S. policies (both domestic and foreign) toward Mexico. Consul Elías Colunga praised the chamber for its efforts in resolving racial antagonism affecting the Mexican communities of Texas. He also read messages from Ambassador Castillo Nájera and Inspector General of the Consulates Adolfo de la Huerta (recall his role in the 1936 citrus pickers' strike). Ambassador Nájera's congratulatory message approached the issue of Texas race relations with tact and grace, smoothing over any frictions and criticisms. In harmony with his superior's message, de la Huerta praised the United States as a protector of Mexicans living within its borders. The northern neighbor, he said, "no longer has imperialist ambitions; rather it is now the giant with a broad smile which is guiding its own people along a path of equity and Christian morality, extending its actions as a benefactor of the peoples of different races." A delighted American consul attending the meeting informed the State Department that he was "pleased to report that the general atmosphere, as well as the tone of the speakers . . . was one of international friendship."[6]

In Mexico political rivalries spiked and, as the Second World War loomed, there was an abrupt change in leadership in the CTM. Backed by incoming President Avila Camacho, former CROM militant Fidel Velásquez ousted his rival Lombardo Toledano (another ex-CROMista) and embarked on a tenure as secretary general of CTM. It was Mexico's largest labor federation and one that was to endure for over half a century. An "iron-handed labor patriarch," Velásquez epitomized the *charro,* the paid professional labor boss working for the PRI, the employer, and, when expedient, for the rank and file.[7] *Charrismo* carries an implication of institutionalized corruption and secret deal making, and part of Velásquez's job was to deliver the labor vote to the PRI and to quell dissident factions and competing unions by any means necessary. Violence was standard procedure.[8]

After the San Antonio congress in 1940, the CTM del Norte lost its momentum as government sponsorship faded. Besides loss of government support, the CTM-dN was also affected by the multiple effects of the Chicano civil rights movement and Velásquez's domestic emphasis. All acted to deter the presence of the CTM among *México de afuera.* However, it remained a viable presence right up to the 1942 Bracero Agreements between Mexico and the United States, which were designed to enable the importation of Mexican labor into the United States and effectively put a brake on all farmworker union activities. The responsibility for transporting such labor across the border was Mexico's. Most studies assign crucial oversight responsibilities to the United States, while Mexico has generally remained peripheral insofar as managing the program was concerned. However, the Bracero program, a binational agreement, legitimized the shipping of cheap Mexican labor, with the Mexican government's active involvement, into the United States. As such, it fits into the time-honored policies of the Mexican government toward its expatriate citizens and extends the decades-long history of consular interventions into the postwar period.

The Bracero Program and the Chicano Community

Diverse forces, set in motion during the Depression and carried forward into the Second World War and beyond, had the effect of altering the socioeconomic character of the Chicano community. The decline of immigration, the repatriation of hundreds of thousands of Mexicans during the thirties, and the economic and politicizing effects of the Second World War were responsible for producing a comprehensive restructuring. The Bracero Program was a significant factor in that evolution. The agreement was a legal device to assist agricultural corporations in resolving an alleged wartime labor shortage. Facilitated by a Mexican government eager to transport a new generation of immigrants across the border, thousands of undocumented Mexican laborers flowed in, lured by the promise of work. Such a plentiful labor supply gave U.S. growers the power to name wages and hours in the workplace. At the same time, the Mexican government guaranteed the supremacy of U.S. agribusiness in labor relations by eliminating government-sponsored CTM union activities among resident agricultural workers. The influx of new workers imported under the Bracero Agreements, by terms of the labor contract, held no rights to organize, to join a union, or bargain for wages. Thus all Mexican workers (resident and bracero) would effectively be delivered to U.S. employers without the right to union representation.

Over the twenty-two-year span of the agreements, nearly five million braceros were contracted as workers, and at various times a greater number of noncontracted laborers worked alongside them. Under the supervision of the Immigration and Naturalization Service (INS), imported Mexican labor, together with "skips" (those who stayed beyond their contract) and so-called "wetbacks" (immigrants without legal papers), rapidly supplanted resident Mexican labor in agriculture, railroad maintenance, and construction. By the terms of the bilateral agreements, bracero labor was contracted for a set period and either recontracted or subject to repatriation. During the contracted period of work, the bracero was stripped of the right to negotiate the wage or conditions of work, join a union, organize a union, strike, cross a picket line, or act as a strikebreaker. Bracero agreements stipulated that the politically neutralized bracero labor force earn no less than the prevailing rate in a given locale. In fact, this rule was seldom enforced, and lower wage rates were the norm. Exploiting the advantages of an overflowing labor pool and unburdened by government oversight, employers were free to set bracero wages at the lowest possible levels and keep them there. In California, for example, because of this privilege wage rates for braceros remained at the same level for ten years in a row: the period between 1950 and 1960 saw no change.[9]

Obligated to work at excessively low surplus-labor wages, braceros were relegated to live in abject poverty. Responsible for the economic status of the Mexican laborers were U.S. agricultural corporations in complicity with federal authorities who consented to it by their inaction. In her comprehensive study of the Bracero programs, Kitty Calavita writes that the federal government acknowledged that wholesale "abuses and lax enforcement produced deplorable living conditions for braceros." The INS "effectively abdicated its border control responsibility" and chose to supervise the border at the pleasure of agricultural enterprises, capitalist interests that have traditionally fought unionization. Neither federal, state, nor local authorities responded to the exploitation of imported Mexican laborers, nor did the Mexican consulate, nor did the ruling regime in Mexico City.[10]

The circumscriptions and conditions of the Bracero Agreements that severely restrained the free wage-labor market applied equally to "legals" and "illegals." In the process of production, legal status mattered only to the extent that it lowered or raised costs and profits. The "wetback" stream provided employers with a continuous flow of the cheapest possible labor—docile, dependable, disciplined. The system worked smoothly: U.S. employers recruited Mexican workers, and the Mexican government, facilitated by binational government sanctions, delivered them. The U.S. labor importing programs and laissez-faire Mexican emigration policies once again demonstrate Mexico's complicity in providing U.S. corporate interests with an unorganized labor supply.

Significantly, in this surplus labor market (created by the Bracero Program), union membership and the powers it conferred became a liability (in terms of hiring) as employers were dead set against unions. Paying union wages (higher than bracero wages) was not only undesirable, it was unnecessary, and resident workers were virtually priced out of the market. Resident Mexican laborers found themselves abruptly marginalized, having been replaced by an influx of even cheaper unorganized labor. In 1949 civil rights leader and agricultural union organizer Ernesto Galarza described the effects of this contract and "wetback" labor on resident Mexican workers and cited the Bracero pacts as a form of misgovernment forged between Washington and Mexico City that put a virtual international ceiling on Mexican agricultural workers' wages:

These agreements were originally signed as a wartime measure, but they have been continued under the insistent pressure of agricultural employers' associations who were looking for a counterpoise to the wage demands of Mexican workers long resident in this country.

The negotiation of these agreements, practically behind closed doors, and the determination of the conditions of such employment by self-appointed arbiters in Washington and Mexico City, establish a form of international economic government without the consent of the governed — in this case the millions of agricultural workers whose wages and standards are immediately affected by such agreements. Relief from this kind of mis-government has not yet been found by the Mexican workers in the United States, either through Washington or through the present administration in Mexico City.[11]

In the forties, as in prior decades, the Mexican government viewed emigration as a device for overcoming national economic and social crises. Officially the Mexican government stood firmly opposed to emigration, but its pronouncements on the subject were belied by their actions. In the end, the monetary benefits of emigration for the Mexican economy were always too tempting to ignore. In 1951 Lyle Saunders and Olin E. Leonard reported that Mexico "maintains a dual position on the wetback situation," an official position opposing emigration on a number of counts: that Mexico needed the workers, that the migration was illegal, that migrants were exploited, that they created a political stir and backlash against Mexicans resident in the United States, and so on. Reading Mexico's behaviors in regard to emigration rather than its political rhetoric reveals an "informal position," an underlying policy that "largely ignores and actually abets the migration." Saunders and Leonard found that "[t]his policy is based upon the belief that temporary [bracero] work in the United States, even illegal, relieves part of the unemployment and underemployment that chronically exists in much of Mexico." They further reported that in several instances the Mexican government, having "magnified the opportunity for illegal migration" by extensively broadcasting employment opportunities, found it necessary to expand transportation capacities for northward travel. In the summer of 1950, for example, an advertising campaign within Mexico produced such a huge surplus of workers that one Mexican newspaper reported that "the [state-owned] railroad companies between Monterrey and Matamoros have been ordered to increase the number of coaches . . . in order to transport, as quickly as possible, the number of workers."[12]

Mexico's bracero emigration policy followed the prescriptions first laid down by Carranza and can be explained if we look at the numbers. The Mexico City daily *Las Ultimas Noticias* reported in its March 5, 1953, edition that "remittances made by the braceros to their homes amounted to 30 million dollars last year and constituted the third largest source of income to Mexico, after the mining industry and tourists." Put another way, the sale of Mexico's surplus labor to U.S. corporate agriculture outperformed manufacturing, agriculture, oil, and other industries in the Mexican economy. Not only did landless and *minifundia* rural migrants bail out the economy, but also, in leaving the country, they released pent-up oppositional political pressure.

Contract bracero workers were bound to the terms of the Bracero Agreements, and in the numerous cases where protections were disregarded, bracero workers paid a price. Some authors contend that Mexico attempted to influence U.S. authorities to respect the worker protection terms of the Agreements.[13] Others disagree. Galarza, an experienced labor organizer, observed that worker "rights under the agreement are but dimly enforced by the United States or by the Mexican officials charged with their supervision."[14] As was true in the Imperial Valley in the thirties, growers generally turned a blind eye toward the conditions under which workers lived and labored. In her scholarly and critical study of the Bracero Program, Kitty Calavita described braceros as "a captive work force" and a "grower's dream."[15] As a result of this wartime–postwar labor importation policy, the term "Mexican wage" reentered market terminology, referring to the very lowest bargain wage.

By maintaining its laissez-faire emigration policy, Mexico continued to stand "shoulder to shoulder" with union-busting agricultural interests and, by extension, with U.S. government policies regarding Mexican labor. Rather than involve itself in labor organizing (notwithstanding that, historically, these "unions" were grower controlled), Mexico had agreed to "sell" its poorest inhabitants to its northern neighbor and acquiesced to their being stripped of their Constitutional rights to organize and bargain collectively. From Brownsville to San Diego, all along the two-thousand-mile border region, Mexican laborers were systematically being used to fill the agricultural labor needs of southwestern and midwestern agricultural interests. As a result, a devastating secondary effect occurred: the aging labor camps, long home to resident workers, were gradually being emptied, squeezed out by an even cheaper—and unorganized—mobile labor supply, the braceros.

Under the terms of the original Bracero Agreement and subsequent renewals, Mexican consulates were responsible for overseeing Mexican labor's compliance with its terms. The Secretariat of Foreign Relations charged consuls with ensuring that their compatriots, bound by contracts, observed Bracero law to the letter. Penalties for noncompliance were severe, especially for workers suspected of union activity. Any overt forms of dissension could be used as grounds for accusations of "agitation" and subject a worker to blacklisting or deportation. These penalties were applied equally to contractual and noncontractual illegal immigrant labor, the so-called wetbacks. As signatory to the Bracero Agreements, the Mexican government represented the braceros. That representation meant ensuring that terms forbidding union organizing were met. Consulates complied and, further, worked to defeat any such efforts. As is evident, the Bracero Agreements in no way altered Mexico's long-standing position in regard to controlling Mexican labor engaged in the United States; as always, Mexico allied itself with U.S. interests.

U.S. employers had access to whatever numbers of braceros were needed for harvests and could convert these workers into strikebreakers if required (an activity forbidden by the Bracero Agreements). Calavita concludes that the steadily rising levels of undocumented and documented braceros "depressed wages and undermined collective bargaining efforts by domestic farm workers." [16] With the tacit, if not open, support of the U.S. and Mexican governments, corporations like California's DiGiorgio Fruit Corporation defeated southwestern unionization drives and strikes in the postwar period. The case of the 1947 National Farm Labor Union strike at the DiGiorgio farms, located in the vast San Joaquin Valley, illustrates the enormous power wielded by employers over labor, a power backed by the authority of the Mexican government.

Eleven hundred unionized workers struck in 1947, and as they walked out of the fields, the braceros followed in a show of loyalty. DiGiorgio managers acted quickly and called in representatives of the Mexican consulate in Fresno (reenter Consul Enrique Bravo) and the Department of Agriculture for assistance to quell the strike. A compliant consul agreed to step in and attempt to persuade the braceros to observe the letter of the Agreement and return to the fields. After a short meeting, the consul induced the reluctant braceros to abandon their fellow workers and return to work. With an inexhaustible supply of labor at their disposal and with the support of the Mexican consulate, the DiGiorgio Corporation broke the strike. A second strike of tomato pickers in San Joaquin County and a third, involving five hundred Imperial Valley harvesters demanding a dollar an hour, demonstrate the overwhelming odds that faced local and imported labor; both strikes went down for reasons similar to those of the DiGiorgio strike. The Bracero factor was key.

In 1951 the National Farm Worker Union called a strike in the Imperial Valley. Again the strike failed, but the loss cannot be credited to an inherent union weakness. The power of the international Bracero Agreement to circumvent unions proved insurmountable. The four thousand braceros in the area were a major obstacle because, in spite of the terms of the Bracero Agreement forbidding braceros to act as strikebreakers, they were used for that purpose. The union hoped to circumvent such actions by reducing the numbers of braceros in the area. To that end the NFWU petitioned the Department of Labor to declare a strike in progress, which would prevent the employment of braceros (i.e., strikebreakers) at farms idled by the strike. However, neither the U.S. Department of Labor nor the Mexican government responded.

Quite the opposite. Calexico Consul Elías Colunga openly confronted the union and sent "an unfavorable and deprecatory report to Mexico City, belittling the efforts of the Union." Mexico City agreed with Colunga's report. Galarza wrote that the "Mexican government allowed matters to take their normal course and continued contracting and strike breaking." [17] Workers up and down the state recognized that growers, backed by the U.S. and the Mexican governments, had an economic and political advantage that could not be overcome. Galarza recorded that workers "sensed the delaying tactics of the Department of Labor and the supportive role of the Mexican government" that would ultimately force them to surrender to the growers.[18] With no backup from either government, the fate of the NFWU was sealed. As we have seen in the actions of Terrazas, Hill, Bravo, and their colleagues, Mexican consuls have a solid history of supporting growers rather than Mexican laborers. This pattern of grower-consul complicity has not changed substantially in nearly a century: Agricultural workers remain in the same economic and political position relative to growers as in the Depression era.

Racial Discrimination

Consigned to the bottom of the economic ladder, Mexican workers suffered social isolation and impoverishment in a climate of extreme racial discrimination. The added burden of racial prejudice effectively robbed them of a place in U.S. society. The agricultural proletariat in particular felt the brunt of this prejudice. Mexico could not ignore racism's impact on the Mexican population living in the United States. And in a political gesture toward addressing the prejudice against Mexicans in Texas, the Mexican government wrote into the 1943 Bracero Agreement a proviso that prohibited the contracting of braceros in that state, charging officially sanctioned discrimination. Discrimination against Mexicans was of course ubiquitous, but in singling out Texas, the agreement suggested that Texas was an anomaly and that racial matters were notably better in other states. In any case, although Texas was declared off limits for braceros from 1943 to 1947, the sanctions had no appreciable affect on the flow of migrant laborers into Texas or on their treatment once they got there.

As one student of the Bracero Program wrote, "it was politically wise and expedient for the Mexican government to . . . forbid braceros to enter

Texas legally but to do little to keep them from entering illegally." To make matters worse, during this four-year period "wetbacks" had no legal recourse when they found themselves victims of discrimination or exploitation. These workers were simply in a "no man's land," so to speak, since terms of the Bracero Agreement did not apply. Thus Texas growers retained their power over labor and were unmoved to alter their racial practices.[19] Nevertheless, in 1947 Mexico officially reversed its decision to deny Texas official access to Bracero Program workers, declaring that Texas had indeed created the necessary racial alterations. Texas public policy had not changed, and neither had Texas social relations involving Mexicans. Racial attitudes were as discriminatory toward Mexicans as before. Hiring practices limited access to all but the lowest-paying jobs, and schools continued to segregate Mexican children. In reversing the ban, perhaps Mexico recognized the hopelessness of its stand; it could not control Texas's racism, nor would it hinder Mexican workers from crossing the border into Texas as "wetbacks."

Bracero Protections

Nevertheless, it remains the case that where Bracero Agreements were in effect throughout the United States, it was only in "exceptional instances" that consuls protested violations, in spite of the fact that consuls were delegated by the Secretariat of Foreign Relations with protecting the braceros and enforcing the contract terms. Even had consuls wished to improve the conditions under which braceros labored and lived, consulates were so understaffed that their ability to intervene was severely limited. In a study of midwestern agricultural workers that devoted considerable attention to braceros, Dennis Nodin Valdés found very few consular protestations against bracero abuses. The reality was that consuls typically committed to the grower rather than to the braceros. In the beet fields of Michigan, for example, Valdés noted that despite deplorable work and living conditions, discrimination, and exploitation, "the consul proved to be of little help" in alleviating the situation. And in Wisconsin, Edmundo Flores, inspector for the Wisconsin War Food Administration, reported that "the performance of the Mexican consulate was thoroughly inadequate. Strangely enough they showed a tendency to blame all the irregularities on the workers."[20] More often, argues Valdés, individuals from the local Mexican communities, and not the consulates, led attempts to redress grievances arising from "widespread contract violations in wages, inadequate housing and health, poor treatment, and discrimination." Unfortunately, continues Valdés, "Most consular officials . . . were timid before U.S. officials and condescending to their own citizens."[21] Inspector Flores stated that over the course of his official duties, the enormous volume of complaints and the nonexistent safeguards made it "almost impossible to do anything about [the violations]."

Generally growers were more than pleased to refer disputes to the consuls for resolution. They recognized that consuls were reluctant to open investigations of Bracero Agreement violations and could feel confident that they were safe from reprimands or demands for redress. They also had nothing to fear from consuls in terms of unionization. Galarza commented that over the twenty-two-year course of the agreements, the union movement among Mexican laborers had little or no impetus. In explaining the lack of a concerted drive to organize agricultural laborers, Galarza refers to the critical "negative role of the Government of Mexico."[22] The United States and Mexico held an uncontested monopoly over the labor market, a market weighted in favor of capital. For twenty-two years the interests of U.S. agricultural enterprises and those of the Mexican government coincided with, and were implemented through, the Bracero Agreements in which Mexico acted as labor contractor for its own people.

The Bracero Agreements were terminated in 1964, but the U.S. practice of tapping into Mexico's cheap labor reserves was not. The new Border Industrialization Program (which superceded the Bracero Program) continued the practice. In this updated binational arrangement, U.S. corporations would now utilize Mexican workers in assembly plants established inside Mexico. U.S. corporations would have exclusive title to factory properties, and infrastructure and plants would be wholly owned and administered by U.S. interests. This new program was primarily designed to benefit U.S. corporations, but it also served to ameliorate Mexico's problems of unemployment and political unrest, just as had emigration. The promise was that the influx of U.S. corporate capital would act to subsidize Mexico's northern border economy and deflect rural discontent. As the plan unfolded, Mexico consistently gave precedence to the cultivation of foreign investment over any protection of Mexican workers. Under CTM-controlled policies, U.S. enterprises were given a free hand to manage Mexican laborers without interference as Mexico abandoned any revolutionary pretense of government oversight. Thus foreign investment was courted and secured, and laborers suffered the consequences.[23]

The Sixties and Seventies

With the instigation of the *maquiladora* Border Industrial Program, a new phase in Mexico–U.S. labor relations began. It was not forgotten, however, that thousands of expatriates constituted a significant political constituency within the United States. Years of labor importation programs had significantly enhanced the resident Mexican population. And in the spirit of the sixties, as various rights groups proliferated, Mexican workers living in the United States became newly politicized. Out of this ferment of discontent and hope, the historic Chicano civil rights movement was born. Denied the right to practice the culture of their parents and grandparents, a generation of sons and daughters of immigrants sought to restore their cultural heritage. In response to a racialized cultural oppression and decades of coerced Americanization in the public schools, many activists romanticized the Mexican Revolution. Moreover, they proclaimed an Aztec homeland and heritage (Aztlán) and espoused the preservation of the Spanish language, Mexican music, dance, and other cultural facets. A number of Chicano cultural symbols resonated with those the Mexican government had proffered since the 1920s in its nationalistic projects.

In Mexico, as in the United States, political ferment raged. To put down the threat to government autocracy, the ruling party of Mexico clamped down violently on outbreaks of rebellion. Student, labor, and peasant movements drew government fire. One such incident in 1968 brought Mexico international censure: In quelling a demonstration in the Plaza Tlatelolco, Mexican militia killed hundreds of unarmed students. In the aftermath of the massacre, the regime sought to offset its tarnished image with a public relations coup. The struggling Chicano Movement, which welcomed support, was perfect for this purpose. Mexico could present its benevolent face to the world by declaring itself the natural ally of Chicanos seeking to return to the culture of *la patria*. Chicano yearnings to return to Mexican roots and their demands for cultural democracy were eminently exploitable. And while celebrating nationalist ideals for the pleasure of the Chicanos, the regime could display potent historic symbols that incidentally reflected the Partido Revolucionario Institucional's (PRI's) nationalist traditions and its political aims. As the situation developed, the Mexican government, with considerable pomp and ceremony, offered its assistance (actually quite limited) to Chicanos. Each party hoped to gain political leverage in the process. Chicano leaders expected to win support from President Luis Echeverría for their cultural and political reforms. Self-interest and expected dividends in the form of international goodwill and approval likewise motivated the regime while it continued to pursue its covert antileftist policies and to suppress dissidents.

President Echeverría (who as Secretary of Gobernación, the Interior, had ordered troops to fire on unarmed students) was well versed in the revolutionary mythology that fitted the nationalistic fervor of the Chicano generation, and he now stepped forward with gestures of support for the cause of the Chicano Movement. Invitations went out to Chicano organizations and their leaders, who descended upon Mexico City for meetings with ranking officials and cabinet members. Through these assemblies the Texas-based La Raza Unida Party and the Reyes Tijerina–led New Mexican land-grant movement, among others, were able to establish a rapport with the Echeverría administration. A La Raza Party leader summarized the sentiment shared by many contemporaries, stating that "Chicanos should not look to Wall Street or Washington to find their destiny. Our destiny is to the south with a people like us. . . . We are a family without borders, we are a family without orphans . . . we are sons of Mexicans." [24]

Such declarations of faith in the Mexican government's support for Chicano issues were perhaps understandable given the persuasive rhetoric of the Echeverrían bureaucracy. But how far support would go toward the Chicano objectives would depend on economic developments. In any case, the Chicano faction hoped to impel the Mexican government to use its powers to take up its cause. On one occasion Tijerina led a caravan of cars loaded with eighty delegates representing the land-grant movement for a meeting with Echeverría officials imploring assistance in their quest to restore titles to original royal Spanish land grants. Such a project would be one of the first to be abandoned when the government found itself in economic straits.

In the early seventies, the Mexican president opened the Office of Mexicans Living Abroad, housed in the Secretariat of Foreign Relations, and charged it with planning and directing the development of a network of Chicano interactions with the Mexican government. Intellectuals and political activists were particularly prominent participants in this government-to-people program. A scholarship program was instituted that brought bright young Chicanos to study in the land of their cultural roots. Libraries at Chicano studies centers in universities and colleges received books and other donations; cultural centers were also established, funded in part by the Mexican government. Thus, the Chicano movement was validated and given limited support from the Mexican government.

Throughout the early sixties and seventies the consulates remained more or less outside of the growing interaction between their Chicano constituency and *la patria,* but as the Mexico-Chicano alliance gained strength under President José López Portillo (1976–1982), consuls were drawn into the movement. The decade of the eighties began with a burst of optimistic publications primarily by Chicano authors on the implicit benefits that would derive from the emerging Chicano-Mexicano connection. Chicano expectations were fed by the anticipation that Mexico's oil production (based on foreign loans) would make Mexico a player among the rich petroleum nations. Chicano academics and political figures, anticipating a future full of potential, were all too easily persuaded by government rhetoric assuring that Chicano interests would be attended to and served. Writing in the early eighties, one prominent political scientist, rejoicing in the maturing bond between Chicanos and Mexico, predicted that "Chicano-Mexican relations will certainly continue, broaden, and intensify. . . . They will enrich Chicanos culturally and may assist Chicanos to become more important actors in internal U.S. political life as well as in U.S.–Mexican relations."[25] In response to the rising Chicano-Mexico clamor, venerable historian Stanley R. Ross augured that "politics in the United States, particularly presidential politics, will assure the presence and importance of the Chicano factor in U.S.–Mexican relations."[26] Such rosy predictions for Chicano-Mexican relations were destined for disappointment and disillusion as Mexico plunged into economic crisis with the abrupt drop in oil prices in the early eighties.

Collapsing Economy, Diminishing Hopes

The collapse of the Mexican economy muzzled proclamations of a Chicano-Mexico political bond. High hopes fizzled, and emerging Chicano academic study programs and promising political dialogue were temporarily weakened. However, in 1982 the Harvard-educated technocrat and PRI presidential candidate Miguel de la Madrid Hurtado revived the tenuously explored linkages. In Mexico a PRI candidacy assures electoral victory, and so a presidential campaign is a pro forma ritual. In these circumstances de la Madrid, acting assertively, appointed a Chicano to "serve as an advisor to the [presidential] campaign on Chicano affairs." Early de la Madrid strategy was to hold a series of three meetings between Chicano and Mexican leaders with the aim of reviving the former sense of interaction between the two entities. At the first meeting held prior to the election, the tone was set for the anticipated alliance. Brought together were leaders from at least nine Chicano and political organizations, including the League of United Latin American Citizens, the Mexican American Legal Defense Fund, and the National Council of La Raza. De la Madrid began the proceedings with a statement of purpose: "This meeting," he began, "should above all else be understood as a reaffirmation of the willingness of the Partido Revolucionario Institucional . . . to fortify, expand, and systematize these linkages that, having their base history and sentiment, can evolve into forms of cooperation even more dynamic and positive."[27]

Treading carefully and diplomatically among topics to be discussed, de la Madrid focused on the least controversial areas of interaction, primarily at the level of culture, in an agenda with fairly conservative political parameters. Education was a safe topic, and taken up were Chicano studies programs, scholarships for Chicano students to study in Mexico, and bilingual programs. As a result of this moderate approach, a more conservative group of Chicanos ultimately joined these meetings. De la Madrid counseled them to follow a course of cultural introspection and to seek their shared identity. The president's ideas for fulfilling Mexico's responsibilities toward its brethren revolved around the usual benefits of reaffirming a Mexican cultural identity, but no specific offers were made. "One manner of defending the rights of these [Mexicano/Chicano] communities," he proclaimed, "is to reaffirm their cultural identity and solidarity produced within these communities because such a reaffirmation gives both of us more leverage in the process of social and political negotiation with the United States."[28] In spite of de la Madrid's culturally based prescriptions and his emphasis on the PRI as the responsible organization within Mexico in the growing discourse, the Chicano connection scarcely took fire. It wasn't until mid-decade that changes in Mexican politics once again made Chicano-to-Mexico relations a viable political issue.

NAFTA, the PRI, and the PRD

The new wave of political change in Mexico was heralded with the selection of Carlos Salinas de Gortari Ponce de León, another Harvard-trained economist, as the PRI presidential candidate in 1988. Mexico now embarked on a campaign of neoliberal reforms centered on the expected passage by the U.S. Congress of the North American Free Trade Agreement (NAFTA), supported in Mexico by a coterie of Ivy League neoliberal technocrats. However, in the late eighties a sizable groundswell of opposition to the liberal Ivy Leaguers arose within Mexico, particularly from the new moderately reformist centrist party, the Partido Revolucionario Democrático. Led by Cuahtémoc Cárdenas, a former PRI governor and senator for the state of Michoacán, son of former president Lázaro Cárdenas, and member of Mexico's elite upper class, the PRD not only opposed NAFTA but also posed a serious threat to the PRI with the possibility of legitimately capturing the 1988 elections. Moreover, the PRD initiated a northern strategy to contest the PRI not only in Mexico, but within the Mexicano/Chicano communities as well. From offices in southern California, northern California, and Chicago, the PRD launched a program of interactive political dialogues that lasted through the nineties.

The PRI and Salinas countered the PRD by seeking to strengthen its own Chicano connection. Salinas also mounted a response to the growing opposition to the trade pact both within the United States and at home in Mexico. This developed into a large-scale intervention into the Mexican communities throughout the United States, a major effort that was funded in part from a $10 million allocation to ensure the passage of NAFTA. As in the past seven decades, domestic politics—in this case, the PRI–PRD political battle over NAFTA and the presidency—determined the international strategy.

Fearing the PRD's anti-NAFTA message, and aware that the PRD was gaining power in the barrios of the Southwest, PRI renewed its efforts to cultivate the Chicano-Mexicano connection. PRI's first objective was to generate Chicano support for the trade agreement, and the second was to undercut endorsement of Cárdenas, the PRD candidate. Cárdenas was feared as a strong challenger to PRI power; it was conceivable that he could win the presidency. The PRI made certain that would not happen.

Thus on July 6, 1988, Salinas was fraudulently elected president of Mexico on a neoliberal program that extolled and widely publicized its Chicano-to-Mexico interaction.[29] As the electoral returns were announced, Salinas's use of the Chicano issue bore fruit. Congratulatory messages arrived in Mexico City from across the Southwest. One from Chicano entrepreneurs and journalists in Colorado typified the reaction: "warm regards on your triumph of July 6, wishing you all the success in the difficult challenge in governing Mexico, you will surely succeed with the support and confidence of Mexicans within and outside of the country." The writers reaffirmed their "unity with the country of their ancestors" and concluded that they "worked for the good of Mexico." The letter made the pages of the Mexico City daily *Excelsior*.[30]

With the promises of a prosperous Mexico under NAFTA, issues of land reform and the nationalization of oil lost their usefulness; they no longer applied. Taking a new tack, the PRI found it expedient to rescue the image of Porfirio Díaz, the long dead dictator, and to depict him as the precursor of the neoliberal modernization policies that the PRI now sought to pursue. Among these pursuits were open-door policies that lowered or eliminated existing barriers to foreign investment and ownership. (The strong resemblance of the present decade to that of the Porfirian era is hard to miss, and it comes as no surprise that the PRI has proposed giving Porfirio Díaz a new reading in Mexico's history books. Historian

Devra Weber recounted to the author that Mexican textbooks have re-defined the previous portrayals of Díaz with favorable reinterpretations that break with Mexican Revolutionary traditions.)

Other parallels with Mexico's modern past began to surface. The presidential inauguration provided one such instance. At Calles's inauguration in 1924, he bowed to unionism, a key political issue of the time, and invited Samuel Gompers, a union leader, to appear on the podium with him. Now years later, at President Salinas's inauguration, the gesture was replicated when he invited prominent Chicanos to stand with him at the gala event.[31] In the former it was the union movement that was being honored; in the latter, the Chicano issue was exhibited. The Salinas message was reassuring: the Mexican government, and therefore the PRI, "stood shoulder to shoulder" with their Chicano brothers and sisters. To launch the new program, the Secretariat of Foreign Relations issued a new directive that not only restated an old principle, an updated version of *mexicanidad* for the nineties, but offered a policy path for consuls to follow: "The relationships [with *México de afuera*] should not remain as they were, subject to changes in administration and the good intentions of numerous isolated initiatives of groups in Mexico and in the United States: the linkages should be actively promoted and deepened."[32] In 1988 Mexico issued statements reaffirming that the causes of its northern Chicano/Mexicano brothers and sisters were Mexico's as well. Mexican consulates in the United States would now administer a revised Chicano/ Mexicano policy.

In marked contrast to previous decades, Mexican consuls were to initiate and manage a multifaceted campaign to stimulate ties of various sorts with intellectuals, businesspeople, administrators, politicians, and community activists. A prestigious Mexican art and archaeological exhibition, "Mexico: Splendor of Thirty Centuries," was assembled and toured major cities with large Mexican settlements. Taped radio programs on Mexican literature accompanied the highly touted exhibition as it traveled. Special government citations were created to be awarded to Chicano leaders in recognition of "distinguished altruistic community service." The Ohtli (from Nahuatl, meaning good path) Award, for instance, was created to celebrate Mexican and Mexican American civic activism. According to a consulate official, "the objective of the award is to expand [Mexico's] relations with Mexicans and persons of Mexican-American descent."[33]

Educational institutions, particularly college and university campuses, received special attention. The Mexican government, in the name of the PRI, donated an endowed chair in Chicano studies as well as books and other materials on Mexico to the University of California at Santa Barbara. Conferences hosted by Mexico brought Chicano and Mexican scholars together to initiate dialogues on matters of common concern. Consulates sought to develop collaborative projects with university Chicano studies programs and proposed cooperative cultural centers to host Mexican art exhibits and events, scholarly presentations, and film festivals. Seeking to promote the emerging interaction, President Salinas assigned official emissaries, including Donaldo Colosio, the ill-fated 1994 presidential candidate for the PRI, and Cecilia Occeli de Salinas, the president's wife. Colosio, the young and energetic Yale Ph.D., toured the United States, especially the southwestern communities with large Mexican populations, to "consolidate [the PRI's] position as the standard-bearer in problems facing immigrants" and to stand as the "vanguard for the interests of the Mexican community abroad." [34]

According to newspaper reports, the president's wife was an effective emissary for her husband's northern strategy. Occeli de Salinas visited southern California schools and health clinics and met with Mexican American women volunteers and bilingual educators. Accompanied by local consulate officials and community figures in the city of Santa Ana, Occeli de Salinas presented a "200 volume set of encyclopedias and other books about Mexico's history and culture" to a barrio elementary school. The school district welcomed this personal envoy from Mexico with displays of Mexican music, folk dancing, and songs. Recapitulating the twenties and thirties, consuls once again played a critical role in the broad-gauged plan and "suddenly became outspoken defenders of the rights and interests of Mexican citizens living in the United States; they boosted immigrant organizations and activities. . . . Mexican governors began making regular trips to meet with their respective emigre colonias and they developed cooperative relationships with them." [35]

California's anti-immigrant "Save Our State" campaign gave the Mexican government a fresh opportunity to display its "protective" face, and officials voiced their strong opposition to Proposition 187. Placed on California ballots in 1995, this proposition, targeting Mexicans and Asians, proposed that public services to undocumented immigrants be banned. In his state-of-the-union address Salinas described the proposition as part of a "xenophobic" campaign, and to allay these xenophobic zealots, he reissued an old invitation to emigrants to return to Mexico and "help build the nation's economy." Mexico extended support to Hispanic groups opposing the measure and even sponsored an advertising campaign to remind California voters of the contributions of Mexicans to their state. However, as one report published in the *New York Times* noted, "the involvement of Mexican officials has remained rhetorical and concentrated on their side of the border." [36] The campaign steered clear of any hint of "meddling" in U.S. affairs, but at the same time Salinas wished to show Mexicans abroad that their government would stand up to the United States, in order to offset "an image of submission for which the Mexican government was widely criticized in negotiations . . . of the North American Free Trade Agreement." According to this *Times* report, Mexico's denunciation of Proposition 187 was "in keeping with the Salinas government's expanding effort to win political support among Mexican migrants to the United States."[37]

Arturo Santamaría Gómez, a sociologist at the Universidad Autónoma de Sinaloa, in studying the Chicano-Mexico political linkages, noted with surprise that today's interactions between consuls and the Mexican American community are much greater than in the sixties and show a greater involvement on every level, politically and socially, than in the past. At the Los Angeles Consulate, Santamaría Gómez notes, "the frequency of political functions attended by . . . powerful Mexican-American leaders from southern California are astonishing. Similarly, the ties between Los Angeles Mexican clubs, associations, and fraternities and the consulate has been greater under Salinas de Gortari than during any of the previous six decades."[38] Los Angeles consulate offices have once again become a hive of political activity as Consul José Angel Pescador Osuna updates the policy first elaborated in the twenties and thirties by his predecessors, Consuls Pesqueira, de la Colina, Hill, and Martínez, and carries it still further.

In the larger communities throughout the United States, cultural centers have sprouted, offering programs promoting Mexican themes. In the late eighties, the Los Angeles Mexican Cultural Institute was founded with the mission of developing a spirit of goodwill between the peoples of Mexico and the United States. The institute's board of directors comprises representatives from the larger Los Angeles community, the director of the Program for the Mexican Communities Living Abroad (acting for Mexico's Secretariat of Foreign Relations), and the consul general, who serves as chairman. Among the institute's programs, the most illustrious was a lecture series on such topics as Mexican archaeology, architecture, history, folk art, and culture. According to an institute flyer, all presentations were given by "members of the prestigious Seminario de Cultura Mexicana, an organization composed of the highest respected scholars in Mexico [sic]."

In the nineties in neighboring Orange County, the Centro Cultural de México serves the same function as the Los Angeles Institute, seeking to "maintain the Mexican heritage alive so as to preserve ourselves as a people." The local consul serves as the "Presidente Honorario," and community volunteers handle the day-to-day administration. Activities include donating library books to local schools with large Spanish-speaking populations, art exhibits, patriotic celebrations, Mexican film festivals, scholarly presentations, and elementary summer school courses taught by visiting Mexican teachers. The tradition of bestowing honorary titles on the consul appears to have been revived. In Santa Ana, the county seat, there are nearly 200,000 Latino inhabitants out of a total of 300,000. A voting-rights group comprised of Chicano professionals made an auspicious entrance in 1996. Prominently listed among the officials of the organization is the local consul, recognized as the "Honorary President."

In the late eighties and early nineties, the PRI struggled to outmaneuver the PRD in a bid to gain the political loyalty of the Chicano community and thus expand its power within the United States. It also specifically sought support for NAFTA as the debate about its passage was taking place in the U.S. Congress. As a tactic for outwitting the PRD in the contest for the Chicano connection, the PRI planned the establishment of fifty pro-PRI organizations across the United States (the first opened in Sacramento, California) and even considered the possibility of offering dual citizenship to Mexicans living abroad. The clash between the PRI and the PRD continues as each party jockeys for position. Which faction will prevail remains to be seen. Most interesting in regard to this analysis is the examination of the political methods employed by both sides. The PRI and the PRD have a long history of organizing involving "transborder" politics. It appears that such policies and practices will continue into the twenty-first century. The PRI's efforts on behalf of NAFTA appear to have been effective. NAFTA was signed by all parties in 1994. Among PRI strategies to win this victory was the use of Latino lobbyists paid to gain key Hispanic caucus votes. A display of bipartisan unity also helped and enabled the U.S. Congress to pass legislation implementing this controversial trade agreement.

That the trade agreement would fail to deliver a fundamental change in the economic condition of Mexican workers as promised comes as no surprise, but no one anticipated the treaty's disastrous consequences for the entire nation. Within weeks of the NAFTA signing, the Mexican economy collapsed, plunging the country into its worst political and economic crisis since the 1910 Revolution. As a bankrupt Mexico foundered, the United States stepped in to rescue its investors. A $50 billion international loan was arranged (some call it a bailout); terms of the loan stipulate that the portion to be repaid to the United States come from Mexico's oil revenues and be deposited directly in U.S. banks. In Mexico a severe austerity program was put into effect. The immediate cost to Mexico's people was enormous: the standard of living fell daily, prices rose, manufacturing and assembly plants closed or downsized, social services shrank or disappeared. Social and political conflict reached staggering proportions as 50 percent of the working population were either unemployed or earning less than $1,000 a year. Street vending, long the province of the unskilled, now attracted the middle class as a way of earning some small income, and even teachers and other former professionals joined the ranks of the down-and-out. Armed peasant rebellions threatened, crime spiraled out of control, the judicial system barely functioned, and vigilante justice became a terrifying presence in rural locales. With each month, the economy sickened further as seventeen thousand small businesses went bankrupt and the state bureaucracy became further mired in such extreme forms of corruption that the government could scarcely be said to govern.

Historically, Mexican society has been bipolar in economic structure, with a few rich and the vast majority poor. But since 1995 the gap has widened catastrophically. The "bottom half of the population receives only 16 percent of all national income" while the top 10 percent receives over 40 percent. It appears that NAFTA had a devastating impact on the poverty levels between 1995 and 1996: those living in extreme poverty numbered twenty-two million people in 1996, an increase of five million in just one year. An estimated one hundred thousand homeless walk the capital's streets searching for food and shelter. The *New York Times* reported that the "degree of [income] disparity is among the worst in the world and is steadily growing more extreme." The eminent historian Lorenzo Mayer is alarmed at the seriousness of the crisis as he observes the "enormous distance and antagonism between the classes and groups that form the Mexican social fabric."[39]

Still another historical tradition within Mexico is that of government corruption at the very highest levels. And here again NAFTA has had a deleterious effect as it plays into the hands of dishonest officials by affording them access to large sums of money. Millions of dollars are being siphoned off as the bureaucracy fattens itself at the expense of the Mexican economy and its people. Drained of these vital dollars, Mexico drifts deeper into poverty and its associated ills. As for the skimmed-off monies, they are stored nearby in U.S. banks or overseas in Swiss banks.

Neither the medieval tributary system rooted in Spanish colonization nor the profligate money barons of the twenties (reported by Beals, Tannenbaum, and Simpson) come anywhere near today's extravagant venality. Apart from NAFTA and other factors, the illegal drug trade alone puts millions of dollars in the pockets of Mexican drug lords and the bureaucrats who are paid (bribed) to look the other way. Feeding the insatiable appetite in the United States for cocaine and marijuana is big business, and the Mexican government shares in the illicit profits and covers

up the connection. Mexican cultural critic Carlos Monsiváis, a participant in the 1968 student movement, commented that "the government
has lost all credibility. . . . The economy is in disarray. Dependence on the
United States is extraordinary."[40] As the unemployed, underemployed,
and underpaid population grows at an ever-increasing rate, these masses
of workers become a serious threat to the PRI. Seeking to stifle the rising
wave of rebellion, the government has prohibited labor demonstrations
(even when workers were members of government-controlled labor federations). Several Labor Day marches were canceled for fear that such
displays would become platforms for mounting political opposition to
the PRI.[41]

Salinas's presidency (1988–1994) was tainted from the start as he
marched his country into the worst economic crisis of modern Mexico.
He was further stained when his brother Raúl was charged with murder
and corruption. With his family in disgrace, Salinas fled the country, seeking solace and protection in exile.

Hopes ran high for political change as Ernesto Zedillo assumed the
presidency in 1994. However, Zedillo's early steps cast doubt on reform.
Will he repudiate the inherited history of corruption and attempt to restore a semblance of democratic order? Judged by recent actions, such an
outcome is doubtful. Zedillo has not hesitated to employ the time-tested
techniques of his predecessors and the PRI; extralegal methods to silence
opposition remain the weapons of choice. The level of government retri-
bution depends on the alleged infractions, but "justice" has ranged from
arbitrary arrest and solitary confinement to threats of loss of employment
and even murder. A former general counsel and special adviser to the
president of the InterAmerican Bank, Jerome Levinson, noted that a dissident labor leader was jailed on trumped-up charges by the government
for attempting to organize a border *maquiladora* in 1991. According to
Levinson, "the message was clear: Conform to the government's low-
wage policy or pay the price."[42] The respected historian Lorenzo Mayer,
for example, was dismissed by the radio station that broadcast his popular program for criticizing Zedillo's continuing close ties to the PRI.
Human-rights activists also felt the sting of government backlash for reporting instances of abuses by security forces, particularly the use of violence "to retain or win political and economic power." Three noted
human-rights advocates were expelled from the country because, stated
an official, their reports "lacked objectivity."[43] As a repressive political
party holds the country hostage and plunders the public treasury, the
Mexican people are caught in a struggle to survive.

As the century closes, Mexico's working class is exploited within its own borders (through NAFTA) and in the United States (through emigration). As before, Mexican consulates sustain alliances with U.S. businesses rather than with the Mexican citizens employed in these enterprises. The laissez-faire principles first enunciated by Carranza in the second decade of the century shape Mexico's emigration policy. At present remittances generated by *México de afuera* total over $4 billion annually, an influx that provides crucial dollars for a broken economy and a discredited nation.

Throughout the twentieth century the United States has been Mexico's main trading partner and bank lender and thus has held economic supremacy over Mexico. One newspaper headline summed up the U.S.–Mexico economic tie: "Trade Knits U.S. and Mexico Ever More Tightly." Another beamed, "Panel Declares NAFTA Success in California," heralding the benefits that have accrued to California and other states along the U.S.–Mexico border. However, promises of economic well-being for Mexico have proved false. True, as planned, foreign-owned companies have provided employment for Mexican laborers. The catch is that once again, that labor is not fairly compensated; a living wage was never guaranteed as part of the deal. The profitability of these capital enterprises is based on cheap labor, and Mexico's oversupply gives to foreign capital the consummate power to control wage levels. Just as agribusiness controlled the level of Mexican wages in the valleys of California in the Depression era, so now do U.S. corporate enterprises exert such control over Mexican labor in Mexico itself.[44]

The net loss is Mexico's as once again the Mexican government delivers its most valuable resource (labor) to U.S. business interests. It would seem that Mexico arranged its own economic suicide when it made its pact with the United States: Mexico now imports U.S. technology in the form of factory components for use in Mexico-based U.S. assembly plants that employ Mexican labor to produce commodities for the U.S. market. By 1996, 80 percent of Mexico's exports to the United States were "intermediate goods" assembled in largely foreign-owned assembly plants. Those U.S. plants employ 875,000 Mexican workers. The typical wage is $28 a week, a fraction of what an American worker is paid for similar work in a plant located in the United States. Moreover, the work week is longer in the Mexican locale, forty-five to fifty-hours, rather than forty as is standard in the United States. The disastrous economic policies pursued by Mexico's ruling elite have robbed this country of its patrimony. Today the economy speeds toward total breakdown. Bringing that day of reckoning ever closer is the *maquiladora* industry. The fastest-growing business in the country is, paradoxically, exacerbating the nation's poverty as "poorly paid jobs with long hours" have ballooned by 60 percent.[45] More people are employed. But as laborers' earnings have declined precipitously, not only is there no gain, there is drastic loss. Since NAFTA, the average Mexican's living standard, already among the lowest among nations, has deteriorated as real wages have fallen by nearly one-third.

Approaching the twenty-first century, Mexico finds itself the focus of international intrigue as the United States fends off competitors (Europe and Japan) for the cheap labor market it considers its own. Mexico began the twentieth century in near complete economic subordination to U.S. capital and now enters the next century in the same relation. Mexico's trading relations with the United States still govern all transactions; no change is in sight. Whichever party rules (or speaks), there is no basis for believing that a favorable economic outcome will take place in Mexico in the near future.

Headlines still project that "U.S. Investment in Mexico Will Continue," in spite of the July 1997 election of PRI defector Cuahtémoc Cárdenas as mayor of Mexico City and the decline of the PRI. Residing in the upper-class Polanco district of Mexico City and often mistaken for a leftist, Cárdenas has recently retreated from his former rejection of NAFTA and instead calls for "fine tuning" of the agreement. U.S. investors, needlessly apprehensive before the election, were "buoyant" afterwards. A confident Wall Street and U.S. State Department took the PRD victories in stride, forecasting that economic and political relations would continue as before without interruption. José de Luis Daza, director of J. P. Morgan's emerging markets research, hummed that the election "results are undoubtedly positive. . . . We will see strong inflows of capital [into Mexico] on a sustained basis."[46] Such is the economic hegemony of the United States over Mexico that aberrations in Mexican politics appear to be irrelevant. It appears that no fundamental change will be forthcoming regardless of the merging of the PRD's and the PRI's economic agendas.

Portents for the Chicano/Mexicano Community

In what ways will Mexico's ruinous economic policies and its internal political struggles impact the Chicano/Mexicano population? We may expect that in this long period of economic depression and political chaos, the contest between PRI and the PRD will intensify as each presses for a political advantage among *México de afuera* as well as at home. Differing and opposing perspectives toward Mexican and Chicano politics will be

a divisive force north of the border. In influencing the political consciousness of the Chicano/Mexicano communities, the party in power will have
a natural advantage. But watched most closely by the Chicano constituencies will be how Mexico responds to the harsh conditions imposed on
them by the United States. A domestic political struggle is already in progress and will dictate government tactics, whether overtly or covertly. Nationalism will surely be used as a rallying cry, especially as the anti–illegal
immigrant campaign launched in the United States looms. The PRI has
already draped itself in the Mexican flag on the immigration issue, proclaiming a defense of the national sovereignty. Within the Chicano/
Mexicano communities, we will see political conflicts similar to those of
the twenties and thirties, where loyalties were strained and trust in their
homeland betrayed as the Mexican government largely abandoned its expatriate citizens, leaving them to the mercy of U.S. capital interests.

It appears that Mexico has become more protective of *México de
afuera* over the past several years and now responds with gestures of support, particularly over the immigrant issue. This is particularly true of
well-publicized events involving police chases and official violence. One
such incident in April of 1996 inflamed the Chicano community: unarmed and restrained Mexican immigrants were arrested and beaten at
Riverside, California. The Los Angeles consulate reacted with outrage to
the attack and took a "highly aggressive stance against law-enforcement
actions." The Los Angeles Consulate's Department of Protections, the
largest such office among Mexican consulates in the United States, sprang
into action, informing investigating reporters that it was mandated to offer protection and assistance to the "growing numbers of Mexican nationals who report alleged police abuse." News coverage depicted the
consul as the lone defender of Mexican nationals against police abuse.

The immigration issue may be the device that binds the Chicano community together as a political force. As for the PRI, it has made a show of
extending cultural ties to Chicanos as well as protections to emigrated
Mexicanos. However, a government that pursues a policy of antidemo-
cratic reforms and threatens or silences those who dare criticize its policies does not realistically inspire faith. Quite the contrary. One of Mexico's leading criminologists, Fernando Tenorio Tagle, comments that the
government's vaunted political reforms have in fact led to greater militarization of society. "We're going from an authoritarian system to a totali-
tarian system," he states, "You see the militarization all over Mexico." [47]
A journalist for the *Boston Globe* writing of Mexico under Zedillo observes that "in the poorest states local strongmen known as caciques run
municipalities like fiefdoms, often enforcing their will with private para-
military attaches known as 'white guards.'" [48] Lamentably, it is a familiar

scene and even one that could have been observed one hundred years earlier.

Adolfo Aguilar Zinser, an independent political figure and scholar, was impressed by the PRI's heralded political pluralism but has reluctantly concluded that "Zedillo's democracy is a sham." [49] A headline in an Orange County newspaper reporting Mexico's 1997 election notes the politics-as-usual strong-arm tactics of the ruling party: "Mexico's Top Party Stifles its Critics. Elections: Rights Activists are Ejected and Opposition Supporters are Muzzled as a Competitive Vote Nears." [50]

Emigration has served as an economic and political crutch for years and continues to do so. Emigrants pump in $4 billion annually and also act as a safety valve in relieving political unrest. Mexico's leaders have told us for eighty years that they despair over the loss of their citizens. But while they publicly weep, privately they smile and do nothing to stem the exodus to the north. As always, emigration serves a multiplicity of political purposes by contributing dollars to a bankrupt economy and reducing the numbers of dissidents. Whichever party is in power will publicly despair of the continuous exodus of its people, all the while aiding and abetting emigration by failing to stop it.

A comment from Ernesto Galarza, written in the mid-forties, defines the twentieth-century Chicano experience, particularly its ties to the Mexican government, and provides a fitting closing for this study. The Mexican, he wrote, "is forced to seek better conditions north of the border by the slow but relentless pressure of United States' agricultural, financial, and oil corporate interests on the entire economic and social evolution of the Mexican nation." [51] The Mexican state has been dominated by the "corrupt and bloated" PRI for nearly seventy years, and a "relentless pressure" has committed the nation to foreign investment and, by extension, to fostering the export of labor migrants and building Mexican/Chicano communities.

Taken together, the Mexican connection in the three agricultural strikes (examined in Chapters 3, 4, and 5) has far-reaching implications and a political significance that goes beyond the fertile acres, the struggling laborers, and the economic lords of that bygone era. Close analysis of today's Chicano community reveals the same international forces at work, and they continue to have an impact upon the political destiny of this expatriate faction. Any understanding of the ethnic consciousness of this group must take into account the international dimensions of their cultural formation.

Mexico remains subordinate to the imperialist capital interests of the United States, with the same ruinous results as in the past. The ruling parties of Mexico have continued to pursue a transborder politics, and whether or not Chicanos and expatriate Mexicanos continue to collaborate or whether divisions and conflicts will erupt over the northern version of Mexican domestic politics remains to be seen. History tells us, however, that political discord generated by Mexico's government and political parties will enter into the political life of the Chicano and Mexicano communities, possibly affecting the minority community's ability to make a single political voice heard in national and state politics.

Notes

Preface and Acknowledgments

1. Mario Gill, *Nuestros buenos vecinos* (Mexico City: Editorial Azteca, 1964), 2–8.

Introduction

1. George Ramos, "Chicano Agenda Getting Bigger Play in Mexico," *Los Angeles Times,* February 2, 1994.

2. Mrs. Vollemeare, Detroit International Institute Interpreter, August 3, 1928, Paul Schuster Taylor Collection, Z R-4 Box 1, Folder "Detroit, Michigan," Bancroft Library.

3. "La Secretaría de Relaciones hace un cálido elogio del cuerpo consular mexicano," *La Opinión,* July 13, 1930. All translations, unless otherwise noted, are mine.

4. Manuel Gamio, *The Mexican Immigrant* (Chicago: University of Chicago Press, 1931; reprint: New York: Arno Press, 1969), 56.

5. Ibid., 216.

6. *Excelsior* (Mexico City), August 14, 1937, clipping in National Archives, Washington, D.C., Record Group 59, Records of the Department of State, 811.5045/476.

7. Mario García, *Memories of Chicano History: The Life and Narrative of Bert Corona* (Berkeley: University of California Press, 1994), 182.

8. "Labor que han desarrollado los cónsules," *La Opinión,* February 3, 1931.

9. Ibid.

10. "La protección del consulado durante junio," *La Opinión,* July 12, 1934.

11. "El cónsul hace un llamado," *La Opinión,* October 19, 1934.

12. Ruth Tuck, *Not with the Fist: Mexican Americans in a Southwest City* (New York: Harcourt Brace and Company, 1946), 168–169.

13. Ignacio López, Foreword, in Tuck, *Not with the Fist,* ix. See also Mario García, "La Frontera: The Border as Symbol and Reality in Mexican American

Thought," in David G. Gutiérrez, ed., *Between Two Worlds: Mexican Immigrants in the United States,* (Wilmington, Del.: Scholarly Resources, 1996), 95.

14. Stuart Jameison, *Labor Unionism in American Agriculture,* United States Department of Labor Bulletin No. 836 (Washington, D.C.: U.S. Government Printing Office, 1945), 76.

15. Francisco Balderrama, *In Defense of La Raza: The Los Angeles Mexican Consulate and the Mexican Community, 1929–1936* (Tucson: University of Arizona Press, 1982), 117. See also Vicki Ruiz, *Cannery Women, Cannery Lives: Mexican Women, Unionization, and the Food Processing Industry, 1930–1950* (Albuquerque: University of New Mexico Press, 1987). Concerning the Los Angeles Mexican Consulate, Ruiz writes that "the Mexican cónsul assigned to Los Angeles . . . organized the Comite de Beneficencia Mexicana as a mechanism for providing relief to those barrio residents hardest hit by the Great Depression" (p. 6). See also Mario García, *Mexican Americans: Leadership, Ideology, and Identity, 1930–1960* (New Haven: Yale University Press, 1989), 150; Arthur F. Corwin, "Mexican Policy and Ambivalence toward Labor Emigration to the United States," in Arthur F. Corwin, ed., *Immigrants and Immigrants: Perspectives on Mexican Labor Migration to the United States* (Westport, Conn.: Greenwood Press, 1978), who writes, "In defending displaced nationals, the Mexican cónsuls since Carranza's time have displayed, all in all, an unmatched dedication" (p. 187); and Zaragosa Vargas, *Proletarians of the North: A History of Mexican Industrial Workers in Detroit and the Midwest, 1917–1933* (Berkeley: University of California Press, 1993), passim. More recently, Francisco Balderrama and Raymond Rodríguez continue the consul-as-protector interpretation in their Ford Foundation–funded study, *Decade of Betrayal: Mexican Repatriation in the 1930s* (Albuquerque: University of New Mexico Press, 1995).

16. Beatrice Griffith, *American Me* (Boston: Houghton Mifflin, 1948), 239.

17. Tuck, *Not with the Fist,* 169.

18. Clete Daniel, *Bitter Harvest: A History of California Farmworkers, 1871–1941* (Ithaca: Cornell University Press, 1981).

19. Devra Weber, *Dark Sweat, White Gold: California Farm Workers, Cotton, and the New Deal* (Berkeley: University of California Press, 1994), 102.

20. Camille Guerin-Gonzales, *Mexican Workers and American Dreams: Immigration, Repatriation, and California Farm Labor, 1900–1939* (New Brunswick, N.J.: Rutgers University Press, 1994); see also R. Reynolds McKay, "The Impact of the Great Depression on Immigrant Mexican Labor: Repatriation of the Bridgeport, Texas Coal Miners," *Social Science Quarterly* 65, no. 2 (1984): 354–363. Balderrama and Rodríguez contend that Mexico's interest was the protection of the repatriates. However, this line of reasoning implies that Mexico acted entirely out of humanitarian impulses. The record, on the other hand, demonstrates that repatriation was a bilateral effort and that responsibility for the campaign must rest on the shoulders of the United States and Mexico (*Decade of Betrayal,* 127–156).

21. Juan Gómez-Quiñones, *Roots of Chicano Politics, 1600–1940* (Albuquerque: University of New Mexico Press, 1994), 379–380; see also Dennis

Nodin Valdés, *Al Norte: Agricultural Workers in the Great Lakes Region 1917–1970* (Austin: University of Texas Press, 1991), 22–23.

22. Ricardo Romo, *East Los Angeles: A History of a Barrio* (Austin: University of Texas Press, 1983), 155.

23. Guerin-Gonzales, *Mexican Workers*, chap. 6.

24. Carlos G. Vélez Ibáñez, *Border Visions: Mexican Cultures of the Southwest United States* (Tucson: University of Arizona Press, 1996).

25. Paul S. Taylor, *Mexican Labor in the United States: Imperial Valley*, University of California Publications in Economics 6, no. 1 (Berkeley: University of California Press, 1928); Linda C. Majka and Theo J. Majka, *Farm Workers, Agribusiness, and the State* (Philadelphia: Temple University Press, 1982), 68–80; see also David G. Gutiérrez, *Walls and Mirrors: Mexican Americans, Mexican Immigrants, and the Politics of Ethnicity* (Berkeley: University of California Press, 1995), 103–105. Other examples include Juan Gómez-Quiñones, *Mexican American Labor, 1790–1990* (Albuquerque: University of New Mexico Press, 1994), part 2.

26. Gilbert G. González, *Labor and Community: Mexican Citrus Worker Villages in a Southern California County, 1900–1950* (Urbana: University of Illinois Press, 1994), chap. 6.

27. George J. Sánchez, *Becoming Mexican American: Ethnicity, Culture, and Identity in Chicano Los Angeles, 1900–1945* (New York: Oxford University Press, 1993), 113.

28. Ibid.

29. Dirk Raat, *Los Revoltosos: Mexico's Rebels in the United States, 1903–1923* (College Station: Texas A&M University Press, 1981), 27–28, 30.

Chapter One

1. James D. Cockcroft, *Mexico: Class Formation, Capital Accumulation and the State* (New York: Monthly Review Press, 1983), 91.

2. Ibid.

3. Roger D. Hansen, *The Politics of Mexican Development* (Baltimore: Johns Hopkins Press, 1971), 14.

4. Cockcroft, *Mexico*, 112.

5. John Womack Jr., "The Mexican Economy during the Revolution, 1910–1920," in Dirk Raat and William H. Beezely, eds., *Twentieth-Century Mexico* (Lincoln: University of Nebraska Press, 1986), 82.

6. Ramón Eduardo Ruiz, *Labor and Ambivalent Revolutionaries: Mexico, 1911–1923* (Baltimore: Johns Hopkins Press, 1976), 2; See also Alan Knight, *The Mexican Revolution*, vol. 2 (Cambridge, Eng.: Cambridge University Press, 1986). Knight argues that the revolution "[p]roduced no ideological blueprint or vanguard party and, above all, seemed to reinforce, rather than subvert, many of the features of the old regime it overthrew" (497). I differ with Knight and most interpreters of the Mexican Revolution who claim that the Mexican Revolution,

based on the Porfirian model, comprised a capitalist project. The Porfirian era hardly resembled a capitalist revolution; on the contrary, it exhibited all the characteristics of a noncapitalist program. Díaz opted to rely on foreign capital for financing modernization—not the development of the home market, the sine qua non of a capitalist society.

7. Helen Delpar, *The Enormous Vogue of Things Mexican: Cultural Relations between the United States and Mexico, 1920–1935* (Tuscaloosa: University of Alabama Press, 1992), 59.

8. Lesley Byrd Simpson, *Many Mexicos* (Berkeley: University of California Press, 1967), 316.

9. Margaret Clark, *Organized Labor in Mexico* (New York: Russell and Russell, 1973; first published by the University of North Carolina Press, 1934), 53, 164.

10. Cockcroft, *Mexico*, 120.

11. Ibid., 135. Historian Jean Mayer adds: "They [revolutionaries] never attacked the principle of the hacienda," and later, "[l]ike many Cardenista reforms, [land reform] was the result of hasty improvisation. . . . It had left the landlords in control of the choice land." "Revolution and Reconstruction in the 1920s," in Leslie Bethell, ed., *Mexico Since Independence* (New York: Cambridge University Press, 1991), 235, 261.

12. John M. Hart, "Agrarian Reform," in Dirk Raat and William H. Beezely, eds., *Twentieth-Century Mexico* (Lincoln: University of Nebraska Press, 1986), 13.

13. Robert Freeman Smith, *The United States and Revolutionary Nationalism in Mexico, 1916–1922* (Chicago: University of Chicago Press, 1972), 34.

14. Ibid., 76.

15. Ibid., 149.

16. Ibid., 201–202.

17. David W. Walker, "Porfirian Labor Politics: Working Class Organizations in Mexico City and Porfirio Díaz, 1876–1902," *Americas* 37 (Jan. 1981): 258.

18. Margaret Clark, *Organized Labor,* 53.

19. Ibid., 76.

20. Gregg Andrews, *Shoulder to Shoulder? The American Federation of Labor, the United States, and the Mexican Revolution* (Berkeley: University of California Press, 1991), 152–57.

21. David W. Walker, "Porfirian Labor Politics," 288–289.

22. American Federation of Labor, Report of the Proceedings of the 47th Annual Convention, Los Angeles, 1927, 276.

23. Ibid., 333.

24. "Organizer Idar to Leave," *Los Angeles Citizen,* March 4, 1928.

25. "Conferences between the Executive Committee of the Pan-American Federation of Labor and Representatives of the Mexican Federation of Labor," October 25, 1923, American Federation of Labor Records, Samuel Gompers Era, Part 2, Reel 127. Gompers described Calles as "the man whom the liberty-loving, humanity-loving people of Mexico should gather to aid in furthering the interest of the Mexican government. . . . I feel that the election of General Calles to the

presidency to succeed President Obregon will do much to extend the freedom of the people of Mexico."

26. Conference on Mexican Affairs with Mexican President-elect Calles and Others, November 1, 1924, American Federation of Labor Records, Samuel Gompers Era, Part 2, Reel 123.

27. Andrews, *Shoulder to Shoulder*, 12.

28. *Los Angeles Citizen*, July 8, 1927; "Mexican Propagandists in the United States," Paul S. Taylor Collection, Z-R4, Box 1, Folder "Mexican Immigration Papers and Reports," Bancroft Library.

29. Ibid., 134.

30. American Federation of Labor, Report of the Proceedings of the 46th Annual Convention, 1926, Detroit, Michigan. Later in his address, he referred to the late Samuel Gompers as "the man who lives in our hearts and whose militant spirit is a stimulant and encouragement to the workers of all the American continent and who succeeded in creating among the workers of Mexico, undying sentiments of fraternity for the American Federation of Labor."

31. American Federation of Labor, Report of the Proceedings of the 47th Annual Convention, 96.

32. "The Foreign Policy of Our Country" (Translation), *El Universal*, February 4, 1933, National Archives Record Group 165, War Department, Records of Army and Navy Intelligence, G-2, 2657–g-733.

33. Ibid.

34. Adolfo de la Huerta to Señor Licenciado Raul Castellanos, May 9, 1938, Archivo General de la Nación (hereafter cited as AGN), Mexico City, Lázaro Cárdenas File, 574/16.

35. Ernesto Hidalgo to José Estrada, February 15, 1939, AGN, Lázaro Cárdenas File, 702, 2/6045.

36. Juan Gómez-Quiñones, "'Piedras contra la luna': México en Aztlán y Aztlán en México: Chicano-Mexican Relations and the Consulates, 1900–1920," in James W. Wilkie et al., *Contemporary Mexico*, Papers of the IV International Congress of Mexican History (Berkeley and Mexico City: University of California Press and El Colegio de México, 1976), 522–523.

37. Carlos V. Ariza, "Su expedientes personal," Archivo de la Secretaría de Relaciones Exteriores (hereafter cited as ASRE), Mexico City, Carlos Ariza Salazar File, 1-7-46.

38. General de División Genovevo de la O to Presidente Alvaro Obregón, December 17, 1920, AGN, Alvaro Obregón File, 809–A-249.

39. José G. Parres to Presidente Alvaro Obregón, December 20, 1920, AGN, Alvaro Obregón File, 809–A 249.

40. Adolfo de la Huerta to Presidente Alvaro Obregón, January 3, 1921, AGN, Alvaro Obregón File, 809–A-249.

41. Anatolio L. Ortega B. to Señor Luis I. Rodríguez, February 24, 1936, AGN, Lázaro Cárdenas File, 702–2/5341.

42. Benjamin Hill to Luis I. Rodríguez, September 9, 1936, AGN, Lázaro Cárdenas File, 702.2/5341.

43. Benjamin Hill to Luis I. Rodríguez, May 20, 1936, AGN, Lázaro Cárdenas File, 702.2/5341.

44. Rodrigo Quevedo to Luis Rodríguez, May 9, 1936, AGN, Lázaro Cárdenas File, 702.2/5341.

45. Eduardo Hay to Luis I. Rodríguez, August 9, 1936, AGN, Lázaro Cárdenas File, 702.2/5341.

46. Brigadier General Manual Ortega to Presidente Lázaro Cárdenas, November 7, 1937, AGN, Lázaro Cárdenas File, 702.2/5341.

47. Manuel H. Ortega to Presidente Lázaro Cárdenas, November 1, 1937, AGN, Lázaro Cárdenas File, 702.2/5341.

48. Ricardo Hill to Fernando Torreblanca, November 11, 1927, AGN, Alvaro Obregón File–Plutarco Elías Calles File, 809–H-147.

49. "Shaw Welcomes New Envoy from Mexico," Newspaper Clipping, AGN, Lázaro Cárdenas File, 544.61/22.

50. Deputy Alejandro Gómez Maganda to Luis I. Rodríguez, Secretary to President Cárdenas, April 4, 1935, AGN, Lázaro Cárdenas File, 544.61/22.

51. Luis I. Rodríguez, Secretary to President Cárdenas, to Deputy Alejandro Gómez Maganda, March 9, 1935, AGN, Lázaro Cárdenas File, 544.61/22.

52. Luis I. Rodríguez, Secretary to President Cárdenas, to Deputy Alejandro Gómez Maganda, March 9, 1935, AGN, Lázaro Cárdenas File, 544.61/22.

53. Alejandro Gómez Maganda to Luis I. Rodríguez, Secretary to President Cárdenas, n.d., AGN, Lázaro Cárdenas File, 544.61/22.

54. "Labor's Parliament to Close Session," *Los Angeles Citizen,* October 14, 1928; American Federation of Labor, Report of the Proceedings of the 47th Annual Convention, Los Angeles, 1927, 96.

55. Margaret Clark, *Organized Labor,* 285.

56. Paul S. Taylor, *A Spanish-Mexican Peasant Community, Arandas in Jalisco, Mexico* (Berkeley: University of California Press, 1933), 44.

57. Ibid., 44.

58. Lawrence Cardoso, *Mexican Immigration to the United States, 1897–1931* (Tucson: University of Arizona Press, 1982), 59–60.

59. Ibid., 82, 109–113.

60. Ibid., 103.

61. Paul Schuster Taylor Collection Z-R4, Box "Reports and Correspondence," Folder "Mexicans in Detroit," Bancroft Library.

62. Interview with Consul Joaquín Terrazas, Detroit, Mich., Paul Schuster Taylor Collection, Z-R4, Box 1, Folder "Detroit, MI, Conversations with Mexicans," Bancroft Library.

63. "Mexican Laborers for Bethlehem Steel," *Manufacturers Record* (May 10, 1923): 73.

64. Consul Rafael de la Colina to Mexican Ambassador, June 10, 1931, ASRE, Los Angeles Consulate File, IV-339–17.

65. "Advertencia Consular a los Trabajadores," *La Opinión,* April 23, 1936.

66. Robert Frazer to the Honorable Secretary of State, July 14, 1931, Paul Schuster Taylor Collection, Z-R4, Box 1, Folder "Mexican Migration–Government Material," Bancroft Library.

67. Samuel Sokobin to the Honorable Secretary of State, November 3, 1931, National Archives, RG 59, Records of the Department of State, 311.1215/26.

68. Enclosure in Edward L. Nathan to the Honorable Secretary of State, November 12, 1931. National Archives, RG 59, Records of the Department of State, 311.1215/27.

69. "En México no quieren a los repatriados," *La Opinión*, October 28, 1932. A July 1931 issue of *La Opinión* reported exploitation at the customs offices, long waits, interminable delays, innumerable stamps and approvals, and bribes.

70. "Explotación inicua a los repatriados," *La Opinión*, July 27, 1931.

71. Edward L. Nathan to the Honorable Secretary of State, November 19, 1931, National Archives, RG 59, Records of the Department of State, 311.1215/29.

72. John S. Littell, "Further Details Regarding Failure of First Two Mexican Repatriate Colonies," May 28, 1934, National Archives, RG 165, Army and Navy Intelligence Files, 2657–g-733.

73. John S. Littell, "Formal Dissolution of Mexican National Repatriation Committee," June 15, 1934, National Archives, RG 59, Records of the Department of State, 311.1215/63.

74. "Dos Puntos Discutibles," *La Opinión* (1936) clipping in Alejandro Gómez Maganda to Luis I. Rodríguez, March 4, 1936, AGN, Lázaro Cárdenas File, 844.61/22.

75. Emory Bogardus, *The Mexican in the United States* (Los Angeles: University of Southern California Press, 1934), 92.

76. "Piden que sea suspendida la repatriación," *La Opinión*, February 11, 1933.

77. Stewart E. McMullin to the Honorable Secretary of State, June 1, 1934, National Archives, RG 59, Records of the Department of State, 311.1215/59.

78. American Consul Edward L. Nathan to the Honorable Secretary of State, November 12, 1931, National Archives, RG 59, Records of the Department of State, 311.1215/27.

79. Wilbur J. Carr to Josephus Daniels, May 9, 1936, National Archives, RG 165, Army and Navy Intelligence, 150.126/377.

80. Homer Cummings to the Secretary of State, April 29, 1936, National Archives, RG 165, 150.26/377.

81. Gordon L. McDonough to Ignacio García Tellez, December 14, 1938, National Archives, RG 165, 855–general.

82. Carey McWilliams, *Southern California: An Island on the Land* (Santa Barbara: Peregrine Smith, 1979), 317.

Chapter Two

1. Manuel Gamio, *The Mexican Immigrant*, 137.

2. Robert E. Cummings, "Mexico. Political," G-2 Report, February, 17, 1933, National Archives, RG 165, Army and Navy Intelligence Records, 2657–g-733.

3. Jorge Prieto Laurens, *Cincuenta años de política mexicana: Memorias políticas* (Mexico City: Editora Mexicana de Periódicos, Libros y Revistas, 1968), 258.

4. Ibid., 260.

5. Ibid., 268.

6. J. E. Hoover to Colonel Stanley H. Ford, March 30, 1929, National Archives, RG 165, Army and Navy Intelligence Records, 2657–g-605.

7. Alejandro Martínez to the Secretariat of Foreign Relations, November 21, 1934, ASRE, Los Angeles Consulate File, IV-317-11; Ricardo G. Hill to Sr. Lic. Luis I. Rodríguez, Nov. 4, 1936, AGN, Lázaro Cárdenas File, 130/165.

8. Efraín G. Domínguez to the Secretary of Foreign Relations, November 18, 1935, AGN, Lázaro Cárdenas File, 559.3/28.

9. Adolfo de la Huerta to Raul Castellano, May 9, 1938, AGN, Lázaro Cárdenas File, 574/16.

10. Untitled 16-page document dated May 19, 1937, AGN, Lázaro Cárdenas File, 559.3/28.

11. Consul Hill to Señor Presidente de la República, September 18, 1935, AGN, Lázaro Cárdenas File, 130/165.

12. Ibid.

13. Consul Alejandro Gómez Maganda to Luis I. Rodríguez, June 3, 1936, AGN, Lázaro Cárdenas File, 544.61/22.

14. Raul G. Domínguez to Raul Castellanos, August 2, 1938, AGN, Lázaro Cárdenas File, 541.1/41.

15. Raul G. Domínguez to General Manuel Avila Camacho, August 2, 1938, AGN, Lázaro Cárdenas File, 541.1/41.

16. Raul G. Domínguez to General Manuel Avila Camacho, August 2, 1938, AGN, Lázaro Cárdenas File, 541.1/41.

17. Consul Alejandro Martínez to the Secretariat of Foreign Relations, January 5, 1935, ASRE, Los Angeles Consulate File, IV-339-11.

18. Ibid.

19. A. Cano del Castillo to the Secretariat of Foreign Relations, March 23, 1938, AGN, Lázaro Cárdenas File, 563.3/31.

20. Juan Andreu Almazán to Presidente de la República, May 16, 1936, AGN, Lázaro Cárdenas File, 573.12/12.

21. Vice-Consul Efraín G. Domínguez to Consul at Douglas, Arizona, October 31, 1935, AGN, Lázaro Cárdenas File, 559.3/25.

22. Vice-Consul Tomás Morlet to Consul de México, Tucson, Arizona, October 31, 1935, AGN, Lázaro Cárdenas File, 559.3/25.

23. Attachment in Lieutenant Colonel F. B. Mallon to Assistant Chief of Staff, G-2, March 18, 1936, National Archives, RG 165, Army and Navy Intelligence Records, 2657–g-657.

24. Ibid.

25. "Consul Belittles Red Talk," *San Antonio Express,* March 25, 1936, in Romeyn Wormuth to the Honorable Secretary of State, March 25, 1936, National Archives, RG 59, 811.5043/49.

26. U.S. Ambassador to the Honorable Secretary of State, March 26, 1936, National Archives, RG 59, 811.5043/53.

27. Ambassador Francisco Castillo Nájera to Assistant Secretary of State Sumner Welles, March 30, 1936, National Archives, RG 59, 811.5043/57.

28. E. B. Nixon to Mr. Fletcher Warren, October 29, 1939, National Archives, RG 59, 811.5045/44.

29. Mr. Welles to Mr. Duggan, September 6, 1939, National Archives, RG 59, 811.5095/44.

30. A. M.—Mr. Warren, September 12, 1939, National Archives, RG 59, 811.5045/44.

31. A.M.—Mr. Warren, October 26, 1939, National Archives, RG 59, 811.5045/45.

32. Cardoso, *Mexican Immigration,* 106; Renato Cantú Lara Personal File, AGN, Lázaro Cárdenas File, 573.1/31.

33. "Mexicans in Sugar Beet Work in the Arkansas River Valley of Kansas," by George T. Edson, September 27, 1927, Paul Schuster Taylor Collection Z-R4, Box 1, Folder "Reports and Correspondence," Bancroft Library.

34. Paul Schuster Taylor Collection Z-R4, Box 1, Folder "Reports and Correspondence," Bancroft Library.

35. "Convención de comisiones honoríficas," *La Opinión,* May 13, 1927.

36. "Conferencia con el Dr. Medina, VI-21-1926," Manuel Gamio Collection, Z-R5, Box 3, Folder "Field Notes," Bancroft Library.

37. Norman D. Humphrey, "The Integration of the Detroit Mexican Colony," *American Journal of Economics and Sociology* 3, no. 2, (Jan. 1944): 158– 159.

38. "Quedó establecida una escuela en Sta. Barbara," *La Opinión,* January 6, 1928; "Una comisión honorífica en Sta. Barbara," *La Opinión,* April 24, 1930.

39. "Son fundadas 3 comisiones honoríficas," *La Opinión,* November 11, 1931.

40. Consul Edmundo L. Aragón to Consul General Alejandro Lubbert, "Informe sobre el establecimiento de la comisión honorífica mexicana," April 30, 1932, ASRE, Calexico Consulate File, IV-338-26.

41. "Una comisión honorífica reinstalada," *La Opinión,* January 31, 1932.

42. "Hay 30 ya, en California," *La Opinión,* October 3, 1926.

43. "Una comisión honorífica en casa blanca," *La Opinión,* June 15, 1932.

44. "Por conducto del consulado," *La Opinión,* March 15, 1929.

45. Francisco Arballo, Comisión Honorífica President, to Consul Joaquín Terrazas, June 30, 1933, ASRE Calexico Consulate File, IV-642-6.

46. "Una escuela y biblioteca para hijos de mexicanos," *La Opinión,* November 26, 1926; "La Escuela 'Mexico,' de Belvedere," *La Opinión,* February 17, 1927.

47. "Un reglamento para escuelas de mexicanos," *La Opinión,* May 27, 1929.

48. "Una labor pro-mexicanismo en California," *La Opinión,* March 20, 1930.

49. "Una escuela en Clearwater," *La Opinión,* August 23, 1927.

50. "La Labor de la comisión honorífica de Watts, Cal.," *La Opinión,* March 4, 1927.

51. "En San Bernardino, Calif., funciona una escuela mexicana," *La Opinión,* January 2, 1928.

52. "Una labor pro-mexicanismo en California," *La Opinión,* March 20, 1930.

53. "Quedó abierta la escuela de Van Nuys, Cal.," *La Opinión,* November 3, 1928.

54. "Las escuelas deberían ser sostenidas por la colonia," *La Opinión,* October 27, 1935.

55. "El consulado pide el apoyo de la colonia," *La Opinión,* April 28, 1935.

56. "Trabajos pro Patria el 16 de septiembre," *La Opinión,* August 27, 1927.

57. "Colectas entre mexicanos," *La Opinión,* April 6, 1927.

58. "Hay 30 ya, en California," *La Opinión,* October 3, 1926.

59. "Como fueron celebrados los días 15 y 16 en Hanford [sic], Cal.," *La Opinión,* September 21, 1927.

60. Ibid.

61. "Invitaciones aceptadas por el señor Pesqueira," *La Opinión,* September 14, 1927.

62. "Un comité de auxilios pro Damnificados," *La Opinión,* March 20, 1933.

63. "Ayuda a los Damnificados," *La Opinión,* March 5, 1931.

64. "Subscripción mexicana en Irwindale," *La Opinión,* January 26, 1927.

65. "Mexicanos en la miseria," *La Opinión,* June 6, 1930.

66. "Pacoima, Calif.," *La Opinión,* October 17, 1931.

67. "La defensa costó $3450 a la colonia," *La Opinión,* December 5, 1930.

68. "El cónsul, en San Bernardino," *La Opinión,* April 16, 1930.

69. "Convención de comisiones honoríficas," *La Opinión,* May 13, 1927.

70. "El consulado ya a la CUOM," *La Opinión,* May 12, 1928.

71. "Gran convención de comisiones honoríficas," *La Opinión,* December 9, 1932.

72. "Una convención de comisiones honoríficas," *La Opinión,* December 29, 1932.

73. "Permiso para hacer vuelos sobre México," *La Opinión,* January 6, 1932.

74. "La misión del Sr. Lupian G. en Estados Unidos," *La Opinión,* April 29, 1933.

75. "El consulado tiene ya otro departamento," *La Opinión,* August 2, 1931, 45.

76. Consul Juan Richer to Julio Quintero, October 26, 1933, ASRE, Los Angeles Consulate File, IV-642-21.

77. Consul F. A. Pesqueira to the Mexican Ambassador in Washington, D.C., August 22, 1929, ASRE, Los Angeles Consulate File, IV-38-10.

78. "Correspondencia entre las cuarenta comisiones honoríficas y el consulado," *La Opinión,* January 9, 1940.

79. Consul Rodolfo Salazar to Consul General Alejandro Lubbert, October 25, 1935, ASRE, Calexico Consulate File, IV-709-19.

80. Anselmo Mena to Consul Alejandro Martínez, August 5, 1933, ASRE, Los Angeles Consulate File, IV-642-21.

81. Consul Rafael de la Colina to the Secretary of Foreign Relations, January 9, 1931, ASRE, Los Angeles Consulate File, IV-339-10.

82. "Beneficencia mexicana en Los Angeles," *La Opinión*, September 30, 1930; also "Los festejos de septiembre," *La Opinión*, July 14, 1927.

83. "Los festejos de septiembre," *La Opinión*, July 14, 1927.

84. "Comité único de festejos patrios para el 16 de Spbre [sic]," *La Opinión*, July 16, 1927.

85. "Los festejos del 5 de mayo," *La Opinión*, April 11, 1927.

86. "Programa para los festejos del 15 y 16," *La Opinión*, September 3, 1928.

87. "El mayor Porter asistirá en los festejos," *La Opinión*, September 17, 1929.

88. "El cónsul de la Colina dará su apoyo a las sociedades de su jurisdicción," *La Opinión*, September 13, 1930.

89. "El cónsul apoya al comité de festejos," *La Opinión*, September 12, 1930.

90. "La nueva mesa de la C. de S. M.," *La Opinión*, March 5, 1930.

91. Ibid.

92. "Annual Report of Secretary-Treasurer, J. W. Buzzell, of the Los Angeles Central Labor Council, for the Fiscal Year 1926–27," *Los Angeles Citizen*, June 24, 1927.

93. Governor C. C. Young's Fact Finding Committee, *Mexicans in California* (San Francisco: State Building, 1930), 123.

94. Ampelio González to General Genaro Estrada, Personal Secretary to the Secretary of Foreign Relations, January 7, 1931, ASRE, Los Angeles Consulate File, IV-339-12.

95. "El programa de la C. de S. Mexicana," *La Opinión*, December 5, 1927.

96. Ibid.

97. "Una iniciativa aprobada por la secretaría de educación," *La Opinión*, November 12, 1927.

98. "Grupo acción de la C. de S. M.," *La Opinión*, November 12, 1927.

99. "El cónsul Pesqueira dejó ya organizada la sucursal de la 'C.R.O.M.' en Los Angeles," *La Opinión*, December 12, 1927.

100. "Mañana saldrá para México el Sr. Pesqueira," *La Opinión*, January 11, 1928.

101. Ibid.

102. Governor C. C. Young's Fact Finding Committee, *Mexicans in California*, 124.

103. Ibid., 125.

104. Ibid.

105. "Respuesta a un mensaje de Gurrola," *La Opinión*, January 25, 1928.

106. Ibid.; see also "Estudiará el problema de los mexicanos y la conveniencia de que se restrinja la emigración," *La Opinión*, January 31, 1928.

107. "So. Cal. Effect in Mex. Lauded by Gov. Elias," *Los Angeles Evening Herald Express*, October 28, 1933.

108. "La AF of L ofrece su ayuda al Pte. Calles para resolver el problema de la emigración," *La Opinión*, February 27, 1928.
109. "California Casual Labor Demands" (address by Dr. George C. Clements), November 13, 1926, George P. Clements Collection, C-B 780, Bancroft Library.
110. U.S. Senate, Subcommittee of the Committee on Education and Labor, Violations of Free Speech and the Rights of Labor, *Hearings*, (Washington, D.C.: U.S. Government Printing Office, 1940) (hereafter cited as *Hearings*), Part 54, 19865.
111. "Mexican Officials, Interview with Consul Pesqueira, Los Angeles, California, October 11, 1928," Paul S. Taylor Collection, 74/187c, Folder "Mexican Officials," Bancroft Library.
112. Governor C. C. Young's Fact Finding Committee, *Mexicans in California*, 128.
113. Ibid., 127.
114. "Quedó ya constituida la F. de Uniones Mexicanas de Oeste," *La Opinión*, March 15, 1928.
115. "Aumenta la imigración de braceros," *La Opinión*, March 24, 1928.
116. Governor C. C. Young's Fact Finding Committee, *Mexicans in California*, 128–129.
117. "Lanzaron manifesto a los obreros mexicanos en E. E., pidiéndonles su cooperacion," *La Opinión*, June 12, 1929.
118. "Actividades Ortizrubistas en California," *La Opinión*, August 13, 1929.
119. Ibid.
120. Ibid.
121. "Asamblea general de Ortizrubistas," *La Opinión*, August 17, 1929.
122. "Trabajos del Ortizrubismo," *La Opinión*, October 10, 1929.
123. "Nueva directiva de la C. S. de M.," *La Opinión*, February 15, 1928; see also "De la Colina dice lo que es la patria," *La Opinión*, March 2, 1931.
124. "Hubo un mitin en pro de la repatriación," *La Opinión*, June 13, 1927.
125. A. M. Villarreal and Armando Flores to Genaro Estrada, Personal Secretary to the Secretary of Foreign Relations, April 28, 1930, ASRE, Los Angeles Consulate File, IV-98-38.
126. "Celebrará el 16 en L.A. el Ortizrubismo," *La Opinión*, September 14, 1929.
127. Ampelio González to General Genaro Estrada, Personal Secretary to the Secretary of Foreign Relations, January 7, 1931, ASRE, Los Angeles Consulate File, IV-339-12.
128. A. M. Villarreal and Armando Flores to Lic. Genaro Estrada, Secretary of Foreign Relations, April 28, 1930, ASRE, Los Angeles Consulate File, IV-98-38.
129. Florencio B. López, President, and A. C. Carvajal, Secretary of the Exterior, to General Abelardo Rodríguez, President of Mexico, March 22, 1933, AGN, Abelardo Rodríguez File, 511/26.

130. "26 manifestantes fueron aprehendidos al acudir un escuadrón de policías," *La Opinión,* January 5, 1930; see also "Habló ayer el cónsul, Señor J. A. Pesqueira," *La Opinión,* June 27, 1930. Demonstrations were also held in Washington, D.C., Detroit, and Hamburg, Germany, according to *La Opinión.*

131. "Preparativos para el Día del Trabajo," *La Opinión,* August 30, 1930.

132. M. F. Obalora, Mayor Official in the Secretariat of Foreign Relations, to Consul Rafael de la Colina, January 12, 1931, ASRE, Los Angeles Consulate File, IV-325-65.

133. Consul Rafael de la Colina to M. F. Oabalora, Oficial Mayor in the Secretariat of Foreign Relations, March 27, 1931, ASRE, Los Angeles Consulate File, IV-325-65.

134. M. F. Obalora, Mayor Official in the Secretariat of Foreign Relations, to Consul Rafael de la Colina, March 27, 1931, ASRE, Los Angeles Consulate File, IV-325-65.

135. "Un llamado a la colonia, del cónsul local," *La Opinión,* February 11, 1931.

136. "En Watts se fundó ya la beneficencia," *La Opinión,* March 25, 1931.

137. "Se acentúa el éxodo de mexicanos," *La Opinión,* April 14, 1931.

138. "Excerpts from the Douglas *Daily Dispatch* of June 21, 1931," Enclosure in "Dispatch" from Lewis V. Boyle, American Consul, to the Honorable Secretary of State, June 24, 1931, National Archives, RG 59, Records of the Department of State, 311, 1215/23.

139. A. G. Arnoll to Mr. C. W. Pheiffer, Secretary, Kansas City Charities Bureau, March 16, 1932, Paul S. Taylor Collection, Z-R4, Box 1, Folder "Statistics for Imperial Valley," Bancroft Library.

140. F. W. Berkshire to Consul Alejandro Martínez, January 29, 1934. Enclosure in "Dispatch" from Edward J. Shaughnessy, INS Deputy Commissioner, to the Honorable Secretary of State, July 2, 1934, National Archives, RG 59, 311.1215/65.

141. "Discutirán el problema de los mexicanos," *La Opinión,* May 20, 1931; "Activan los trabajos de repatriación," *La Opinión,* March 14, 1931.

142. "Un festival benéfico el 5 de Mayo," *La Opinión,* March 22, 1931.

143. "La labor de la beneficencia," *La Opinión,* November 17, 1931.

144. "Se discute en la Conferencia de Santa Mónica la situación de los mexicanos en EE.UU.," *La Opinión,* December 6, 1931.

145. "Conferencias organizadas por el Partido L. Mexicano," *La Opinión,* November 25, 1931; see also "Mañana hablará en un mitin el cónsul, Sr. de la Colina," *La Opinión,* December 12, 1931.

Chapter Three

1. Rodolfo Acuña, *Occupied America: A History of Chicanos* (New York: Harper and Row, 1981); Balderrama, *In Defense of La Raza;* Daniel, *Bitter Harvest;* Abraham Hoffman, "The El Monte Berry Pickers' Strike, 1933: International

Involvement in a Labor Dispute" *Journal of the West* 5, no. 7 (Jan. 1973): 71–84; Ronald W. López, "The El Monte Berry Strike of 1933," *Aztlán: Chicano Journal of the Social Sciences and the Arts* (Spring 1970): 101–114; Douglas Monroy, "Anarquismo y Comunismo: Mexican Radicalism and the Communist Party in Los Angeles During the 1930s," *Labor History* 24, no. 1 (1983); Charles B. Spaulding, "The Mexican Strike at El Monte, California," *Sociology and Social Research* 18 (July 1934): 571–580; Devra Weber, "The Organizing of Mexicano Agricultural Workers: Imperial Valley and Los Angeles, 1928–1934, An Oral History Approach," *Aztlán: Chicano Journal of the Social Sciences and the Arts* 3, no. 2 (1973); Charles Wollenberg, "Race and Class in Rural California: The El Monte Berry Strike of 1933," *California Historical Quarterly* 51 (Summer 1974): 155–164.

2. "El cónsul Pesqueira dejó ya organizada la surcursal de la CROM en Los Angeles," *La Opinión*, December 12, 1927; also see Governor C. C. Young's Fact Finding Committee, *Mexicans in California*, 126.

3. "Los obreros de México son apoyados aquí," *La Opinión*, May 1931; A. M. Villareal and Armando Flores to Genero Estrada, Secretary of Foreign Relations, April 28, 1930, ASRE, Los Angeles Consulate File, IV-98-38.

4. "Actividades de sociedades mexicanas," *La Opinión*, June 25, 1932.

5. "Una asamblea Ortiz Rubista," *La Opinión*, September 7, 1929.

6. "Celebrará el 16 en Los Angeles el Ortizrubismo," *La Opinión*, September 14, 1929.

7. ASRE, Ricardo Hill File, Document 21-6-4.

8. Ibid.

9. Daniel, *Bitter Harvest*, 148–149.

10. Carey McWilliams, *Southern California: An Island on the Land* (Santa Barbara, Calif.: Peregrine Smith, 1979), 236.

11. Los Angeles Chamber of Commerce, Agriculture Department, "Crop Acreage Trends for Los Angeles County and Southern California, 1925–1957" (Los Angeles County Board of Supervisors, 1957), 6.

12. Mazakawa Iwata, *Planted on Good Soil: A History of the Issei in the United States Agriculture*, Vol. 1 (New York: Peter Lang, 1992), 268.

13. McWilliams, *Southern California*, 321.

14. John Modell, *The Economics and Politics of Racial Accommodation: The Japanese of Los Angeles, 1900–1942* (Urbana: University of Illinois Press, 1977), 120–123.

15. Governor C. C. Young's Fact Finding Committee, *Mexicans in California*, 179.

16. Ibid., 214.

17. Charles B. Spaulding, "Mexican Strike," 571–572.

18. "Raspberry and Potato Pickers Answer the Call," *Western Worker*, June 12, 1933.

19. Ibid.

20. "Huelga de 125 mexicanos aquí," *La Opinión*, June 4, 1933.

21. "Fijan como mínimo 30 cts. la hora," *La Opinión*, June 5, 1933.

22. "Apoyan el movimiento en El Monte," *La Opinión,* June 6, 1933.

23. Ibid.

24. "Tres líderes capturados en Sawtelle," *La Opinión,* June 7, 1933.

25. "Ranks of the Southern California Berry Strikers Solid," *Western Worker,* August 7, 1933.

26. Quoted in Modell, *Economics and Politics,* 122.

27. U.S. Senate, *Hearings,* Part 64 (Washington, D.C.: U.S. Government Printing Office, 1940): 23629.

28. "Ya tienen esperanzas de arreglo," *La Opinión,* June 10, 1933.

29. Ibid.

30. Ibid.

31. "Indignation Grows at Sell Out by Mexican Consul, Labor Dept.," *Western Worker,* August 7, 1933.

32. "Ranks of Southern California Berry Strikers Solid," *Western Worker,* August 7, 1933.

33. "Berry Strike Gets Violent," *Los Angeles Times,* June 10, 1933.

34. "Indignation Grows at Sell Out by Mexican Consul, Labor Dept.," *Western Worker,* August 7, 1933.

35. "Ya tienen esperanzas de arreglo," *La Opinión,* June 10, 1933; "Action to End Strike Begun," *Los Angeles Times,* July 1, 1933.

36. Josephus Daniels to the Honorable Secretary of State, June 23, 1933, National Archives, RG 59, Records of the Department of State, 511, 5045/129.

37. Ibid.

38. "Seven in Berry Strike Jailed," *Los Angeles Times,* June 11, 1933.

39. "Plagían a siete huelguistas en El Monte," *La Opinión,* June 11, 1933.

40. "Seven in Berry Strike Jailed," *Los Angeles Times,* June 11, 1933.

41. "Action to End Strike Begun," *Los Angeles Times,* July 1, 1933.

42. Consul Alejandro Martínez to President Abelardo Rodríguez, July 1, 1933, AGN, Abelardo Rodríguez File, 561–4/18.

43. "Farm Strikers to Start Drive," *Los Angeles Times,* June 25, 1933.

44. Memorandum from Dr. J. M. Causaranc to President Abelardo Rodríguez, July 1, 1933, AGN, Abelardo Rodríguez File, 561, 4/18.

45. "Expectación hoy cesa el ultimátum," *La Opinión,* June 12, 1933.

46. E. L. Fitzgerald and E. P. Marsh to Director H. L. Kerwin, July 3, 1933, National Archives, RG 280, Federal Mediation and Conciliation Service Records (hereafter cited as FMCS) File, 170/8983.

47. "El consulado unifica a los huelguistas," *La Opinión,* June 13, 1933.

48. Armando Flores to President Franklin D. Roosevelt, June 14, 1933, National Archives, RG 280, FMCS File, 170/8983.

49. H. L. Kerwin to Consul Martínez, June 21, 1933, National Archives, RG 280, FMCS File, 170/8083.

50. U.S. Senate, *Hearings,* Part 53, 19487; Dr. Clements to Mr. Gast, June 27, 1933, George C. Clements Papers, Box 64, Special Collections, University Research Library, University of California, Los Angeles.

51. Commissioners W. H. Fitzgerald and E. P. Marsh to Director H. L. Kerwin, June 27, 1933, National Archives, RG 280, FMCS File, 170/8083.

52. W. H. Fitzgerald and E. P. Marsh to Director H. L. Kerwin, July 3, 1933, National Archives, RG 280, FCMS File, 170/8083.

53. "Otro llamado del comité de la huelga," *La Opinión*, June 16, 1933.

54. "Envían un mensaje al presidente," *La Opinión*, June 16, 1933.

55. Ibid.

56. "La CROM da apoyo a los huelguistas," *La Opinión*, June 18, 1933.

57. "Calles envía dinero a los huelguistas," *La Opinión*, June 21, 1933.

58. Ibid.

59. Ibid.

60. Ibid.

61. Ibid.

62. "Gran interés por la huelga de pizcadores," *La Opinión*, June 24, 1933.

63. Ibid.

64. Memorandum from Secretary J. M. Puig to President Abelardo Rodríguez, July 1, 1933, AGN, Abelardo Rodríguez File, 561, 4/18.

65. Consul Alejandro Martínez to President Abelardo Rodríguez, July 9, 1933, AGN, Abelardo Rodríguez File, 561, 4/18.

66. "Acuerdos del comité de los huelguistas," *La Opinión*, June 27, 1933.

67. "Dan nuevo impulso al movimiento," *La Opinión*, June 20, 1933.

68. "$600 más de Calles a los huelguistas," *La Opinión*, June 29, 1933.

69. Ibid.

70. "El consulado y el comité abren una investigación," *La Opinión*, June 30, 1933.

71. "Dos representantes de Mister Rolph investigan desde ayer el movimiento" *La Opinión*, July 1, 1933.

72. General Plutarco Calles to President Franklin D. Roosevelt, July 6, 1933, National Archives, RG 59, Records of the Department of State, 811.5045/133.

73. Dr. Clements to Mr. Arnoll, July 26, 1933, George C. Clements Papers, Box 64, Special Collections, Research Library, University of California, Los Angeles.

74. Dr. Clements to Mr. Findlay, August 9, 1933, George C. Clements Papers, Box 64, Department of Special Collections, University Research Library, University of California, Los Angeles.

75. H. R. Bursley to Mr. Johnson, July 28, 1933, National Archives, RG 59, 811.5045/140.

76. "Along the Camino Real," *Los Angeles Times*, July 6, 1933.

77. "Distinción a funcionarios de Los Angeles," *La Opinión*, December 5, 1931. Less than ten years had passed when Officer Duran Ayres earned a Captain's insignia and the position of the chief of a special police unit, the Foreign Relations Bureau. Notwithstanding the "cordial relations," Captain Ayres gained notoriety upon publication of a bureau report that explained innate behavioral and cultural traits of Mexicans:

The Caucasian . . . especially the Anglo-Saxon, when engaged in fighting, particularly among youths, resort to fisticuffs and may at times kick each other, which is considered unsportive: but this Mexican element considers all that to be a sign of weakness, and all he knows and feels is a desire to use a knife or lethal weapon. In other words, his desire is to kill, or at least let blood. . . . When it is added to this inborn characteristic, the use of liquor, then we certainly have crimes of violence." (as quoted in Carey McWilliams, *North from Mexico: The Spanish Speaking People in the United States* (Philadelphia: J. B. Lippincott, 1949), 234)

78. Alejandro V. Martínez to Señor General Guillermo M. Palma, Police Inspector General, January 27, 1933, AGN, Abelardo Rodríguez File, 611/11.

79. Mr. Harman to Dr. Clements, August 23, 1933, George C. Clements Papers, Box 64, Special Collections, University Research Library, University of California, Los Angeles.

80. Dr. Clements to Mr. Arnoll, November 23, 1937, George C. Clements Collection, Box 80, Special Collections, University Research Library, University of California, Los Angeles.

81. See Dr. Clements to Mr. Arnoll re: Mexican Labor, July 12, 1933, George C. Clements Papers, Box 64, Folder "El Monte Berry Strike"; also Dr. Clements to Mr. Arnoll re: Mexican Berry strike, July 17, 1933.

82. Dr. Clements to Mr. Harman, August 22, 1933, George C. Clements Papers, Box 64.

83. President Abelardo Rodríguez to Consul Alejandro Martínez, July 4, 1933, AGN, Abelardo Rodríguez File, 561.4/18.

84. Francisco Gaxiola to President Abelardo Rodríguez, July 7, 1933, AGN, Abelardo Rodríguez File, 561.4/18.

85. "Los pizcadores ganaran 20 cts. la hora, como mínimo, $1.50 por día," *La Opinión*, July 7, 1933.

86. Frank G. MacDonald to Mr. V. Cuevas López, Secretary General, Council of Labor, Tampico, Mexico, July 19, 1933, National Archives, RG 59, 811.5045/140.

87. "D. Joaquín Terrazas cónsul en N. Orleans," *La Opinión*, July 20, 1935.

88. Official Bulletin of the Ministry of Foreign Affairs *[sic]* (translation), in Josephus Daniels to Honorable Secretary of State, August 25, 1933, National Archives, RG 59, 811.5045/142.

89. Ibid.

90. Weber, "Organizing," 331.

91. "Volvieron al trabajo 6000 huelguistas," *La Opinión*, July 8, 1933.

92. Ambassador Josephus Daniels to Secretary of State, July 5, 1933, National Archives, RG 59, 811.5045/135.

93. Dr. Clements to Mr. Arnoll, July 20, 1933, National Archives, RG 59, 811.5045/139.

94. Unsigned note to Mr. Johnson, July 22, 1933, National Archives, RG 59, 811.5045/139.

95. H. S. Bursley to Mr. Johnson, July 28, 1933, National Archives, RG 59, 811.5045/139.

96. Unsigned note in response to the Mexican Office of Foreign Affairs Bulletin, Department of State, September 2, 1933, National Archives, RG 59, 811.5045/142.

97. Guillermo Velarde to Mr. Towne Nylander, Assistant Secretary, Los Angeles Regional Labor Board, 1934, National Archives, RG 280, National Labor Relations Board (hereafter cited as NLRB), 15–21.

98. Weber, "Organizing," 343.

99. See González, *Labor and Community,* chapter 5.

100. J. B. Nathan, "Report on the Citrus Strike," in Citrus Strikes, Paul Schuster Taylor Collection, C-B 893, Bancroft Library.

101. Arthur E. Clark to Stuart Strathman, April 22, 1936, Exhibit 12611–B, U.S. Senate, *Hearings,* Part 70.

102. J. A. Prizer to Members of the Orange County Protective Association, July 17, 1936, U.S. Senate, *Hearings,* Exhibit 12739, Part 70, 25953.

103. W. Maxwell Burke to Mr. Edward H. Fitzgerald, June 26, 1936, National Archives, RG 17, File 182/1525.

104. "Velarde in Battle to Halt Peace," *Santa Ana Register,* July 17, 1936.

105. "New Pact Is Reached at Meeting," *Orange Daily News,* July 25, 1936.

106. David Price, "Orange County Strike," *Pacific Weekly* 5 (August 24, 1936): 116–17.

107. "Orange County Licks Three Governments," *Pacific Rural Press,* August 1, 1936, 100.

108. "Mexican Consul Flayed by Union," *Western Worker,* August 13, 1936.

109. Stuart Strathman to Consul Ricardo Hill, June 25, 1936, ASRE, Ricardo Hill File, 21–6–4.

110. W. Maxwell Burke to Mr. Edward H. Fitzgerald, June 26, 1936, National Archives, RG 280, FMCS, Case Files 182/1525.

111. Secretary Frances Perkins to Secretary of State Cordell Hull, July 1, 1936, National Archives, RG 59, 811.5045/196.

112. E. H. Fitzgerald to Mr. H. L. Kerwin, June 25, 1936, National Archives, RG 280, FMCS, Case Files 182/1525.

113. John F. Dolan to Mr. McGroarty, in John Stephan McGroarty to Mr. Edward Reed, June 19, 1936, National Archives, RG 59, 811.5045/193.

114. Secretary of State Cordell Hull to Secretary of Labor Frances Perkins, July 7, 1936, National Archives, RG 170, Department of Labor, Frances Perkins Files.

115. Luis Quintanilla to Secretary to President Lázaro Cárdenas, n.d., ASRE, Ricardo Hill File, Document 21–6–4.

116. Luis I. Rodríguez to Ricardo Hill, July 13, 1936, AGN, Lázaro Cárdenas File, 130/165.

117. Ricardo G. Hill to Luis I. Rodríguez, June 30, 1936, AGN, Lázaro Cárdenas File 130/165.

Chapter Four

1. Daniel, *Bitter Harvest,* 184–185.

2. Paul S. Taylor, *On the Ground in the Thirties* (Salt Lake City: Peregrine Smith, 1983), p. 32.

3. Weber, *Dark Sweat, White Gold,* 27.

4. Paul S. Taylor and Clark Kerr, "Documentary History of the Cotton Pickers in California, 1933," typed manuscript in the Paul Schuster Taylor Collection, C-R3 Carton 1, Folder Documentary History of the Strike, Bancroft Library, p. 6.

5. Weber, *Dark Sweat, White Gold,* 39–40.

6. Federal Writers Project, "Labor in California Cotton Fields," 1939, Bancroft Library, 70.

7. Ibid., 48.

8. Paul S. Taylor, *Mexican Labor in the United States: Migration Statistics II,* University of California Publications in Economics, vol. 12, no. 2 (Berkeley: University of California, 1933), 1.

9. Ibid., 16–18.

10. Bertha Underhill, "A Study of 132 Families in California Cotton Camps with Reference to Availability to Medical Care" (Division of Child Welfare Services, California Department of Social Welfare, 1936), 1–2.

11. Ibid., 3.

12. Ibid., 3.

13. See, for example, the work of Ruth Allen, *The Labor of Women and Families in the Production of Cotton,* Ph.D. diss., University of Chicago, 1933 (reprint, New York: Arno Press, 1975), chapter 7.

14. U.S. Senate, *Hearings,* Part 62, Supplementary Exhibits, Exhibit 9578, 22645.

15. Underhill, "Study of 132 Families," 1.

16. Ibid., 2.

17. Ibid., 3.

18. Ibid., 8.

19. Taylor, *Mexican Labor in the United States: Migration Statistics II,* 20–21.

20. Underhill, "Study of 132 Families," 18.

21. Ibid.

22. Ibid., 31.

23. Ibid., 16.

24. "Piden que en Fresno halla un consulado," *La Opinión,* January 18, 1931.

25. "Gran recepción concedido al nuevo cónsul de Fresno," *La Opinión,* February 21, 1931.

26. Ibid.

27. Ibid.

28. Consul Enrique Bravo to Señor Don Manuel G. Otaloria, Oficial Mayor de la Secretaría de Relaciones Exteriores, September 29, 1931, ASRE, Enrique Bravo File, Su expediente personal, 7-27-34.

29. Ibid.

30. "Varios miles secundan el movimiento," *La Opinión,* October 7, 1933.

31. "Cotton Pickers Threaten Strike," *Berkeley Daily Gazette,* September 18, 1933.

32. Quoted in Daniel, *Bitter Harvest,* 184.

33. "Cotton Pickers Strike," *Western Worker,* October 9, 1933.

34. Ibid.; see also Taylor and Kerr, "Documentary History," in U.S. Senate, *Hearings,* Part 54, 19962.

35. "Valley Cotton Men Organize to Fight Strikers' Wage Demands," *Visalia Times-Delta,* October 6, 1933.

36. Taylor and Kerr, "Documentary History," in U.S. Senate, *Hearings,* Part 54, 19963–19964.

37. "Growers Plan to Drive Out Agitators," *Visalia Times-Delta,* October 9, 1933.

38. U.S. Senate, *Hearings,* Part 75, 27601–27602.

39. "Field Notes," Paul S. Taylor Collection, C-R3, Carton 1, Folder Unmarked #2, Bancroft Library.

40. C. H. Ernest to Honorable Franklin D. Roosevelt, President of the United States, October 9, 1933, National Archives, RG 170, Department of Labor, Perkins Files.

41. Quoted from the *San Francisco News,* October 11 [1933], in Taylor, *On the Ground,* 84–85.

42. Ibid.

43. Interview by Paul S. Taylor in his *On the Ground,* 90.

44. E. H. Fitzgerald to H. L. Kerwin, Director of Conciliation, October 13, 1933, National Archives, RG 170, Department of Labor, Perkins File.

45. Taylor, *On the Ground,* 101.

46. "Report of State Labor Commissioner Frank C. MacDonald to Governor James Rolph, Jr. on the San Joaquin Cotton Strike," U.S. Senate, *Hearings,* Part 54, 19901.

47. Ibid.

48. Quoted from *Fresno Bee,* October 14, [1933], in Taylor, *On the Ground,* 100.

49. "Officials Complete Plans for Mediation of Cotton Strike," *Visalia Times-Delta,* October 14, 1933.

50. "Mexican Consul Says Nationals Ready to Go Back to Work," *Visalia Times-Delta,* October 13, 1933.

51. "Should Have Mediated Before and Not After the Strike," *Visalia Times-Delta,* October 13, 1933.

52. "Gross Misrepresentations of Strike Conditions by Metropolitan Press," *Visalia Times-Delta,* October 14, 1933.

53. "Cotton Strike to End in 48 Hours; Rolph Told; Towns Quiet," *San Francisco Examiner,* October 13, 1933.

54. "Strike Bull Pen Seen in Cotton Area," *San Francisco Chronicle,* October 18, 1933.

55. Quoted from the *Tulare Times,* October 14, [1933], in Taylor, *On the Ground,* 30.

56. "Todos en masa a patrullar el cónsul," n.d., Simon Julius Lubin Papers, Carton 5, CAWIU Materials, 1933, Bancroft Library.

57. "Strike Bulletin," October 27, 1933, in the Simon Julius Lubin Society Papers, Carton 5, Bancroft Library.

58. Taylor, *On The Ground,* 55.

59. Ibid, 71.

60. Ibid.

61. "Rancheros amenazan de muerte al cónsul en Fresno," *La Opinión,* October 15, 1933.

62. Taylor, *On the Ground,* 71.

63. Licenciado Enrique Jiménez D., Oficial Mayor del Despacho de Relaciones [Exteriores], to Presidente Abelardo Rodríguez, October 14, 1933, AGN, Abelardo Rodríguez File, 561.4/26.

64. "Martial Law Faces Cotton Strike Area," *San Francisco Chronicle,* October 15, 1933.

65. "Official Notice, Visalia, California, October 16, 1933," National Archives, RG 280, FMCS Files, Dispute Case Files 1913–1948, File 176–35.

66. Ibid.

67. "Ultimátum de los rancheros a los pizcadores en huelga," *La Opinión,* October 14, 1933.

68. "Armed Gangs Speeding to Strike Area," *San Francisco Examiner,* October 17, 1933.

69. "Mediation Board Fails to Meet; One Member in East," *Visalia Times-Delta,* October 17, 1933.

70. "Idleness in Cotton Fields Continue *[sic]* in Face of Arbitration," *Visalia Times-Delta,* October 16, 1933.

71. "Mediators Hanna and Knowles Leave; Will End Tomorrow," *Visalia Times-Delta,* October 20, 1933.

72. "Hearings Held on the Cotton Strike in San Joaquin Valley," in Paul Schuster Taylor Collection, C-R3, Box 1, Folder Unmarked, Bancroft Library.

73. Paul S. Taylor to Monroe Deutsch, October 27, 1933, Paul S. Taylor Collection, C-R3, Box 1, Folder #14, Bancroft Library.

74. "Calles apoya a los pizcadores," *La Opinión,* October 23, 1933.

75. "Strike Zone Invaded by Armed Band," *San Francisco Chronicle,* October 17, 1933.

76. "Rolph Acts to Clean up Strike Area," *San Francisco Chronicle,* October 28, 1933.

77. "Strikers Defy Officers," *Visalia Times-Delta,* October 26, 1933.

78. Daniel, *Bitter Harvest,* 215.

79. George Creel, Administrator, District Recovery Administration, to Mr. W. A. Simpson, President, Los Angeles Chamber of Commerce, October 28, 1933, National Archives, RG 25, NLRB, Case File 16–3, San Francisco Region.

80. F. J. Palomares, Manager, Agricultural Labor Bureau, to George Creel,

October 25, 1933, National Archives, RG 25, NLRB, Case File 16-3, San Francisco Region.

81. San Diego Fruit and Produce Company to George Creel, October 20, 1933, National Archives, RG 25, NLRB, Case File 16-3.

82. George Creel to San Diego Fruit and Produce Co., Castroville, Calif., October 20, 1933, National Archives, RG 25, NLRB, Case File 16-3.

83. W. V. Buckner and R. E. Springer to President Abelardo Rodríguez, October 30, 1933, AGN, Abelardo Rodríguez File 561.4/26.

84. R. E. Springer, Chief of Police, Corcoran, California, to General Plutarco Elías Calles, ASRE, Enrique Bravo Caro File, Su Expediente Personal, IV-363-4.

85. Frank C. MacDonald, "Report of the State Labor Commissioner to Governor James J. Rolph, Jr. on San Joaquin Cotton Strike, September–October 1933," November 3, 1933, U.S. Senate, *Hearings,* Part 54, 19905.

86. Consul General Alejandro Lubbert to Secretario de Relaciones Exteriores, November 3, 1933, AGN, Abelardo Rodríguez File, 561.4/26.

87. Alejandro Lubbert to Javier Gaxiola, Secretario Personal del Sr. Presidente de la República, November 3, 1933, AGN, Abelardo Rodríguez File, 561.4/26.

88. Consul Enrique Bravo to the Secretariat of Foreign Relations, October 31, 1933, ASRE Enrique Bravo Caro File, Su Expediente Personal, IV-651-11.

89. ASRE, Enrique Bravo Caro File, Su Expediente Personal, ASRE IV-363-4.

90. Juan Briones and Andrés Saavedra to the Secretariat of Foreign Relations, January 1, 1935, ASRE, Enrique Bravo Caro File, Su Expediente Personal, 7–27–34.

91. "Trials, Visalia, California, January 16, 17, 1933," Paul Schuster Taylor Collection, C-R3, Box 1, Folder #14, Bancroft Library.

92. Baltazar Estrada and Herculano Ramos to Primer Magistrado de la República Mexicana (Abelardo Rodríguez), October 20, 1933, ASRE, Enrique Bravo Caro, 7–27–34.

93. "Dos cónsules son atacados en California," *La Opinión,* May 13, 1934.

94. *Western Worker,* November 6 [1933], quoted in Taylor, *On the Ground,* 140.

Chapter Five

1. R. E. Hodges, "Imperial Valley, Active and Very Promising," *Pacific Rural Press,* November 25, 1933, 423; see also Helen Hosmer, "Triumph and Failure in the Colorado Desert," *American West* 3, no. 1 (1966): 34.

2. George H. Shoaf, "Imperial Valley Outrage," *Open Forum,* July 5, 1930, 1.

3. Quoted in Secretary of Labor Frances Perkins to Honorable Lewis W. Douglas, Director of the Budget, April 1934, National Archives, RG 170, Department of Labor Records, Perkins File.

4. U.S. Senate, *Hearings,* Part 55, 20129.

5. *Hearings,* Part 55, 20137. The following were listed among the largest landowners in the Valley: Balfour-Guthrie Investment Company of San Francisco,

4,234 acres; Equitable California Holding Company of Los Angeles, 3,316 acres; Missouri-State Life Insurance Company of St. Louis, Missouri, 3,536 acres; Security First National Bank of Los Angeles, 4,194 acres; Southern Pacific Land Company of San Francisco, 42,558 acres; Times-Mirror Company of Los Angeles, 8,885 acres; Bank of America of San Francisco, 4,113 acres; State Life Insurance Company of Los Angeles, 10,177 acres. *Hearings*, Part 55, 20289–20290.

6. Taylor, *Mexican Labor in the United States Imperial Valley*, 3–35.

7. U.S. Senate, *Hearings*, Part 55, 20128.

8. Quoted in Secretary of Labor Frances Perkins to Honorable Lewis W. Douglas, Director of the Budget, April 1934, National Archives, RG 170, Department of Labor Records, Perkins File.

9. Taylor, *Mexican Labor in the United States: Imperial Valley*, 32; also see: R. E. Hodges, "Kaleidoscope Imperial Valley," *Pacific Rural Press*, October 25, 1930.

10. "8 mexicanos murieron de isolación," *La Opinión*, July 26, 1929.

11. "Muertos de calor, en Calexico," *La Opinión*, June 30, 1929.

12. Twenty-second Biennial Report of the Bureau of Labor Statistics of the State of California, 1925–1926, Sacramento: California State Printing Office, 1926, 116, in Paul Schuster Taylor Collection, Z-R4 Box 1, Folder "Statistics for Orange County," Bancroft Library.

13. Paul S. Taylor, *Mexican Labor in the United States: Imperial Valley*, 28.

14. Ibid., 38.

15. Campbell MacCulloch, "Labor Conditions in the Valley," January 19, 1934, typewritten report in C. B. Hutchison Papers, C-B 84, Box 1, Folder "Miscellany A–Z," Bancroft Library.

16. J. L. Leonard, Will J. French, and Simon Lubin, "Report to the National Labor Board by Special Commission," February 11, 1934 (hereafter cited as Lubin Report), AGN, Abelardo Rodríguez File, 561.8/326.

17. MacCulloch, "Labor Conditions in the Valley," 6.

18. Secretary of Labor Frances Perkins to Honorable Lewis W. Douglas, Director of the Budget, April 1934, National Archives, RG 170, Department of Labor Records, Perkins File.

19. MacCulloch, "Labor Conditions in the Valley," 6; Lubin Report, 6.

20. Timothy A. Reardon, California State Department of Industrial Relations, "Report to the Governor's Council," April 1934, National Archives, RG 170, Perkins File.

21. Taylor, *Mexican Labor in the United States: Imperial Valley*, 38.

22. MacCulloch, "Living Conditions," 4.

23. For accounts of the 1928 events in the Valley, see Taylor, *Mexican Labor in the United States: Imperial Valley;* Charles Wollenberg, "Huelga 1928 Style: The Imperial Valley Cantaloupe Workers' Strike," *Pacific Historical Review* 28 (Feb. 1969): 45–58; Governor C. C. Young's Fact Finding Committee, *Mexicans in California;* and Jameison, *Labor Unionism.*

24. American Consulate General to the Honorable Secretary of State, July 14, 1931, Memorandum no. 241, in the Paul Schuster Taylor Collection, Z-R4, Box 1, Folder "Mexican Migration, Government Materials," Bancroft Library.

25. Governor C. C. Young's Fact Finding Committee, *Mexicans in California,* 137–138.

26. Taylor, *Mexican Labor in the United States: Imperial Valley,* 53.

27. U.S. Works Projects Administration, Federal Writers Project, "Organizational Efforts of Mexican Agricultural Workers," Oakland, Calif., 1939, 16, Bancroft Library.

28. Taylor, *Mexican Labor in the United States: Imperial Valley,* 53.

29. Governor C. C. Young's Fact Finding Committee, *Mexicans in California,* 140.

30. *Imperial Valley Press,* May 10, 1928.

31. Governor C. C. Young's Fact Finding Committee, *Mexicans in California,* 140.

32. Consul Hermolao Torres to the Mexican Secretariat of Foreign Relations, May 19, 1928, Oficio no. 617, AGN, Calexico Consulate File, IV-261-19.

33. *Imperial Valley Press,* May 12, 1928.

34. Consul Rendón Quijano to Alejandro Lubbert, Consul General, November 22, 1928, AGN, Calexico Consulate File, IV-26119.

35. Frank Spector, *Story of the Imperial Valley* (New York: International Labor Defense, 1930), 18–19.

36. "Celebraron ya un pacto de solidaridad para lograr la regularización de salarios," *La Opinión,* December 29, 1929.

37. Letter from Charles T. Connell to Honorable H. L. Kerwin, Director, Conciliation Service, Department of Labor, January 17, 1930, National Archives, RG 280, FMCS File, 170/5463.

38. *Brawley News,* January 13, 1930.

39. *Brawley News,* January 14, 1930; Charles T. Connell to Hon. H. L. Kerwin, January 17, 1930, National Archives, RG 280, File 170/5463; Spector, *Story of the Imperial Valley,* 19.

40. Spector, *Story of the Imperial Valley,* 18–19.

41. Charles T. Connell to Hon. H. L. Kerwin, April 24, 1930, National Archives, RG 280, File 170/5463.

42. Ambassador Manuel C. Tellez to Secretary of State Stimson, January 14, 1930, National Archives, RG 59, Department of State Records File, 811.5045/120.

43. Summary of Final Report of Commissioner of Conciliation, National Archives, RG 280, FMCS File, 170/5463.

44. "Sean expulsados del Valle Imperial los comunistas," *La Opinión,* January 16, 1930.

45. "Esperan facilidades de transporte en el Valle Imperial para regresar a México," *La Opinión,* February 2, 1930.

46. "8 comunistas en la huelga del V. Imperial," *La Opinión,* January 15, 1930.

47. *La Opinión* article titles (here translated) illustrated the change of attitude: "Great Invasion of Filipinos in California," (March 27, 1930); "Invasion of Filipinos in the Imperial Valley," (October 23, 1930); "[Growers] Prefer Oriental Labor," (February 19, 1931).

48. Porter Chaffee, "The Imperial Valley Strikes of January and February 1930," in *A History of the Cannery and Agricultural Workers Industrial Union*, Vol. 1, Federal Writers Project Collection, Bancroft Library, 6.

49. Ibid., 8.

50. Charles T. Connell to Hon. H. L. Kerwin, February 19, 1930, National Archives, RG 280, FMCS File, 170/5463.

51. "Mexican Consul Here; Reported after Radicals," *Brawley News*, January 10, 1930.

52. James Gray, "The American Civil Liberties Union of Southern California and Imperial Valley Agricultural Labor Disturbances, 1930–1934," Ph.D. diss., University of California, Los Angeles, 1966, 32.

53. A. N. Jack to Charles T. Connell, January 27, 1930, National Archives, RG 280, FMCS File, 170/5463.

54. Charles T. Connell to Honorable H. L. Kerwin, Director of the Conciliation Service, April 24, 1930, National Archives, RG 280, FMCS File, 170/5463.

55. Consul Edmundo Aragón to Alejandro Lubbert, Consul General, August 11, 1930, AGN, Calexico Consulate File, IV-338-26.

56. Edmundo Aragón to Alejandro Lubbert, Consul General, April 30, 1932, AGN, Calexico Consulate File, IV-338-26.

57. A. A. Heist to Miss Frances Perkins, Secretary of Labor, March 31, 1934, National Archives, RG 170, Records of the Department of Labor, Perkins Files.

58. Monroe Sweetland, "Red Paint in the Imperial Valley," *The World Tomorrow*, June 14, 1934, 310.

59. Joaquín Terrazas, Su Expediente Personal, ASRE, Joaquín Terrazas Personal File, 21-4-5.

60. Interview with Mr. Terrazas, Mexican Consul, 713128, Paul Schuster Taylor Collection, Z-R4, Box 1, Folder "Detroit, Michigan. Conversations with Mexicans," Bancroft Library.

61. Consul Howard A. Bowman to the Honorable Secretary of State, April 16, 1934, NA, RG 59, 811.5045/145.

62. "Brawley Lettuce Strike Settled," *Imperial Valley Press*, October 18, 1933; "Mexican Wage Scale Adopted at Conference," *Brawley News*, October 18, 1933.

63. *Brawley News*, October 18, 1933.

64. Ibid.

65. Ibid.; also "Agree on New Wage Scale for Lettuce," *Calexico Chronicle*, October 19, 1933.

66. "Reds Show Hand in Attempted Valley Strike," *Brawley News*, November 23, 1933.

67. Ibid.

68. Ibid.

69. "Otra huelga de pizcadores en Brawley," *La Opinión*, January 10, 1934.

70. Report of the Special Investigating Committee, "The Imperial Valley Farm Labor Situation," Sacramento, Calif., April 16, 1934, in Glassford Papers, Box 25, Department of Special Collections, University of California, Los Angeles; also, "Otra Huelga de Pizcadores en Brawley," *La Opinión*, January, 10, 1934.

71. P. D. Glassford to Mr. Ernest Besig, June 20, 1934, Federal Writers Project Collection, C-R2, Glassford Report Folder, Carton 34, Bancroft Library.

72. MacCulloch, "Living Conditions in the Imperial Valley," 4.

73. A. L. Wirin, "'Direct Action' in Imperial Valley," *Open Forum*, January 27, 1934, 1.

74. "Motines en las calles," *La Opinión*, January 13, 1934.

75. Wirin, "'Direct Action'"; "Workers Defy Terror," *Western Worker*, January 22, 1934; also, "Motines en las calles," *La Opinión*, January 13, 1934.

76. *Open Forum*, April 7, 1934.

77. "Reds Gird for New Clash in Imperial Valley Strike War," *Los Angeles Illustrated Daily News*, January 22, 1934.

78. "Strike of Lettuce Workers Believed to Have Been Weakened," *Imperial Valley Press*, January 11, 1934; "Say Strike Is Nearly at an End," *Calexico Chronicle*, January 11, 1934.

79. *Brawley News*, January 12, 1934.

80. "Call for Militia Is Rescinded" and "Terrazas Will Help Quell Strike Trouble," *Calexico Chronicle*, January 12, 1934.

81. "Strike Quiet Observed as Injunction Is Sought," *Calexico Chronicle*, January 22, 1934; January 23, 1934.

82. "Radical Leader Leaves Valley Today after Kidnapping at Brawley," *Calexico Chronicle*, January 24, 1934.

83. *Open Forum*, February 3, 1934, 1.

84. "T. A. Reardon Reports No Serious Conditions," *Calexico Chronicle*, January 27, 1934.

85. "Move to Have Valley Facts in Hands of Authorities," *Brawley News*, January 25, 1934.

86. *Open Forum*, February 3, 1934.

87. Campbell MacCulloch to the National Labor Board, January 25, 1934, National Archives, RG 25, NLRB Case File, Cases 15.28-15.57, Box No. 3, "Vegetable Shippers of Imperial Valley" (1934).

88. "Suggested Avenues of Inquiry Imperial Valley Survey," National Archives, RG 25, NLRB Case File, Cases 15.28 to 15.29, Box No. 3, "Vegetable Shippers of Imperial Valley" (1934).

89. J. L. Leonard to Mr. Lubin, February 20, 1934, National Archives, RG 25, NLRB Case File, Cases 15.28 to 15.57, Box No. 3, "Vegetable Shippers of Imperial Valley" (1934).

90. *Brawley News*, January 29, 1934.

91. "U.S. Report Vindicates ACLU," *Open Forum*, February 24, 1934; *San Diego Union*, February 18, 1934.

92. "Inquiries of Strike Complete," *Calexico Chronicle*, February 7, 1934; "Labor Inquiry Is Ended," *Brawley News*, February 7, 1934; "Valley's Big Crop of Peas Now Periled by Agitators," February 14, 1934.

93. A. G. Arnoll, Managing Secretary, Los Angeles County Chamber of Commerce, to President Abelardo Rodríguez, February 12, 1934, AGN, Abelardo Rodríguez File, 561.8/326.

94. Campbell MacCulloch to Joaquín Terrazas, February 15, 1934, National Archives, RG 25, NLRB Case File, Cases 15.28 to 15.57, Box No. 3 (1934).

95. Joaquín Terrazas to Campbell MacCulloch, February 15, 1934, National Archives, RG 25, NLRB Case File (1934).

96. Chester Williams, "The Imperial Valley Crisis Nears," *Open Forum,* April 14, 1934, 1.

97. "Consul Tells Rotary Club about Mexico," *Brawley News,* February 1, 1934.

98. "Union of Laborers is Sought," *Calexico Chronicle,* February 16, 1934.

99. "Consul Terrazas Starts Sane Movement," *Brawley News,* February 23, 1934. See also Gray, "American Civil Liberties Union," 109–111.

100. "Growers Organize to Combat Red Menace during Cant Harvest," *Calexico Chronicle,* March 15, 1934.

101. "Se espera una nueva huelga de pizcadores," *La Opinión,* March 14, 1934.

102. Ibid.

103. *Los Angeles Times,* January 16, 1934.

104. Williams, "The Imperial Valley Crisis Nears," 2.

105. "Anti-Reds Take Over Assembly," *Calexico Chronicle,* March 26, 1934.

106. "Terrazas Will Organize Brawley Field Workers," *Calexico Chronicle,* March 10, 1934.

107. Gray, "American Civil Liberties Union," 111.

108. Ernest Besig's Report, Wednesday, March 21 to Thursday, March 27, 1934, 3, FWPC, BANC MSS C-R2, Carton 14, Folder #602, Bancroft Library.

109. Ibid., 1–2.

110. Ibid., 3.

111. Ibid.

112. Ibid., 4.

113. Ibid., 3.

114. Ibid., 5.

115. Ibid., 4.

116. Ibid.

117. Ibid.

118. "Imperial Valley Growers and Shippers Protective Association" (1934), Glassford Papers, Box 25, Special Collections, University of California, Los Angeles.

119. "Boletín de la Asociación Mexicana del Valle Imperial," National Archives, RG 25, NLRB Case File, Cases 15-28 to 15-57, Box No. 3 (1934). See also *Open Forum,* April 28, 1934.

120. "Goodwill Tour Is Called Off," *Brawley News,* April 28, 1934.

121. Howard A. Bowman to the Secretary of State, April 16, 1934, National Archives, RG 59, 811.5045/145.

122. "Imperial Valley Growers and Shippers Protective Association" (1934), Glassford Papers, Box 25, Special Collections, University of California, Los Angeles.

123. "Local Labor Preference Will Rule in 'Can't Season,'" *Brawley News,* March 28, 1934.

124. "Boletín de la Asociación Mexicana del Valle Imperial," National Archives, RG 25, NLRB Case File, Cases 15-28 to 15-57, Box No. 3 (1934).

125. Alejandro Lubbert to Sr. Lic. Francisco Xavier Gaxiola (Secretary to President Abelardo Rodríguez), April 16, 1934, AGN, Abelardo Rodríguez File, 561. 8/326.

126. Consul General Alejandro Lubbert to President Abelardo Rodríguez, April 16, 1934, AGN, Abelardo Rodríguez File, 561-8/236.

127. "Glassford Hears All Who Come," *Calexico Chronicle,* April 5, 1934.

128. Richard Bransten, *The New Masses,* May 15, 1934, Federal Writers Project Collection, BANC MSS C-RZ, Carton 14, Folder 604, Bancroft Library.

129. Randall Henderson to A. N. Jack, July 20, 1934, Exhibit 8918, U.S. Senate, *Hearings,* Part 55, 20312.

130. Howard A. Bowman to the Secretary of State, April 16, 1934. National Archives, RG 59, 811.5045/145.

131. EWR to Mr. Bursley, April 22, 1934. National Archives, RG 59, 811.5045.

132. "Investigators Find No Valley Strikes," *Brawley News,* April 12, 1934; "Mediator Blames Labor Agitators," *Calexico Chronicle,* April 12, 1934.

133. "Gen. Glassford Goes Wrong on One Point," *Brawley News,* April 13, 1934; *Calexico Chronicle,* April 12, 1934.

134. U.S. Senate, *Hearings,* Part 55, 20136–20137.

135. Ibid., 20136.

136. P. D. Glassford to Imperial Valley Growers and Shippers Association and the Asociación Mexicana del Valle Imperial, May 23, 1934, Glassford Papers, Box 25, Special Collections, Research Library, University of California, Los Angeles.

137. "Agricultural Unrest Traced Directly to Agitators' Activities," *Calexico Chronicle,* April 20, 1934.

138. "Goodwill Tour Is Called Off," *Brawley News,* April 28, 1934; see also Gray, "American Civil Liberties Union."

139. *Open Forum,* March 24, 1934; "We Want C&AWIU Imp. Valley Mass Meeting Demands," *Western Worker,* April 2, 1934; *San Diego Sun,* April 2, 1934.

140. Helen Marston to Campbell MacCulloch, March 20, 1932, National Archives, RG 25, NLRB Case Files, Cases 15-28 to 15-57, Box 3.

141. Campbell MacCulloch to Helen D. Marston, March 21, 1934, National Archives, RG 25, NLRB Case Files, Cases 15-28 to 15-57, Box 3.

142. T. A. Reardon to Frances Perkins, May 3, 1934. National Archives, RG 170, Perkins Files.

143. James Rolph Jr. to Frances Perkins, May 8, 1934, National Archives, RG 170, Perkins Files.

144. Frances Perkins to James Rolph Jr., May 14, 1934, National Archives, RG 170, Perkins Files, Federal Intervention in Imperial Valley, 1934–1935.

145. "Highways Guarded to Intercept 'Dynamite' Cargo of Communists,"

Calexico Chronicle, May 1, 1934; see also Gray, "American Civil Liberties Union," 200–202.

146. "Glassford Is Against New Labor," *Calexico Chronicle,* May 11, 1934.

147. C. B. Moore to President Abelardo Rodríguez, July 11, 1934, ASRE, Joaquín Terrazas File, 21-4-5.

148. "The Mexican Consul and the Harvest Strike" (Editorial), *Morning Post,* August 5, 1936.

149. Consul General Alejandro Lubbert to Secretariat of Foreign Relations, Department of Commercial and Protection, June 5, 1934, ASRE, Joaquín Terrazas, Su Expediente Personal.

150. Alberto Robles et al. to President Abelardo Rodríguez, May 1934, AGN, Abelardo Rodríguez File, 561.8/236.

151. Anonymous Strikers to Secretary of Foreign Relations, March 12, 1934, ASRE, Joaquín Terrazas, Su Expediente Personal, 21, 4–5.

152. *Workman's Bulletin of Imperial Valley* (San Diego) 1, no. 1 (April 2, 1934), Glassford Papers, Box 25/26, Special Collections, University of California, Los Angeles.

153. Helen Marston to Campbell MacCulloch, March 20, 1932, National Archives, RG 25, NLRB Case Files, Cases 15-28 to 15-57, Box 3.

154. "Lessons of the Imperial Valley Strike," *Western Worker,* February 19, 1934.

155. González, *Labor and Community,* chap. 6.

Chapter Six

1. Rebecca Taylor and Barney Egan to Secretary of Labor Frances Perkins, March 23, 1938, National Archives, RG 25, NLRB File, XVI-C-221. See also "Consul's Strike Stand Protested," *San Antonio Express,* March 24, 1938.

2. Hobart Spalding Jr., *Organized Labor in Latin America* (NY: New York University Press, 1977), 122–123.

3. Ibid., 129. See also Evelyn P. Stevens, "Mexico's PRI: The Institutionalization of Corporatism?" in James M. Malloy, ed., *Authoritarianism and Corporatism in Latin America* (Pittsburgh: University of Pittsburgh Press, 1977), 232.

4. James B. Stewart to the Honorable Secretary of State, December 21, 1939, National Archives, RG 59, Department of State Records File, 811.504/550.

5. Confederación de Trabajadores Mexicanos de Norte America, "Informe," January 7, 1940, AGN, Mexico City, Lázaro Cárdenas File, 433/467.

6. Enclosure to William P. Blocker to the Honorable Secretary of State, April 21, 1941, National Archives, RG 59, 811.5045/320.

7. "Mexican Labor Titan Dies at 97," *Orange County Register,* June 22, 1997.

8. Cockroft, *Mexico,* 154; see also Francisco Zapata, "Labor and Politics: The Mexican Paradox," in Edward C. Epstein, ed., *Labor Autonomy and the State in Latin America* (Boston: Unwin Hyman, 1989), 179.

8

9. Ernesto Galarza, *Merchants of Labor: The Mexican Bracero Story* (Charlotte, N.C.: McNally and Loftin, 1964), 208–211.

10. Kitty Calavita, *Inside the State: The Bracero Program, Immigration, and the I.N.S.* (New York: Routledge, 1992), 110.

11. Ernesto Galarza, "The Mexican American: A National Concern: Program for Action," *Common Ground* 10, no. 4 (1949): 29–30.

12. Lyle Saunders and Olin E. Leonard, *The Wetback in the Lower Rio Grande Valley of Texas,* Inter-American Education Occasional Papers, 7 (July 1951; reprint, New York: Arno Press, 1976), 92.

13. Manuel García y Griego, "The Importation of Mexican Contract Laborers to the United States, 1942–1964," in David G. Gutiérrez, ed., *Between Two Worlds: Mexican Immigrants in the United States* (Wilmington, Dela.: Scholarly Resources, 1996).

14. Ernesto Galarza, "Big Farm Strike: A Report on the Labor Dispute at the Di Giorgio's," *Commonweal* (June 4, 1948): 180.

15. Calavita, *Inside the State,* 70, 74.

16. Ibid., 2.

17. Galarza, *Merchants of Labor,* 217.

18. Ibid.

19. Johnny Mac McCain, "Contract Labor as a Factor in United States–Mexican Relations, 1942–1947," Ph.D. diss., University of Texas, Austin, 1970, 288–289.

20. Quoted in Valdés, *Al Norte,* 103–104.

21. Ibid.

22. Galarza, *Merchants of Labor,* 220.

23. See Richard Craig, *The Bracero Program: Interest Groups and Foreign Policy* (Austin: University of Texas Press, 1971), 60.

24. Arturo Santamaría Gómez, *La política entre México y Aztlán: Relaciones chicano mexicanas del 68 a Chiapas 94* (Culiacán: Universidad Autónoma de Sinaloa, 1994), 60.

25. Rodolfo de la Garza, "Chicano-Mexican Relations: A Framework for Research," *Social Science Quarterly* 63, no. 2 (March, 1982): 128.

26. Stanley R. Ross, "Introduction," in Richard D. Erb and Stanley R. Ross, eds., *United States Relations with Mexico: Content and Context* (Washington, D.C.: American Enterprise Institute For Public Policy Research, 1981), 6.

27. Armando Gutiérrez, "The Chicano Elite in Chicano-Mexicano Relations," in Tatcho Mindeola and Max Martínez, eds., *Chicano-Mexicano Relations* (University Park, Tex.: University of Houston, 1986), 56.

28. Ibid., 57.

29. Many invited international observers testified that widespread violations of the electoral code occurred. Lynne Halpin, coordinator of Witness for Peace, found little that could be categorized as democratic in the 1994 elections. Halpin reported extensive deliberate violations, including withholding of "benefits from government programs impacting rural areas, union pressure and requirements of vote for the government party, landowners present at voting precincts, . . . creden-

tial confiscation, . . . people voting who were not on the lists and on and on."
Letter to the editor, *Los Angeles Times,* September 3, 1994.

30. Santamaría Gómez, *La Política,* 207.

31. Ibid., 208.

32. Ibid., 211.

33. Eduardo Ruiz, "México premia dos mexicamericanos de Orange con el reconocimiento," *Excelsior* (Santa Ana, Calif.), May 3, 1997.

34. As quoted in Santamaría Gómez, *La Política,* 217.

35. David Ayon, "How Mexico's Ruling Party Outflanked Its Opposition in U.S.," *Los Angeles Times,* October 13, 1996.

36. "Mexico Assails Prop. 187, Offers Opponents Support," *Orange County Register,* October 4, 1994.

37. Reprinted in ibid.

38. Santamaría Gómez, *La Política,* 212.

39. Anthony de Palma, "Mexico's Rich Richer, Poor Angrier," *Orange County Register,* July 21, 1996.

40. Steve Fainaru, "Mexico's War Within," *Boston Globe,* September 17, 1996.

41. "Fearing Worker Unrest, Unions Cancel Parade," *Los Angeles Times,* March 31, 1995; "Mexican Labor Leader and Kingmaker Dies at 97," *Los Angeles Times,* June 27, 1997.

42. Jerome I. Levinson, "Give Mexican Workers Their Due," *Los Angeles Times,* September 29, 1992.

43. Sam Dillon, "Mexico's Top Party Stifles Its Critics," *Orange County Register,* May 2, 1997.

44. Mary Beth Sheridan, "Trade Knits U.S. and Mexico Ever More Tightly," *Los Angeles Times,* May 5, 1997; and Art Pine, "Panel Declares NAFTA Success in California," *Los Angeles Times,* April 29, 1997.

45. Mary Beth Sheridan, "Riding Ripples of a Border Boom," *Los Angeles Times,* June 9, 1997.

46. "U.S. Investments in Mexico Will Continue," *Orange County Register,* July 9, 1997.

47. Mark Fineman, "Mexico's Crime Rate Rises Despite Crackdown," *Los Angeles Times,* December 15, 1996.

48. Steve Fainaru, "Mexico's War Within," *Boston Globe,* September 17, 1996.

49. Adolfo Aguilar Zinser, "Zedillo's Democracy Is a Sham," *Los Angeles Times,* September 4, 1996.

50. *Orange County Register,* May 2, 1997.

51. Galarza, "The Mexican American," 31.

Bibliography

Archival Collections

Archivo de la Secretaría de Relaciones Exteriores (ASRE), Mexico City. Carlos Ariza Salazar file; Enrique Bravo file; Calexico (California) Consulate file; Rafael de la Colina file; Ricardo Hill file; Los Angeles Consulate file; Alejandro Lubbert file; Alejandro Martínez file; Fernando Alfonso Pesqueira file; Vicente Rendón Quijano file; Joaquín Terrazas file.

Archivo General de la Nación (AGN), Mexico City. Abelardo Rodríguez file; Alvaro Obregón/Plutarco Elías Calles file; Lázaro Cárdenas file.

Bancroft Library, University of California, Berkeley. Federal Writers Project collection; Manual Gamio collection; C. B. Hutchison papers; C. B. Hutchison photo collection; Simon Julius Lubin Society papers; Jim McCrary papers; Paul Schuster Taylor collection; James Earl Wood papers.

Bobst Library, Tamiment Library/Wagner Library, New York University. Sam Darcy collection.

Department of Special Collections, University Research Library, University of California, Los Angeles. George P. Clements papers; Pelham Davis Glassford collection; Dorothy Healey papers; Carey McWilliams collection.

Imperial County Historical Society, Imperial, California. Joan S. Thagard Scrapbook.

National Archives, Washington D.C. Army and Navy Intelligence–G2 Records; Department of Labor Records; Department of State Records; Federal Mediation and Conciliation Service (FMCS) Records; National Labor Relations Board (NLRB) Records; National Recovery Administration Records.

Southern California Library for Social Studies and Research, Los Angeles. Film and Photo League documentary film collection.

Walter P. Reuther Library, Archives of Labor and Urban Affairs, Wayne State University, Detroit, Michigan. Film and Photo League *Century of Progress* film documentary.

Newspapers and Periodicals

Berkeley Daily Gazette
Boston Globe
Brawley News
Calexico Chronicle
California Citrograph
Excelsior (Santa Ana, Calif.)
Fresno Bee
El Heraldo de México (Los Angeles, Calif.)
Imperial Valley Farmer (El Centro, Calif.)
Labor Defender
Los Angeles Citizen
Los Angeles Evening Herald Express
Los Angeles Illustrated Daily News
Los Angeles Times
Morning Post (El Centro, Calif.)
Oakland Tribune
La Opinión (Los Angeles, Calif.)
Orange County Register (Calif.)
Orange Daily News (Calif.)
Pacific Weekly
La Prensa (San Antonio, Tex.)
San Antonio Express
San Diego Sun
San Diego Union
San Francisco Chronicle
San Francisco Examiner
San Francisco News
Santa Ana Register (Calif.)
Visalia Times-Delta
Western Worker

Books, Articles, and Other Publications

"Agrarian Revolt in California" (Correspondence). *The Nation* 137 (September 1933): 272.

Acuña, Rodolfo. *Occupied America: A History of Chicanos.* New York: Harper and Row, 1981.

Adams, R. L. *Seasonal Labor Requirements for California Crops.* Bulletin 623. Berkeley: University of California College of Agriculture, Agricultural Experiment Station, 1938.

Andrews, Gregg. *Shoulder to Shoulder? The American Federation of Labor, the United States, and the Mexican Revolution, 1910–1924.* Berkeley: University of California Press, 1991.

Arroyo, Luis Leobardo. "Mexican Workers and American Unions: The Los Angeles AFL, 1890–1933." Working Paper Series 107. Berkeley: University of California Chicano Political Economy Collective, 1981.

Balderrama, Francisco. *In Defense of La Raza: The Los Angeles Mexican Consulate and the Mexican Community*. Tucson: University of Arizona Press, 1982.

Balderrama, Francisco, and Rodríguez, Raymond. *Decade of Betrayal: Mexican Repatriation in the 1930s*. Albuquerque: University of New Mexico Press, 1995.

Bethell, Leslie, ed. *Mexico Since Independence*. New York: Cambridge University Press, 1991.

Blackwelder, Julia Kirk. *Women in the Depression: Caste and Culture in San Antonio, 1929–1939*. College Station: Texas A&M University Press, 1984.

Bogardus, Emory. *The Mexican in the United States*. Los Angeles: University of Southern California Press, 1934.

Bustamante, Jorge A. "Chicanos: Biografía de una toma de conciencia." *Cuadernos Políticos* 6 (Oct.–Dec. 1975): 25–43.

Calavita, Kitty. *Inside the State: The Bracero Program, Immigration, and the I.N.S.* New York: Routledge, 1992.

Camarillo, Albert. *Chicanos in California: A History of Mexican Americans in California*. San Francisco: Boyd and Fraser, 1984.

Cardoso, Lawrence. *Mexican Immigration to the United States, 1897–1931*. Tucson: University of Arizona Press, 1982.

Chacón, Ramón. "Labor Unrest and Industrialized Agriculture in California: The Case of the 1933 San Joaquín Valley Cotton Strike." *Social Science Quarterly* 65, no. 2 (1984): 336–353.

Clark, Margaret. *Organized Labor in Mexico*. New York: Russell and Russell, 1973. First published by the University of North Carolina Press, 1934.

Cockcroft, James D. *Mexico: Class Formation, Capital Accumulation and the State*. New York: Monthly Review Press, 1983.

Corwin, Arthur. *Immigrants and Immigrants: Perspectives on Mexican Labor Migration to the United States*. Westport, Conn.: Greenwood Press, 1978.

Corwin, Arthur F. "Mexican Policy and Ambivalence toward Labor Emigration to the United States." In *Immigrants and Immigrants: Perspectives on Mexican Labor Migration to the United States*. Ed. Arthur F. Corwin. Westport, Conn.: Greenwood Press, 1978.

Craig, Richard. *The Bracero Program: Interest Groups and Foreign Policy*. Austin: University of Texas Press, 1971.

Daniel, Clete. *Bitter Harvest: A History of California Farm Workers, 1871–1941*. Ithaca: Cornell University Press, 1981.

de la Garza, Rodolfo. "Chicano-Mexican Relations: A Framework for Research." *Social Science Quarterly* 63, no. 2 (March 1982): 113–130.

———. "Chicanos and U. S. Foreign Policy: The Future of Chicano-Mexican Relations." In *Mexican–U.S. Relations: Conflict and Convergence*. Ed. Carlos Vásquez and Manuel García y Griego. Los Angeles: UCLA Chicano Studies Research Center Publications and Latin American Center Publications, 1983.

de la Garza, Rodolfo, and Jesus Velasco, eds. *Bridging the Border: Transforming Mexico–U.S. Relations.* New York: Rowman and Littlefield, 1997.

Decker, Caroline. "California Workers Undefeated." *The Nation* 140 (1934): 481–482.

Delpar, Helen. *The Enormous Vogue of Things Mexican: Cultural Relations between the United States and Mexico, 1920–1935.* Tuscaloosa: University of Alabama Press, 1992.

Epstein, Edward C. *Labor Autonomy and the State in Latin America.* Boston: Unwin Hyman, 1989.

Erb, Richard D., and Stanley R. Ross, eds. *United States Relations with Mexico: Content and Context.* Washington, D.C.: American Enterprise Institute for Policy Research, 1981.

Galán, Israel. "Los chicanos, el petróleo mexicano y una alianza posible." In *Las Relaciones México–Estados Unidos,* vol. 1. Ed. David Barkin et al. Editorial Nueva Imagen and Universidad Autónoma de México, 1981.

Galarza, Ernesto. "Big Farm Strike: A Report on the Labor Dispute at the Di Giorgio's." *Commonweal,* June 4, 1948, 178–182.

———. *Merchants of Labor: The Mexican Bracero Story.* Charlotte, N.C.: McNally and Loftin, 1964.

———. "The Mexican American: A National Concern: Program for Action." *Common Ground* 10, no. 4 (1949): 27–38.

Gamio, Manuel. *The Mexican Immigrant.* Chicago: University of Chicago Press, 1931; reprint, New York: Arno Press, 1969.

García, Mario. "La Frontera: The Border as Symbol and Reality in Mexican American Thought." In *Between Two Worlds: Mexican Immigrants in the United States.* Ed. David Gutiérrez. Wilmington, Dela.: Scholarly Resources, 1996.

———. *Memories of Chicano History: The Life and Narrative of Bert Corona.* Berkeley: University of California Press, 1994.

———. *Mexican Americans: Leadership, Ideology, and Identity, 1930–1960.* New Haven: Yale University Press, 1989.

García y Griego, Manuel. "The Importation of Mexican Contract Laborers to the United States, 1942–1964." In *Between Two Worlds: Mexican Immigrants in the United States.* Ed. David G. Gutiérrez. Wilmington, Dela.: Scholarly Resources, 1996.

García-Acevedo, María Rosa. "Return to Aztlán: Mexico's Policies Toward Chicanos/as." In *Chicanas/os at the Crossroads.* Ed. David R. Maciel and Ysidro D. Ortiz. Tucson: University of Arizona Press, 1996.

Gill, Mario. *Nuestros buenos vecinos.* Mexico City: Editorial Azteca, 1964.

Gómez-Quiñones, Juan. *Mexican American Labor, 1790–1990.* Albuquerque: University of New Mexico Press, 1994.

———. "Notes on an Interpretation of the Relations between the Mexican Community in the United States and Mexico." *In Mexican–U.S. Relations: Conflict and Convergence.* Los Angeles: UCLA Chicano Studies Research Center Publications and the Latin American Center Publications, 1983.

———. "'Piedras contra la luna': México en Aztlán y Aztlán en México: Chicano-Mexican Relations and the Consulates, 1900–1920." In *Contemporary Mexico*. Papers of the IV International Congress of Mexican History. Ed. James W. Wilkie et al. Berkeley and Mexico City: University of California Press and El Colegio de México, 1976.

———. *Roots of Chicano Politics, 1600–1940.* Albuquerque: University of New Mexico Press, 1994.

González, Gilbert G. . *Labor and Community: Mexican Citrus Worker Villages in a Southern California County, 1900–1950.* Urbana: University of Illlinois Press, 1994.

Griffith, Beatrice. *American Me.* Boston: Houghton Mifflin, 1948.

Guerin-Gonzales, Camille. *Mexican Workers and American Dreams: Immigration, Repatriation, and California Farm Labor, 1900–1939.* New Brunswick, N.J.: Rutgers University Press, 1994.

Gutiérrez, Armando. "The Chicano Elite in Chicano-Mexicano Relations." In *Chicano-Mexicano Relations.* Ed. Tatcho Mindiola and Max Martínez. University Park, Tex.: University of Houston, 1986.

Gutiérrez, David. *Walls and Mirrors: Mexican Americans, Mexican Immigrants, and the Politics of Ethnicity.* Berkeley: University of California Press, 1995.

———, ed. *Between Two Worlds: Mexican Immigrants in the United States.* Wilmington, Dela.: Scholarly Resources, 1996.

Hansen, Roger D. *The Politics of Mexican Development.* Baltimore: Johns Hopkins Press, 1971.

Hart, John M. "Agrarian Reform." In *Twentieth-Century Mexico.* Ed. Dirk Raat and William H. Beezely. Lincoln: University of Nebraska Press, 1986.

Hodges, R. E. "Imperial Valley, Active and Very Promising." *Pacific Rural Press,* November 25, 1933, 423.

Hoffman, Abraham. "The El Monte Berry Pickers' Strike, 1933: International Involvement in a Labor Dispute." *Journal of the West* 5, no. 7 (Jan. 1973): 71–84.

Hoffman, Abraham. *Unwanted Mexican Americans in the Great Depression: Repatriation Pressures, 1929–1939.* Tucson: University of Arizona Press, 1974.

Hosmer, Helen. "Triumph and Failure in the Imperial Valley." *American West* 3, no. 1 (1966): 34–79.

Humphrey, Norman D. "The Integration of the Detroit Mexican Colony." *American Journal of Economics and Sociology* 3, no. 2 (1944): 155–166.

———. "The Migration and Settlement of Detroit Mexicans." *Economic Geography* 19, no. 4 (1943): 358–361.

Iwata, Mazakawa. *Planted on Good Soil: A History of the Issei in the United States Agriculture.* Vol. 1. New York: Peter Lang, 1992.

Jameison, Stuart. *Labor Unionism in American Agriculture.* United States Department of Labor Bulletin No. 836. Washington, D.C.: U.S. Government Printing Office, 1945.

Knight, Alan. *The Mexican Revolution,* vols. 1 & 2. Cambridge, Eng.: Cambridge University Press, 1986.

————. *U.S. Mexican Relations, 1910–1940*. San Diego: Center for U.S. Mexico Studies, University of California, San Diego, 1987.

Krenn, Michael L. *U.S. Policy toward Economic Nationalism in Latin America, 1917–1929*. Wilmington, Dela.: Scholarly Resources, 1990.

Lembcke, Jerry Lee. "Labor History's 'Synthesis Debate': Sociological Interventions." *Science and Society* 59, no. 2 (1995): 137–173.

Levenson, Lew. "California Casualty List." *The Nation* 139 (August 29, 1934): 243–245.

López, Ronald W. "The El Monte Berry Strike of 1933." *Aztlán: Chicano Journal of the Social Sciences and the Arts* 1 (Spring 1970): 101–114.

Majka, Linda C., and Theo J. Majka. *Farm Workers, Agribusiness, and the State*. Philadelphia: Temple University Press, 1982.

Mallory, James M., ed. *Authoritarianism and Corporatism in Latin America*. Pittsburgh: University of Pittsburgh Press, 1977.

Marston, Helen. "A Case Study in Social Conflict." *Advance* (June 21, 1934), 236.

Mayer, Jean. "Revolution and Reconstruction in the 1920s." In *Mexico Since Independence*. Ed. Leslie Bethell. New York: Cambridge University Press, 1991.

McKay, R. Reynolds. "The Impact of the Great Depression on Immigrant Mexican Labor: Repatriation of the Bridgeport, Texas Coal Miners." *Social Science Quarterly* 65, no. 2 (1984): 354–363.

McWilliams, Carey. *North from Mexico: The Spanish Speaking People in the United States*. Philadelphia: J. B. Lippincott, 1949.

————. *Southern California: An Island on the Land*. Santa Barbara: Peregrine Smith, 1979.

"Mexican Laborers for Bethlehem Steel." *Manufacturers Record* (May 10, 1923): 73.

Mindeola, Tatcho, and Max Martínez, eds. *Chicano-Mexicano Relations*. University Park, Tex.: University of Houston Press, 1986.

Modell, John. *The Economics and Politics of Racial Accommodation: The Japanese of Los Angeles, 1900–1942*. Urbana: University of Illinois Press, 1977.

Monroy, Douglas. "Anarquismo y Comunismo: Mexican Radicalism and the Communist Party in Los Angeles during the 1930s." *Labor History* 24, no. 1 (1983): 35–59.

Price, David. "Orange County Strike." *Pacific Weekly* 5 (August, 1936): 116–117.

Prieto Laurens, Jorge. *Cincuenta años de política mexicana: Memorias políticas*. Mexico City: Editora Mexicana de Periódicos, Libros y Revistas, 1968.

Raat, Dirk. *Los Revoltosos: Mexico's Rebels in the United States, 1903–1923*. College Station: Texas A&M University Press, 1981.

Raat, Dirk, and William Beezely, ed. *Twentieth-Century Mexico*. Lincoln: University of Nebraska Press, 1986.

Reisler, Mark. "Mexican Unionization in California Agriculture, 1927–1936." *Labor History* 14, no. 4 (1973): 562–579.

Romo, Ricardo. *East Los Angeles: A History of a Barrio*. Austin: University of Texas Press, 1983.

Ross, Stanley R. "Introduction." In *United States Relations with Mexico: Content and Context.* Ed. Richard D. Erb and Stanley R. Ross. Washington, D.C.: American Enterprise Institute for Public Policy Research, 1981.

Rothenberg, Irene Fraser. "Mexican-American Views of U.S. Relations with Latin America." *Journal of Ethnic Studies* 6, no. 1 (1978): 62–78.

Ruiz, Ramón Eduardo. *Labor and Ambivalent Revolutionaries: Mexico, 1911–1923.* Baltimore: Johns Hopkins Press, 1976.

―――. *The People of Sonora and Yankee Capitalists.* Tucson: University of Arizona Press, 1988.

Ruiz, Vicki. *Cannery Women, Cannery Lives: Mexican Women, Unionization, and the Food Processing Industry, 1930–1950.* Albuquerque: University of New Mexico Press, 1987.

Sánchez, George J. *Becoming Mexican American: Ethnicity, Culture, and Identity in Chicano Los Angeles, 1900–1945.* New York: Oxford University Press, 1993.

Santamaría Gómez, Arturo. *La política entre México y Aztlán: Relaciones chicano mexicanas del 68 a Chiapas 94.* Culiacán: Universidad Autónoma de Sinaloa, 1994.

Schoaf, George. "Imperial Valley Outrage." *Open Forum,* July 5, 1930, 1.

Seiler, Conrad. "Cantaloupes and Communists." *The Nation* 131 (September 3, 1930): 243–244.

Simpson, Lesley Byrd. *Many Mexicos.* Berkeley: University of California Press, 1967.

Smith, Robert Freeman. *The United States and Revolutionary Nationalism in Mexico, 1916–1922.* Chicago: University of Chicago Press, 1972.

Spalding, Hobart Jr. *Organized Labor in Latin America.* New York: New York University Press, 1977.

Spaulding, Charles B. "The Mexican Strike at El Monte, California." *Sociology and Social Research* 18 (July 1934): 571–580.

Spector, Frank. *Story of the Imperial Valley.* New York: International Labor Defense, 1930.

Stevens, Evelyn P. "Mexico's PRI: The Institutionalization of Corporatism?" In *Authoritarianism and Corporatism in Latin America.* Ed. James M. Malloy. Pittsburgh: University of Pittsburgh Press, 1977.

Stokes, Frank. "Let the Mexicans Organize." *The Nation* (December 19, 1936): 731–732.

Sufrin, Sidney. "Labor Organization in Agricultural America, 1930–1935." *American Journal of Sociology* 43 (1938): 544–559.

Sweetland, Monroe. "Red Paint in the Imperial Valley." *The World Tomorrow,* June 14, 1934, 310.

Taylor, Paul S. *Mexican Labor in the United States: Imperial Valley.* University of California Publications in Economics, vol. 6. Berkeley: University of California, 1930.

―――. *Mexican Labor in the United States: Migration Statistics II.* University of California Publications in Economics, vol. 12, no. 2. Berkeley: University of California, 1933.

―――. *On the Ground in the Thirties* (Salt Lake City: Peregrine Smith, 1983).

———— ⸳. *A Spanish-Mexican Peasant Community, Arandas in Jalisco, Mexico.* Berkeley: University of California Press, 1933.

Taylor, Paul S., and Clark Kerr. "Uprisings on the Farms." *Survey Graphic* 24 (January 1935): 19–22, 44.

Tennayuca, Emma, and Homer Brooks. "The Mexican Question in the Southwest." *The Communist* (March 1939): 257–268.

Tuck, Ruth. *Not with the Fist: Mexican Americans in a Southwest City.* New York: Harcourt Brace and Company, 1946.

Valdés, Dennis Nodin. *Al Norte: Agricultural Workers in the Great Lakes Region, 1917–1970.* Austin: University of Texas Press, 1991.

Vargas, Zaragoza. *Proletarians of the North: A History of Mexican Industrial Workers in Detroit and the Midwest, 1917–1933.* Berkeley: University of California Press, 1993.

Vélez Ibáñez, Carlos G. *Border Visions: Mexican Cultures of the Southwest United States.* Tucson: University of Arizona Press, 1996.

Walker, David W. "Porfirian Labor Politics: Working Class Organizations in Mexico City and Porfirio Díaz." *Americas* 37 (June 1981): 257–289.

Weber, Devra. *Dark Sweat, White Gold: California Farm Workers, Cotton, and the New Deal.* Berkeley: University of California Press, 1994.

Weber, Devra. "Oral Sources and the History of Mexican Workers in the United States." *International and Working Class History* 23 (Spring 1983): 47–50.

———. "The Organizing of Mexicano Agricultural Workers: Imperial Valley and Los Angeles, 1928–1934, An Oral History Approach." *Aztlán: Chicano Journal of the Social Sciences and the Arts* 3, no. 2 (1973): 307–343.

Wilkie, James W., Michael C. Meyer, and Edna Monzón de Wilkie, eds. *Contemporary Mexico.* Papers of the IV International Congress of Mexican History. Berkeley and Mexico City: University of California Press and the Colegio de México, 1976.

Williams, Chester. "Imperial Valley Mob." *New Republic* 78 (February 21, 1934): 39–41.

———. "Imperial Valley Prepares for War." *The World Tomorrow* 17 (April 26, 1934): 199–201.

Winter, Ella. "California's Little Hitlers." *New Republic* 77 (1933): 188–190.

Wollenberg, Charles. "Huelga 1928 Style: The Imperial Valley Cantaloupe Workers' Strike." *Pacific Historical Review* 28 (1969): 45–58.

———. "Race and Class in Rural California: The El Monte Berry Strike of 1933." *California Historical Quarterly* 51 (Summer 1974): 155–164.

Womack, John Jr. "The Mexican Economy during the Revolution, 1910–1920." In *Twentieth-Century Mexico.* Ed. Dirk Raat and William H. Beezely. Lincoln: University of Nebraska Press, 1986.

———. *Zapata and the Mexican Revolution.* New York: Alfred A. Knopf, 1970.

Zamora, Emilio. "Chicano Socialist Labor Activity in Texas, 1900–1920." *Aztlán: Chicano Journal of the Social Sciences and the Arts* 6, no. 2 (1975): 221–236.

———. *The World of the Mexican Worker in Texas.* College Station: Texas A&M University, 1993.

Zapata, Francisco. "Labor and Politics: The Mexican Paradox." In *Labor Autonomy and the State in Latin America*. Ed. Edward Epstein. Boston: Unwin Hyman, 1989.

Zazueta, Carlos H. "Mexican Political Actors in the United States and Mexico: Historical and Political Contexts of a Dialogue Renewed." In *Mexican–U.S. Relations: Conflict and Convergence*. Ed. Carlos Vásquez and Manuel García y Griego. Los Angeles: UCLA Chicano Studies Research Center Publications and Latin American Center Publications, 1983.

Theses and Dissertations

Allen, Ruth. "The Labor of Women and Families in the Production of Cotton." Ph.D. diss., University of Chicago, 1933. Reprint, New York: Arno Press, 1975.

Fearis, Donald Friend. "The California Farm Worker, 1930–1942." Ph.D. diss., University of California, Davis, 1971.

Gray, James. "The American Civil Liberties Union of Southern California and Imperial Valley Agricultural Labor Disturbances: 1930–1934." Ph.D. diss., University of California, Los Angeles, 1966.

Halcomb, Ellen Lois. "Efforts to Organize the Migrant Workers by the Cannery and Agricultural Workers Industrial Union in the 1930's." M.A. thesis, Chico State College, Chico, California, 1963.

Lowenstein, Norman. "Strikes and Strike Tactics in California Agriculture: A History." M.A. thesis, University of California, Los Angeles, 1940.

McCain, Johnny Mac. "Contract Labor as a Factor in United States–Mexican Relations, 1942–1947." Ph.D. diss., University of Texas, Austin, 1970.

Pichardo, Nelson Alexander. "The Role of Community in Social Protest: Chicano Working-Class Protest, 1848–1933." Ph.D. diss., University of Michigan, Ann Arbor, 1990.

Pycior, Julie Leininger. "La Raza Organizes: Mexican American Life in San Antonio, 1915–1930 as Reflected in Mutualista Activities." Ph.D. diss., University of Notre Dame, 1979.

Shapiro, Harold Arthur. "The Workers of San Antonio, Texas, 1900–1940." Ph.D. diss., University of Texas, Austin, 1952.

Walton, Roger M. V. "A Study of Migratory Mexican Peapickers in Imperial Valley." Ph.D. diss., University of California, Los Angeles, 1940.

Wolf, Jerome. "The Imperial Valley as an Index of Agricultural Labor Relations in California." Ph. D diss., University of California, Los Angeles, 1964.

Reports and Proceedings

American Federation of Labor. Records, Samuel Gompers Era. Shields Library, University of California, Davis.

————. Report of the Proceedings of the Forty-Seventh Annual Convention, Los Angeles, California, 1927. Shields Library, University of California, Davis.

————. Report of the Proceedings of the Forty-Sixth Annual Convention, Detroit, Michigan, 1926. Shields Library, University of California, Davis.

Chaffee, Porter M. "A History of the Cannery and Agricultural Workers Union." Federal Writers Project collection, Bancroft Library.

Cramp, Kathryn, Louise Shields, and Charles A. Thompson. "Study of the Mexican Population of the Imperial Valley, California." New York: Council of Women for Home Missions, 1926.

Governor C. C. Young's Fact Finding Committee. *Mexicans in California*. San Francisco: State Building, 1930.

Los Angeles Chamber of Commerce, Agriculture Department. "Crop Acreage Trends for Los Angeles County and Southern California, 1925–1957." Los Angeles County Board of Supervisors, 1957.

Pan-American Federation of Labor. Report of the Proceedings of the Fourth Congress, Mexico City, 1924.

Saunders, Lyle, and Olin E. Leonard. *The Wetback in the Lower Rio Grande Valley of Texas*. Inter-American Education Occasional Papers 7, July 1951. Reprint, New York: Arno Press, 1976.

Underhill, Bertha. "A Study of 132 Families in California Cotton Camps with Reference to Availability to Medical Care." California Department of Social Welfare, Division of Child Welfare Services, 1936.

U.S. Senate. Subcommittee of the Committee on Education and Labor. Violations of Free Speech and the Rights of Labor. *Hearings*. Parts 53–75. Washington, D.C.: U.S. Government Printing Office, 1940.

Index

ACLU: 178; labor defense, 181–182. *See also* A. L. Wirin; Helen Marston
AFL: alliance with CROM, 18, 20; and CUOM, 67; and hemispheric economic hegemony, U.S., 19; recommends immigration restriction, Mexico, 65; ties to President Alvaro Obregón, 20
Agricultural Labor Bureau, San Joaquin Valley: 127–128, 138, 144; setting wages, 131; strategy to end strike, 154
Aguilar Zinser, Adolfo: 227
Alvares Acosta, Miguel: 201
anarchism: 20
Anderson Clayton Company: 126. *See also* land tenure; corporate farming
Aragon, Edmundo: 51; and Comisión Honorífica, 169, 173
Ariza, Carlos V.: appointed consul, 23; organizing labor union, 166; and repatriation, 32
Arvin, CA: 142
Asiatic Exclusion Act: 107. *See also* Chamber of Commerce, Los Angeles County
Asociación Mexicana del Valle Imperial: and consul leadership, 176–179, 183, 185, 188; union contract, 192–193. *See also* Carlos Ariza
Asociación Mutual del Valle Imperial: 168; and Crom, 169–171
Asociación Nacional México Americana: 3
Associated Farmers of California: 118
Atlanta, GA: 26

Austin, TX: 201, 203
Avelyra, Rafael: 62
Avila Camacho, Miguel: 204; spying, 44
Ayres, Edward Duran: 108

Bakersfield, CA: 157
Balderrama, Francisco: 5, 230n20
Bank of America: cotton loans, 126
Batten, James: research on Mexicans, 90–91
Beals, Carlton: 13, 222
Besig, Ernest: as ACLU investigator, Imperial Valley, 187–188
Bethlehem Steel: 30
Biscailuz, Eugene: 108; strike strategies, 110
Border Industrial Program: 212, 223–224
Bracero Agreements: 198, 204; promote union busting, 206, 210; Texas sanctions, 210; wages under, 208; worker rights under, 209, 211–212
Bravo, Enrique: 6; alliance with growers, 144; attempts to lead cotton strike, 144–146, 148; conflicts with Mexican community, 136–138; Fresno Mexican community reception, 134–135
Brawley, CA: 51, 163, 169, 173, 176, 180, 187
Brownsville, TX: 44
Bucareli Agreements: 40
Bureau of Labor Statistics, California: 168

Calavita, Kitty: views on the Bracero Agreements, 206, 208

Calexico, CA: 24, 32, 46, 48, 53, 62, 166, 175, 180, 184–188, 210

Callahan, Pat: negotiates strike demands, 138

Calles, Plutarco Elias: 7, 14, 103; CROM political ties with, 22; in exile, 43; orders CUOM founding, 65; and the Partido Nacional Revolucionario, 22; personal wealth, 218; strike involvement, Los Angeles County, 102, 105, 107

Cannery and Agricultural Workers Industrial Union (CAWIU): 113, 159; and conflicts with consuls, 93–94, 98–100, 195–196; Federal government opposition to, 183; Imperial Valley strike, 173–174, 188; organizing, San Joaquin Valley, 123, 137; strike negotiations, 150; union headquarters in Hicks Camp, 91

Cantú Lara, Renato: 49

Cárdenas, Cuahtémoc: 216, 225. See also NAFTA; PRD

Cárdenas, Lázaro: 7, 22, 26–27; Calles' exile, 44; and the CTM, 200, 202; land reform, 14; and Mexican emigrants, 3, 34; selecting consular personnel, 25

Cardoso, Lawrence: 29

Centro Cultural de México, Orange County, California: 220

Chamber of Commerce, El Monte: 103

Chamber of Commerce, Imperial County: 167, 170

Chamber of Commerce, Los Angeles County: 166; accuses consulate of meddling, 113–115, 119; and Mexican contract labor, 30, 71; racializing, 109; repatriation, 32, 80–81; and strike mediation, 102; supports Consul Terrazas, 184

Chambers, Pat: 124, 180; indicted, Criminal Syndicalism charges, 143

Charity. See Comité de Beneficencia; comisiones honoríficas

Charrismo: 204

Chicago, IL: 75

Chicano Movement: 198; and Chicano Studies, 214; cultural symbols, 213, 216; and La Raza Unida Party, 214; relations with the PRI, 214

Chicano Studies: and the PRI, 218–219

child labor: in the Imperial Valley, 162; San Joaquin Valley, 130–131

Clark, Margaret: 14, 17; and Mexican emigration, 28

Clements, George C.: 109, 113

Cockroft, James D.: 13, 14

Colossio, Donaldo: 1, 219

Colunga, Elías: 203

comisiones honoríficas: 69, 175; consulate control over, 51–52; duties of, 50, 58–59; integrating locals of, 59–60; and nationalization of Mexico's oil, 55–56; number in southern California, 51; political activities of, 55, 75. See also Mexican Schools; Comité de Beneficencia

Comité de Beneficencia Mexicana: 79–80, 84

Communist Party, USA: 92; and farm labor, 173; and opposition to Mexicanization, 78. See also CAWIU

community, Mexican: 37; families, 129–130; organizations, 129. See also labor camps

Conciliation and Mediation Service: 102, 105, 169

Confederación de Sociedades Mexicanas (CSM): 201; and charity, 62; consular oversight, 62–63; founding of, 62; and the Mexican ruling party, 38, 74; objectives of, 62

Confederación de Trabajadores Mexicanos (CTM): organizing in the southwest, 198–204

Confederación de Uniones Obreros Mexicanos (CUOM): 7, 166; founding convention and objectives, 65–66, 71; relations with the AFL, 65–66; ties to CROM, 67–68

Confederación de Uniones Obreros y Campesinos Mexicanos (CUCOM): founding of, 111; relations with consulates, 38, 118; strike, Los Angeles County, 83; strike, Orange County, 115. See also William Velarde

Confederación Regional Obrero Mexicano (CROM): allied with the AFL, 19, 21; corruption in, 17–18; and CUOM, CUCOM, 186; and J. Edgar Hoover, 18; leadership hierarchy, 17–

19; ties to the Asociación Mexicana del Valle Imperial, 196

Connell, Charles T.: 169–170

Corcoran camp: 128, 141, 153, 154–155; visited by Consul Bravo, 147

Corporatism, Mexico: 22, 114; and emigrants, 37

Corwin, Arthur F.: 230n15

Corona, Bert: 3

Corporate farming, Imperial Valley: 160–161

cotton production, San Joaquin Valley: 125–126, 148

Creel, George: 144, 154

Cross, Ira B.: 151

Dallas, TX: 201

Daniel, Clete: 6, 85–86, 124

Daniels, Josephus: 105; reviews Los Angeles county strike, 112–113

Darcy, Sam: 124

Decker, Caroline: 124, 150–151

De la Colina, Rafael: 51, 62; and the Communist Party, 78–79; and the Confederacion de Sociedades Mexicanas, 64; cooperates with employment agents, 30; spying by, 43

de la Huerta, Adolfo: 203; on consular requirements, 22–23, 43; in opposition to William Velarde, 117–118

de la Madrid, Miguel: 215

Delano, CA: 137

de la O, Genovevo: 24

Department of Social Welfare, CA: 132

Depression, Great: 73, 88–89, 131; and Mexican Schools, 55

Detroit, MI: 30, 51, 135, 175

Detroit International Institute: 2

Díaz, Porfirio: opens door to foreign investments, 11, 15; political exiles, 9

Dolan, John F.: 117; negotiates citrus picker strike, 119–120

Domínguez, Efraín G.: 42

Domínguez, Raul G.: 44

Douglas, AZ: 79

East Los Angeles, CA: 7

Echeverría, Luis: 213

Edson, George T.: 49

El Centro, CA: 163, 179–180, 195

El Monte, CA: 82–83, 91–93, 103

El Paso, TX: 35, 39–40, 59, 203

emigration, Mexico: 12; consular assistance, 30; CROM and AFL agreements to restrict, 27–28; Mexican government policy on, 8, 28, 207–208; spying on exiles, 40

Ensenada, Baja California, México: 106

family labor: 82, 89; ethnic integration, 133, 162; health and medical care, 133; in Los Angeles County, 90–91; in the San Joaquin Valley, 130–132; in the Imperial Valley, 162

Farm Bureau Federation, California: 150

farmers, Japanese: 96; land restrictions upon, 88–89. *See also* Chamber of Commerce, Los Angeles

farm workers, Black: and the CAWIU, 177, 180; as cotton pickers, 122; on cotton strike committee, 124; ethnic unity, 158; in labor camps, 132; migrations of, 132

farm workers, Filipino: 92, 89, 122, 124; and the CAWIU, 177, 180; competing with Mexican labor, 166, 169; unions of, 170–171

farm workers, Japanese: 92, 111

Federal Bureau of Investigation (FBI): 203. *See also* J. Edgar Hoover

Fitzgerald, Edward H.: 144, 148–149; defends Consul Hill, 119; as Federal mediator, 105, 143

Flores, Armando: 113; leads CUCOM, 111; leader of Partido Liberal Mexicano, 77; meets with Plutarco Elías Calles, 106; political history of, 84; pro-consul strike leader, 93–94, 103–104; strike settlement, 112

Fresno, CA: 109, 122, 128–129, 135

Frisselle, S. Parker: testimony before Congressional committiees, 71, 128

Galarza, Ernesto: 206; on the Bracero Agreements, 208–209; on causes of Mexican emigration, 227; views of Mexican government, 210; on worker rights, 212

Galveston, TX: 45

Glassford, Pelham D.: and the ACLU,

191; critique of the CAWIU, 194; as Federal Conciliator, Imperial Valley, 190
Gómez Maganda, Alejandro: 26
Gómez Quiñonez, Juan: 6
Gompers, Samuel: 19; political goals in Mexico, 20, 232n25. *See also* AFL; CROM
Griffith, Beatrice: critiques consuls, 6
Growers and Shippers Association, Imperial Valley: 173, 188, 192, 194; cooperates with consulate, 176
Growers Association, Japanese: 106
Grupo Acción: 21, 68. *See also* CROM; CUOM
Guerin-Gonzales, Camille: 6
gun running: consular surveillance of, 45

haciendas, Mexico: analysis of, 12. *See also* land reform
Hammet, Bill: blacklisted, 155; critiques Consul Bravo, 146; as union leader, 124
Hanford, CA: 56–57, 128, 135
Hart, John W.: 15
Hay, Eduardo: 25
Hicks camp, El Monte, CA: 82, 94, 97–99. *See also* CAWIU; Ricardo Hill
Hill, Benjamin: 25
Hill, Ricardo: 42, 55; appointed consul, 26; appointed to Mexican Congress, 120–121; and comisiones honoríficas, 60; cooperates with labor recruiters, 31; family ties to ruling party, Mexico, 85; intervention in Los Angeles County strike, 83, 86, 100, 111, 115–116. *See also* comisiones honoríficas
Hispanic Caucus, U.S. Congress: and NAFTA passage, 221
Hoover, Herbert: 15
Hoover, J. Edgar: 41. *See also* FBI
Hull, Cordell: 120, 199

immigrants: Asian, 2; European, 2; Japanese, 92
immigrants, Mexican: 1, 2; employment of, 90; and segregation, 90
immigration, Mexican, restrictions upon: urged by the AFL, 21, 68, 70, 72; urged by CUOM, 69. *See also* repatriation

Immigration and Housing, California Division of: 129
Immigration and Naturalization Service: and braceros, 205–206
imperialism, U.S.: economic domination of Mexico, 10, 13, 16, 227; foreign investments in Mexico, 12. *See also* NAFTA; AFL
Industrial Relations, California Department of: 181
International Ladies Garment Workers Union (ILGWU): 198–199

Jameison, Stuart: on consular protections, 5

Kansas City, MO: 2
Kelly, Joe: and CROM, 20
Knight, Alan: 230–231n6

labor camps: 150; distribution of, Imperial Valley, 163; evictions, 139–140; housing, Imperial Valley, 163–164; living conditions in, San Joaquin Valley, 129, 132–134
labor contractors: 130; in the Imperial Valley, 164
land reform, Mexico: and ejidos, 14; failure of, 14–15; large estates protected from, 14; and Lázaro Cárdenas, 15; and peasant rebellions, 15, 28; plans for, 14–15
land tenure: in the Imperial Valley, 160–161; in Los Angeles County, 87–89; in Mexico, 12, 14–15, 208; in the San Joaquin Valley, 125. *See also* land reform
Laredo, TX: 46–47, 60
law enforcement: antilabor bias of in Imperial Valley, 178; Los Angeles Police Department, 96–97, 181–182; Mexicali Police and unions, 186; Peace Officers Association, California, 140; progrower bias of, 186; and violence against unions, 179–181, 183
League of United Latin American Citizens: 215
Leonard, Olin E.: on braceros, 207
Liekens, Enrique: 40
Lombardo Toledano, Vicente: 3
Long Beach, CA: 58

Lopez, Ignacio: critiques consuls, 4
López Portillo, Jose: 214
Lubbert, Alejandro: 148, 189; reports on
   Consul Bravo, 156; reports on Consul
   Terrazas, 195; serves as employment
   agency, 30
Lucio, Lucas: citrus picker strike activities
   of, 116, 118; CUCOM criticism of,
   118; as official in Confederación de
   Sociedades Mexicanas, 75

MacCulloch, Campbell: on police vio-
   lence, 182; on unions, 185
MacDonald, Frank: 144, 153; report on
   Consul Bravo, 156
Majka, Linda C.: 7
Majka, Theo J.: 7
Marston, Helen: 181; opinions of Consul
   Terrazas, 193
Martínez, Alejandro: 4, 42, 45, 100, 108;
   and comisiones honoríficas, 61; role in
   Los Angeles County strike, 83; and
   spying, 41
McAllen, TX: 46
Mexicali, Baja California, México: 175
Mexican American Legal Defense and
   Education Fund (MALDEF): and
   Mexican government overtures, 215
Mexican Cultural Institute, Los Angeles:
   influence of Mexican government, 220
Mexicanismo (Mexicanization): 9–10;
   and the Chicano Movement, 218; and
   the communist Left, 78; conflicts created by, 4–5; and CUOM, 66; discussion of, 38, 86; as a political tool, 81.
   See also Mexican Schools
Mexican Schools: and the consulates, 53;
   as tool for Mexicanization, 53–54
Mexico City: 34, 40, 56, 71–72, 105,
   120, 134–135, 148, 156, 167, 189,
   206, 225
México de afuera: 1, 4; and domestic policy, Mexico, 9
Meyer, Jean: 232n11
Meyer, Lorenzo: 223
migration labor: family, 129; in the Imperial Valley, 161–162. See also community; labor camps
militarization, Mexico: 226
military intelligence, United States: consular surveillance, 46–49

Monsiváis, Carlos: 223
Monterrey, Nuevo Leon, Mexico: 33
Morones, Luis: and the AFL, 20; as
   CROM leader, 17; political opportun-
   ism of, 18
Mujica, Emilio: 72
Mutualistas: 2

Nathan, J. B.: on consulate intervention,
   116
National Council of La Raza: 215
National Farm Labor Union: 209
National Labor Relations Board (NLRB):
   182, 198; and citrus picker strike,
   118; opposes the CAWIU, 193; pro-
   poses government unions, 185
New Orleans, LA: 39
1910 Mexican Revolution: 9–10; continues Díaz-era policies, 17; critiques of,
   13; labor policy, 16–17; land reform,
   14–15; and U.S. foreign domination,
   16, 21
Nogales, AZ: 38, 175
North American Free Trade Agreement
   (NAFTA): 216, 224; as cause of Mexico's economic collapse, 221–222; and
   the Hispanic Caucus, 221; resemblance to Díaz-era policies, 217

Oakland, CA: 75
Obregón, Alvaro: 7, 24, 37; assassination
   of, 73; and Bucareli Agreements, 16;
   ordered to form comisiones honorífi-
   cas, 49
Occeli de Salinas, Cecilia: 219
Office of Mexicans Living Abroad: 214
Oñate Laborde, Santiago: 1
Orange County, CA: 50, 198, 220
Ortiz Rubio, Pasqual: 75; as presidential
   candidate, 73

Padres, Gustavo, Jr.: 48
Palomares, Frank: 127
Pan American Federation of Labor: 21,
Partido Laborista Mexicana: 75
Partido Liberal Mexicana (PLM): 9; and
   Mexican Schools, 55; and 1929 elec-
   tions, 76–77
Partido Nacional Revolucionario (PNR):
   106; founding, 22
Partido Revolucionario Democratico

(PRD): 216; contests the PRI, 225; on NAFTA, 217, 221

Partido Revolucionario Institucional (PRI): 1, 200, 204, 225; and Ernesto Zedillo, 213, 223; and NAFTA, 221; opposition to, 217; political reforms of, 227; relations with the Chicano Movement, 218

Partido Revolucionario Mexicano (PRM): 200, 203

Pasadena, CA: 75

Perkins, Frances: on farm workers' health, 164; and federal grievance, Chamber of Commerce, Los Angeles, 119–120

Pescador Osuna, José Angel: 220

Pesquiera, F. Alfonso: 170, 220; and government loyalty, 52; and labor immigration controls, 71–72; organizes comisiones honoríficas, 51, 61; organizes Confederación de Uniones Mexicanas, 65, 68; participation of in Confederación de Sociedades Mexicanas, 64; and patriotic celebrations, 57

Pineda, José G.: allied with company union, 199

Pixley, CA: 142, 150, 158

Plaza Tlatelolco: 213

Portes Gil, Emilio: 73

Prieto Laurens, Jorge: 39

Proposition 187: 219; exploited by the PRI, 220

Protective Association, Imperial Valley: 189

Protective Association, Orange County: 116

Puig Causaranc, José M.: 97, 101; issues strike directives, 104

Raat, Dirk: 9

Ray, Dorothy: 180

Reardon, Timothy A.: 181

relations of production: affected by consular policy, 197

remittances, immigrant: Consul Terrazas on significance of, 30; filling an economic need in Mexico, 29, 207

repatriation: Confederación de Uniones Mexicanas lobbies for, 69; consuls blame Filipinos, 80; difficulties

encountered in returning, 33–34; U.S.-Mexico cooperation in, 31–32, 35–36, 70

Richer, Juan B.: control over comisión honorífica, 61; and labor unions, 61; military surveillance on, 46–47

Riverside, CA: 52

Rodríguez, Abelardo: 38, 77, 95, 103; on Consul Terrazas, 195; directs consuls to end strike, 111; instructions to consuls, 22

Rolph, James: 106, 144

Romo, Ricardo: 7

Ross, Stanley R.: 215

Ruiz, Ramón Eduardo: on the Mexican Revolution, 13, 16

Salazar, Rodolfo: 62

Salinas, Raul: 223

Salinas de Gortari, Carlos: 216; and neoliberalism, 218

Saltillo, Coahuila, Mexico: 33

San Antonio, TX: 25, 41, 198–199, 201

San Bernardino, CA: 59

Sanchez, George: 6; on consular leadership, 8

San Diego, CA: 44

San Francisco, CA: 2, 75

San Marcos, TX: 49

Santa Ana, CA: 50, 75

Santa Barbara, CA: 51

Santa Maria, CA: 61

Santamaría Gómez, Arturo: 220

Santa Monica, CA: 95

Santa Paula, CA: 58

Santibáñez, Enrique: 41

Saunders, Lyle: on braceros, 207

Scharrenberg, Paul: on immigration restriction, Mexico, 21

Secretariat of Foreign Relations, Mexico: and comisiones honoríficas, oversight, 52, 60–62; consular selection process, 22–27; defends consuls, 4; directs Los Angeles strike, 101; instructions to Consul Bravo, 148; and spying, 37, 43, 47

Servin, Manuel: favors repatriation, 80

Simpson, Lesley Byrd: 14, 222

Smith, Robert Freeman: 16

Spalding, Hobart, Jr.: 200, 201

spying: by consuls, 38–49; consuls' paid informants, 45; by the Partido Nacional Revolucionario, 41
St. Louis, MO: 84

Tannenbaum, Frank: 222; on government unions, Mexico, 18
Taylor, Paul Schuster: 7; on Black labor migrations in California, 132; on causes of Mexican migration, 28–29; on the CAWIU, 124; on corporate farming, 161; describes strike hearings, 152; on Mexican migration in California, 128; on vigilantism, 142–143
Terrazas, Joaquín: 53, 174–175; bribery allegations, 175; discusses emigrant remittances, 30; negotiates labor agreement, 176; organizes company union, 186–189
Texas Infant Manufacturing Company: 198–199
Tokyo, Japan: 84
Toledano, Vicente Lombardo: 200; ties to Lázaro Cárdenas, 204
Torres, Hermolao: 52
Trade Union Unity League (TUUL): as the Agricultural Workers Industrial League (AWIL) in the Imperial Valley, 168–169, 171–173; and the CAWIU, 82; organized by Communist Party, 78
Tuck, Ruth: critiques consuls, 6; opposes Mexicanismo, 4
Tucson, AZ: 24, 42, 46
Tulare, CA: 128, 141, 147

Unión de Repatriados: 35
Unión de Trabajadores del Valle Imperial: 165–166

Van Nuys, CA: 54
Vasconcelos, José: and 1929 presidential campaign, 74, 76
Velarde, William: conflicts with Consul Hill, 117; opposes Los Angeles County strike settlement, 112; political ideology of, 115–116
Velásquez, Fidel: 204
Vélez Ibáñez, Carlos G.: 7
Venice, CA: 93
vigilantes: examined by Paul S. Taylor, 147; kidnapping of A. L. Wirin by, 181; murders by, 141–142; supported by the press, 191; union actions suppressed by, 180

wages, farm workers': in Imperial Valley, 164–165; in Los Angeles County, 90–91; in San Joaquin Valley, 131–132
Walker, David: 16–17
Washington, D.C.: 70, 102, 114, 190, 206
Watts, CA: 54
Weber, Devra: 6, 127; on NAFTA and Mexican education, 218
Wilson, Woodrow: 15
Wirin, A. L.: counsel for the CAWIU, 151; kidnapped by vigilantes, 181; report on police tactics, 178
Womack, John, Jr.: 13
Woodville, CA: 140
working conditions: in Imperial Valley, 162–164; in Los Angeles County, 90–91; in San Joaquin Valley, 133–134

Young Communist League: in Hicks camp, 95; in the Imperial Valley, 188

Zedillo, Ernesto: and democratic reforms, 223, 226–227